Transforming Businesses With Bitcoin Mining and Blockchain Applications

Dharmendra Singh Rajput
VIT University, India

Ramjeevan Singh Thakur
Maulana Azad National Institute of Technology Bhopal, India

Syed Muzamil Basha
Sri Krishna College of Engineering and Technology, India

A volume in the Advances in Finance, Accounting, and Economics (AFAE) Book Series

IGI Global
DISSEMINATOR OF KNOWLEDGE

Published in the United States of America by
IGI Global
Business Science Reference (an imprint of IGI Global)
701 E. Chocolate Avenue
Hershey PA, USA 17033
Tel: 717-533-8845
Fax: 717-533-8661
E-mail: cust@igi-global.com
Web site: http://www.igi-global.com

Library of Congress Cataloging-in-Publication Data

Names: Rajput, Dharmendra Singh, 1985- editor. | Thakur, Ramjeevan Singh, 1974- editor. | Basha, Syed, 1986- editor.
Title: Transforming businesses with bitcoin mining and blockchain applications / Dharmendra Rajput, Ramjeevan Thakur, and Syed Basha, editors.
Description: Hershey, PA : Business Science Reference, [2020] | Summary: "This book examines the use of bitcoin mining and blockchain applications in business"-- Provided by publisher.
Identifiers: LCCN 2019018096 | ISBN 9781799801863 (hardcover) | ISBN 9781799801870 (paperback) | ISBN 9781799801887 (ebook)
Subjects: LCSH: Electronic commerce. | Electronic funds transfers. | Digital currency. | Business enterprises--Finance. | Bitcoin. | Blockchains (Databases)
Classification: LCC HF5548.32 .T7245 2020 | DDC 658.15--dc23
LC record available at https://lccn.loc.gov/2019018096

This book is published in the IGI Global book series Advances in Finance, Accounting, and Economics (AFAE) (ISSN: 2327-5677; eISSN: 2327-5685)

British Cataloguing in Publication Data
A Cataloguing in Publication record for this book is available from the British Library.

All work contributed to this book is new, previously-unpublished material.
The views expressed in this book are those of the authors, but not necessarily of the publisher.

For electronic access to this publication, please contact: eresources@igi-global.com.

Advances in Finance, Accounting, and Economics (AFAE) Book Series

ISSN:2327-5677
EISSN:2327-5685

Editor-in-Chief: Ahmed Driouchi, Al Akhawayn University, Morocco

MISSION

In our changing economic and business environment, it is important to consider the financial changes occurring internationally as well as within individual organizations and business environments. Understanding these changes as well as the factors that influence them is crucial in preparing for our financial future and ensuring economic sustainability and growth.

The **Advances in Finance, Accounting, and Economics (AFAE)** book series aims to publish comprehensive and informative titles in all areas of economics and economic theory, finance, and accounting to assist in advancing the available knowledge and providing for further research development in these dynamic fields.

COVERAGE

- Accounting information systems
- Interest Rates and Annuities
- Economics of Migration and Spatial Mobility
- Applied Finance
- Public Finance
- Theoretical Issues in Economics, Finance, and Accounting
- Comparative Accounting Systems
- Economics of Natural and Environmental Resources
- Accounting Standards
- Health economics

IGI Global is currently accepting manuscripts for publication within this series. To submit a proposal for a volume in this series, please contact our Acquisition Editors at Acquisitions@igi-global.com or visit: http://www.igi-global.com/publish/.

The Advances in Finance, Accounting, and Economics (AFAE) Book Series (ISSN 2327-5677) is published by IGI Global, 701 E. Chocolate Avenue, Hershey, PA 17033-1240, USA, www.igi-global.com. This series is composed of titles available for purchase individually; each title is edited to be contextually exclusive from any other title within the series. For pricing and ordering information please visit http://www.igi-global.com/book-series/advances-finance-accounting-economics/73685. Postmaster: Send all address changes to above address.

Titles in this Series

For a list of additional titles in this series, please visit:
https://www.igi-global.com/book-series/advances-finance-accounting-economics/73685

Migration and Urbanization Local Solutions for Global Economic Challenges
Denis Ushakov (Suan Sunandha Rajabhat University, Thailand)
Business Science Reference • copyright 2020 • 365pp • H/C (ISBN: 9781799801115) • US $245.00 (our price)

Financial Technology and Disruptive Innovation in ASEAN
Muhammad Anshari (Universiti Brunei Darussalam, Brunei) Mohammad Nabil Almunawar (Universiti Brunei Darussalam, Brunei) and Masairol Masri (Universiti Brunei Darussalam, Brunei)
Business Science Reference • copyright 2020 • 331pp • H/C (ISBN: 9781522591832) • US $195.00 (our price)

International Trade Policies in the Era of Globalization
Ahu Coşkun Özer (Marmara University, Turkey)
Business Science Reference • copyright 2020 • 363pp • H/C (ISBN: 9781522595663) • US $205.00 (our price)

Management Accounting Standards for Sustainable Business Practices
Ionica Oncioiu (Titu Maiorescu University, Romania) Gary Cokins (Analytics-Based Performance Management LLC, USA) Sorinel Căpuşneanu (Titu Maiorescu University, Romania) and Dan Ioan Topor (1 Decembrie 1918 University, Romania)
Business Science Reference • copyright 2020 • 360pp • H/C (ISBN: 9781799801788) • US $215.00 (our price)

Handbook of Research on Economic and Political Implications of Green Trading and Energy Use
Ramesh Chandra Das (Vidyasagar University, India)
Business Science Reference • copyright 2019 • 421pp • H/C (ISBN: 9781522585473) • US $225.00 (our price)

For an entire list of titles in this series, please visit:
https://www.igi-global.com/book-series/advances-finance-accounting-economics/73685

IGI Global
DISSEMINATOR OF KNOWLEDGE

701 East Chocolate Avenue, Hershey, PA 17033, USA
Tel: 717-533-8845 x100 • Fax: 717-533-8661
E-Mail: cust@igi-global.com • www.igi-global.com

Editorial Advisory Board

Table of Contents

Detailed Table of Contents

Since the advent of the web, the number of users who started using the internet for everyday purpose has increased tremendously. Most of the common purposes are to access their data whenever they want and wherever they want. So many companies have started providing these services to normal users. These companies store huge volume of data in the data centers. So protecting the integrity of the data is the main responsibility of these companies. Blockchain is one of the trending solutions that gives storage immutability to the users. This chapter starts with the working of blockchain and smart contracts and advantages and disadvantages of blockchain and smart contracts and then goes on to explain how blockchain can be integrated into the internet of things (IOT). This chapter ends with an architecture based on the proof-of-concept for access management, which is blockchain-based fully distributed architecture.

Blockchain is the new "buzz" word that has attracted the attention of industries and businesses. It is an innovative technology that provides information exchange in an efficient and transparent manner. It has a wide range of application varying from cryptocurrency, healthcare, risk management, education, financial services, internet of things (IoT), border security to public services. However, security issues and threats of this novel technology is also an important topic. In this chapter, the authors provide a comprehensive study of applications, challenges, and issues and how to combat them in the blockchain. Major areas of concern are security, scalability, cryptocurrency's malicious attacks, etc.

Internet of things (IoT) technology plays a vital role in the current technologies because IoT develops a network by integrating different kinds of objects and sensors to create the communication among objects directly without human interaction. With the presence of internet of things technology in our daily comes smart thinking and various advantages. At the same time, secure systems have been a most important concern for the protection of information systems and networks. However, adopting traditional security management systems in the internet of things leads several issues due to the limited privacy and policies like privacy standards, protocol stacks, and authentication rules. Usually, IoT devices has limited network capacities, storage, and computing processors. So they are having more chances to attacks. Data security, privacy, and reliability are three main challenges in the IoT security domain. To address the solutions for the above issues, IoT technology has to provide advanced privacy and policies in this large incoming data source. Blockchain is one of the trending technologies in the privacy management to provide the security. So this chapter is focused on the blockchain technologies which can be able to solve several IoT security issues. This review mainly focused on the state-of-the-art IoT security issues and vulnerabilities by existing review works in the IoT security domains. The taxonomy is presented about security issues in the view of communication, architecture, and applications. Also presented are the challenges of IoT security management systems. The main aim of this chapter is to describe the importance of blockchain technology in IoT security systems. Finally, it highlights the future directions of blockchain technology roles in IoT systems, which can be helpful for further improvements.

Internet of things (IoT) is ready to change human life and release tremendous financial benefits. It may be that lack of information security and the belief of the current IoT are actually restricting its selection. Blockchain changes in an appropriated and secure record holds reliable records of information in various areas and possibly resolves information security concerns in the IoT system. This chapter presents a thorough review on the existing blockchain progress with an accent on IoT applications. The authors first give an overview of blockchain architecture including blockchain technologies and key characteristics of blockchain. The authors then discuss the blockchain for the internet of things including blockchain for IoT: technologies. Furthermore, they list some challenges and problems that will hinder blockchain development and summarize some existing approaches for solving these problems. Some possible future directions are also discussed. Future research bearings are ordered for a viable mix of blockchains in the IoT system.

Blockchain technology is very trending and promising. It can revolutionize the traditional way of manipulation of data in many industries. There are industries which blockchain can disrupt: banking, cyber security, smart contract, insurance,

pages; requester information like which type of search engines is used, keywords and top referring sites, and so on. In general, the website administrator uses this kind of knowledge to make the system act better, helping in the manipulation process of site, then also forgiving marketing decisions support. Most of the advanced web mining systems practice this kind of information to take out more difficult or complex interpretations using data mining procedures like association rules, clustering, and classification.

The global naming systems are used to resolve the DNS (domain name system) queries by providing the IP address of a particular domain. Humans are familiar in remembering the text rather than numbers. So the DNS servers help in resolving the human-readable domain names into system understandable IP address. In the current DNS architecture, there are several threats that cost a lot of damage to the organizations. At the earlier stage, DNS protocol lacks security assurance in place. To solve this issue, they introduced DNSSEC (subsequent DNS) as an additional layer of trust on top of DNS by providing authentication. Still, the current DNS servers couldn't address issues such as DoS/DDoS attacks. To address all these issues, blockchain technology offers an innovative method to handle those challenges. The existing naming systems are centralized, which is a major problem in achieving security.. The main aim of this chapter is to provide an overview of blockchain technology and a brief introduction to blockchain-based naming and storage systems.

Bitcoin has brought a revolution in digital market. Bitcoin doesn't follow any supervisory body or central authority to control it. Unlike any country's currency, it is not supervised by a government. It flows on networks and is managed by decentralized actors. Like any other innovation, bitcoin also has pros and cons associated with it. In this chapter, the authors discuss all the opportunities and challenges related to bitcoin and its impact on the world economy.

Section 3
Security and Applications of Blockchain

In today's world, we deal with various online services, where each person deals with various technologies. These technologies are made for people to make our access to the new world easily. There is a tremendous use of online applications, websites which require large storage. Large data is handled by the online systems. The collection of data in the whole world is about 20% in the last few years. The data is captured from the user, controlled by the systems, and operations are performed on data. It requires more system accuracy and protection to personal data. But the person does not know about the data, where and how it is used where it is stored or whether the data is handled by some organisations for their own use or data is been hacked by another person. This chapter explores protection of data using the decentralized privacy of blockchain.

Technology is a boon to mankind in this fast-growing era. The advancement in technology is the predominant factor for the sophisticated way of living of the people. In spite of technology, revolution happens across the world, and mankind still suffers due to various health issues. Healthcare industries take immense measures to improve the quality of life. An enormous volume of digital data is being handled every day in the healthcare industry. There arises a need for the intervention of technology in the healthcare industry to be taken to a greater extent. The prime duty of any healthcare industry is to store and maintain those data in the form of electronic health records (EHR) in a secured manner.

Blockchain technology is a distributed framework for sharing data that is validated through cryptographic functions. The nodes of the network come to a consensus regarding addition of data to the blockchain. Every blockchain operation requires a processing fee. This fee makes storing of large data on the blockchain infeasible. An indirect alternative for this challenge could be use of IPFS, which is a decentralized peer-peer network that facilitates storage of file. This is accomplished by storing the hash of the IPFS as data on the blockchain.

The global popularity of digital cryptocurrencies and research in a decentralized system have led to the foundation of blockchain, which is fundamentally a public digital ledger to share information in a trustworthy and secure way. The concept and applications of blockchain have now spread from cryptocurrencies to various other domains, including business process management, smart contracts, IoT, and so on. Cryptocurrency is a mechanism designed to work for the online secure payments system using cryptography. Cryptography maintains confidentiality, integrity, and authentication. Cryptocurrency has come as a novel way of making payments that keep all the transactions secure and safe, which avoids any type of intermediaries such as a bank. This chapter will shed light on the concept of blockchain technology, security, and its applications in various domains.

Preface

In 2009, Bitcoin was introduced as one of the decentralized digital currency and worked like cash. It has become the world's biggest bank with no cash. It can use Information Technology Infrastructure to reinvent business models. The success of many companies proves that IT continues to dominate and transform businesses. Hence entrepreneurs, of tomorrow need to understand, how these technologies work to identify innovation opportunities and thrive in an increasingly competitive environment. This Book is therefore designed to provide the understanding of four timely and foundational topics in IT Infrastructure and emerging trends. Cloud computing, Mobile communications, Information security, and Blockchains. This book explains all about, how this currency works and how users can mine Bitcoins. Where, Bitcoins mining is a tough process, it is almost impossible to create Bitcoins on the simple computer. There is a need for specialist hardware to generate Bitcoins. A deeper conceptual understanding of these technologies from this Book be able to appreciate and identify and apply and manage IT solutions as needed. The Topics covered in this Book are: Features of the Cloud, Considerations in Cloud Adoption, Cloud Computing Realizations, Terminal Services, Virtualization, Cloud Computing Service Models (SaaS, PaaS, IaaS), Applications of Mobile Technologies, Economic Issues, Mobile Communications, Information Security (Threats and Attacks), Cyber Defense (Shared Private key encryption, Public Key encryption, Encryption benefits), Vulnerability Disclosure process, Future of Data Security, Emerging Trends: Blockchains, The cryptography Behind Bitcoin, Bitcoin Mining, Applications of Blockchain (Blockchain Mining Rigs).

To make readers understand the Technology of Blockchain Management including the challenges and opportunities . This understanding should help the readers in analyzing and extract information from Bitcoin network and security issues involved in transferring Bitcoin currency. It provides the necessary steps required to design the open blockchain. It is expected that under the umbrella of well-defined specifications, blockchain modules created by various members will be pluggable into each other's technology environment. These include standard functional modules and defined interfaces. Re-use of common building blocks, Diverse developer community, Rapid experimentation, extensible codebases, and flexible modification of any component.

This Book is used by students, having Network Security as the mainstream of course at VIT University which offers 25 Undergraduate, 30 Postgraduate, 4 Integrated Programmes, and 4 Research programmes. In addition to full-time/part-time Ph.D., M.S. (BY RESEARCH) Degrees in Engineering and Management Disciplines, M.Phil, Ph.D., in Science and Languages, Integrated Ph.D. programmes also offered for engineering disciplines in selected schools. Additionally, this can be useful to the student and research Community of all over India and abroad.

CHAPTER 1: INTRODUCTION OF BLOCKCHAIN AND USAGE OF BLOCKCHAIN IN INTERNET OF THINGS

Since the advent of the web, the number of users who started using the internet for everyday purpose has increased tremendously. Most of the common purpose is to access their data whenever they want and wherever they want. So many companies have started providing these services to normal users. These companies store huge volume of data in the data centers. So to protect the integrity of the data is the main responsibility of these companies. Blockchain is one of the latest trending solutions which gives storage immutability to the users. This chapter starts with the working of blockchain and smart contracts and advantages and disadvantages of blockchain and smart contracts and then goes on to explain how blockchain can be integrated into the Internet of Things (IOT). This chapter ends with an architecture based on the proof-of-concept for access management which is blockchain-based fully distributed architecture.

CHAPTER 2: THE ROLE OF BLOCKCHAIN TECHNOLOGY TO MAKE BUSINESS EASIER AND EFFECTIVE

Blockchain is the new "buzz" word that has attracted the attention of industries and businesses. It is an innovative technology which provides information exchange in an efficient and transparent manner. It has a wide range of application varying from cryptocurrency, helthcare, risk management, education, financial services, Internet of Things (IoT), border security to public services. However, security issues and threats of this novel technology is also an important topic. In this chapter, we will provide a comprehensive study of applications, challenges and issues and How to combat them in the blockchain. Major areas of concern are security, scalability, cryptocurrency's malicious attacks etc.

CHAPTER 3: TOWARDS THE INTEGRATION OF BLOCKCHAIN AND IOT FOR SECURITY CHALLENGES IN IOT - A REVIEW

IoT devices has limited network capacities, storage and computing processors. So they are having more chances to attacks. Data security, privacy and reliability, there are three main challenges in the IoT security domain. To address the solutions for the above issues, the IoT technology has to provide advanced privacy and policies in this large incoming data source. Blockchain is the one of the trending technologies in the privacy management to provide the security. So in this chapter, focused on the blockchain technologies which can be able to solve several IoT security issues. This review mainly focused on the state of the art IoT security issues and vulnerabilities by existing review works in the IoT security domains. The taxonomy is presented about security issues in the view of communication, architecture and applications. Also presented challenges of IoT security management systems. Finally highlights the future directions of blockchain technology roles in IoT systems which can be helpful for further improvements.

CHAPTER 4: A NOVEL SURVEY ON BLOCKCHAIN FOR INTERNET OF THINGS

Internet of Things (IoT) is ready to change human life and release tremendous financial benefits. It may be that, lack of information security and the belief of the current IoT are actually restricting its selection. Blockchain changes in an appropriated and secure record, holds reliable records of information in various areas, and possibly resolves information security concerns in the IoT system. This chapter presents a thorough review on the existing Blockchain progress with an accent on IoT applications. Authors first give an overview of blockchain architecture including blockchain technologies and key characteristics of blockchain. Authors then discuss the Blockchain for the Internet of Things including Blockchain for IoT: Technologies. Furthermore, they list some challenges and problems that will hinder blockchain development and summarize some existing approaches for solving these problems. Some possible future directions are also discussed. Future research bearings are ordered for a viable mix of blockchains in the IoT system.

CHAPTER 5: A FRAMEWORK ON ENTERPRISE-GRADE SMART CONTRACT USING BLOCK CHAIN

Block chain technology is very trending and promising. It can revolutionize the traditional way of manipulation of data in many industries. There are industries which block chain can disrupt, few examples can be Banking, Cyber Security, Smart Contract, Insurance, Cloud Storage, Government, Healthcare, Media Streaming. The decentralized approach of block chain using Peer-to-Peer system to verify the correct record of the ledger, which builds a trust in the system. A system can be compiled and made to get adopted with the concept of Smart Contract. The aim of the paper is to develop a system that is flexible enough to get implemented in the Industries like Finance, Cyber Security, Data Storage, Buying and selling of Properties, Healthcare etc. This will use a one way encryption method known as SHA-256. A block with the 256 character code bind with the other metadata of the block will be termed as a smart contract for the item

CHAPTER 6: AN APPLICATION OF BLOCKCHAIN IN STOCK MARKET

Blockchain is one of the most growing technology which is used for financial management system. As it is well known that financial data must be kept secure otherwise it can create a huge loss. So whenever security features or technologies are developed they keep financial security as a priority. Stock market management is another area of finance sector which works on two concepts that is minimize the risk and maximize the profit. In this chapter we will discuss how blockchain technology is used for stock market analysis. Mainly blockchain will help us to make optimal stock exchanges through automation and decentralization. Stock market across the globe is rapidly using blockchain technology for the market transaction. Some of the country is still preparing themselves to use the blockchain technology. This technology offers huge potential for tracing securities lending, margin financing and surveillance of system risk.

CHAPTER 7: A MODEL FOR EXTRACTING MOST DESIRED WEB PAGES

Weblog analysis takes raw data from access log and performs study on this data for extracting statistical information. These info incorporates a variety of data for the website activity such as average no. of hits, total no. of user visits, failed &

successful cached hits, average time of view, average path length over a website and analytical information such as page was not found errors and server errors, server information which includes exit and entry pages, single access pages and top visited pages, requester information like which type of search engines is used, keywords and top referring sites and so on. In general, the website administrator uses this kind of knowledge to make better the system act, helping in the manipulation process of site, then also forgiving marketing decisions support. Most of the advanced Web mining systems practice this kind of information to take out more difficult or complex interpretation those take learning, using data mining procedures like association rules, clustering, and classification etc

CHAPTER 8: GLOBAL NAMING AND STORAGE SYSTEM USING BLOCKCHAIN

The global naming systems are used to resolve the DNS (Domain Name System) queries by providing the IP address of a particular domain. Humans are familiar in remembering the text rather than numbers. So the DNS servers help in resolving the human-readable domain names into system understandable IP address. In the current DNS architecture, there are several threats that cost a lot of damage to the organizations. At the earlier stage, DNS Protocol lacks security protection in place. To solve this issue, they introduced DNSSEC (Subsequent DNS) as an additional layer of trust on top of DNS by providing authentication. Still, the current DNS servers couldn't address issues such as DoS/DDoS attacks. To address all these issues, Blockchain technology offers an innovative method to handle those challenges. The existing naming systems are centralized, which the major problem to achieve security. The main aim of this chapter is to provide an overview of blockchain technology and a brief introduction to Blockchain based naming and storage systems.

CHAPTER 9: IMPACT OF BITCOIN ON THE WORLD ECONOMY – OPPORTUNITIES AND CHALLENGES

Since 2008, world became evident of dramatically changed economical scenario due to the emergence of Bitcoin, a crypto currency. Bitcoin has brought a revolution in digital market that itself showing its value and impact. Bitcoin doesn't follow any supervisory body or central authority to control it, unlike any country's currency is supervised by its government. It flows on network and managed by decentralized actors. Like any other innovation, Bitcoin also has pros and cons associated with it.

In this chapter we are going to discuss all the opportunities and challenges related to Bitcoin and its impact on world economy.

CHAPTER 10: PROTECTION TO PERSONAL DATA USING DECENTRALIZING PRIVACY OF BLOCKCHAIN

In today's world, we deal with various online services, where each person deals with various technologies. These technologies are made for people to make our access to new world easily. There is a tremendous use of online applications, websites which require large storage. Large data is handled by the online systems. The collection of data in the whole world is about 20% in the last few years. The data is captured from the user, controlled by the systems and operations are performed on data. It requires more system accuracy and protection to personal data. Ex. Email, WhatsApp, Instagram, Facebook, Bank transactions, Real-time estate etc. But the person is unknown about the data, where and how it is used where it is stored or whether the data is handled by some organisations for their own use or data is been hacked by other person. Since the protection towards the personal data is been decreasing day by day.

CHAPTER 11: PRESERVING DATA PRIVACY IN ELECTRONIC HEALTH RECORDS USING BLOCK CHAIN TECHNOLOGY

Technology is a boon to mankind in this fast growing era. The advancement in technology is the predominant factor for the sophisticated way of living of the people. In spite of technology, revolution happens across the world, mankind still suffers due to various health issues. Healthcare industries take immense measures to improve the quality of life. An enormous volume of digital data is being handled every day in the healthcare industry. There arises a need for the intervention of technology in the healthcare industry to be taken to a greater extent. The prime duty of any healthcare industry is to store and maintain those data in the form of Electronic Health Record (EHR) in a secured manner.

CHAPTER 12: DECENTRALIZING PRIVACY USING BLOCKCHAIN TO PROTECT PRIVATE DATA AND CHALLENGES WITH IPFS

Blockchain technology is a distributed framework for sharing data that is validated through cryptographic functions. The nodes of the network come to a consensus regarding addition of data to the blockchain. Every blockchain operation requires a processing fee. This fee makes storing of large data on the blockchain infeasible. An indirect alternative for this challenge could be use of IPFS which is a decentralized peer-peer network that facilitates storage of file easier. This is accomplished by storing the hash of the IPFS as a data on the blockchain.

CHAPTER 13: CONCEPTUAL INSIGHTS IN BLOCKCHAIN TECHNOLOGY – SECURITY AND APPLICATIONS

The global popularity of digital cryptocurrencies and research in a decentralized system has led to the foundation of Blockchain which is fundamentally a public digital ledger to share information in a trustworthy and secure way. The concept and applications of Blockchain have now spread from cryptocurrencies to various other domains, including business process management, smart contracts, IoT and so on. Cryptocurrency is a mechanism designed to work for the online secure payments system using cryptography. Cryptography maintains confidentiality, integrity, and authentication. Cryptocurrency has come as a novel way of making payments that keep all the transactions secure and safe which avoids any type of intermediaries such as a bank. This chapter will shed light on the concept of blockchain technology, security and its applications in various domains.

CHAPTER 14: HEALTHCARE INFORMATION EXCHANGE THROUGH BLOCKCHAIN-BASED APPROACHES

Nowadays blockchain is one of the fast growing and most important technologies in the world. Most of the people think that blockchain is all about cryptocurrency or bitcoin but we can say it is much beyond that. It is a technology that creates immutable and distributable data records that is shared between peer to peer in network database systems and records digital event in such a way that it cannot be altered or recognized until it reaches the recipient. In recent times many of the industries are using blockchain as a tool to innovate their functionality. Some of the well known industries are banking sector, real estate, healthcare, Internet-of Things,

Insurance and many more. Out of these industries healthcare is one of the industry which is adopting blockchain very rapidly. So this chapter will discuss about the block chain and how it has transformed the healthcare industry.

A deeper conceptual understanding of these technologies from this book be able to appreciate and identify and apply and manage IT solutions as needed. Towards providing an overview of different application domains of blockchain technologies in the Internet of Things. The Topics covered in this Book are: Features of the Cloud, Considerations in Cloud Adoption, Cloud Computing Realizations, Terminal Services, Virtualization, Cloud Computing Service Models (SaaS, PaaS, IaaS), Applications of Mobile Technologies, Economic Issues, Mobile Communications, Information Security (Threats and Attacks), Cyber Defense (Shared Private key encryption, Public Key encryption, Encryption benefits), Vulnerability Disclosure process, Future of Data Security, Emerging Trends: Blockchains, The cryptography Behind Bitcoin, Bitcoin Mining, Applications of Blockchain (Blockchain Mining Rigs).

Acknowledgment

The editors would like to express appreciation to the numerous individuals who saw us through this book; for all those who provided support, talked things over, read, composed, offered remarks, allowed us to cite their comments and assisted in the editing, proofreading and design. Without their support, this book would not have become a reality.

I believe that the team of authors provides the perfect blend of knowledge and skills that went into composing this book. I thank each of the authors for devoting their time and effort towards this book; I believe that it will be a great asset to the community! Much obliged for everything, I look forward to writing the second edition soon! The editors wish to acknowledge the significant commitments of the reviewers regarding the improvement of quality, coherence, and content presentation of chapters. Some of the authors also served as referees; we highly appreciate their twofold undertaking.

We would like to thank to our mentors Dr. Kamal Raj Pardasani, Dr. KanakSaxena, Dr. J Janet, Dr. Vivek Tiwari, Dr.Thippa Reddy G, Dr. Rajesh Kaluri, Dr. Harshita Patel, Dr. Praveen Kumar Reddy, Dr. Krishna Kumar Mohbey, Dr. Pradeep Chouksey, Dr. Bharth Bhushan, Dr. Varsha Namdeo, Dr. Goutam Singh Lalotra and Dr. Chiranjilal Choudhary. They have been our inspiration and motivation for continuing to improve our knowledge and experience. We are likewise exceptionally appreciative to all for providing all support and faith when required.

Last and not least: I beg forgiveness of all those who have been with me over the course of the years and whose names I have failed to mention.

Dharmendra Singh Rajput
VIT University, India

Ramjeevan Singh Thakur
Maulana Azad National Institute of Technology, Bhopal, India

Syed Muzamil Basha
Sri Krishna College of Engineering and Technology, India

Ramjeevan Singh Thakur
Maulana Azad National Institute of Technology, Bhopal, India

Syed Muzamil Basha
Sri Krishna College of Engineering and Technology, India

Introduction

This book explains all about, how bitcoin currency works and how users can mine Bitcoins. Where, Bitcoins mining is a tough process, it is almost impossible to create Bitcoins on the simple computer. There is a need for specialist hardware to generate Bitcoins. A deeper conceptual understanding of these technologies from this book be able to appreciate and identify and apply and manage IT solutions as needed.

Blockchain is one of the latest trending solutions which gives storage immutability to the users. This books starts with the working of blockchain and smart contracts and advantages and disadvantages of blockchain and smart contracts and then goes on to explain how blockchain can be integrated into the Internet of Things (IOT). It has a wide range of application varying from cryptocurrency, healthcare, risk management, education, financial services, Internet of Things (IoT), border security to public services.

It presents a thorough review on the existing Blockchain progress with an accent on IoT applications.

The Topics covered in this Book are: Features of the Cloud, Considerations in Cloud Adoption, Cloud Computing Realizations, Terminal Services, Virtualization, Cloud Computing Service Models (SaaS, PaaS, IaaS), Applications of Mobile Technologies, Economic Issues, Mobile Communications, Information Security (Threats and Attacks), Cyber Defense (Shared Private key encryption, Public Key encryption, Encryption benefits), Vulnerability Disclosure process, Future of Data Security, Emerging Trends: Blockchains, The cryptography Behind Bitcoin, Bitcoin Mining, Applications of Blockchain (Blockchain Mining Rigs).

Section 1
Blockchain With IoT

Chapter 1
Introduction of Blockchain and Usage of Blockchain in Internet of Things

Chandrasekar Ravi
National Institute of Technology Puducherry, India

Praveensankar Manimaran
https://orcid.org/0000-0003-3614-5722
National Institute of Technology Puducherry, India

ABSTRACT

Since the advent of the web, the number of users who started using the internet for everyday purpose has increased tremendously. Most of the common purposes are to access their data whenever they want and wherever they want. So many companies have started providing these services to normal users. These companies store huge volume of data in the data centers. So protecting the integrity of the data is the main responsibility of these companies. Blockchain is one of the trending solutions that gives storage immutability to the users. This chapter starts with the working of blockchain and smart contracts and advantages and disadvantages of blockchain and smart contracts and then goes on to explain how blockchain can be integrated into the internet of things (IOT). This chapter ends with an architecture based on the proof-of-concept for access management, which is blockchain-based fully distributed architecture.

DOI: 10.4018/978-1-7998-0186-3.ch001

INTRODUCTION

Blockchain is a peer to peer network which is distributed among the untrustworthy peers and the untrustworthy peers can interact with each other. The interactions will be verified using some form of cryptographic mechanisms. Blockchain enables applications to run in a decentralized manner without any need for centralized authority. Blockchain makes it possible to do transactions between trustless parties without the need for centralized authorities (Christidis & Devetsikiotis, 2016). Blockchain uses cryptographic techniques to provide authentication functionality to peers. Smart contracts have been defined as "self-executing scripts" and usually smart contracts will be stored on the blockchain which can provide automated workflows in the network.

BLOCKCHAIN

Blockchain is similar to the database which is distributed among the peers participating in the network and the network structure it forms is peer to peer network so there is no need of centralized entity. Blockchain is a digital decentralized ledger (Novo, 2018). Blockchains are important because they provide a safe and secure way for people to make any type of transaction without having to trust anyone. Blocks in a blockchain can be thought of as a sheet of paper. Blocks, just like paper, can hold any type of data on them. The first block in the blockchain is called genesis block. The genesis block will be initialized when the blockchain network starts for the first time. The second block will have the transactions and the cryptographic hash value of the first block. Next blocks will follow the same.

Each block(other than genesis block) will include the hash value of the preceding blocks. This will form a linked list in which the node is a block. It is shown in Figure 1. Each block will have id associated with it. Each node will hold a copy of the blockchain. Each node can be used by a single user or more than one user. Bitcoin introduced blockchain architecture to solve the double-spending problem (Nakamoto, 2008).

Figure 1. Blockchain structure

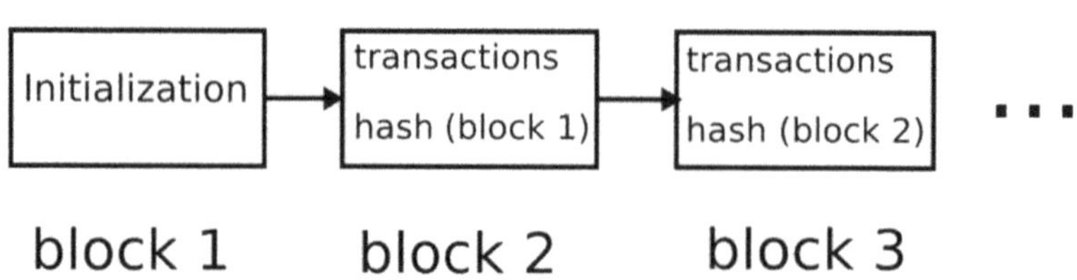

Since different peers will have the same copy of the blockchain, each peer will try to create the next block for the blockchain. Once the peers created a new block, the new block will be broadcasted to all other peers in the network. If two peers have created two different blocks then the latest and the longest block will be chosen as the next block. This process is called forks. The discarded block is called orphan blocks. Based on the total difficulty of blockchain, the longest block is chosen.

Each user will have a pair of a private key and public key (Hellman, 2002). Using those keys the user can access the blockchain. Transactions will be signed by the peers using the peer's private key. Once the transaction is signed and verified it will be included in the block. Once a transaction is added to the block it will be broadcasted to the other peers or users in the blockchain. Peers can validate the transactions by using the creators public key. After the validation and verification of transactions, the transaction will be ordered based on consensus mechanism and the transactions will be packed into a block and it will be broadcasted to the other peers in the network.

Blocks contain a set of transactions. Each transaction transfers the values from one entity to another entity. Pool miners are solo miners who mine the blocks. Mining operation bundles the set of transactions into blocks. Miners are chosen based on the consensus(proof-of-work in the case of bitcoin) mechanism. Once the miners finished mining they will be rewarded with transaction fees which is usually some amount of bitcoin in the bitcoin network. In the Proof-of-work(POW) approach difficulty level is increased after a certain amount of blocks mined. To avoid the double-spending issue, all the peers in the blockchain network will verify the transactions. Each peer will get an update from the network and it will verify the block by checking the validity of the transactions and previous block hash. Then the peer will append the block to its local blockchain. Each peer will have a set of rules for validating transactions. Using these rules the peer nodes can validate the transactions.

Properties of the Blockchain Technology

- Rules are determined by decentralized peers. Peers can decide the consensus algorithm. Peers can determine the properties of the blockchain network.
- All the peers can see and verify the transactions which had occurred in the blockchain network. Since all the peers can see the transaction non-repudiation is enforced. Public key cryptography is used for verifying the transaction.
- All the peers in the blockchain network will hold the copy of the blockchain ledger. Since all the peers hold the ledger even if one or more peers are compromised the remaining peers can preserve the integrity of the data.

- Transactions are validated by the peers chosen based on the decentralized consensus mechanism.
- Ledger is tamper-proof. Since all the peers will have the ledger to modify the data more than half of the peers should be compromised.

Types of Blockchain Network

The first type of blockchain network is a public blockchain network. Any node can participate in the public blockchain provided it has a valid private key-public key pair from the authorized certificate authority. Any node can participate in the consensus mechanism. The second type of blockchain network is private blockchain network. It is mostly used by the organizations where the transactions are business to business and only the authorized entities can participate in the transaction.

Advantages of Blockchain Technology

Blockchain is fully distributed peer to peer network where no central authority is used. Since it uses consensus algorithm to choose the node for mining the next block to modify the data the consensus mechanism has to be compromised. So it preserves the integrity of the data. Once a node created a block or added transaction to the block it can be verified by any node in the network. So even though the nodes are not trustworthy it can't fake the transactions. So it allows the interactions between non-trusting parties.

Techniques to Preserve Blockchain for Users

Use unique public key for each transaction. Since each transaction uses the unique public key the miner can always verify the block contents using the miner's private key. In private blockchain, if entities involved are competitors of each other use different network so that it can control the entities participating in the network.

CONSENSUS

It is an agreement between two or more agents. When transactions are added to the block, the order of these transactions is very important. All the nodes should agree on some common order then only it can be added to the block. In Proof-of-Work(POW) to add each block to the network, the node should solve a computationally hard cryptographic problem. In Proof of Stake(POS), only those peers who stake the specified amount of cryptocurrency can participate in the mining operation. If consensus is not maintained different nodes will have different states of the blockchain. To maintain consistency in the blockchain network distributed consensus algorithm is needed. Order of the transactions for the next block will be decided by the validating nodes. Whichever order is supported by the majority of the nodes that order will be chosen. In a public blockchain network, this will lead to "Sybil attack" (Douceur, 2002). Because a single malicious entity can use multiple ids and influence voting.

If a single entity uses multiple identities it can take over the network. Bitcoin solves this problem by using a computationally expensive mining operation. Bitcoin uses a consensus mechanism called proof-of-work. Proof of stake is used in ethereum. Private blockchain networks don't need computationally expensive consensus mechanisms because all the nodes are trustworthy. Practical Byzantine Fault Tolerance(PBFT) (Castro & Liskov, 1999) is used in most of the private blockchain networks. The main property of the PBFT is that it will be assumed that at least two-thirds of the nodes are honest and the remaining nodes can be faulty (n). So It will need at least 3n +1 nodes. In Juno blockchain network ("Juno", 2019) Tangaroa algorithm is used. " unique nodes list " is used in Ripple (Armknecht, Karame, Mandal, Youssef, & Zenner, 2015).

ASSETS

Assets can be represented in the table as digital assets. Each peer will use the public key for its identification. Transactions are used to modify the asset. Assets are introduced by some special transaction by a node or set of nodes which can be used only for this purpose. In private blockchain whichever node configures the blockchain network can create assets. That node can give permission for asset creation to other nodes also. All the nodes in the system should agree on how the assets are generated and how the assets are exchanged.

SMART CONTRACTS

The definition of Smart Contract is given as "computerized transaction protocol that executes the terms of contract" (Szabo, 1997) by Nick Szabo. In most of the blockchain implementations, smart contracts will be stored along with the data in the blockchain network itself (Christidis & Devetsikiotis, 2016). When two parties are doing a transaction smart contract can be used to reduce the need for a trusted middleman.

Smart Contract Properties and Usage

- Business logic can be expressed using smart contracts.
- Smart should be ready for all possible inputs.
- Smart Contracts are deterministic.
- All peers can see the code of the smart contract.
- The behavior of smart contracts should always be predictable.

EXISTING BLOCKCHAIN TECHNOLOGIES

Bitcoin

It is a cryptocurrency. It uses public-key cryptography and Proof-of-Work(POW) consensus mechanism. The transactions will be verified using the POW algorithm. A new block is created every 10 mins. When someone receives bitcoin it is recorded as UTXO (unspent transaction outputs). UTXO contains the bitcoin amount and locking script which can be used to send cryptocurrency from the amount.The minimum amount of cryptocurrency that can be sent is called “satoshi”.

Ethereum

It is designed by Vitalik Buterin (Wood, 2014).”Ether” the cryptocurrency used in ethereum. Smart contracts on ethereum can be programmed using the programming language called “solidity”.It uses the “Proof of Stake” consensus mechanism. Block creation time is 12 approximately seconds.

Hyperledger Fabric

It is a private blockchain (Androulaki et al., 2018) which is mainly used for business to business applications. It uses practical byzantine fault tolerance consensus mechanism.

USAGE OF BLOCKCHAIN IN IOT

In the manufacturing industry, the current centralized model has a high maintenance cost. Using blockchain software updates can be distributed so that even after the support for the device is stopped, the device can receive updates from the peers. A smart contract can be used to control and monitor the distribution process autonomously.

The peers who supply the software update can bill the other peers which need the software update if the blockchain network supports cryptocurrency.

FileCoin (Benet & Greco, 2018) can be used to rent the disk space of the user. EtherApis (“EtherAPIs”, 2019) can be used to bill the devices which need the API services.

CHALLENGES OF USING BLOCKCHAIN IN IOT

- high latency - since all the nodes should have updated copy of the ledger it will take a lot of time for a transaction to be propagated throughout the whole blockchain network.
- low throughput - only one block can be mined at a time it won’t be efficient if there are more number of blocks to be mined at the same time.
- Confidentiality of the data - Since all the nodes can look at the transaction the privacy of the user is compromised. To enforce the confidentiality the data should be encrypted with the user’s private key before adding it to the blockchain.
- Verifying the identity of the miners - since any node can become the miner it would be troublesome if the attackers took control of more than half of the mining nodes. So to solve this issue the number of nodes should be more in such a way that it would be impossible to take control of more than half of the nodes.
- Regulations - It is a very new technology. The government doesn’t have any regulations in place to handle all the situations.

BLOCKCHAIN IN IOT SECURITY

IBM is providing blockchain services in the supply chain domain so that it can efficiently track items when they are moving from source to destination. In IBM Watson IOT platform (Kaul, 2016) selected IOT data can be added to a private blockchain network. IOT devises data is converted into the format given by the blockchain network. The data can be accessed and supplied by the user’s of the network and they can verify the integrity of transactions. In IBM Watson IOT platform the users of the blockchain are mostly business partners who are using the IOT services.

Provence uses blockchain to provide trust between parties when they are using supply chain. Filament uses in-house built wireless sensors called “Taps” which can communicate with computers within 16 km. Taps create a mesh network in which blockchain is used to store the identification of devices. It uses smart contracts for communication using blockchain-backed identities because of that it doesn't rely on cloud services. Foxconn Technology, Robert Bosch, Cisco, Bank of New York Mellon and some other companies have formed a ground which focuses on securing IOT using blockchain technologies. IOT devises firmware and other important software's hash values can be stored in private or public blockchain. No one other than authenticated users can perform software updates on those devices. Before performing updates the software's integrity can be verified. IP spoofing and IP address forgery attacks can be prevented by using Identity and access control systems which are based on the blockchain technology. IOT security can be improved by using identity systems and access control systems which are based on the blockchain technology (Kshetri, 2017).

ADVANTAGES OF BLOCKCHAIN OVER CLOUD IN IOT

In the cloud model, most operations are performed in the servers in the cloud. Those servers identify and authenticate IOT devices. In the cloud model, the cost is very high. That is the biggest constraint when the cloud model is integrated into IOT. In 2016 every day 5.5 million new devices (Van Der Meulen, 2015) were connected to the IOT network, estimated by Gartner. Each node in the IOT network is vulnerable to various attacks which can compromise the whole IOT network (Banafa, 2016). Most prominent attacks in IOT are stealing the sensor data, modifying the sensor data, taking control of the IOT devices and DDOS attacks. Smart water meters can be used to monitor the water usage and alert users of any water leakage. But hackers can use this information to determine whether the user is at home or not. If there is no water usage for some specified period, then the hacker will determine that the user/consumer is not at the home. Centralized cloud models are susceptible to manipulation if the cloud service provider wants to modify something or remove some data to reduce the cost. Int 2014 in the city of Flint, Michigan flint authorities altered sample data taken by researchers to analyze the lead level in the drinking water.

In the Bitcoin network, the message exchanges between the nodes can be compared to the financial transactions. Messages are exchanged by smart contracts. Smart contracts ensure that messages are sent by the valid sender. This technology can eliminate another crisis as same as above. Blockchain eliminates the need for centralized authority which maintains the IOT network so it can save cost. By using decentralized architecture server downtime can be removed. The integrity of the data in the blockchain is preserved by using cryptographic keys and digital signature.

BLOCKCHAIN FOR SUPPLY CHAIN SECURITY IN IOT

Using blockchain the product can be traced from fully functional product to raw materials used. If some part is defective the products which are having the defective part are identified and tracked and the replacement for those parts can be done quickly and efficiently. If any of those products is compromised because of some security breach, those products can be traced back and security updates can be sent to only those products. Internet-connected cameras by Hangzhou Xiongmai Technologies recalled its products which are affected by Mirai malware (Antonakakis et al., 2017). If blockchain-based supply is used it would have become so easy to trace the users who are using vulnerable cameras and provide software updates or replacement to those users.

BLOCKCHAIN FOR ACCESS CONTROL IN IOT

Centralized access control systems are well suited for the traditional human-machine internet-based communication systems. In IOT devices are mobile (Sun & Ansari, 2016) and may be handled by different "management communities" from time to time. So centralized access control systems won't work for these type of systems. In IOT devices' battery,CPU and storage are limited. When devices are querying the access management system very frequently and the devices' access control system needs frequent updates centralized architecture will fail.

Advantages of Decentralized Access Control System

- Devices can be grouped into clusters. Each cluster can have separate access control policies.
- In centralized system access control, managers use sleep pattern to save energy. In this approach even if one system is sleeping another node can take care of the access control management.
- Multiple managers can also be possible.
- This approach is highly scalable.

The implementation uses a single smart contract. Blockchain stores and distributes access control information. So all the nodes will have a copy of the access control details. IOT devices are size constrained so it won't be able to have a copy of the blockchain.so "management hub" will act as an intermediary between IOT devices and blockchain. In this system, all the functionalities will be defined in the smart contract itself. To manage the smart contract, special nodes called "managers" will be used.

Decentralized Access Control Architecture

The blockchain-based decentralized access control system is shown in Figure 2 (Novo, 2018). Its components are explained to subsequent sections.

IOT Network

It allows communication between devices which are constrained in terms of power. All IOT devices would have a public key. The IOT devices are not part of the blockchain.

Managers

The permission for all the IOT devices will be controlled by the managers. The managers won't store the blockchain and won't participate in the mining operations. So these are lightweight nodes. So even one or a group of IOT devices can take the role of managers. Or some kind of edge devices can be used for this purpose. Managers can interact with the blockchain network only when it is required. All the IOT devices should be under manager's control. One or more IOT devices can be under a single manager. More than one manager can manage a single IOT device. Manager can specify access control permission for all the IOT devices it managers.

Agent Node

The smart contract is defined and deployed in the blockchain by the agent nodes. The smart contract will have an address and once the smart contract is accepted in the blockchain network, the address of the smart contract will be returned to the agent node.

Smart Contract

Transaction triggers the operations defined by the smart contract. Only managers can modify the smart contract. The smart contract controls all the operations are being performed in the blockchain network.

Figure 2. Blockchain based access control

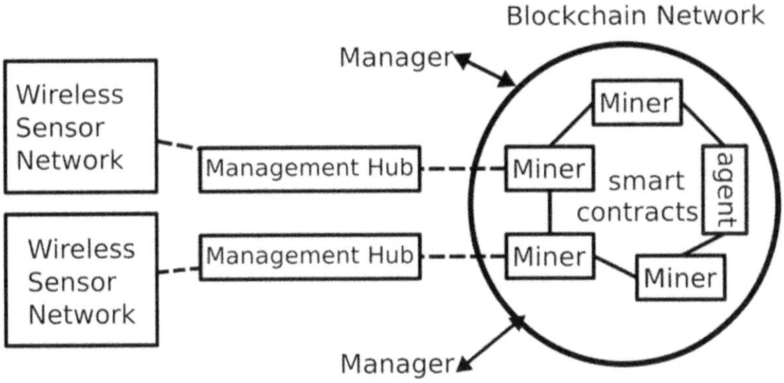

Blockchain Network

A private blockchain is used in this system. Any node can access the values in the blockchain network. But adding data in the blockchain network will be done by a specified set of nodes. Special miner nodes will perform the transactions in the blockchain.

Management Hubs

Management hub acts as an interface between the IOT device and block network(miner). It converts the message from the COAP format to JSON format. A single management hub can manage one or more wireless sensor networks. A single miner can have a connection with one or more management hubs. constrained devices can't become management hubs because it needs to process a huge number of simultaneous requests at once. IOT device should know the location of the management hub and management hubs should be able to verify IOT devices.

Interfaces Provided by the System

Smart Contract

Each manager will have set of a public keys. Each IOT device will have a set of public keys.
Policy p(s,t.r) - an IOT device 's' have access for resource 'r' of IOT device 't'
Functionalities provided by the smart contract is given below:

- RegisterManager (public key of manager): Registers new manager

- RegisterDevice: Registers an IOT device
- AddManagertoDevice: for IOT device it sets a manager
- RemoveManagerFromDevice: from IOT device it removes a manager. (manager can only self remove itself no other option)
- AddAccessControl: Add access control policies for a device by its manger
- DeregisterManager: Removes a manager(self removal)
- DeregisterDevice: Removes a device(done by any of its manager)
- RemovePermission: Remove IOT device access for a resource held by another IOT device
- QueryManager: Returns list of devices managed by a manager
- QueryPermission: Returns access control permissions for an IOT device

Management Hub

It will be used to query whether an IOT device can access a resource held by another IOT device.

System Workflow

There are 4 phases:

- Blockchain network initialization
- Registration of the nodes
- Defining access policies
- Discovering policies

Blockchain Network Initialization

Blockchain network is created for the access management system. Once the network is created then the smart contract will be deployed on the blockchain by the agent node and the address of the smart contract will be returned to that agent node. All managers will use this address to register itself as managers and to define access policies for a set of IOT devices it manages(this address is hard-coded in the managers and management hubs). The management hub will look for the miner node and it will connect to the closest miner node. All the management hubs will have set IOT devices associated with it.

Registration of the Nodes

Any node can be registered as a manager. Manager node can register IOT devices for which it can define access policies. A manager can manage any number of nodes. If an IOT device wants to register under a manger then it can verify the authenticity of the manager.

Management of the Nodes

Multiple managers can control the same IOT device. Managers can remove itself for an IOT device under its control. Only the manager can add another manager to the IOT device it manages. But it can't remove other managers.

Defining Access Control Policies

Managers can define access control policies for IOT devices it manages. Access control policy specifies which resource can be accessed by which IOT device. Each policy may have an expiry time.

Updating Access Control Policies

Manager can delete and modify the policy at any time.

Resource Request

If any device wants to access the resource of the other device it will query the management hub for this information. Management hub will query the miner which then queries the blockchain(it doesn't perform any transaction) and returns the answer to that query. Once the management hub gets the answer, it will pass the answer to the IOT device which asked for access permission details.

Limitations

Miners need to be paid for maintaining the blockchain network running.so it will increase the cost for the users who are using the blockchain. Since all the nodes should have updated content it will the processing time is very high. (12s for each transaction)(only the manager node will do the transaction. Management hub will not perform any transaction).

CONCLUSION

This chapter has briefly explained the concept of blockchain technology and the way the smart contract is used to control the blockchain. Origin of the blockchain technology has also been explained along with the use of blockchain technology. This chapter then has explained how blockchain can be integrated into IOT and what is the security issues it solves in IOT and about the performance penalty that the system incurs because of the addition of blockchain in IOT. This chapter has finally ended with a decentralized access control system which solves some of the problems the centralized access control system faces because of the huge growth of a number of IOT devices.

REFERENCES

Androulaki, E., Barger, A., Bortnikov, V., Cachin, C., Christidis, K., De Caro, A., ... Muralidharan, S. (2018, April). Hyperledger fabric: a distributed operating system for permissioned blockchains. In *Proceedings of the Thirteenth EuroSys Conference* (p. 30). ACM. 10.1145/3190508.3190538

Antonakakis, M., April, T., Bailey, M., Bernhard, M., Bursztein, E., Cochran, J., . . . Kumar, D. (2017). Understanding the mirai botnet. In *26th USENIX Security Symposium (USENIX Security 17)* (pp. 1093-1110). USENIX.

Armknecht, F., Karame, G. O., Mandal, A., Youssef, F., & Zenner, E. (2015, August). Ripple: Overview and outlook. In *International Conference on Trust and Trustworthy Computing*(pp. 163-180). Springer. 10.1007/978-3-319-22846-4_10

Banafa, A. (2016). *A secure model of IoT with Blockchain*. OpenMind.

Benet, J., & Greco, N. (2018). *Filecoin: A decentralized storage network*. Protoc. Labs.

Castro, M., & Liskov, B. (1999, February). *Practical Byzantine fault tolerance* (Vol. 99). OSDI.

Christidis, K., & Devetsikiotis, M. (2016). Blockchains and smart contracts for the internet of things. *IEEE Access: Practical Innovations, Open Solutions*, *4*, 2292–2303. doi:10.1109/ACCESS.2016.2566339

Douceur, J. R. (2002, March). The sybil attack. In *International workshop on peer-to-peer systems* (pp. 251-260). Springer. 10.1007/3-540-45748-8_24

EtherAPIs: Decentralized Anonymous Trustless APIs. (2019). Retrieved from https://etherapis.io/

Hellman, M. E. (2002). An overview of public key cryptography. *IEEE Communications Magazine*, *40*(5), 42–49. doi:10.1109/MCOM.2002.1006971

Juno: Smart Contracts Running on a BFT Hardened Raft. (2019). Retrieved from https://github.com/kadena-io/juno

Kaul, A. (2016). *IBM Watson IoT and its integration with blockchain*. Academic Press.

Kshetri, N. (2017). Can blockchain strengthen the internet of things? *IT Professional*, *19*(4), 68–72. doi:10.1109/MITP.2017.3051335

Nakamoto, S. (2008). *Bitcoin: A peer-to-peer electronic cash system*. Retrieved from http://bitcoin. org/bitcoin. pdf

Novo, O. (2018). Blockchain meets IoT: An architecture for scalable access management in IoT. *IEEE Internet of Things Journal*, *5*(2), 1184–1195. doi:10.1109/JIOT.2018.2812239

Sun, X., & Ansari, N. (2016). EdgeIoT: Mobile edge computing for the Internet of Things. *IEEE Communications Magazine*, *54*(12), 22–29. doi:10.1109/MCOM.2016.1600492CM

Szabo, N. (1997). The idea of smart contracts. *Nick Szabo's Papers and Concise Tutorials, 6*.

Van Der Meulen, R. (2015). Gartner says 6.4 billion connected 'things' will be in use in 2016, up 30 percent from 2015. Gartner.

Wood, G. (2014). Ethereum: A secure decentralised generalised transaction ledger. *Ethereum project yellow paper, 151*, 1-32.

Chapter 2
The Role of Blockchain Technology to Make Business Easier and Effective

Vartika Koolwal
Central University of Rajasthan, India

Sunil Kumar
Central University of Rajasthan, India

Krishna Kumar Mohbey
https://orcid.org/0000-0002-7566-0703
Central University of Rajasthan, India

ABSTRACT

Blockchain is the new "buzz" word that has attracted the attention of industries and businesses. It is an innovative technology that provides information exchange in an efficient and transparent manner. It has a wide range of application varying from cryptocurrency, healthcare, risk management, education, financial services, internet of things (IoT), border security to public services. However, security issues and threats of this novel technology is also an important topic. In this chapter, the authors provide a comprehensive study of applications, challenges, and issues and how to combat them in the blockchain. Major areas of concern are security, scalability, cryptocurrency's malicious attacks, etc.

DOI: 10.4018/978-1-7998-0186-3.ch002

INTRODUCTION

The escalating popularity of digital crypto-currency has led to the foundation of blockchain (Staff, 2016). The blockchain is a distributed public ledger that maintains transaction between two parties in a permanent and verifiable way (Iansiti & Lakhani, 2017). It is a bedrock mechanics for the successful implementation of virtual currency i.e. Bitcoin (Nakamoto, 2008). Bitcoin is awarded as the best-performing currency for the year 2015 and 2016 (Desjardins, 2017) and it has total bitcoin (sum of all bitcoins) of 17,523,954 BTC with its monetary value of $ 59,561,046,878 USD by bitinfochart[1] in February, 2019. Bitcoin, along with its underlying technology, has exhibited promising operational prospects which have attracted the interest of industries and academia. This technology can be put forward into many domains like finance (Eyal, 2017; Guo & Liang, 2016), healthcare (Ekblaw, Azaria, Halamka, & Lippman, 2016; Yue, Wang, Jin, Li, & Jiang, 2016), internet of things (Huh, Cho, & Kim, 2017), software engineering (Xu et al., 2016; Nordström, 2015), infrastructure (Shrier, Wu, & Pentland, 2016) and many more.

Financial institutions, BAWT and GAFA companies (Baidu, Alibaba, Weibo, Tencent, Google, Amazon, Facebook, Apple, respectively) or some government bodies tend to implement this distributed technology for their operation. Facebook has shown keen interest in blockchain and has a devoted team for blockchain. It may this disruptive technology to issue its own crypto-currency or have faster payment channel or for storing the user details and many more[2]. Microsoft, has created 'Coco' blockchain construct to work in big business framework to render solutions to institutional clients[3]. Google is working in blockchain related to cloud business to make data more secure[4]. IBM has Fabric blockchain-project[5] to give support for the implementation of blockchain solutions.

Despite all these promising potentials, it has encountered many security attacks, data tampering, and privacy breach. Due to network interconnectivity, more than 500,000 new malware and spyware variants surface on an ordinary level. Majority of these are polymorphic malware which is cryptic to penetrate the latest detection program in the market (Gallagher, 2014). Cryptocurrency hacks have become more prominent and valuable with more than $10M+ hacks happening regularly after mid-2016 when crypto-market started taking off (Raul, 2018). Recently, there was a crypto hack on Japanese exchange, Coincheck Inc., (BBC News, 2018), stating a $500M digital tokens were stolen. This was regarded as world biggest theft ever in digital currency. Recently, the government of India has taken the measures to ban bitcoins due to tax issues and criminal activity[6]. Such an incidence throws light on the need for a safer and secure system.

The aim of this chapter is to summaries the implementation of blockchain and similar digital distributed ledger technology in different businesses beyond its application in finance. We are not proposing any framework or new implementation of this technology. The overall journey is divided into the section where we focus on blockchain and its key features in section 2. Section 3 depicts the application and opportunities of this technology in domain specific areas. In section 4, states the issues, challenges, and solutions. Lastly, conclusion and future work is included in section 5.

BLOCKCHAIN

In recent years, the advancement in the distributed computing and cryptography has laid the foundation for the innovative Blockchain technology. Nakomoto (2008) proposes a model which is the collection of nodes with distributed ledger and secure database. This novel technology is the result of skillful craftsman of above mention approaches. It is now a general-purpose technology, which has diffused in various walks of life.

Blockchain is a series of time-stamped and immutable records that is managed by distributed cluster of computers. Figure 1 shows the basic blockchain concept. Each block is secure and bound together by cryptographic chain. It consists of two parts i.e. blocks and transactions. Block is a collection of stored data which is associated with timestamp, sequence, hash, etc. Transaction is the action provoked by the user. Bitcoin is the successful implementation of the blockchain technology. Public and private blockchain can be deployed in industry in numerous ways.

For ease of convenience, blockchain is categories according to the purpose and usage (Swan, 2015). It is evolved from blockchain 1.0 of crypto-currency, deployment of digital currencies and related operations like remittances, money transfer, digital payment system etc. Then, is blockchain 2.0 of smart-contract. It reduces the cost

Figure 1. Basic blockchain concept

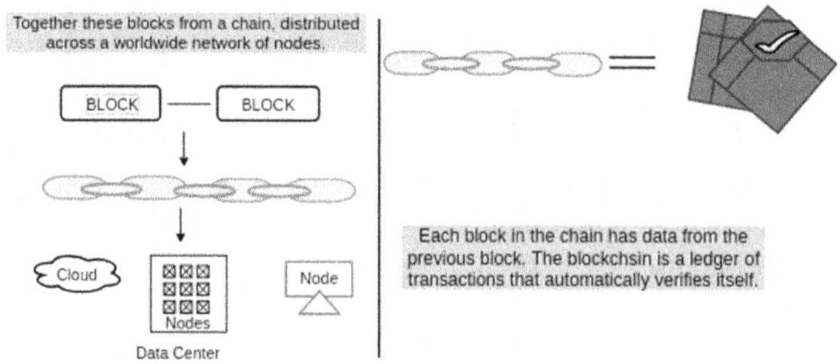

cash agreements. It deals with the potential activities in areas of stocks, titles, smart property which could be automatically handled by contract. Blockchain 3.0 is all other than finance. It deals with flourishment of blockchain in different ventures of works such as government, health, education etc.

Key features of blockchain are:

1. Decentralization

In traditional system, each deal needs to be verified by the centralized management system which is cumbersome resulting in efficiency bottleneck. But, in blockchain there is a peer-to-peer transactions conducted in a distributed manner. It reduces the server costs and alleviates the performance barrier of central server.

2. Automatic Execution Contract

Blockchain has automatic execution code stored to facilitate the operation of the transaction that is, smart contract. It can complement or substitute, for legal contracts. It helps in faster completion of the tasks.

3. Auditability

Each of the transaction is recorded with a timestamp making it easily validated, verified and traceable from the previous records. Each record can be traversed to previous record iteratively. It improves the traceability and reduces the chances of fraud.

4. Persistent

As each transaction is stored after validating it from previous hashed records, tampering of the data is very difficult. So, it allows the records to be distributed freely but doesn't allow it to be copied.

5. Anonymity

Each user with the generated address can communicate with the blockchain network. Moreover, a user can produce multiple address to prevent identity exposure. There is no centralized record keeping system. This preserves the privacy of the transaction to a certain level.

APPLICATIONS

Entrepreneurs have grasped the promising potentials of blockchain. They have already commenced on the journey to get benefit from this novel technology. Figure 2 is an overview of diverse application of blockchain technology in different economic domain.

3.1 Government

There are numerous operations being probe in blockchain technology to aid the government functionality and to take e-government to the next level. Auditability, transparency and integrity are some blockchain key attributes which can go long way for better management of government affairs.

1. E-Voting

Blockchain and smart contract can be used as a service for e-voting system. The voting booth is downloaded by the voters where, they securely submit the identity information for verification, entitling them as a valid voter. The voter casts the vote and submits their ballot to a secure ballot box based blockchain which provide ballot secrecy and anonymity.

Hjalmarsson et al. (2018) has set up Go-Ethereum and permissioned Proof-of-Authority (PoA) blockchain for novel e-voting system. Figure 3 show the structure of the blockchain where district node represents the voting district. Bootnode is a coordination service that helps the district nodes to discover one another and

Figure 2. Blockchain application in different economic ventures

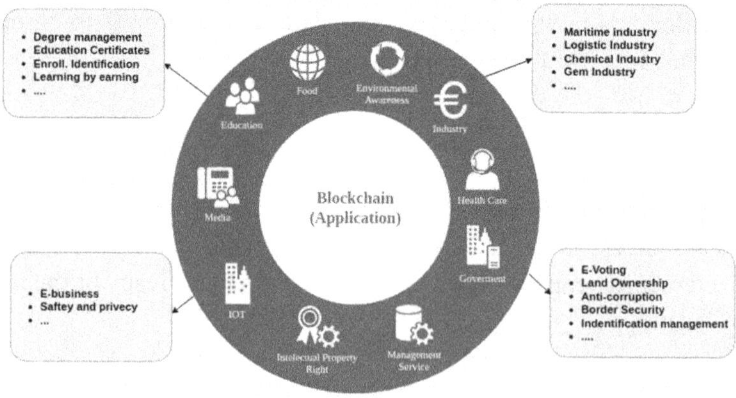

Figure 3. E-Voting structure

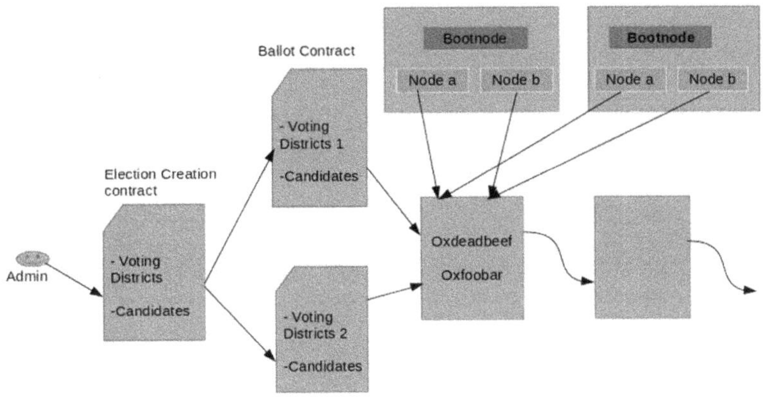

communicate. After, the initial set up we have smart contract for the election agreement (voter, election agreement), process (voter registration) and voting transactions. Dagher et al implements BroncoVote (Marella, Mohler, & Milojkovic, 2017) a university-level blockchain-based voting system It is implemented using Ethereum blockchain, smart contract and homomorphic encryption.

2. Land Title

More than 70% of the population lacks "legally registered titles" to their lands, according to the World Bank (2017). For effective land management only one-third of world-wide countries track land ownership digitally (Deininger, 2018). People will face difficulty to justify their purchase on land without formal access to a land registry, thereby, constantly living in fear to lose their land. Strong land management and safe record keeping is necessary.

According to CNBC, an Indian state, Andra Pradesh has partnered with Swedish company ChromaWay to build blockchain based solutions to fight against land fraud (Browne, 2017). Another, is the small blockchain technology collaboration project to form a land registry in the city of Panchkula, in Haryana, India (Oprunenco & Akmeemana, 2018). The government of Georgia has shown strong interest in land-based project titling to move on blockchain platform. The new blockchain system takes 10 min for land registry where citizen carry out operations from smartphones using modern verification scheme (Shang & Price, 2019). Figure 4 presents the land titling via blockchain is faster and better. The government stores operation on smart contract which increases transparency and public trust. In 2018, a total of 1.5 million land titles were published on the blockchain in the Republic of Georgia which provide security and immutability to the data (Weiss & Corsi, 2017).

Figure 4. Land titling in Republic of Georgia

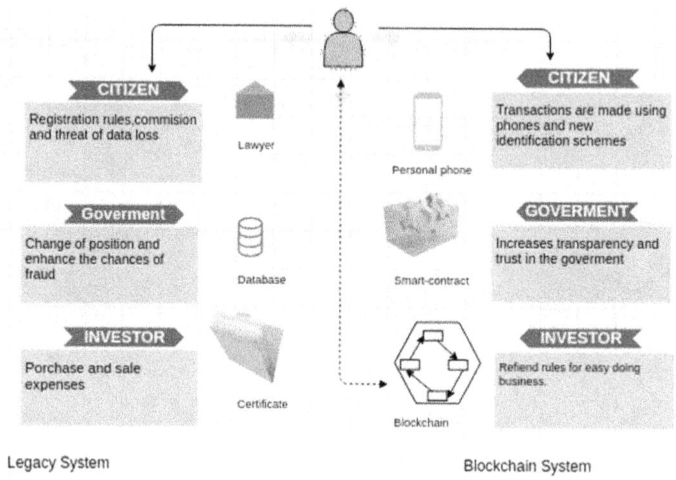

3. Border Security

Blockchain can provide support in anti-terrorism activity by providing the facility of blacklisting in a smart contract. A hash of biometric ID and travel document of an individual need to be stored in blockchain. When a travel document is blacklisted, it will be immediately made available to all the agencies and border security points thus rendering immediate control over suspicious travel moment (Bashir, 2018). Figure 5 presents the procedure of the border security using the blockchain. Passport is scanned using the RFID reader and is verified using the hash and unique id from the records stored in the smart contract blockchain. If the passport is already blacklisted it is rejected else the person to travel is safe.

The UN's World Food Program (WFP) has used blockchain to support refugees. Instead of the recipients, money was paid directly to the merchants. Banks were not involved and beneficiaries receive goods directly from the merchants (Menezes, 2017).

4. ID-Card

Central online database has many times proven that citizen personal information is vulnerable, tampered and insecure. Blockchain implemented record keeping allows control over personal information access. User can know who have seen or utilized their personal records for what purpose. Blockchain serves as a platform for using single ID for various purpose like pension, marriage registration, tax or benefit (Bashir, 2018). Deng et al. (2019) proposed a cloud-based framework for

Figure 5. Passport verification using blockchain as a border security measure

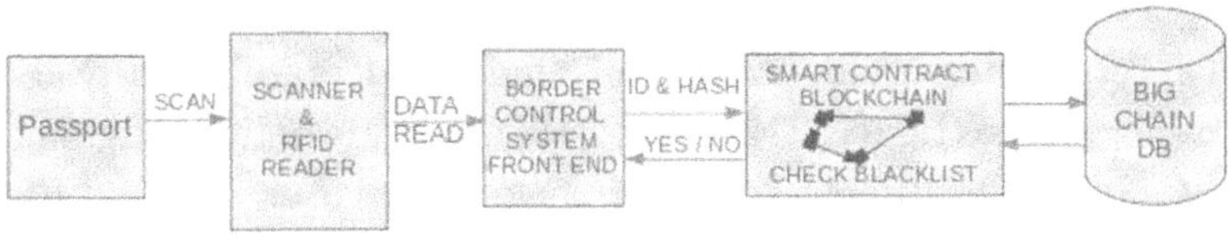

preservation of the trusted electronic records in blockchain. They have used proof of retrievability to guarantee the credibility.

3.2 Education

Some universities and schools have implemented this distributed ledger technology in education. To manage student's certificates given from MOOC platforms, the University of Nicosia uses blockchain technology (Sharples & Domingue, 2016). Stanford University has around 10 blockchain-related courses like "Cryptocurrencies and Blockchain Technologies" and "Cryptography" and have started their own Center for Blockchain Research. Cornell University offers 9 courses blockchain-related courses like "Introduction to Blockchains, Cryptocurrencies, and Smart Contracts" (Martin, 2018).

1 Learning By Earning

It means students will get rewards for their efforts in learning. Many schools are implementing such approach for motivating student to learn. In Sharples and Domingue (2016), the authors claim for "Kudos", an Educational Reputational currency. Kudos can be used for measuring learning outcomes and will be stored in digital wallet. Moreover, real-time awards can be given by the instructors to the student through some simple clicks. Student will get some kind of rewards as virtual currency according to smart contract. This reward can be stored in educational blockchain wallet which may later be used to pay fees, tuitions, or could even exchange with real money.

2 Degree Management

Blockchain helps in reducing fraud of degree. It could be used to grand and manage the student's degree. The data is verified with user ID and is stored in blockchain. The stored data are checked, validate, and maintained by efficient miners from all around the world. Blockchain ledger are immutable and trustworthy. Thus, frauds are reduced as reliability and authority are ensured (Chen, Xu, Lu, & Chen, 2018).

3 Education Certificate

Educational certificates are indication of student's learning ability. Education Certificate Blockchain (ECBC) (Xu et al., 2017) supports high throughput and low delay. ECBC is drafted with transaction format to protect user's privacy. Blockchain manages each educational certificate storing certificate holder name, holder's contact details, type of certificate etc., all this information in encrypted form.

3.3 Industry

As one of the technologies of fourth industrial revolution, since the invention of engine, electricity, and Internet, blockchain utility need to be exploited further. G20 is an international platform of governments, central banks and European Union. It has New Industrial Revolution Action Plan which acknowledges the implementation of public and private blockchain (Maupin, 2017). Some instances of implementation of this innovative technology in economic sector are listed below.

1. Maritime Industry

The success story of blockchain implementation in other industries has provided confident for its adoption in maritime commerce. 80% of the routine consumed goods are carried by maritime industry. More than $4 trillion valued goods are shipped every year[7].

Czachorowski et al. (2019) has proposed ways to diffuse blockchain in marine industry. Blockchain renders full transparency between contracting party involve in proof of work. It provides class society inspection and port state management and audit compliance. Public blockchain TrustMe™ is used for new verified gross mass. It can solve the problem of faster creation of Bill of Landing (BOL), which is important for cargo delivery. Shirani (2018) proposed a web client application using proof-of-concept. It is build using Hyperledger Sawtooth Linux framework, to explain the application of a maritime logistic blockchain. It also hints about positive future of implementing blockchain in this area.

2. Logistic Industry

Kuperberg et at. (2019) introduced implementation of blockchain in decentralized railway control and simplifies usage of billing. Trains can determine likely routes and book them directly. It is based upon transparent and binding smart contract which provide conflict-fee resource booking. Immutability of blockchain can be used as a proof for vehicle management (Hofman & Brewster, 2019). Vehicle driving in the specific road when the traffic ticket was issued, can be recorded to trace it.

3. Chemical Industry

A change from a technology-oriented to a value-driven methodology for blockchain-based implementation is needed (Maxeiner, Martini, & Sandner, 2018). It can help to increase the profits and secure future growth by improving productivity, minimizing cost, and enhance company visibility. Leaders in the chemical industry can pilot and operate blockchain technology to test the possible positive returns. It can join business partners, suppliers, customers, sellers, equipment, manufactures, etc. US company, Walmart considers the use of blockchain to trace chemicals[8]. German chemical company BASF, who is working on supply chain tracking. The project goal was to render position and movement information of the goods in the supply chain. It highlighted the idea that the project could track, like car parts that go missing or all shipments shared between all points in manufacturing pipeline[9].

4. Gem Industry

To increase transparency and traceability of in the diamond, colored stone and pearl industries blockchain technologies are been explored. Such methods could be used in quality control and process improvement, to correctly identify, describe, disclose treated, synthetic materials, and fulfill demand for rock's origin information (Cartier, Ali, & Krezemnicki, 2018). Data is added to the blockchain, each transactional step is verified. Ownership is attributed and the record is timestamped, encrypted and stocked permanently in immutable chain. Tracr[10] company is setting the standard for blockchain traceability solutions in diamond industry. It has tracked diamonds from mine- to- finger through blockchain.

3.4 Media

Copyrights and transfer issues can smoothly be managed by blockchain. It provides a network where digital data (song or movie) is cryptographically guarantee to be owned only by the party who pays for it (Bashir, 2018). The illegal copying of digital music files can be removed by blockchain's immutability. Smart contract can manage the distribution and payment to all concerned players in the industry. Original matter is at times, edited for creative subject formation or tampered to embed false propagation over digital media. Bhowmik et al. (2017) presents a novel watermarking- based multimedia blockchain structure that can address such problems. Its framework contains a cryptographic hash (includes transactional histories) and image hash (contains original media content). If, the watermark is obtained, then first part is placed on a distributed ledger, and latter part is used to identify the tampered area.

3.5 Food

Distributed ledger technology has increase international trade agreement in the field of agriculture, like World Trade organization agreements, provisions contracts, Paris agreement on climate Changes, Basel agreement (Maupin, 2017). It emphasizes on transparency and responsibility to compliance of such agreements. Food frauds are acknowledged internationally due to health hazards, resulting in importance of food traceability. In a pilot project done by Walmart and IBM, they were able to trace a mango in a store to its origin from a farm through distribution process, import/export channels, transportation system, warehouse in Mexico in record breaking time of 2.2 seconds (Yinnas, 2018). Moreover, they have conducted similar test on Pork in china farm to Walmart store. Such capability will ensure rapid processing of recalls. It will also limit possible exposure to affected products. Tian (2017) introduces agri-food chain traceability system using blockchain and IoT. The chain interlinks all the possible hazard center and collects information about food storing, transferring, sharing.

3.6 Sustainable Environment

Blockchain technology can be used in power and energy for sustainable environment. Brooklyn Microgrid model electricity transaction among customer using blockchain (Sawa, 2018). Smart meters were used to measure excess PV power and deliver crypto-tokens. Consumers offer for clean energy through transaction on Ethereum smart contracts. These transactions are managed and monitored to prevent double-spending problem. Energy Blockchain lab Inc.[11] of IBM, has created efficient and transparent platform that permits high-emission organizations to oversees carbon footprints. It allows high emitters to meet quotas by purchasing credits from low emitters. It produces more efficient green energy marketplace with blockchain technology.

Panda Green Energy Group Company, is the world's leading eco-development solution has started smart power plant blockchain management project[12]. Along with, the development of Pandacoin digital currency used for trading in new energy i.e. solar, hydropower and wind.

3.7 Intellectual Property Management

Intellectual property means protection of ideas and information which has commercial value. For the problem of royalty stability, we can use 'pegged cryptocurrencies' whose value is endorsed by stable assets (Ito & O'Dair, 2018). This innovative technology can be used to manage the intellectual property. Firstly, due to authenticity as metadata can be tangled to the original file such as song or film. Secondly, due traceability property can get to ownership and usage. Lastly, enables faster payment of royalties (O'Dair & Beaven, 2017).

3.8 Internet of Things (IoT)

Blockchain can solve the problems in the IoT especially in data security and reliability (Wang et al., 2019). IoT tools can connect with blockchain network to provide primary function of blockchain such as generation of raw sensory data, validating dealings, and mining blocks (Sharma, Moon, & Park, 2017). IOTA is a blockchain solution for IoT networks[13].It is based on 'Tangle' technology which has no blocks, chains or fees. It has anti-tampering distributed ledger with Direct Acyclic Graph (DAG) structure. In this, transactions are the only storage units.

In Yinnas (2018), the authors proposed a food supply chain based on Radio Frequency Identification (RFID), Hazard Analysis and Critical Control Points (HACCP) and blockchain technology. It uses IoT based mechanism to gather, store and manage data of food products on BigchainDB. The food chain members are suppliers, producers, retailers, wholesalers, distributers, consumers and certificates. All the members have the power to add, update and verify the information on the BigchainDB, after registration as a user. Each food product is associated with a distinct digital identifier tag (RFID) to connect physical item with the virtual existence. Product profile information providers the virtual identity. Users data is also store in the system which has location, certifications, relation with the item. The suggested framework is managed by set of rules which define the user interaction with the system, data sharing rights, storage of data. Rules can be altered by broadcasting it to all nodes and verified by the majority. Figure 6 presents the food blockchain where the user register using cryptographic keys. User can then access to the products associated with tags and can trace them.

ISSUES AND CHALLENGES

As a budding technology, blockchain faces a number of problems which are listed below.

Figure 6. Agri-food chain process

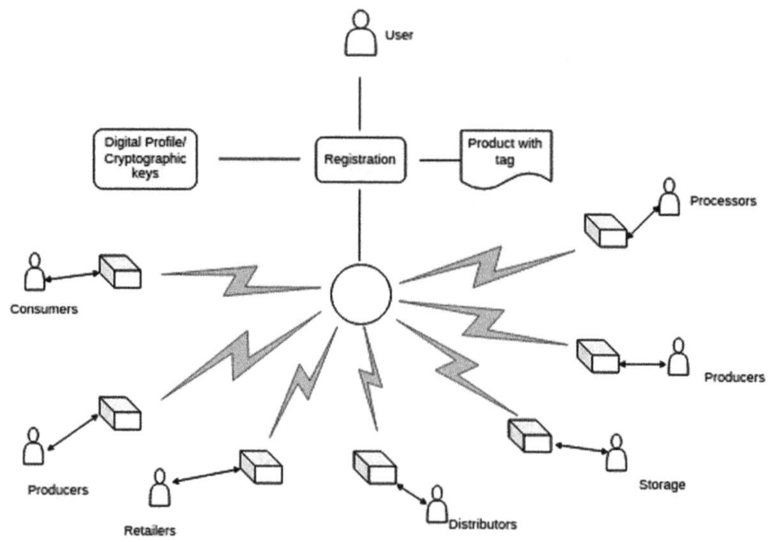

4.1 Scalability

As blockchain and cryptocurrencies are gaining popularity and creating public awareness, there are more likely chances it may not keep up with the growing demands and have hit the scalability limit. Bitcoin blockchain is exponentially growing since its introduction in 2009 to starting of January 2019 with approximately 197 gigabytes in size (Statista, 2019) signifies the need to deal with future demands of the resources (storage, response time, consensus delay, cost). Bitcoin, used as an actual global payment system suffers from its low capacity transactional throughput which is, 7 transactions per seconds (Croman et al., 2016).

Effort recommended to deal with scalability issue: -

1. Forks Increase Network Transaction:

The fork is the process of changing the consensus protocol of the bitcoin process in order to increase the network transaction processing limit. They occur due to the decentralized node version. They could be of hard or soft. Hard forks are formed when a group of nodes is upgraded or a new version is run on them, they are incompatible with the old version. Moreover, the old nodes can't run on the new version, as a result, one chain is split into two. Ex Bitcoin Cash, Bitcoin XT, Bitcoin Classic are hard to fork increasing the maximum block size.

Similarly, there is Soft fork means minimal changes in the present technology which will have only point effect allowing it to run with old nodes. In this node can upgrade to the new version gradually. Unlike hard fork soft node will only have one chain. Ex Ethereum is a soft fork. Figure 7 displays the hard and soft forks.

2. Rebuild Blockchain Using Scalable Protocol

Eyal et al (2016) proposed a new scalable protocol Bitcoin-NG (Next Generation). This protocol achieves improved result due to the decoupling of the conventional block into two segments: key block for electing a leader and microblock to backlog all transactions. One of the competing miner will become the leader which will be responsible for the microblock generation until a new leader shows up. In this, longest chain strategy with a count of key block and microblock scarring, no weight is extended. Moreover, can use the GHOST protocol of Sompolinsky and Zohar (2013) to improve scalability by chaining its chain selection rule. Redesigning of the blockchain to tradeoff between the block size and network security can also be done.

3. Sharding

Sharding is a layer 1 solution for scalability which divides the block verification process into segments and running parallel segments to collate the complete data. Luu et al. (2016) proposes ELASTICO -a distributed protocol for permission-less blockchain which scales transaction rates linearly. Similarly, Gencer, van Renesse, and Sirer (2017) suggest ASPEN which shares to scale with a high number of

Figure 7. Hard and soft fork creation

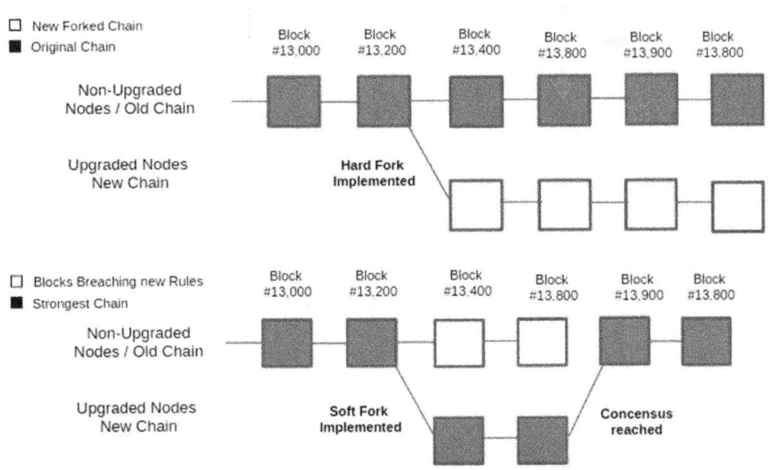

transactions. It reforms scalability by solving non-miner participants (service users) from the duty of processing, storing and proliferate irrelevant data to test the validity of interested services. In this, a coffee shop need not bother itself with land and deed records to certify the payment system.

4. Plasma

Plasma is a scalable Ethereum blockchain. It utilizes a group of smart contracts to create sidechains hierarchical trees called subchains (Poon & Buterin, 2017). These subchains live inside the root blockchain and regularly communicate with the Ethereum parent-chain. The subchains are offline so they could be as many as desired. Plasma could support nearly infinite scaling (Imbrex, 2017). Ethereum's Plasma will cut down irrelevant data from root-chain, resulting in less time and power needed to process the transactions.

5. Lighting Network

Lighting Network[14] is a smart contract functionality using a decentralized network in the blockchain. It is capable of billions of transactions per seconds over the network (Poon & Dryja, 2016). For this to work, there is a need to make a multi-signature wallet where the transacting user can access it with their own private keys. After, creating a wallet, the transacting user can perform infinite transactions among them which is a redistribution of the stored funds in the wallet. The real distribution of funds is done when the channel gets closed. So, the Lighting network gives the user the opportunity to perform zillions of transactions outside the root blockchain, recording them as one single transaction only after the channel is closed. It provides information about its initial and final situation on the blockchain. This concept is widely adopted to scale the blockchain.

6. Segregated Witness (SegWit)

Segregate means segregate and Witnesses are transaction signatures. Therefore, Segregated Witness implies to separate transaction signatures. SegWit is the technology which helps to increase the limit of block size in the blockchain by removing signature data from transactions. This frees up space when certain parts of a transaction are cleared up. This free space can be used to add more transactions to the chain (Frankenfield, 2018). It expands the block size limit to 4Mb, implying a single block can store the records of over 8,000 transactions.

4.2 Security

Blockchain, being the basic technology for bitcoin, are becoming part of the mainstream. The blockchain is one of the core technologies of the finance industry, its security is the utmost priority. Numerous security attacks and vulnerabilities have been reported. Table 1 shows the overview of security issues. According to the Center for Strategic and International Studies and McAfee reported that nearly and Cyber-attacks was projected to get 1% of the global GDP ($600 billion) is lost to cybercrime each year (Palmer, 2018). Recently, in starting of 2019, Economics times (Zraick, 2019) reported that the Canadian CEO of crypto-Exchange died, where the company can't pay investors as only, he had the password, making people loss around $250 million. This arises the questions of How can we guarantee that our money in the digital currency will return back to us? or Can't we access our own money?

Some of the security issues in blockchain are discussed below:

1. 51% Vulnerability

This is one of the major concerns as it targets the mining process. Blockchain-based on PoW model, if an individual miner's hashing capacity is more than 50% of the computing capacity in the mining process, then such individual will be able to modify, exclude, and self-reverse transactions and could stop some or all 'mining' of the authentic blocks for their selfish benefit. Such an attack also stimulates other attacks. Some researcher has claimed that even with 40% of the computational resources, they can overcome 6-deep confirmed transactions with successes probability of 50% (Malhotra, 2013).

We can use checkpoints so that the transactions done before the checkpoints can't be altered. We could also use Application-specific integrated circuits (ASIC) miner to bring down the hashing power. This will enhance the mining hardware which has outperformed the standard mining hardware (CPU's and GPU's). Another solution of this would be to raise the number of confirmations before taking in account the fully complete transactions. BTC on Feathercoin to combat such attacks increase number of confirmations from usual 6 to 100 and the Reddcoin merchants' hike from 6 to 60.

2. Double Spending:

Double spending means when the user uses same cryptocurrency multiple times for different transactions making the correct transaction as invalid. This normally happen in "fast payment" mode. There was intrusion on May 2018, Bitcoin-Gold undergo through 51% attack and double spending problem for several days causing the stealing of more than $18 million (Faridi, 2018). This problem is likeable to be possible in all proof-of-work chains as a result of consensus rules inherited from bitcoin. Figure 8 shows the double spending situation where buyer makes transaction with coin to the seller X. At the same time, with the same coin it again conducts a dealing with seller Y by changing the timestamp to make this fraud transaction look like genuine. Since, bitcoin associate will not allow multiple transaction with the same input, they will put forward the first transactions and reject all the other. Thereby, original receiver will not be able to continue the transactions.

The proposed measure could be to change the Satoshi consensus of longest chain rule by making it more expensive to double spend. Garoffolo, Stabilini, Viglione, and Stav (2018) introduced a penalty system on delayed block submission in correspondence to the amount of time the block was concealed from the public network. Time is measured in block intervals rather than, generally, timestamp.

3. Time-Jacking Attack

Time-jacking is altering the network time counter of the node in order to make them reject the valid block. Every node maintains its own network time internally which is the median time of a node's neighbor. The network time and system time are synchronized regularly. An attacker can possibly speed up or slow down the network counter time of the nodes by associating multiple peers and broadcasting inaccurate timestamp (Garoffolo et al., 2018). To attempt such attack hackers, need to create time gap by lagging segment of the system until either the target or unaffected node made a block itself, or operators interrupt or reset the clock between the mining machine and target node. Such result in dropping of valid block and money lost or stolen. This malpractice leads to wastage or computational time and double-spending problem.

The potential solutions could be using system time instead of the node time to determine the accepted time range of the valid block (Boverman, 2011). We could

Figure 8. Double-spending attack

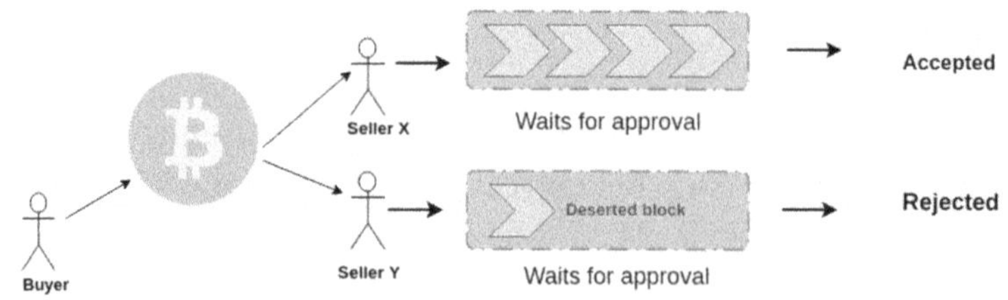

also narrow down the acceptable time ranges. Moreover, we should use only the trusted peers for medium time calculation.

4. Selfish Mining

Selfish mining is a strategy where a group of miners conspire to expand their revenue. They misguide other honest miners, leading them to exhaust their computing power in false direction (Solat & Potop-Butucaru, 2016). The attacker keeps some privately mined block hidden and forks them to create a private chain longer than public chain. This private branch will be broadcasted to the public chain and it would be accepted by all miners as it is longer than public chain. Before the private blockchain broadcasting, all the honest miners were wasting their resources on the futile branch whereas selfish miners add blocks in private chain without competition. Thereby, selfish miners tend to crop up more revenues.

Selfish mining is shown in Figure 9, where mining is done separately on private blockchain, then when it grows stronger it is broadcasted to public and becoming the largest chain to mine further.

Selfish-Mine is the strategy suggested by Ittay et al. (Eyal & Sirer, 2014), allowing honest miners to mine on stale public blockchain by adapting the blockchain protocol to decrease the success possibility of selfish mining.

Figure 9. Selfish mining

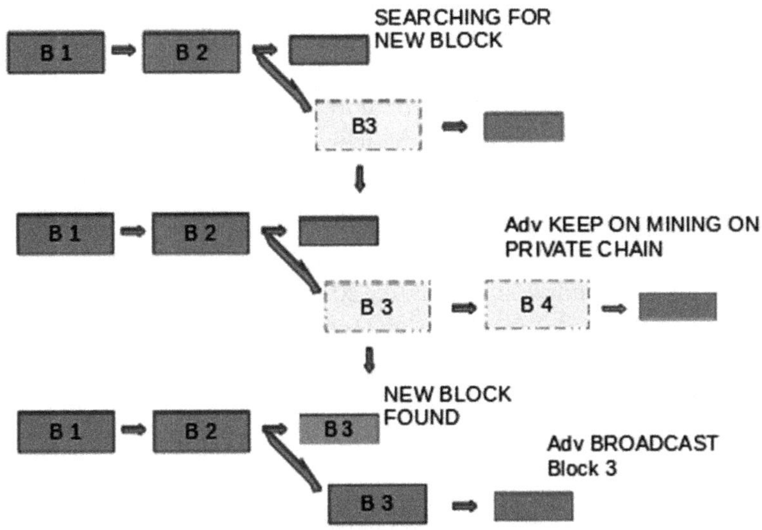

5. DDoS Attack

Distributed Denial of Services due to legitimate users are denied the services due to high number of illegitimate users. Multiple DDoS mugger start the attack simultaneously. Malicious miners perform this attack to honest miners taking fighting miner out of the network. This makes the malignant miners to increase mining at effective hash rate.

To resolve this, can implement the Proof of activity as blockchain protocol which validate all the transactions are valid and genuine (Bentov, Lee, Mizhari, & Rosenfeld, 2014). Every user reach at a consensus on the actual public ledger. Moreover, in Neudecker, Andelfinger, & Hartenstein (2015), put forward the idea of network partitioning, hence isolating the honest nodes by decreasing their reputation from the network.

6. Private Key Security

Private key is considered as identity of the user on the blockchain. User have to create, generate and manage the key on their own. However, this private key can be hacked and misused to manipulate any transaction or is at the risk of being tampered. If the key is stolen, it is tough to keep track of criminal activity and regain the altered blockchain transaction.

7. Criminal Smart Contracts (CSC)

CSC is simply a smart contract made for criminal purposes. They could be used to spill the intimate information, theft of cryptographic keys and other crimes (e.g. arson, murder, terrorism). Jules, Kosba, and Shi (2016) shows how enforcing smart contract has functionally increase and made more robust already present criminal contracts. Moreover, how can we practically use them in an Ethereum system. Criminals can take advantages of CSC to make 0-day vulnerable transaction. A zero-day exploit (0-day) is a chunk of code that accomplishes a target piece of software through a vulnerability which are as yet not known to the developers resulting in inability of patches. Terrorists group like al-Qaeda have leverage the CSC to get digital fund transfer from unknown individuals (Malik, 2018).

To counter with CSC effectively we use bitcoin on the Darknet with the an The Onion Router (Tor), an anonymizing software to expand security and anonymity (Mueller, 2017). We should also have better rules and regulations in cybercrime. We should study the link between cryptocurrency and terrorism.

8. Vulnerabilities in the Smart Contract

As program run on blockchain, smart contracts undergo security vulnerable due to program fault. Smart contract suffers from call to the unknown, out-of-gas sent, exception disorder irregularity, type cast, immutable bug etc. Luu et al. (2016) developed OYENTE to inspect security concerning bugs of smart contracts and proposed set of rules of security improvement on the Ethereum protocol. They stated that 8833 out of 19366 Ethereum based smart contracts are prone to attack.

QuillAudit[15], is a platform which is created to audit smart contracts for the vulnerabilities and smooth running. Mythril (Mueller, 2017) – a detailed toolkit to detect bugs and secure smart contracts can also be used.

With such current security threats and anonymous identity, the need of an hour is to develop secure systems or strength the blockchain-bitcoin framework. Such as Yin et. al. (2019) has designed the supervised machine learning approach for de-anonymizing bitcoin blockchain. Gradient boosting algorithm is implemented with accuracy of 80.42% is gained. Moreover, Maksutov, Alexeev, Fedorova, & Andreev (2019) have worked on the identification of transactions for money laundering and alteration in payment transaction using decentralized COIN JOIN methodology. While, Hari, Kodialam, and Lakshman (2019) designed ACCEL to improve the latency and boosting the throughput and deterministic confirmation of blockchain of bitcoin. They have used singular block identification to save time which lower the block spacing. Providing incentive to honest miners as one of the reputational approaches done by Tang, Wu, Wen, and Zheng (2019) to mitigate the attack and reduce the malicious activities.

CONCLUSION AND FUTURE WORKS

Blockchain is used worldwide as secure peer-to-peer distributed infrastructure. It is undergoing a transformation and manages rising operational costs. It has attained space into various business applications and discussion arousing interest of eminent entrepreneurs to make business easier and effective. It has a positive future ahead where further possibilities to exploit this innovative technology can be done. In this chapter we represented the use of blockchain in business process like food chain, border security, education, gem mining and many more, for effective management, immutable record keeping and reducing the cost. However, it has certain limitation such as scalability, security attacks, privacy etc. which are highlighted and some mitigation measures are suggested.

Table 1. Overview of security issues

S. No.	Security Issues	Description	Major target	Side-effects	Mitigation
1	**51% vulnerability**	More than 50 hashing power	Users, mining process,	Mining process, DoS, consensus protocol, lead to double spending	Use checkpoints, Raise number of confirmations.
2	**Double spending**	Same cryptocurrency for different transactions	Users wallets	Wallet theft, proof-of-work chains, "fast-payment" channel	Penalty system on delayed block submission (Garoffolo et al., 2018)
3	**Time-jacking attack**	Adversary speed-up or slow down the majority of minor's clock.	Minors	Seclude a miner and waste its resources.	Use system time (Boverman, 2011), time sampling on the input taken from trusted peers and Network time protocol (NTP) (Mills, Martin, Burbank, & Kasch, 2011)
4	**Selfish mining**	Malicious miners mining to increase revenue	Honest miners, users	honest miner wasting their resources, malicious miners increase revenue	Selfish-mine (Eyal & Sirer, 2014), monitor long private chain
5	**DDoS attack**	legitimate users are denied the services	Miners and users	Isolate or drive away miners and allow malicious miners to mine at higher rate	Network portioning (Neudecker, Andelfinger, & Hartebsteubm 2915) and proof-of-activity (Bentov et al., 2014), fast verification system
6	**Private key security**	stole or destroy private key of user	Business or Individual user	Bitcoin from the user wallet, modify the transactions	Password-Protected Secret Sharing (Jarecki et al., 2016) (PPSS)
7	**Criminal Smart Contracts (CSC)**	Smart contracts for criminal use	Users,	Spill confidential information, zero-day exploit, theft of cryptographic keys	The Onion Router (Tor) for more security (Mueller, 2017), cyberlaws
8	**Vulnerabilities in the smart contract**	Prone to attacks due to program fault	Program -code, mining process,	from call to the unknown, exception disorder irregularity, type-cast	QuillAudit, OYENTE (Luu et al., 2016), Mythril (Mueller, 2017)

In the future direction, blockchain is growing fast and many applications are proposed which are yet to be practically implemented. We plan to investigate in-depth for blockchain in future and may suggest some blockchain-based new framework.

REFERENCES

Bashir, I. (2018). *Mastering Blockchain: Distributed ledger technology, decentralization, and smart contracts explained*. Packt Publishing Ltd.

BBC News. (2018). *Coincheck: World's biggest ever digital currency 'theft'*. Retrieved from https://www.bbc.com/news/world-asia-42845505

Bentov, I., Lee, C., Mizrahi, A., & Rosenfeld, M. (2014). Proof of Activity: Extending Bitcoin's Proof of Work via Proof of Stake. *IACR Cryptology ePrint Archive, 2014*, 452.

Bhowmik, D., & Feng, T. (2017, August). The multimedia blockchain: A distributed and tamper-proof media transaction framework. In *22nd International Conference on Digital Signal Processing (DSP)* (pp. 1-5). IEEE. 10.1109/ICDSP.2017.8096051

Boverman, A. (2011). *Timejacking & Bitcoin*. Retrieved from https://culubas.blogspot.com/2011/05/timejacking-bitcoin_802.html

Browne, R. (2017). *An Indian state wants to use blockchain to fight land ownership fraud*. Retrieved from https://www.cnbc.com/2017/10/10/this-indian-state-wants-to-use-blockchain-to-fight-land-ownership-fraud.html

Cartier, L. E., Ali, S. H., & Krzemnicki, M. S. (2018). Blockchain, Chain of Custody and Trace Elements: An Overview of Tracking and Traceability Opportunities in the Gem Industry. *The Journal of Geology*, *36*(3).

Chen, G., Xu, B., Lu, M., & Chen, N. S. (2018). Exploring blockchain technology and its potential applications for education. *Smart Learning Environments*, *5*(1), 1. doi:10.118640561-017-0050-x

Croman, K., Decker, C., Eyal, I., Gencer, A. E., Juels, A., Kosba, A., ... Song, D. (2016, February). On scaling decentralized blockchains. In *International Conference on Financial Cryptography and Data Security* (pp. 106-125). Springer. 10.1007/978-3-662-53357-4_8

Czachorowski, K., Solesvik, M., & Kondratenko, Y. (2019). The Application of Blockchain Technology in the Maritime Industry. In *Green IT Engineering: Social, Business and Industrial Applications* (pp. 561–577). Cham: Springer. doi:10.1007/978-3-030-00253-4_24

Deininger, K. (2018). *For Billions without Formal Land Rights, the Tech Revolution Offers New Grounds for Hope*. Retrieved from http://blogs.worldbank.org/developmenttalk/billions-without-formal-land-rigtechrevolution-offers-new-grounds-hope

Deng, Z., Ren, Y., Liu, Y., Yin, X., Shen, Z., & Kim, H. J. (2019). Blockchain-Based Trusted Electronic Records Preservation in Cloud Storage. *Computers. Materials & Continua*, *58*(1), 135–151. doi:10.32604/cmc.2019.02967

Desjardins, J. (2017). *Bitcoin: The Top Performing Currency For a Second Year in a Row*. Retrieved from http://money.visualcapitalist.com/bitcoin-top-performing-currency-second-year/

Ekblaw, A., Azaria, A., Halamka, J. D., & Lippman, A. (2016, August). A Case Study for Blockchain in Healthcare: "MedRec" prototype for electronic health records and medical research data. In Proceedings of IEEE open & big data conference (p. 13). IEEE.

Eyal, I. (2017). Blockchain technology: Transforming libertarian cryptocurrency dreams to finance and banking realities. *Computer*, *50*(9), 38–49. doi:10.1109/MC.2017.3571042

Eyal, I., Gencer, A. E., Sirer, E. G., & Van Renesse, R. (2016). Bitcoin-ng: A scalable blockchain protocol. In *13th USENIX Symposium on Networked Systems Design and Implementation (NSDI 16)* (pp. 45-59). USENIX.

Eyal, I., & Sirer, E. G. (2014). Majority is not enough: Bitcoin mining is vulnerable. In N. Christin & R. Safavi-Naini (Eds.), Financial cryptography and data security (pp. 436–454). Academic Press.

Faridi, O. (2018). *In Altcoins, Bitcoin Gold Hit With 51% and Double Spend Attacks, $18 Million Stolen*. Retrieved from https://www.cryptoglobe.com/latest/2018/05/bitcoin-gold-hit-with-51-and-double-spend-attacks-18-million-stolen/

Frankenfield, J. (2018). *SegWit (Segregated Witness)*. Retrieved from https://www.investopedia.com/terms/s/segwit-segregated-witness.asp

Gallagher, S. (2014). *New "Shellshock" patch rushed out to resolve gaps in first fix*. Retrieved from https://arstechnica.com/information-technology/2014/09/new-shellshock-patch-rushed-out-to-resolve-gaps-in-first-fix/

Garoffolo, Stabilini, Viglione, & Stav. (2018). *Horizon Proposal to modify satoshi concensuss to enhance protection against 51% attacks*. Academic Press.

Gencer, A. E., van Renesse, R., & Sirer, E. G. (2017, April). Short paper: Service-oriented sharding for blockchains. In *International Conference on Financial Cryptography and Data Security* (pp. 393-401). Springer. 10.1007/978-3-319-70972-7_22

Guo, Y., & Liang, C. (2016). Blockchain application and outlook in the banking industry. *Financial Innovation*, *2*(1), 24. doi:10.118640854-016-0034-9

Hari, A., Kodialam, M., & Lakshman, T. V. (2019, April). ACCEL: Accelerating the Bitcoin Blockchain for High-throughput, Low-latency Applications. In *IEEE INFOCOM 2019-IEEE Conference on Computer Communications* (pp. 2368-2376). IEEE.

Hjalmarsson, F. P., Hreioarsson, G. K., Hamdaqa, M., & Hjalmtysson, G. (2018, July). Blockchain-Based E-Voting System. In *2018 IEEE 11th International Conference on Cloud Computing (CLOUD)* (pp. 983-986). IEEE. 10.1109/CLOUD.2018.00151

Hofman, W., & Brewster, C. (2019). The Applicability of Blockchain Technology in the Mobility and Logistics Domain. In *Towards User-Centric Transport in Europe* (pp. 185–201). Cham: Springer. doi:10.1007/978-3-319-99756-8_13

Huh, S., Cho, S., & Kim, S. (2017, February). Managing IoT devices using blockchain platform. In *2017 19th international conference on advanced communication technology (ICACT)* (pp. 464-467). IEEE. 10.23919/ICACT.2017.7890132

Iansiti, M., & Lakhani, K. (2017). R. (2017). The truth about blockchain. Harvard Business Review. *Harvard University*, *27*(9).

Imbrex. (2017). *Sharding, Raiden, Plasma: The Scaling Solutions that Will Unchain Ethereum*. Retrieved from https://medium.com/imbrexblog/sharding-raiden-plasma-the-scaling-solutions-that-will-unchain-ethereum-c590e994523b

Ito, K., & O'Dair, M. (2018). *A Critical Examination of the Application of Blockchain Technology to Intellectual Property Management. In Business Transformation through Blockchain* (pp. 317–335). Cham: Palgrave Macmillan.

Jarecki, S., Kiayias, A., Krawczyk, H., & Xu, J. (2016, March). Highly-efficient and composable password-protected secret sharing (or: How to protect your bitcoin wallet online). In *2016 IEEE European Symposium on Security and Privacy (EuroS&P)* (pp. 276-291). IEEE 10.1109/EuroSP.2016.30

Juels, A., Kosba, A., & Shi, E. (2016, October). The ring of gyges: Investigating the future of criminal smart contracts. In *Proceedings of the 2016 ACM SIGSAC Conference on Computer and Communications Security* (pp. 283-295). ACM. 10.1145/2976749.2978362

Kuperberg, M., Kindler, D., & Jeschke, S. (2019). *Are Smart Contracts and Blockchains Suitable for Decentralized Railway Control?* arXiv preprint arXiv:1901.06236

Luu, L., Chu, D. H., Olickel, H., Saxena, P., & Hobor, A. (2016, October). Making smart contracts smarter. In *Proceedings of the 2016 ACM SIGSAC Conference on Computer and Communications Security* (pp. 254-269). ACM. 10.1145/2976749.2978309

Luu, L., Narayanan, V., Zheng, C., Baweja, K., Gilbert, S., & Saxena, P. (2016, October). A secure sharding protocol for open blockchains. In *Proceedings of the 2016 ACM SIGSAC Conference on Computer and Communications Security* (pp. 17-30). ACM. 10.1145/2976749.2978389

Maksutov, A. A., Alexeev, M. S., Fedorova, N. O., & Andreev, D. A. (2019, January). Detection of Blockchain Transactions Used in Blockchain Mixer of Coin Join Type. In *2019 IEEE Conference of Russian Young Researchers in Electrical and Electronic Engineering (EIConRus)* (pp. 274-277). IEEE.

Malhotra, Y. (2013). *Bitcoin Protocol: Model of 'Cryptographic Proof' Based Global Crypto-Currency & Electronic Payments System*. Academic Press.

Malik, N. (2018). *How Criminals And Terrorists Use Cryptocurrency: And How To Stop It*. Retrieved from https://www.forbes.com/sites/nikitamalik/2018/08/31/how-criminals-and-terrorists-use-cryptocurrency-and-how-to-stop-it/#5675830c3990

Marella, P. B., Mohler, J., & Milojkovic, M. (2017). *BroncoVotes: Secure Voting System using Ethereum's Blockchain*. Academic Press.

Martin, J. (2018). *Top Tier Colleges Offering Blockchain Education*. Retrieved from https://blockchain.wtf/2018/11/blog/top-tier-colleges-offering-blockchain-education/

Maupin, J. (2017). *The G20 countries should engage with blockchain technologies to build an inclusive, transparent, and accountable digital economy for all (No. 2017-48)*. Economics Discussion Papers.

Maxeiner, L. S., Martini, J. P., & Sandner, P. (2018). Blockchain in *the Chemical Industry*. Retrieved from https://medium.com/@philippsandner/blockchain-in-the-chemical-industry-ecf703237ba6

Menezes, N. (2017). *UN Uses Ethereum to Distribute Funds to Jordanians*. Retrieved from https://btcmanager.com/un-uses-ethereum-todistribute-funds-to-jordanians

Mills, D., Martin, J., Burbank, J., & Kasch, W. (2011). *Network time protocol version 4: Protocol and algorithms specification*. RFC 5905. Internet Engineering Task Force.

Mueller, B. (2017). *Mythril—Reversing and Bug Hunting Framework for the Ethereum Blockchain*. Retrieved from https://hackernoon.com/introducing-mythril-a-framework-for-bug-hunting-on-the-ethereum-blockchain-9dc5588f82f6

Nakamoto, S. (2008). *Bitcoin: A peer-to-peer electronic cash system*. Academic Press.

Neudecker, T., Andelfinger, P., & Hartenstein, H. (2015, May). A simulation model for analysis of attacks on the bitcoin peer-to-peer network. In *2015 IFIP/IEEE International Symposium on Integrated Network Management (IM)* (pp. 1327-1332). IEEE. 10.1109/INM.2015.7140490

Nordström, E. (2015). *Personal Clouds: Concedo*. Retrieved from http://www.diva-portal.org/smash/get/diva2:1029288/FULLTEXT02.pdf

O'Dair, M., & Beaven, Z. (2017). The networked record industry: How blockchain technology could transform the record industry. *Strategic Change*, *26*(5), 471–480. doi:10.1002/jsc.2147

Oprunenco, A., & Akmeemana, C. (2018). *Using blockchain to make land registry more reliable in India*. Retrieved from https://www.undp.org/content/undp/en/home/blog/2018/Using-blockchain-to-make-land-registry-more-reliable-in-India.html

Palmer, D. (2018). *Cybercrime drains $600 billion a year from the global economy*. Retrieved from https://www.zdnet.com/article/cybercrime-drains-600-billion-a-year-from-the-global-economy-says-report/

Poon, J., & Buterin, V. (2017). *Plasma: Scalable autonomous smart contracts*. White Paper.

Poon, J., & Dryja, T. (2016). *The bitcoin lightning network: Scalable off-chain instant payments*. Academic Press.

Raul. (2018). *The Speed of Crypto Hacks is Picking Up: This Month Alone Thieves Stole*. Retrieved from https://howmuch.net/articles/biggest-crypto-hacks-scams

Sawa, T. (2018). Blockchain technology outline and its application to field of power and energy system. *Electrical Engineering in Japan.*

Shang, Q., & Price, A. (2019). A Blockchain-Based Land Titling Project in the Republic of Georgia: Rebuilding Public Trust and Lessons for Future Pilot Projects. *Innovations: Technology, Governance, Globalization, 12*(3-4), 72–78. doi:10.1162/inov_a_00276

Sharma, P. K., Moon, S. Y., & Park, J. H. (2017). Block-VN: A Distributed Blockchain Based Vehicular Network Architecture in Smart City. *JIPS, 13*(1), 184–195.

Sharples, M., & Domingue, J. (2016, September). The blockchain and kudos: A distributed system for educational record, reputation and reward. In *European Conference on Technology Enhanced Learning* (pp. 490-496). Springer. 10.1007/978-3-319-45153-4_48

Shirani, A. (2018). Blockchain for global maritime logistics. *Issues in Information Systems, 19*(3).

Shrier, D., Wu, W., & Pentland, A. (2016). Blockchain & infrastructure (identity, data security). *Massachusetts Institute of Technology-Connection Science, 1*(3).

Solat, S., & Potop-Butucaru, M. (2016). *Zeroblock: Preventing selfish mining in bitcoin.* arXiv preprint arXiv:1605.02435

Sompolinsky, Y., & Zohar, A. (2013). Accelerating Bitcoin's Transaction Processing. Fast Money Grows on Trees, Not Chains. *IACR Cryptology ePrint Archive, 2013*(881).

Staff, E. (2016). Blockchains: The great chain of being sure about things. *The Economist, 18.*

Statista. (2019). *Size of the Bitcoin blockchain from 2010 to 2019, by quarter*. Retrieved from https://www.statista.com/statistics/647523/worldwide-bitcoin-blockchain-size/

Sun Yin, H. H., Langenheldt, K., Harlev, M., Mukkamala, R. R., & Vatrapu, R. (2019). Regulating cryptocurrencies: A supervised machine learning approach to de-anonymizing the bitcoin blockchain. *Journal of Management Information Systems, 36*(1), 37–73. doi:10.1080/07421222.2018.1550550

Swan, M. (2015). *Blockchain: Blueprint for a new economy.* O'Reilly Media, Inc.

Tang, C., Wu, L., Wen, G., & Zheng, Z. (2019). Incentivizing Honest Mining in Blockchain Networks: A Reputation Approach. *IEEE Transactions on Circuits and Wystems. II, Express Briefs*, 1. doi:10.1109/TCSII.2019.2901746

Tian, F. (2017, June). A supply chain traceability system for food safety based on HACCP, blockchain & Internet of things. In *International Conference on Service Systems and Service Management* (pp. 1-6). IEEE.

Wang, X., Zha, X., Ni, W., Liu, R. P., Guo, Y. J., Niu, X., & Zheng, K. (2019). Survey on blockchain for Internet of Things. *Computer Communications*, *136*, 10–29. doi:10.1016/j.comcom.2019.01.006

Weiss, M., & Corsi, E. (2017). Bitfury: Blockchain for government. *HBS Case Study*.

World Bank. (2017). *Why Secure Land Rights Matter*. Retrieved from http://www.worldbank.org/en/topic/land

Xu, X., Pautasso, C., Zhu, L., Gramoli, V., Ponomarev, A., Tran, A. B., & Chen, S. (2016, April). The blockchain as a software connector. In *2016 13th Working IEEE/IFIP Conference on Software Architecture (WICSA)* (pp. 182-191). IEEE. 10.1109/WICSA.2016.21

Xu, Y., Zhao, S., Kong, L., Zheng, Y., Zhang, S., & Li, Q. (2017, October). ECBC: A high performance educational certificate blockchain with efficient query. In *International Colloquium on Theoretical Aspects of Computing* (pp. 288-304). Springer. 10.1007/978-3-319-67729-3_17

Yiannas, F. (2018). A New Era of Food Transparency Powered by Blockchain. *Innovations: Technology, Governance, Globalization*, *12*(1-2), 46–56. doi:10.1162/inov_a_00266

Yue, X., Wang, H., Jin, D., Li, M., & Jiang, W. (2016). Healthcare data gateways: Found healthcare intelligence on blockchain with novel privacy risk control. *Journal of Medical Systems*, *40*(10), 218. doi:10.100710916-016-0574-6 PMID:27565509

Zraick, K. (2019). *Crypto-Exchange CEO dies in India, platform can't pay investors as he had the passwords*. Retrieved from https://economictimes.indiatimes.com/small-biz/startups/newsbuzz/crypto-exchange-ceo-dies-in-india-platform-cant-pay-investors-as-he-had-the-passwords/articleshow/67861832.cms

ENDNOTES

1 Bitinfochart https://bitinfocharts.com/bitcoin/

2 Toshendra Kumar Sharma, 1 octomber,2018 https://www.blockchain-council.org/blockchain/facebook-field-blockchain/

[3] Microsoft. 2017. The Coco Framework. 2017, Whitepaper, https://github.com/Azure/coco-framework

[4] GOOGLE CLOUD, https://www.blog.google/products/google-cloud/building-a-better-cloud-with-our-partners-at-next-18/

[5] IBM https://www.ibm.com/blockchain/hyperledger

[6] Business Today, June 7 2019, Draft anti-crypto law proposes 10-year jail for dealing in Bitcoin, cryptocurrencies, https://www.businesstoday.in/current/policy/draft-anti-cryptocurrency-law-10-year-jail-bitcoin/story/354334.html

[7] Digitizing global trade with maersk and IBM—blokchain unleashed, Jan 2018 https://www.ibm.com/blogs/blockchain/2018/01/digitizing-global-trade-maersk-ibm.

[8] Leigh Stringer, Global Business Editor, 21 June 2018, Walmart considers blockchain technology for tracing chemicals https://chemicalwatch.com/67911/walmart-considers-blockchain-technology-for-tracing-chemicals

[9] Wolfie Zhao, Jul 28, 2017, German Chemical Company Pilots Supply Chain Blockchain, https://www.coindesk.com/german-chemical-company-pilots-supply-chain-blockchain

[10] Tracr, https://www.tracr.com/

[11] IBM Energy Blockchain Labs Inc. https://www.ibm.com/case-studies/energy-blockchain-labs-inc

[12] Panda Green Energy Group http://www.pandagreen.com/show-1416.html

[13] IOTA https://www.iota.org/

[14] Lighting Network https://lightning.network/

[15] Quillhash https://www.quillhash.com/

Chapter 3
Towards the Integration of Blockchain and IoT for Security Challenges in IoT:
A Review

K. Dinesh Kumar
https://orcid.org/0000-0003-0843-1561
VIT University, Chennai, India

Venkata Rathnam T.
Annamacharya Institute of Technology and Sciences, Tirupati, India & Jawaharlal Nehru Technological University, Anantapur, India

Venkata Ramana R.
Sri Venkateswara College of Engineering, Tirupati, India & Jawaharlal Nehru Technological University, Anantapur, India

M. Sudhakara
https://orcid.org/0000-0002-2559-4074
VIT University, Chennai, India

Ravi Kumar Poluru
https://orcid.org/0000-0001-8591-5266
VIT University, India

ABSTRACT

Internet of things (IoT) technology plays a vital role in the current technologies because IoT develops a network by integrating different kinds of objects and sensors to create the communication among objects directly without human interaction. With the presence of internet of things technology in our daily comes smart thinking and

DOI: 10.4018/978-1-7998-0186-3.ch003

various advantages. At the same time, secure systems have been a most important concern for the protection of information systems and networks. However, adopting traditional security management systems in the internet of things leads several issues due to the limited privacy and policies like privacy standards, protocol stacks, and authentication rules. Usually, IoT devices has limited network capacities, storage, and computing processors. So they are having more chances to attacks. Data security, privacy, and reliability are three main challenges in the IoT security domain. To address the solutions for the above issues, IoT technology has to provide advanced privacy and policies in this large incoming data source. Blockchain is one of the trending technologies in the privacy management to provide the security. So this chapter is focused on the blockchain technologies which can be able to solve several IoT security issues. This review mainly focused on the state-of-the-art IoT security issues and vulnerabilities by existing review works in the IoT security domains. The taxonomy is presented about security issues in the view of communication, architecture, and applications. Also presented are the challenges of IoT security management systems. The main aim of this chapter is to describe the importance of blockchain technology in IoT security systems. Finally, it highlights the future directions of blockchain technology roles in IoT systems, which can be helpful for further improvements.

INTRODUCTION

The Internet of Things (IoT) has created a remarkable role in all environments of our daily lives. The Internet of Things technology already adopted in several fields to create the flexible environments like automobiles, healthcare, entertainments, sports, industries and homes etc. The adoption of IoT technology in daily activity environments, makes the life comfortable and easy. The main idea of the IoT technology is, all physical objects connected with each other under one network. So that, connected objects analyse the data and makes the proper decisions by sharing the information with each other. The IoT technology transforms these objects as a smart things by using the several technologies like sensors networks, internet protocols, communication technologies, ubiquitous computing, embedded devices and applications. Smart things along with supported technologies perform the tasks while using data analytical models and ubiquitous computing services. The complete concept of the IoT technology is, each and every connected application has to interact with other independent services to make the proper decisions. For example, smart traffic system will enable the vehicles to automatically respond when vehicles met with accidents. To get this potential technology and innovation, the traffic system application need to improve and growth. Additionally, the vehicles need to be manufactured to match the system requirements and robust communication protocols has to be developed for proper communication among different kinds of things. With this vision, traditional devices has become autonomous and smart intelligence and developing technology towards smart cities, smart homes, smart vehicles and smart everything.

The further development of IoT technology is more important to everyday life. This can be rapidly grows the evolution of hardware techniques like increasing the bandwidth by integrating the connected based networks to address issue of underutilization of bandwidth spectrum. The supporting technologies to IoT technology like Cloud computing, Bigdata analytics, Wireless sensor networks and Machine-to-Machine have now developed rapidly as supporting components for the IoT development. On the other hand, the privacy and security issues related to Machine-to-Machine, Cloud computing and Wireless sensors networks remain to increasing in the view of challenges in communication protocols with the IoT. So, the complete architecture of IoT needs to be robust and secured from several attacks which may arise the issues to integrity, privacy and confidentiality of collected data. Still adopting traditional secure paradigms in IoT technology which can lead major issues, because IoT is a collection of heterogeneous devices and several collections of interconnected computer networks. Additionally, the IoT things have sensors which may have limited memory and power. Due to the limited power of sensors, having more chances to get the vulnerable from attackers. In this context, many literature reviews are addressed the security issues in IoT such as author (Alaba et al., 2017) classified the security issues in the view of architecture, application, data, and communication. Authors presented the taxonomy of classification of IoT security issues and also presented attacks on IoT hardware, application components, and networks. In another literature review (Granjal et al., 2015) author presented the analysis of security and privacy issues of IoT protocols. This analysis presented about several privacy key management systems with cryptographic algorithms. In the same way (Yi et al., 2015) and (Wang et al., 2015) authors presented different kinds of security issues for fog computing. Authors (Abduvaliyev et al., 2013), (Butun et al., 2014), and (Mitchell et al., 2014) presented a comparative analysis of intrusion detection system in IoT.

In distributed systems, providing privacy without third-parties is an advanced management that can increase the potential power of IoT based organizations. The IoT technology has taking the advantages of cloud computing and bigdata computing to overcome the limitations. In the same way blockchain technology also increase the potential growth of IoT security systems. Blockchain is a trending technology in security management system which can provide a strong and robust privacy solutions and maximum level of security standards (Banerjee et al., 2018). The developers of blockchain technology argue that this approach is secured by design. In a blockchain technology, not required to store the data with third party organizations. Every record of information is stored in interlocked computers. Now a days, blockchain technology can be used in different applications to authorize, authenticate, and audit data which is collected from different devices. Additionally, blockchain is having decentralization characteristic which can helps to avoid the third party involvement. The main aim of the blockchain technology is, develops a decentralization process as a security measurement to develop a secure index for all transactions in a network. This characteristic helps to improve the IoT security management system.

Many literature reviews addressed the security issues and solutions of IoT security management system, but not completely presented in the view of effective security management system. This chapter presents a complete review on the Internet of Things, IoT security issues and challenges, and blockchain based solutions for IoT security management system. The main contributions of this chapter are:

- A systematic literature review on Internet of Things and Blockchain technologies.
- The taxonomy and classification of security issues in IoT is presented.
- Presented a characteristics of the blockchain based security solutions.
- This chapter focused on the classification of different solutions for the applications of Blockchain technology in an IoT environment.

The rest of the chapter is organized as follows. Section 2 presented about overview of Internet of Things and architecture. In section 3, presented a taxonomy of different kinds of security issues and challenges of IoT security management system. Section 4 describes about blockchain technology and their basic characteristics, whereas, Section 5 presented a different solutions for the application of blockchain in an IoT environment. Future directions for IoT security issues is presented in Section 6. Finally presented a conclusion of this chapter in Section 7.

INTERNET OF THINGS

The Internet of Things term defines the huge category of internet applications and communication protocols developed on top of the interconnected networks whereas billions of things connected under one network (Ammar et al., 2018). Usually the 'Internet of Things' term is a combination of two major parts such as 'Internet' and 'Things'. By this sentence it-self can understand Internet of Things is, each and every object having the capability of connecting to the internet such as sensors, multimedia devices etc., is able to communicate with each other and exchanging the information from anywhere at any time. Ubiquitous computing is the major requirement of IoT and to achieve this, IoT application need to be support all kinds of multimedia devices and communication protocols. Also it requires integration of sensors, edge computing devices like hubs and routers, and multimedia devices. The main idea of this integration of all physical object is exchange the data with each other object so that can make the proper decisions. This integration feature allows managing all connected devices from remote location with less human interactions in connected network infrastructure (Kouicem et al., 2018). The IoT technology transforms these devices from classical to smart by exploring the supporting technologies like communication capabilities, ubiquitous computing, applications, and internet protocols. Figure 1 represents the advanced architecture of IoT where every application is connected with another application in the network. The IoT communication protocols plays a major role in communication among devices to exchange the data and selection of proper function that comply with the different kinds of functionalities of each connected device. In the next level, applications performs the data granularity operations to process the data which is generated from devices for analytics purpose. The IoT structure is a combination of protocols, rules

Figure 1. IoT connected network

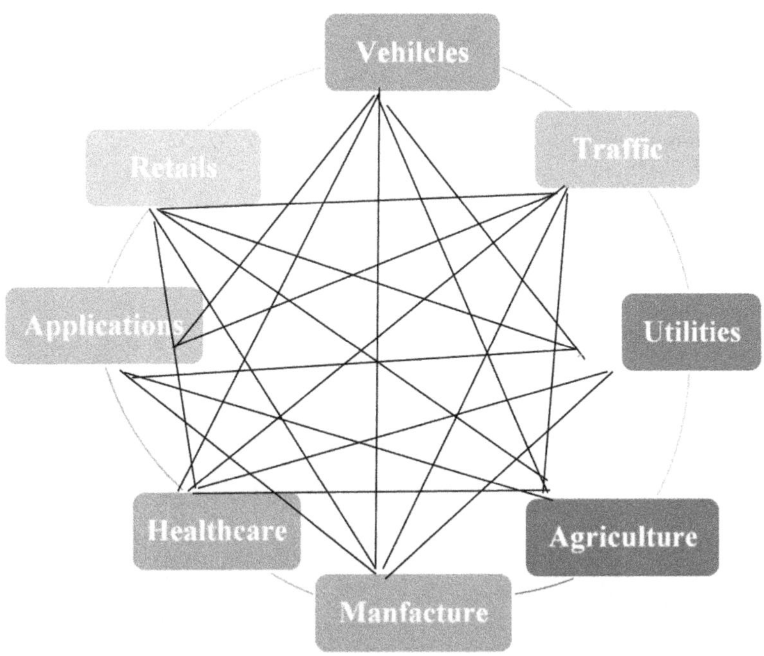

and regulations, performs the analysis of data and exchange information among all connected devices. Based on the survey which is conducted by RnRMarketResearch, the IoT market will be worth nearly $1500 billion by 2020, with Internet of Nano Things. The IoT technology playing a major role in the future technology. In this context, several industries has planned to invest billions of dollars on IoT research. According to the Statista survey, 75.44 billion devices will be connected in worldwide IoT network by 2025. Figure 2 represents the IoT connected devices installed base worldwide from 2015 to 2025.

The IoT architecture could be different from application to application, according to the solution which is intend to build. But, the basic IoT architecture mainly consists of four components, such as Sensors, Gateways, Devices, and Applications. These four components would be used at four stages. At the first stage, data would be collected from different kinds of devices like sensors, actuators, wearable devices, cameras and, multimedia devices. These devices collects the data from the objects or environments and forwards to management services with the help of gateways and networks. These gateways can be Wifi, Ethernet, and WAN networks. Once the data has been aggregated and digitized, it is ready to further processing which performs in-depth analysis. After analysing the data, it is forwarded to cloud based systems or physical datacenters to provide the information to application interfaces. Figure 3 represents the IoT architecture where can see different stages of IoT architecture.

The IoT architecture has another three important aspects such as Wireless sensors networks (WSN's), Addressing, and middleware. The WSN's is the major component in the IoT environment which is collection of sensors networks. These networks have different kinds of sensors, RFID's (Radio frequency identifications),

Figure 2. Statista survey on IoT connected devices by 2025.

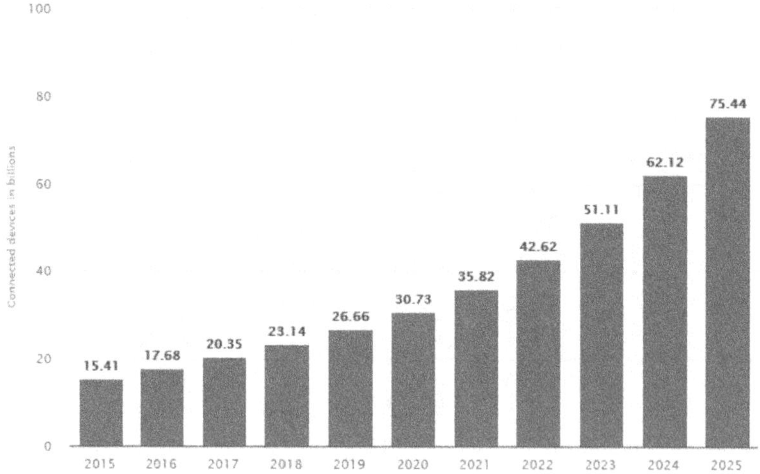

Figure 3. IoT architecture

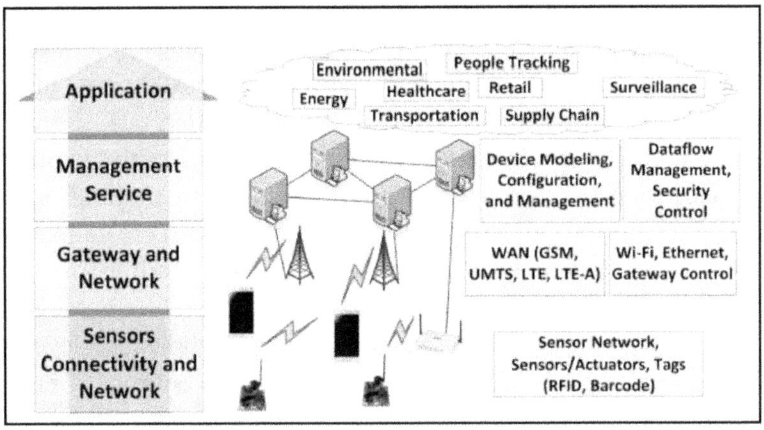

and multimedia devices. These devices exchanges the information together to getting information about temperature, position, and movement etc. WSN's plays a major role to provide useful data and utilized in different areas like environmental services, healthcare, traffic system, government, agriculture and, defence etc. Addressing is the second major aspect of IoT environment. In IoT network each object transforms from classical to smart thing. This transformation creates the smart environment, but identifying the things with unique address is a challenging task for the success of IoT environment. Reliability, scalability, uniqueness and persistence represent challenging features for creation of a unique address for each IoT device. So, IPv6 is the new extension of IPv4 which can solve the some of the device identification issues. Finally, middleware which is third major aspect of IoT environment. In IoT network, connected things has limited processing capabilities and storage. So these middleware services provides the several services like management services, object abstraction, security control, and service composition.

SECURITY ISSUES IN IOT ENVIRONMENT

The IoT concept changing the technology rapidly day by day. Additionally, many other technologies giving support for growth of IoT such as wireless sensors networks, cloud computing, and bigdata analytics etc. (Butun et al., 2014). The automation of devices and Machine-to-Machine another two technologies plays major role in the IoT environment. With the help of these two technologies IoT providing flexible services in several domains such as healthcare, agriculture environments, smart intelligent transportation, smart grids, and smart cities etc. In these applications, things communicate with each other device, including human beings and exchanging the information with each other. Here every transaction of data must be secured and protected by robust methods and algorithms, so that providing the confidence to the users that users data is properly secured. But, providing robust security management to the IoT, is a major challenging task and also demanding task. Security is the primary concern in all networks, but in IoT environments security paradigm is the most important parameter. Because the IoT network built by millions of connected things. With this connectivity and availability, attackers can create many chances to attack the network with malwares (Granjal et al., 2015). Still IoT networks have lots of chances to be affected by several kinds of threats at different levels such as physical level, network level, communication level, and application level (Alaba et al., 2017). So different kinds of attacks at different levels, makes IoT environment as an insecure.

Issues at Physical Level

At physical level of IoT environment, several kinds of hardware devices connected which includes sensors, RFID's, multimedia devices, Bluetooth, and ZigBee etc. The sensor nodes and RFID tags are major devices in IoT environment to detection and identification. These devices plays key role in exchanging the information among several devices in IoT network. But sensors and RFID tags may compromise to attacks and threats which includes repudiation, tracking, DoS, spoofing and counterfeiting etc. (Mitchell & Chen, 2014) These kind of attacks and threats from attackers which can leads data theft issue from sensors and tags. Even these devices having the issue of tracking. Once attacker gets the accessibility of device, attackers can track the information. ZigBee is another component which is used in IoT network frequently to collect the information. It is a one kind of micro controller and protocol. Due to the limited processing power, these devices are having more chances to get attacks and threats. Usually these devices have the information of packets and keys. By getting the accessibility of these devices, attackers can perform hacking, packet manipulation, and key exchange. Bluetooth is the device which is used for data exchange between devices. But few kinds of attacks to Bluetooth devices leads data theft issues and DoS, eavesdropping, Bluesnarfing, and Bluebugging attacks creates more vulnerable to attacks and threats.

Issues at Network Level

At Network level, communication can be done either wired network or wireless networks in IoT environment. In wired network, data can be exchanged by network adapters, routers, and cables between connected IoT devices. This kind of communication completely based on wired network and it develops the reliability, security, and ease of use. But, attackers making the IoT networks as a vulnerable by threats and attacks (Abduvaliyev et al., 2013). Various attacks to wired medium such as extortion hack, data manipulation, equipment hijacking, malicious attacks, and malware signalling systems etc., proven that IoT wired networks also compromises to threats and attacks. On the other hand, wireless medium networks utilizes transmitters, radio communication channels, and receivers to exchange the data in between IoT devices. This wireless connection networks transforms the connectivity from classical connectivity to smart connectivity. However, a wireless network communication channel also compromises to threats and attacks such as data hacking, misconfiguration, DoS attacks, signal loss issues, Man-in-the-Middle attack, protocol tunnelling, and war dialling etc. In IoT networks, security issues at network level makes maximum loss for users. Once data can be hacked from IoT networks, attackers may get the accessibility of entire IoT network. Because, in IoT networks, all applications has the connectivity with each other. So, threats and attacks at network level in IoT networks which leads the several issues (Khan et al., 2018).

Issues at Application Level

In IoT network, several applications have the connectivity with each other and each application have several kinds of supporting IoT devices. The applications in IoT network such as smart grids, smart intelligent transport system, smart cities, smart healthcare, smart agriculture, and smart surveillance etc. Each and every application, have different kinds of connected devices to collect the data from environment. For example, Smart city idea is the new evolution of the technology and includes smart street lights, smart cameras, smart e-governance, smart waste management, and smart water management etc. This kind of environment provides flexible services and makes human lives as an easy and also improves the economic development of city. But, IoT devices in smart city environment are open to several attacks and threats. For example, by data manipulation which is collected by smart cameras from traffic environment, attackers can able to give wrong information to travellers. And also fake disaster detection, DoS attacks, and fake seismic detection creates many issues for human lives (Huckle et al., 2016). Smart grid also one of the good idea of IoT technology. It improves the reliability in smart energy systems. However, smart grid also has possibility to threats and attacks. These attacks in smart grid environments makes maximum loss. For example, malicious attacks in traditional power devices collapse the entire power management system. Smart agriculture is the great idea for farmers, but lack of the knowledge about attacks and threats, farmers may face wrong assumption issues. Another application of IoT environment is smart healthcare management system, it enhance the services for patients.

However, smart health cards have the chances to vulnerable. Data manipulations and data misusing of healthcare cards creates several issues. The smart intelligent transport system controls traffic, transportation and smart parking etc. But due to the malware attacks, DoS attacks, and cyber-attacks, attackers get the accessibility of traffic management system.

Additionally, several attacks at other levels makes IoT networks as a vulnerable (Zarpelao et al., 2017). If consider the DoS attacks which makes the IoT devices as a vulnerable to users so that users gets interruptions frequently. These DoS attacks are categorized into several types which includes collision of data, signal jamming, and malware internal attacks. Eavesdropping is another kind of attack, it can be attack on communication channel in either wired network or wireless network. The main aim of this attack is, interruption of communication by extract the data from communication channel. Counterfeiting attack also major concern in security issues in IoT environments. By using this method attacker can do forgery of information, which means attacker can create the duplication of content. Man-in-the-Middle attack is one of the challenging attacks in network environments. By using this approach, attacker can access the data from IoT devices. Figure 4 represents, the taxonomy of security issues in IoT environment. This chapter mainly focused on three levels where can get the several security attacks and threats.

BLOCKCHAIN TECHNOLGY

The Blockchain technology has been rapidly growing in security management system over the past three years (Miraz et al., 2018). As per Statista survey reports, in global market blockchain technologies creates the business worth of $2000 billion by 2020. In next five years, blockchain technology creates huge evolution in security management system. Bitcoin is one of the applications of blockchain technology which transforms the crypto-currency system throughout world. Bitcoin is the digital currency which was developed based on the decentralized management system. In peer-to-peer network, bitcoin transactions can be done by exchanging with public key cryptography. These public keys are will be created based on cryptography rules and can be used for transactions of bitcoins. All these transactions which have done by users, needs to validate and store the information into blockchain. In blockchain, every block acts as a ledger and it stores all the transactions of users. Likewise, every user in peer-to-peer network verifies and stores the information into blockchain. The main advantage of the blockchain technology in crypto-currency system is, avoiding the interactions of third party organizations and their charges for transactions which is done by user. The blockchain technology, also avoids the centralized information storage and centralized control system (Panarello et al.,

Figure 4. Security issues in IoT environment

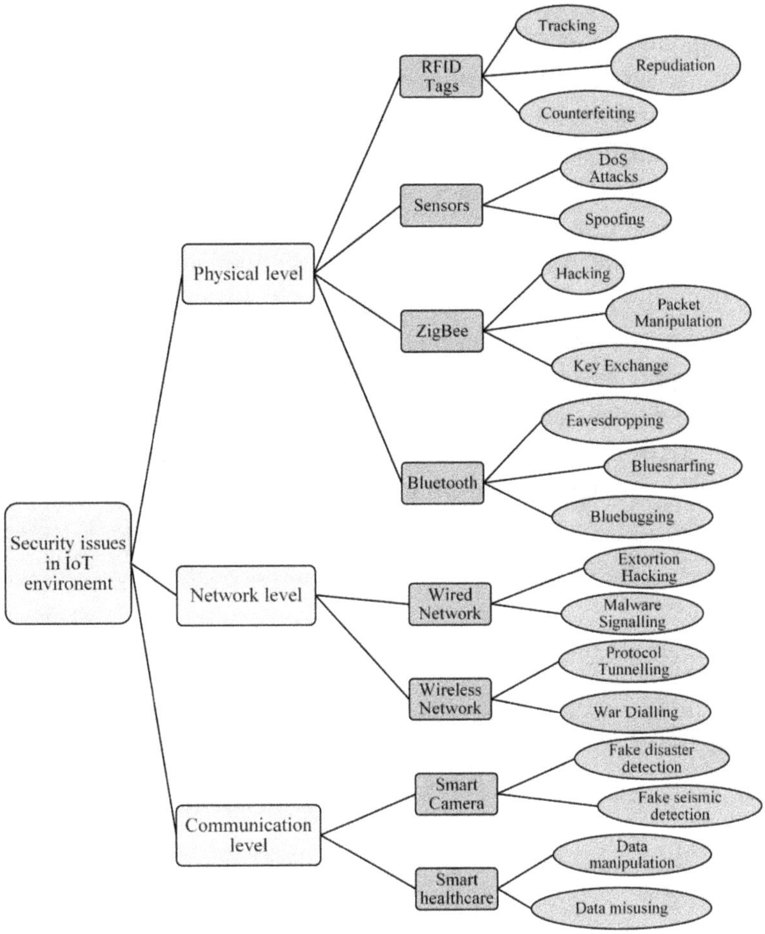

2018). After that, a transaction based state machine was presented to support the blockchain technologies. Based on these features such as security, privacy, integrity, auditability, system transparency, authorization, and fault tolerance etc., blockchain technology can be adopted in several environments like supply chain management system, agriculture, mobile crowd sensing, smart intelligent transport system, and identity management (Dorri et al., 2016).

In peer-to-peer network, each and every node receives two types of keys such as public key and private key. The public key is used for encryption of message which is sent by users to another user in a network, usually this concept is called encryption method. The private key is used to read a received message which is called decryption method. Likewise, in blockchain technology every node of blockchain has the information of transaction and it has to be sent to every user in blockchain network. To get the information of transaction user needs the private key to authenticate the transaction. Once user receive the information of transaction, that node sends the broadcast message to other users about this transaction. Then users verifies the transaction and stores the information in ledger with previous block of the chain. If validation is not fulfilled, the block will be discarded. The blockchain architecture is mainly composed with a sequence of blocks. These blocks are connected with each other with their hash function values. In ledger, users stores the information of authorized transactions. As shown in the figure 5, every user has a public key and private key. Private key used for signing into blockchain transaction while public key used for represent their address. Once the transaction is validated according to the cryptographic rules, a special node represents as a miners, stores the valid transactions into a time-stamped block. These time-stamped blocks comes back to the blockchain network and it will be verified by hash function value. In this manner, blockchain will be updated with valid transactions (Fernandez-Carames et al., 2018).

Figure 5. The working process of blockchain technology

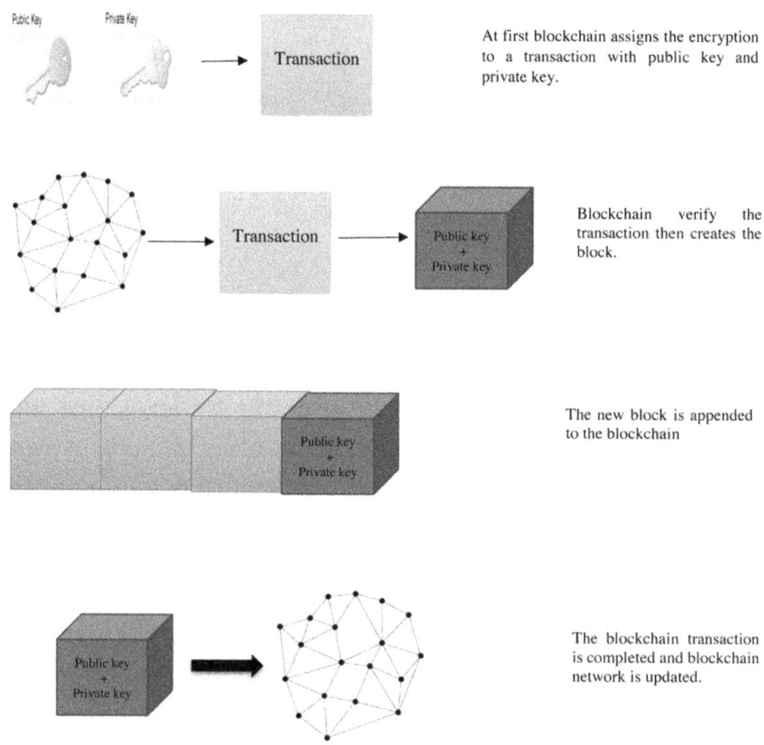

The blockchain technology mainly can be categorized into two ways such as either in public manner or in private manner. However, users can able to categorize into several types based on the availability of data and actions can be performed on data (Fernandez-Carames et al., 2018). In public blockchain networks, any user can perform the actions in blockchain network and able to act as a node or miner node. On the other hand in private blockchain networks, the network administrator has to authorize the user to perform the action. But types of blockchain networks are based on decentralized management system. These also provides high level of privacy and security against threats and malicious attacks. The main differences between public and private is different execution of authorizations of users, ledger maintenance, and protocols. The examples of public blockchain network are Bitcoin, Litecoin, and Ethreum etc., these blockchain networks also called as a permission-less blockchain networks. The private blockchain also called as a permissioned blockchain platform and examples are Corda, Hashgraph, and Ripple or Hyperledger etc.

BLOCKCHAIN BASED SOLUTIONS FOR IOT ENVIRONMENT

A shown in the figure 2, IoT devices connectivity will keep on grow and it will reach 75 billion by 2025. In IoT network, each device acts like internet thing and provide the information to other device in a network. With all these connected devices, data generates in huge volume and processing of that data is a challenging task for researchers. On the other hand, security issues for production data also becomes another challenging task (Sfar et al., 2018). Usually, IoT network is a distributed architecture and each node has the possibilities to allow the attacks and threats. Every infected node can collapse the IoT network in fraction of seconds. This kind of centralized environment collapse the entire idea of IoT technology. This problem statement motivated the authors to propose the blockchain based solutions for IoT environment.

The main aim of the blockchain technology is to free users from any kind of third parties those who are regulate and manage the all kind of transactions. This technology plays major role in controlling, managing, and also provides the security and privacy to IoT devices. The blockchain technology provides the key solutions for several security issues in IoT environment (Jesus et al., 2018). An integration of blockchain and IoT technology brings many features in different kinds of environments such as trading, crypto-currency, machine-to-machine transactions, device tracking systems, supply chain management systems, certifications, government records management, and digital identity systems etc. (Panarello et al., 2018). So many industries like IBM working hard to develop blockchain frameworks in IoT industries. The following characteristics of blockchain technology transforms the IoT technology as a more robust.

- The decentralization is one of the primary and main characteristic of the blockchain technology. This feature increase the scalability, reliability, and robustness of the IoT devices. The main advantage of this characteristic is avoids one-to-many or many-to-one traffic flows of network while supporting the participation of all nodes in network. So that, it eliminates network delay issues and issue of a single node of failure.
- The second characteristic of the blockchain technology is anonymity. This feature keeps the IoT devices data as a private. In IoT environment secure of IoT devices data is, most important thing. So anonymity feature does supports to IoT devices, data should be kept private.
- Finally, security is the third characteristic of the blockchain technology. Making the IoT network as a secured from unauthorized users and devices, increase the robustness of the IoT network.

However, integration of these two technologies is not an easy task due to the different challenges like increment of number of nodes and block mining (Reyna et al., 2018). However, the huge efforts of researchers on these challenges, brings the tremendous evolution in technology (Kshetri, 2017). In this context, the following features of the blockchain technology solves the security issues in IoT environment (Khan & Salah, 2017).

Authorization and Authentication

Blockchain technology supports the decentralized management system, so this characteristic can be able to provide the decentralized authorization and authentication rules to IoT devices. So that IoT devices can be able to adopt multi authorization rules for users. Compare with traditional authorization and authentication protocols such as OMA DM, OpenID, LWM2M, OAuth 2.0, and RBAC etc., the blockchain authorization protocols provides secured access protocols to make connection with IoT devices while have less complexity. Additionally, privacy of IoT devices data also increase by accessing blockchain authorization rules and providing the accessibility of data to only authenticated users. These protocols also helps to upgrade, update, reset the IoT devices, allocation of new keys, and change ownership etc.

Address Space

The blockchain technology supports the 160-bit address space and 160-bit hash of the public key which is generated by Elliptic curve digital signature algorithm. With these both features, blockchain technology can able to allocate the addresses for approximately 1.46 * 10^{48} IoT devices (Khan & Salah, 2017). Generally, 10^{48} addresses avoids the issues of unique identification. That means when allocating the addresses to IoT devices, verification is not required. At present, Internet assigned numbers authority governance allocating the IPv4 and IPv6 address globally. In future, blockchain technology solves the issues of unique addresses for IoT devices.

Secure Communication

In IoT wired or wireless networks, communication protocols helps to communicate devices with each other. The traditional protocols in IoT networks such as HTTP, CoAP, MQTT, and RPL etc., are not provides robust security and privacy. These protocols integrates with other protocols to provide privacy and secure communication. But, blockchain technology transforms the concept of communication from traditional to advanced secure communication. Blockchain technology provides uniqueness of address and asymmetric key pair to IoT devices. So that, no need to exchange and handle the public key infrastructure certificates unlike in traditional communication. Additionally, IoT devices increases the computing process and memory resources.

Cryptography Algorithms

Due to the limited power of processing capabilities and memory resources, IoT devices not be able to handle the advanced cryptographic rules efficiently. Many cryptography algorithms consuming much power of IoT devices, so that IoT devices regularly gets the issues of shutting down. So, power consumption is one of the main parameter to consider when adopting the cryptography algorithm for IoT devices. Blockchain technology uses sophisticated algorithms for security and privacy while using hash functions. These hash functions are very flexible to implement in IoT devices. For example, SHA-256 is one of the blockchain hash functions which can be used in several IoT devices. Additionally, it also helps to avoid the issues about heavy power consumption of IoT devices.

Identity and Access Management

The identity and access management for IoT devices, is a challenging task due to the ownership of IoT devices. The ownership of IoT devices changes from user to user. Each and every IoT device have some parameters like manufacturer details, device type, serial number, and location etc. In some cases, changes of IoT device parameters, is not possible and creates another kind of issues when users make them as a vulnerable. With the help of blockchain technology, can able to solve these kind of issues easily, and efficiently. Generally, blockchain technology provides secure identity registration, monitoring of nodes, and ownership tracking. So, blockchain technology provide identity registration to IoT connected devices and stores the information about each and every parameter of IoT device into blockchain ledger.

The blockchain technology can be adopted in in several environments and use cases (Ferrag et al., 2018). At first, blockchain technology used for crypto-currency system, and later based on the flexible and secure features this technology providing the services in many fields such as data storage management system, user identity management system, smart intelligent transport management system, smart agriculture, and smart living applications etc. (Fernandez-Carames et al., 2018). In supply management also, blockchain using in IoT environments to transport the goods safely to destination. Likewise, the power management sector also taking the advantages of blockchain to IoT devices by providing smart and intelligent hardware components. Another application is smart health care system, the blockchain technology adding some more features to IoT devices to validate the records of patients. In this context, the following section presents how each IoT application utilizing the blockchain features and giving strengthen to IoT devices (Panarello et al., 2018).

Smart City

The smart city can be able to manage the things with intelligently like mobility, vehicles, surveillance cameras, and environmental resources etc. These things acts as intelligent devices, for example smart surveillance cameras captures the accidents on roads and gives the instructions to traffic management system and emergency management system. This kind of system needs data exchange process among connected IoT devices continuously. So attackers targets the devices to access the information of devices so that, attackers can perform unauthorized actions. The blockchain technology provides the secure solution for this issue. The collected data would be divided into several packets and distributes to connected devices in smart city environment. The blockchain cryptographic methods adds the certification rules to these packets which contains the original data. By adding this rules to packets, packets gets the hash of the collected data from IoT devices. Finally, the owner rebuilds the original data from received packets. For the communication also among IoT devices, blockchain uses Telehash protocol to control the devices from the surveillance cameras to traffic management system. This protocol adds authentication rules to IoT devices, so that they communicate with each other without interaction of central authority.

Smart Healthcare System

The integration of IoT technology and blockchain technology brings the evolution in healthcare system and provides the several flexible services to users. In smart healthcare system, the IoT network architecture builds with several kind of sensors, RFID tags, and routers etc. In healthcare system, record maintenance of patients, data communication from connected devices to computing processors, and monitoring the live conditions of patients etc., are very important things and kept as a private. Once the attacker gets the accessibility of IoT network, attacker may misuse the information of patients. The blockchain gives the solution for this issue by providing the secure communication among IoT devices. For example, IoT devices should authenticate with each other to intercommunication. The protocols like SSL or TLS, should be authenticated by public key infrastructure. Few authors (Biswas & Muthukkumarasamy, 2016) proposed a multilayer blockchain based framework for IoT networks. The aim of the proposed systems is data protection from unauthorized users. This architecture supports three layers for blockchain frameworks, the first layer for data storage based on the blockchain blocks, second layer for secure communication in IoT devices, and third layer for data management with access control system.

Smart Home

The IoT technology giving the automation system ability to devices, to enhance the lifestyle of human lives while providing safety, and flexibility. With this ability people can handle and manage several works from outside the home. However, due to the lack of the knowledge about internal functions of IoT network, consumers may get the issues from attackers. For example, if attacker gets the accessibility of one of the IoT devices from smart home then attacker gets the private and confidential data of consumers. Even Man-in-the-Middle attack can be access the information from home routers and sensors etc. So blockchain provides the solution for these attacks by providing public key infrastructure system. Author (Dorri et al., 2016) proposed a multi-layer architecture to overcome the security and privacy issues in IoT environment while adopting the blockchain technology. The main aim of the proposed system is providing the availability, confidentiality, integrity, and reliability of data. This framework have three layers such as smart home, network, and cloud storage system. Likewise bitcoin technology, the miner creates the block when new device is added to IoT network. This block contains the information of block header and policy header. At second layer, devices communicate with each other by secure communication protocol. Finally, with the help of secured hash values data could be stored in cloud storage. This framework aims to provide the confidentiality, integrity, and reliability of data. Another integration of IoT and blockchain technology framework (Jentzsch et al., 2018) proved that, blockchain features provides more strength to IoT networks. This framework proposed an automatic authentication technique to smart IoT devices. The main aim of this proposed framework is, providing the possibilities to users to monitor and control the IoT devices and other goods with the help of blockchain rules. This technique allows the external devices into network and authenticating by smart IoT devices. And also used for authorizing the payments without help of intermediate points.

Smart Transactions

At first blockchain technology mainly used for transactions of crypto-currency, now different kinds of fields also trying to adopt the blockchain features in their environment. The blockchain architecture providing the several possibilities to IoT devices, in such way smart devices can able to make the secure and privacy transactions. In this context, (Wilkinson et al., 2014) proposed the framework for secure and privacy transactions. This framework uses p2p protocol to provide private, secure and encrypted cloud storage system. The main of this framework is, allowing the users to give rent their infrastructures to another users by using blockchain features.

FUTURE RESEARCH DIRECTIONS

Presents several advantages of integration of blockchain and IoT, and it helps to many researchers to solve the various security and privacy issues in IoT environment. But, this integration concept needs further investigations to enhance the research directions (Fernandez-Carames et al., 2018). In this context, the following points helps to researchers for further improvements. The future research directions of integration of blockchain technology and IoT are as follows:

- Still many challenges and issues to be addressed in integration of blockchain and IoT, such as cryptographic algorithms enhancement, security, reliability of data, integrity, and scalability etc. These constraints are very important things in the view of blockchain based IoT applications. Additionally, blockchain technology design processes have the limitations in validation protocols, transaction capacity, and implementation of public key infrastructure rules.

- The development of blockchain architecture rules in IoT environments, need to be approval of all management holders to achieve interoperability. And also has to integrated with legacy polices. An international standards also should be support the integration implementations to provide authorization, authentication, protection polices, and access control etc.
- A sophisticated infrastructure will be needed to implement the integration of blockchain and IoT technologies. To fulfil the requirements of IoT security management system by blockchain based rules, infrastructure or framework should be supports control and inter domain rules.
- The IoT network builds with different kinds of devices, architectures, protocols, and several standard rules etc. So, these networks have more chances to become vulnerable, even at single point of failure. Researchers needs to be develop robust standard protocols and cryptographic algorithms.
- Due to the low limited processing power, IoT devices have the chances to become vulnerable. An advanced security algorithms for hardware vulnerabilities, needs to be implement in intermediaries for malfunctioning, verification of packet processing, and routing etc.
- An advanced and robust rules should be provide for supply management methods. The blockchain technology can be used for supply management system. Adopting these rules in IoT environment, blockchain itself may get the challenges such as efficiency, scalability, reliability, regulations, and integration of data.

CONCLUSION

Now a days, IoT technology growing rapidly to provide the flexible services to human lives. This IoT concept brought the evolution in technology. On the other side, IoT devices are becomes vulnerable and losing the capabilities of defending due to the limited processing power and resources. These issues are raising due to the lack of sophisticated standards, secure protocols, and secure software and hardware designs. To resolve these issues, blockchain technology can offer secure standards, secure protocols, and robust cryptographic algorithms to IoT applications. This chapter focused on blockchain based solutions for IoT platforms. At first, presented about IoT technology and IoT architecture. In the next section, presented about several security and privacy issues in IoT platforms. The taxonomy also created to represents about security issues in IoT environment. An examined about blockchain technology and working process, proposed blockchain based solutions for IoT platforms like smart cities, smart healthcare systems, smart home, and smart transactions. Additionally, future research directions were discussed to provide few ideas to developers and researchers for further blockchain based solutions. The main of this chapter is, to provide technological innovation and secure solutions for IoT platforms based on blockchain technology.

REFERENCES

Abduvaliyev, A., Pathan, A. S. K., Zhou, J., Roman, R., & Wong, W. C. (2013). On the vital areas of intrusion detection systems in wireless sensor networks. *IEEE Communications Surveys and Tutorials*, *15*(3), 1223–1237. doi:10.1109/SURV.2012.121912.00006

Alaba, F. A., Othman, M., Hashem, I. A. T., & Alotaibi, F. (2017). Internet of Things security: A survey. *Journal of Network and Computer Applications*, *88*, 10–28. doi:10.1016/j.jnca.2017.04.002

Alvi, S. A., Afzal, B., Shah, G. A., Atzori, L., & Mahmood, W. (2015). Internet of multimedia things: Vision and challenges. *Ad Hoc Networks*, *33*, 87–111. doi:10.1016/j.adhoc.2015.04.006

Ammar, M., Russello, G., & Crispo, B. (2018). Internet of Things: A survey on the security of IoT frameworks. *Journal of Information Security and Applications*, *38*, 8–27. doi:10.1016/j.jisa.2017.11.002

Antonopoulos, A. M. (2014). *Mastering Bitcoin: unlocking digital cryptocurrencies*. O'Reilly Media, Inc.

Banerjee, M., Lee, J., & Choo, K. K. R. (2018). A blockchain future for internet of things security: A position paper. *Digital Communications and Networks*, *4*(3), 149–160. doi:10.1016/j.dcan.2017.10.006

Biswas, K., & Muthukkumarasamy, V. (2016). Securing smart cities using blockchain technology. In *2016 IEEE 18th international conference on high performance computing and communications; IEEE 14th international conference on smart city; IEEE 2nd international conference on data science and systems (HPCC/SmartCity/DSS)* (pp. 1392-1393). IEEE. 10.1109/HPCC-SmartCity-DSS.2016.0198

Botta, A., De Donato, W., Persico, V., & Pescapé, A. (2016). Integration of cloud computing and internet of things: A survey. *Future Generation Computer Systems*, *56*, 684–700. doi:10.1016/j.future.2015.09.021

Butun, I., Morgera, S. D., & Sankar, R. (2014). A survey of intrusion detection systems in wireless sensor networks. *IEEE Communications Surveys and Tutorials*, *16*(1), 266–282. doi:10.1109/SURV.2013.050113.00191

Dorri, A., Kanhere, S. S., & Jurdak, R. (2016). *Blockchain in internet of things: challenges and solutions.* arXiv preprint arXiv:1608.05187

Fernández-Caramés, T. M., & Fraga-Lamas, P. (2018). A Review on the Use of Blockchain for the Internet of Things. *IEEE Access: Practical Innovations, Open Solutions*, *6*, 32979–33001. doi:10.1109/ACCESS.2018.2842685

Ferrag, M. A., Derdour, M., Mukherjee, M., Derhab, A., Maglaras, L., & Janicke, H. (2018). *Blockchain technologies for the internet of things: Research issues and challenges*. IEEE Internet of Things Journal.

Granjal, J., Monteiro, E., & Silva, J. S. (2015). Security for the internet of things: A survey of existing protocols and open research issues. *IEEE Communications Surveys and Tutorials*, *17*(3), 1294–1312. doi:10.1109/COMST.2015.2388550

Huckle, S., Bhattacharya, R., White, M., & Beloff, N. (2016). Internet of things, blockchain and shared economy applications. *Procedia Computer Science*, *98*, 461–466. doi:10.1016/j.procs.2016.09.074

Jentzsch, C., Jentzsch, S., & Tual, S. (2018). *Slock.IT*. Available online: https://slock.it

Jesus, E. F., Chicarino, V. R., de Albuquerque, C. V., & Rocha, A. A. D. A. (2018). A survey of how to use blockchain to secure internet of things and the stalker attack. *Security and Communication Networks*.

Kalra, S., & Sood, S. K. (2015). Secure authentication scheme for IoT and cloud servers. *Pervasive and Mobile Computing*, *24*, 210–223. doi:10.1016/j.pmcj.2015.08.001

Khan, M. A., & Salah, K. (2018). IoT security: Review, blockchain solutions, and open challenges. *Future Generation Computer Systems*, *82*, 395–411. doi:10.1016/j.future.2017.11.022

Kouicem, D. E., Bouabdallah, A., & Lakhlef, H. (2018). Internet of things security: A top-down survey. *Computer Networks*, *141*, 199–221. doi:10.1016/j.comnet.2018.03.012

Kshetri, N. (2017). Blockchain's roles in strengthening cybersecurity and protecting privacy. *Telecommunications Policy*, *41*(10), 1027–1038. doi:10.1016/j.telpol.2017.09.003

Kumar, K. D., & Umamaheswari, E. (2017). *An Authenticated, Secure Virtualization Management System in Cloud Computing. Asian Journal of Pharmaceutical and Clinical Research.*

Kumar, K. D., & Umamaheswari, E. (2018). Prediction methods for effective resource provisioning in cloud computing: A Survey. *Multiagent and Grid Systems, 14*(3), 283–305. doi:10.3233/MGS-180292

Kumar, K.D., & Umamaheswari, E. (2018). Efficient Cloud Resource Scaling based on Prediction Approaches. *International Journal of Engineering & Technology, 7*(4.10).

Miraz, M. H., & Ali, M. (2018). *Applications of blockchain technology beyond cryptocurrency.* arXiv preprint arXiv:1801.03528

Mitchell, R., & Chen, R. (2014). A survey of intrusion detection in wireless network applications. *Computer Communications, 42*, 1–23. doi:10.1016/j.comcom.2014.01.012

Panarello, A., Tapas, N., Merlino, G., Longo, F., & Puliafito, A. (2018). Blockchain and iot integration: A systematic survey. *Sensors (Basel), 18*(8), 2575. doi:10.339018082575 PMID:30082633

Reyna, A., Martín, C., Chen, J., Soler, E., & Díaz, M. (2018). On blockchain and its integration with IoT. Challenges and opportunities. *Future Generation Computer Systems, 88*, 173–190. doi:10.1016/j.future.2018.05.046

Sfar, A. R., Natalizio, E., Challal, Y., & Chtourou, Z. (2018). A roadmap for security challenges in the Internet of Things. *Digital Communications and Networks, 4*(2), 118–137. doi:10.1016/j.dcan.2017.04.003

Sicari, S., Rizzardi, A., Grieco, L. A., & Coen-Porisini, A. (2015). Security, privacy and trust in Internet of Things: The road ahead. *Computer Networks, 76*, 146–164. doi:10.1016/j.comnet.2014.11.008

Wang, Y., Uehara, T., & Sasaki, R. (2015). Fog computing: Issues and challenges in security and forensics. In *2015 IEEE 39th Annual Computer Software and Applications Conference* (Vol. 3, pp. 53-59). IEEE.

Weber, R. H. (2015). Internet of things: Privacy issues revisited. *Computer Law & Security Review, 31*(5), 618–627. doi:10.1016/j.clsr.2015.07.002

Wilkinson, S., Boshevski, T., Brandoff, J., & Buterin, V. (2014). *Storj a peer-to-peer cloud storage network.* Academic Press.

Yi, S., Qin, Z., & Li, Q. (2015). Security and privacy issues of fog computing: A survey. *International Conference on Wireless Algorithms, Systems, and Applications*, 685–695. 10.1007/978-3-319-21837-3_67

Zarpelao, B. B., Miani, R. S., Kawakani, C. T., & de Alvarenga, S. C. (2017). A survey of intrusion detection in Internet of Things. *Journal of Network and Computer Applications*, *84*, 25–37. doi:10.1016/j.jnca.2017.02.009

Chapter 4
A Novel Survey on Blockchain for Internet of Things

Jay Kumar Jain
Sagar Institute of Research and Technology, India

Varsha Jain
Bansal Institute of Science and Technology, Bhopal, India

ABSTRACT

Internet of things (IoT) is ready to change human life and release tremendous financial benefits. It may be that lack of information security and the belief of the current IoT are actually restricting its selection. Blockchain changes in an appropriated and secure record holds reliable records of information in various areas and possibly resolves information security concerns in the IoT system. This chapter presents a thorough review on the existing blockchain progress with an accent on IoT applications. The authors first give an overview of blockchain architecture including blockchain technologies and key characteristics of blockchain. The authors then discuss the blockchain for the internet of things including blockchain for IoT: technologies. Furthermore, they list some challenges and problems that will hinder blockchain development and summarize some existing approaches for solving these problems. Some possible future directions are also discussed. Future research bearings are ordered for a viable mix of blockchains in the IoT system.

DOI: 10.4018/978-1-7998-0186-3.ch004

INTRODUCTION

A blockchain is a decentralized, distributed database that is used to maintain a continuous growing list of records, which is called a block. This is a digital ledger of records which is shown in a network to capture transactions between different parties. For use as a distributed ledger, a blockchain is autonomously managed by a peer-to-peer network, which adheres to a protocol for inter-node communication and validates new blocks and after its creation includes all transactions. Each block contains a cryptographic hash of the past block, a timestamp, and exchange information. All members like businesses or people, utilizing the common database are "hubs" associated with the blockchain each keeping up an indistinguishable duplicate of the record. Each section into a blockchain is an exchange and all these exchanges show a trade of significant worth among members (i.e., an advanced resource that demonstrate rights, commitments or proprietorship). By and by, a wide range of sorts of blockchains are being developed and tried. Nonetheless, most blockchains pursue this essential system and approach. When one member needs to make an exchange with another, the various hubs in the system speak with one another utilizing a pre-decided component to watch that the new exchange is legitimate.

This mechanism is referred to as an assent calculation. When a transaction has been acknowledged by the system, all duplicates of the record are refreshed with the new data. Different exchanges are generally joined into a "hinder" that is attached to the record. Each square contains data that alludes back to past squares and along these lines all squares in the steel together in the dispersed indistinguishable duplicates. Taking an interest hub can include new, time-stepped exchanges, however, members can't erase or adjust the passages once they have been approved and acknowledged by the system. On the off chance that a hub changed a past square, it would not synchronize with the remainder of the system and would be prohibited from the blockchain. A legitimately working blockchain is in this manner changeless in spite of coming up short on a focal head.

Blockchain Architecture

According to Lee KuoChuen, D. et al. (2015), Blockchain is a series of blocks, which carries a complete list of transaction records like a traditional public ledger. Figure 1 outlines the case of a blockchain. Each block indicates the immediately previous block via a reference that is fundamentally a hash value of the previous block known as parent block. According to Buterin, et al. (2014) it is worth noting that uncle blocks (offspring of the block's predecessor) hashes will likewise be stored in ethereum blockchain. The initial block of a blockchain is known as genesis block which has no parent block. The author then presents the block structure in

Figure 1. Sequence of blocks.

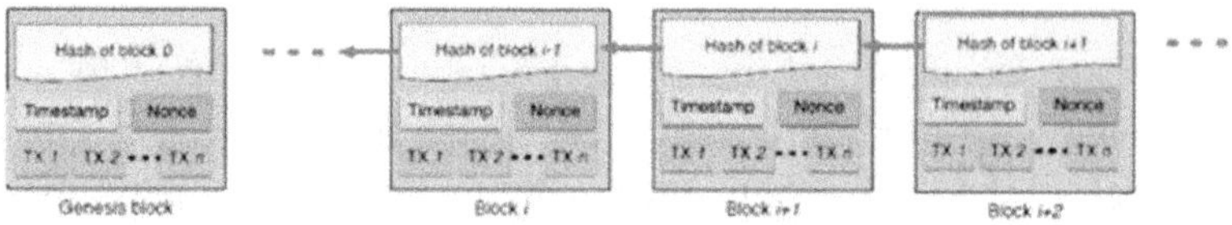

section 2.1, digital signature working in section 2.2. Additionally, authors also give a precise of blockchain key attributes in section 2.3. Also, Blockchain taxonomy is shown in section 2.4.

Block

A block comprises of the block header and the block body as mentioned in Figure 2. In particular, the block header includes:

1. Block version: implies which set of block validation rules to pursue.
2. Parent block hash: it is 256-bit hash values that indicate to the previous block.
3. Merkle tree root hash: the hash value of all the transactions in the block.
4. Timestamp: current timestamp as seconds since 1970-01-01T00:00 UTC.
5. nBits: current hashing target in a minimal format.
6. Nonce: a 4-byte field, which usually starts with 0 and increases for every hash computation.

The block body is made out of a transaction counter and transactions. The maximum transaction that a block can contain relies upon the block size and the measure of each transaction. Blockchain utilizes an asymmetric cryptography mechanism to validate the authentication of transactions. An asymmetric cryptography-based digital signature is used in an unfaithful situation. Author next quicky explains digital signature.

Digital Signature

Each user holds a set of the private key and public key. The private key is used to sign a transaction. The digital signed transactions are spread all over the entire network and afterward are accessed by public keys, which are shown to everyone in the network. Figure 3 shows an example of a digital signature used in blockchain. The classic digital signature includes two phases: the signing phase and the verification phase. Take Figure 3 for instance again. When a user Alice wants to sign a transaction, Firstly she generates a hash value obtained from the transaction. Then she encrypts

Figure 2. Block Structure

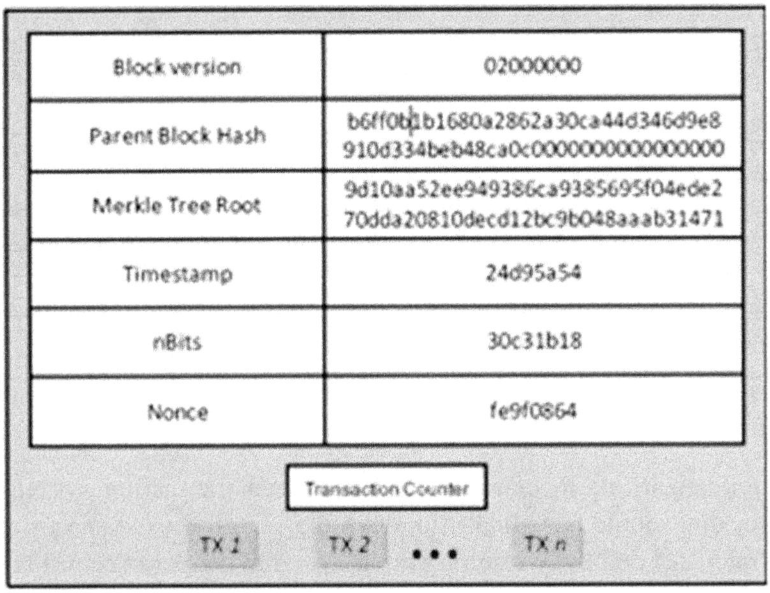

the hash value by utilizing her private key and is included transfer to another user Bob the encrypted hash with the original data. Bob verifies the received transaction by comparing the decrypted hash (by using Alice's public key) and the hash value generated from the received data by the same hash function as Alice's. The typical digital signature algorithms utilized in blockchains incorporate elliptic curve digital signature algorithm (ECDSA) defined by Johnson et al. (2001).

Key Characteristics of Blockchain

Precisely, blockchain has the following key properties:

Figure 3. Digital signature used in Blockchain

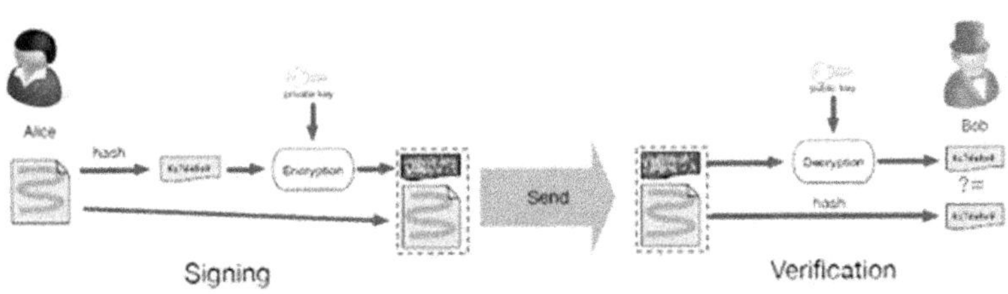

Table 1. Differentiate among public blockchain, consortium blockchain, and private blockchain

Property	Public blockchain	Consortium blockchain	Private blockchain
Consensus Determination	All miners	Selected set of nodes	One organization
Read permission	Public	Could be public or restricted	Could be public or restricted
Immutability	Nearly impossible to tamper	Could be tampered	Could be tampered
Efficiency	Low	High	High
Centralized	No	Partial	Yes
Consensus process	Permissionless	Permissioned	Permissioned

- **Decentralization:** In conventional centralized transaction systems, every transaction should be validated through the central trusted agency (e.g., the central bank) definitely resulting in the cost and the performance hold-up at the central servers.

Differently, a transaction in the blockchain network can be regulated in between any two peers (P2P) without the authentication by the central agency. In this manner, blockchain can considerably diminish the server costs (including both development and operation cost) and reduce the performance bottlenecks at the central server.

- **Persistency:** Since every transaction spreading over the network should be verified and recorded in blocks distributed in the entire network, it is nearly impossible to tamper. Additionally, each broadcasted block will be approved by other nodes and transactions will be checked. So any falsification will be diagnosed easily.
- **Anonymity:** Each user can interact with the blockchain network using a generated address. Further, a user will generate multiple addresses to avoid identity exposure. There is no longer any central party keeping users' private information. This mechanism preserves a definite amount of privacy on the transactions included in the blockchain. Note that blockchain cannot ensure the ideal privacy preservation due to the constitutional constraint.
- **Auditability:** Since all the transactions on the blockchain is verified and recorded with a timestamp, users can easily validate and trace the previous records by accessing any node in the distributed network. In Bitcoin blockchain, every transaction can be detected to previous transactions

iteratively. It enhances the traceability and the transparency of the data stored in the blockchain.

Taxonomy of Blockchain Systems

Current blockchain systems can be roughly classified into three types: public blockchain, private blockchain and consortium blockchain. Buterin et al. (2015) compare all the three types of blockchain from different perspectives. The comparison is shown in Table 1.

- **Consensus Determination**: In the public blockchain, every node can participate in the consensus process. And the selected group of nodes are responsible for validating the block in consortium blockchain. As for the private chain, it is fully managed by one organization who can determine the final consensus.
- **Read Permission**: Transactions in a public blockchain are visible to the public while the read permission rely on a private blockchain or a consortium blockchain. The consortium or the organization can umpire whether the stored information is public or restricted.
- **Immutability**: Since transactions are stored in multiple nodes in the distributed network, therefore, it is certainly impossible to tamper the public blockchain. However, if most of the consortium or the ruling organization wants to tamper the blockchain, then the consortium blockchain or private blockchain can be reversed or tampered.
- **Efficiency**: It takes enough time to propagate transactions and blocks because there are a huge number of nodes on the public blockchain network. Taking network safety into consideration, limitation on the public blockchain will be much more severe. Hence, transaction throughput is restricted and the latency is high. With fewer validators, consortium blockchain and private blockchain can be much efficient.
- **Centralized**: The chief difference in between the three types of blockchains is that public blockchain is decentralized, consortium blockchain is partially centralized and private blockchain is fully centralized as it is governed by a single group.
- **Consensus Process**: Everyone in the globe can join the consensus process of the public blockchain. Apart from public blockchain, both consortium blockchain and private blockchain are permissioned. One node should be certificated to join the consensus process in consortium or private blockchain.

Since public blockchain is exposed to the world, it can mesmerize many users. The communities are .also very active. Several public blockchains emerge day by day. As for consortium blockchain, it can be applied to several business applications. Currently Hyperledger (2015), Hyperledger is evolving business consortium blockchain frameworks. Ethereum also has provided tools for constructing consortium blockchains. As for private blockchain, there are still a few companies applying it for efficiency and auditability.

EXISTING BLOCKCHAIN TECHNOLOGIES

Blockchain furnished decentralized data storage service with a tamper-resistant ledger having blocks chained in serial in distributed networks. It can record and secure transactions or transactional events with cryptography. The first Blockchain was suggested by Satoshi Nakamoto et al. (2008) and implemented in 2009 as the sanction technique for the proliferating cryptocurrency-Bitcoin (2007).

The data is recorded in a secure and distributed manner in the blockchain. The fundamental unit of records in Blockchain is the transaction. Every time a new transaction is generated, it is broadcast to the whole Blockchain network. Nodes receiving the transaction can validate the transaction by verifying the signature attached to the transaction, and mine validated transactions into cryptographically secured blocks. Such nodes are called block miners (or miners for short). To permit a miner to construct a block, a consensus problem required to be solved in a distributed way. The miners that manage to resolve the consensus problem broadcast their new blocks into the network. Upon the receipt of a new block, the miners yet to be able to resolve the consensus problem append the block to their own chains of blocks locally maintained at the miners, after all the transactions enclosed in the block are validate and the block is also proven to provide the right answer to the consensus problem. The new block consists of a link to the previous block in the chains, just by exploiting cryptographic means. All miners can synchronize their chains on a general basis, and specific terms are defined to ensure the consistent ledger shared among the distributed network, e.g., Bitcoin Blockchain keeps the longest chain only, in the case where there is discrepancy into the chains. In the following, few more detailed descriptions are given on these key components of Blockchain, i.e., the data structure, the consensus protocol, smart contracts and the security analysis on Blockchain.

BLOCKCHAIN FOR THE INTERNET OF THINGS

As described in ITU Report, (2015), the Internet of Things (IoT) refers to the network of many physical objects (20 billion by 2020, according to Gartner et al. (2016) which are given with Internet connection. Those devices acquire information about the surrounding environment, and they communicate with each other and with software systems by the Internet. As a result of such rich interaction, they also generate a large amount of data, in turn, usable to enable dependent services.

Instead of the benefits provided by these services, critical privacy issues may arise. It is because the connected devices (the things) spread sensitive personal data and disclose the behaviors and preferences of their owners. People's privacy is definitely at risk when such sensitive data are directed by centralized companies, which can make an illegal use of them: as a matter of fact, Edward Snowden's revelations showed that people's data stored by Internet and telecommunication companies have been exploited within a mass surveillance program, i.e, the PRISM program.

To prevent this situation, the goal of our research is to encourage a decentralized and private by- design IoT, where privacy is ensured by the technical design of the systems. Authors believe that this can be accomplished by adopting Peer-to-Peer (P2P) systems. In particular, the blockchain could be very helpful in constructing such privacy preserving IoT. S. Nakamoto et al. (2009) said the blockchain is a P2P ledger, initially used in the Bitcoincryptocurrency for economic transactions.

It is tamper-proof and consists only authentic information; additionally, since it is P2P, it is not handled by any single centralized entity. Because of these reasons, cryptocurrencies are just one of the possible applications of all this technology.

A private-by-design IoT could be fostered by the merging of the blockchain and a P2P storage system. Sensitive data generated and exchanged among IoT devices are stored in such a storage system, whose P2P nature could guarantee privacy, robustness, and absence of single points of failure. Including with this storage system, the blockchain has the basic role to register and authenticate all operations performed on IoT devices data. Every operation on data (creation, modification, deletion) is registered in the blockchain: this could guarantee that any abuse on data can be detected. Moreover, access policies can be specified and enforced by the blockchain, preventing unauthorized operations on data. In this system, people are not required to entrust IoT data generated by their devices to centralized companies: data could be securely stored in different peers, and the blockchain could ensure their authenticity and prevent unauthorized access.

Limitations of IoT Security

M. Pticek et al. (2016) said that IoT network prevails with its ability to interconnect several devices possessing multiple sensing and computing abilities with little human interventions. Sensing and actuating devices form heterogeneous IoT networks to provide several applications. Typical IoT applications consist of smart home, smart transport, eHealth and smart grid discussed by C. Perera et al. (2014).

A typical IoT architecture includes Perception, Networking, Service, and Interface Layers, from bottom to top. The Perception layer also called the sensor layer in other IoT architectures summarized in, contain sensors and actuators collecting and processing environmental information to execute functions, such as querying temperature, location, motion, acceleration. The perception layer is an indispensable part of a variation of IoT applications. Multiple types of end devices can be adopted in the perception layer to bridge the physical world and the digital world. Classic end devices include Radio- Frequency Identification (RFID), wireless sensors and actuators, Near Field Communications (NFC), and mobile phones. For example, the RFID tag is a small microchip linked to an antenna. By attaching RFID tags to objects, the object can be identified, tracked, and monitored during logistics, retailing, and supply chain. The Networking layer is responsible for connecting other smart things, network devices, and servers. The Service layer constructs and manages specific services to meet the IoT application requirements. The Interface layer facilitates data use interactions with objects for certain applications.

BLOCKCHAINFOR IOT: APPLICATIONS

IoT networks are data-centric, where data are uploaded by a huge number of end devices. This makes both data and devices be the prey of potential attacks on IoT. Sensory data in an IoT system can be personal or sensitive, e.g., medical IoT; or from national applications, e.g., the IoT-based smart grid proposed by W.L. Chin et al. (2017) and nuclear factory by R. Langner et al. (2011). The integrity and privacy of the data are important. Blockchain is believed to hold the key to fix security, data integrity and reliability concerns in the IoT network. Provided ensured data integrity, Blockchain has drawn a lot of attention for multiple IoT applications (e.g., supply chain management defined by K. Korpela et al. (2017) and smart city by K. Biswas et al. (2016)), beyond the cryptocurrency. Blockchain technologies handle security risks on both aspects of sensory data and end-devices.

The correctness of sensory data. The data in Blockchain powered IoT networks can be separated into Blockchain-related data, e.g., account, balance and transaction fee, and IoT-related data, e.g., sensory data. The Blockchain-related data can be validated based on previous transactions, e.g., the expense must be fewer than the balance of an account, as done in other typical Blockchain applications. The IoT-related data are secured by signatures in a transactional fashion, which guarantees that only the messages sent by the authorized IoT devices are recorded and exploited. On the other hand, the correctness of IoT-related data can be ensured by the Oracle service which gives an authenticated data feed. The backward-linked hashed structure to increase the trustworthiness of sensory data recorded in IoT-Blockchain ledgers. Malicious functionality of IoT devices. The malicious behaviors of end devices in IoT-Blockchain can be summarized as the following three types: (1) sending transactions with false signatures, which can be detected, punished and rejected by the Blockchain system; or (2) sending transactions with invalid data but correct signatures, which can be removed by false data detection algorithms and punishing the transactions source nodes; or (3) consuming resources, e.g., DoS, which can be prevented by transaction fee mechanisms.

BLOCKCHAIN FOR IOT: TECHNOLOGIES

In this section, authors describe typical technologies of Blockchains which can be used in IoT applications. Firstly, they present three categories of current Blockchain networks and map IoT applications into suitable Blockchain categories. After that the core function of Blockchain, namely, the consensus protocol, is analyzed from two key points, followed by representing Blockchain projects compared in the suitability in IoT applications. Based on access controls of the Blockchain networks, the state-of-the-art Blockchains can be classified into public Blockchain, private Blockchain, and hybrid Blockchain which mixes of the former two.

- **Public Blockchain:** The main class of Blockchain is public Blockchain in which, with no access control, any uncertified, untrustworthy node can read and record transactions, and take part in mining blocks and contributing to Blockchain. Designed for open access to public distributed networks, public Blockchains can give strong scalability. However, preserving the consistent records of public Blockchain becomes increasingly tough, as the network scales up, and would compromise the block creation rate of public Blockchain consequently. This is due to the fact that, without access control, public networks do not have strict control policy on the identification and certification of any participants according to V. Buterin et al. (2015), and therefore the executed consensus protocols have to scarify the block creation rate for security. Specifically, PoW and PoX are normally used in public Blockchain as consensus protocols, achieving lower block generation rate compared with PBFT algorithm utilized in private Blockchain, which will be analyzed in detail later in this section. Current public Blockchain projects, containing Bitcoin and Ethereum, also specify the openness and capacity-limited attributes. Public Blockchain is best suited for the IoT applications with open access or flexible peers at a large scale, such as VANET and supply chain.

- **Private Blockchain:** Another well-known class of Blockchain is private Blockchain which resides in closed proprietary networks with stringent access control and read/write permission, as well as participant identification and certification. Private Blockchains can meet the privacy needs and has been increasingly drawing attention from financial institutions. The proprietary networks, on which private Blockchains operate, can be efficient for high speed and low latency. For instance, high speed of up to tens of thousands of transactions every second can be achieved in private Blockchains. Private Blockchain acquires BFT protocols, i.e., PBFT and its variability, as consensus protocols, which give higher capacity with restricted access control. The access control given by private Blockchain further protects IoT applications from external adversaries. In general, private Blockchain is best suited for IoT applications with the small scale of miners, because of both the high communication complexity and overhead of BFT protocols. When the network size goes beyond twenty, the capacity of private Blockchain exponentially slows down. Apart from multiple BFT consensus protocols, private Blockchain can use other efficient consensus protocols, e.g., Paxos and Raft, in response to particular types of failures, e.g., crash failures and fail-stop failures.
- **Hybrid Blockchain:** Another category of Blockchain is hybrid Blockchain which was proposed to leverage the advantages of public and private Blockchains, to be more specific, the block create rate of private Blockchain and the scalability of public Blockchain. Another recent example of hybrid Blockchain is ByzCoin which dynamically forms hash power-proportionate consensus groups to gather recently-successful block miners. Communication trees can be employed to optimize transaction commitment and verification under normal operation. More examples of hybrid Blockchain consist a resilience optimal Byzantine consensus algorithm that Crain et al. proposed for consortium Blockchain which relies on neither a leader nor a signature or randomization. The proposed consensus protocol companies reducing multivariate Byzantine consensus to binary Byzantine consensus satisfying a validity property. The property is that, if all the non-faulty processes propose a similar value, no other value can be decided. The hybrid Blockchain is attractive to IoT applications due to the complexity and heterogeneity of IoT

networks. A hierarchical Blockchain structure was introduced for the smart home applications, where a private Blockchain, maintained by resourceful ''miners'', runs at each home and public Blockchain runs on the ''miner'' network.

BLOCKCHAIN SOLUTIONS FOR IOT SECURITY

Blockchain technology has been showcased by industry and research community as a disruptive technology that is ready to play a major role in overseeing, controlling, and most importantly securing IoT devices. This section discusses how blockchain can be a key enabling technology for providing practical security solutions to today's challenging IoT security problems. Firstly, the section gives a concise background about blockchain, and after that outlines open research IoT security problems and challenges which blockchain may give solutions for. Also, the section gives the literature of blockchain-based solutions for IoT security problems.

Background

A blockchain is basically a decentralized, distributed, shared, and immutable database ledger that stores registry of assets and transactions throughout a peer-to-peer (P2P) network. It contains chained blocks of data that have been timestamped and verified by miners. The blockchain works on elliptic curve cryptography (ECC) and SHA-256 hashing to give solid cryptographic proof for data authentication and integrity discussed by A.M. Antonopoulos et al. (2014). Fundamentally, the block data consists of a list of all transactions and a hash to the previous block. The blockchain has a full history of all transactions and gives a cross-border global distributed trust.

Trusted Third Parties (TTP) or centralized authorities and services can be disrupted, compromised or hacked. They can also misbehave and become immortal in the future, despite the fact that they are trustworthy now. In the blockchain, each transaction in the shared public ledger is validated by a majority consensus of miner nodes which are actively incorporated in verifying and validating transactions. In a bitcoin network, miners validate the block by calculating a hash with leading zeros to meet the difficulty target. Once transactions are verified and validated by consensus, block data are immutable, i.e. data can never be erased or modified. Blockchain can be built as (1) permissioned (or private) network that can be prohibited to a specific group of participants, or (2) permission-less or public network which is open for anyone to join in. Permission blockchains outfit more privacy and better access control Fig. 4 illustrate a typical design structure of a Blockchain. The design structure is mainly composed of the block header and the block body which

Figure 4. Blockchain design structure showing chained blocks with header and body fields

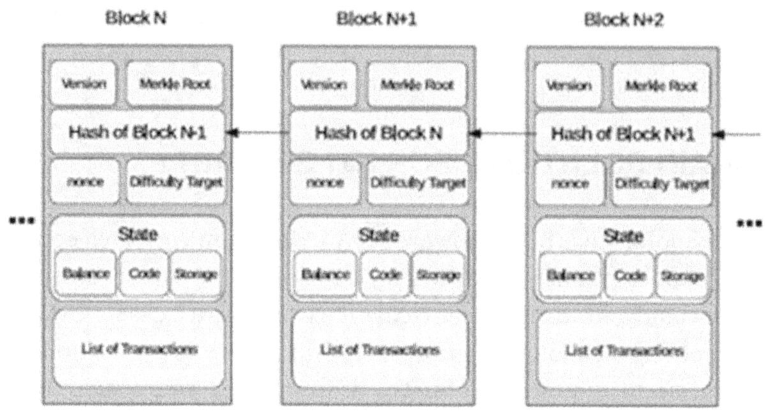

consists of a list of transactions. The block header consists of multiple fields, one of which is a version number to track software of protocol upgrades. Also, the header consists of a timestamp, block size, and the number of transactions. Merkle root field showcases the hash value of the current block. Merkle tree hashing is commonly used in distributed systems and P2P networks for efficient data verification. The nonce field is used for the proof-of-work algorithm, and it is the trial counter value that created the hash with leading zeros. The difficulty target enumerates the number of leading zeros and is used to keep the blocktime approximately 10 min for BitInfoCharts, Block - Bitcoin Wiki, (2016) and Ethereum Average BlockTime Chart, (2016). The difficulty target is adjustable periodically and is grown (with more leading zeros) as the computation power of hardware grows over time. The blocktime is set by design to account for the propagation time of blocks to reach every miner, and for every miner to reach a consensus.

Bitcoin is one of the first and the most famous applications that execute on the top of blockchain infrastructure. In general, the bitcoin blockchain has been the underlying platform and technology of several of today's most popular cryptocurrencies. However, with the advent of the Ethereum blockchain, which enacts smart contracts, the potential use of space for blockchain has become endless. Ethereum blockchain was introduced and opened for use to the public in July 2015. Subsequently, similar smart-contract blockchain platforms have lately emerged. Those consist of Linux-Foundation (2017), C. Kuhlman (2016), Stellar, Stellar network overview, (2014), Ripple, Ripple network, (2013) and Tendermint [2017]. In contrast to bitcoin blockchain which is primarily used for digital currency transactions, Ethereum blockchain has the potential to store records and more importantly run smart contracts. The term smart contracts were first introduced by Nick Szabo in 1994. A smart contract is basically a computerized transaction protocol that runs the terms of the contract. In the simplistic definition, smart contracts are programs written by users to be uploaded and run on the blockchain. The scripting or programming language for smart contracts is known as Solidarity which is a JavaScript-like language.

Ethereum Blockchain provides EVM (Ethereum Virtual Machines) which are basically the miner nodes. These nodes are able to provide cryptographically tamper-proof trustworthy execution and enforcement of these programs or contracts. Ethereum supports its own digital currency which is known as Ether. As in bitcoin, in Ethereum, users can send coins to each other using normal transactions which get recorded on the ledger, and for such transactions, there is no requirement for a blockchain state in bitcoin.

However, for Ethereum to assist smart contract execution, a blockchain state is used. A smart contract consists of its own account and address, and associated with it is its own executable code and balance of Ether coins. The storage is perceptual and holds the code to be executed on the EVM nodes. EVM storage is relatively costly, and for a large storage to be uploaded to the blockchain, another remote decentralized data store like BitTorrent, IPFS, or Swarm can be used. The smart contracts, however, can hold a validation hash of such remotely stored data. The possible use cases and applications of smart-contract blockchain applications are vast and endless, extending from cryptocurrency and trading to autonomous machine-to-machine transactions, from supply chain and asset tracking to automated access control and sharing, and from digital identity and voting to certification, management, and governance of records, data, or items discussed by J. Mattila et al. (2016). Based on blockchains, commercial deployments are increasing rapidly. For instance, Safeshare releases (2016) have offered insurance solution using blockchain based on bitcoin. Similarly, as per linux foundation, (2017), IBM has launched its blockchain framework using Hyperledger Fabric platform. The framework supports the development of blockchain applications, and in contrast to other frameworks, it does not need cryptocurrency. The IBM blockchain is being used commercially into banks, supply chain systems, and cargo shipping companies.

Potential Blockchain Solutions

In the context of IoT, blockchain depends on smart contracts is expected to play a noteworthy role in managing, controlling, and most importantly securing IoT devices. In this section, authors discuss and summarize a few of the intrinsic features of blockchain that can be immensely useful for IoT in general, and IoT security in particular. Address Space. Blockchain has a 160-bit address space, instead of IPv6 address space which consists 128-bit address space according to A.M. Antonopoulos et al. (2014). A blockchain address is 20 bytes or a 160-bit hash of the public key created by ECDSA (Elliptic Curve Digital Signature Algorithm). With the 160-bit address, blockchain can generate and allocate addresses offline for around 1.46*1048 IoT devices. The probability of address collision is approximately 1048, which is considered adequately safe to provide a GUID (Global Unique Identifier) which requires no registration or uniqueness verification when assigning and allocating an address to an IoT device. With blockchain, centralized authority and governance, like that of the Internet Assigned Numbers Authority (IANA), is removed. Currently, IANA oversees the allocation of global IPv4 and IPv6 addresses, Furthermore, blockchain gives 4.3 billion addresses more than IPv6, therefore making blockchain a more scalable solution for IoT than IPv6.

Lastly, it is worth noting that several IoT devices are constrained in memory and computation capacity, and therefore will be unfit to run an IPv6 stack.

Identity of Things (IDoT) and Governance. Identity and Access Management (IAM) for IoT must address various challenging issues in an efficient, safe, and reliable manner. One primary challenging issues deal with ownership and identity relationships of IoT devices. Ownership of a device changes during the lifetime of the device from the manufacturer, supplier, retailer, and consumer proposed by I. Friese et al. (2014). The consumer ownership of an IoT device can be changed or revoked, if the device gets resold, decommissioned, or compromised. Managing of attributes and relationships of an IoT device is another challenge. Attributes of a device can be consist of the manufacturer, make, type, serial number, deployment GPS coordinates, location, etc. Aside from attributes, capabilities, and features, IoT devices have relationships. IoT relationships may consist of the device to- human, device-to-device, or device-to-service. An IoT device relationships can be deployed by, used by, shipped by, sold by, upgraded by, fixed by, sold by, etc.

Blockchain has the capability to solve these challenges effectively, securely, and efficiently. Blockchain has been used widely for giving trustworthy and authorized identity registration, ownership tracking and monitoring of products, goods, and assets. According to P. Otte et al. (2017), approaches like Trust Chain are proposed to enable trusted transactions using blockchain while providing the integrity of the transactions in a distributed environment. IoT devices are no exception. Blockchain can be used to register and give identity to connected IoT devices, with a set of parameters and complex relationships that can be uploaded and stored on the blockchain distributed ledger.

Blockchain also gives trustworthy decentralized management, governance, and tracking at every point in the supply chain and lifecycle of an IoT device, as portrayed in Fig. 5. The supply chain can incorporate multiple players such as factory, vendor, supplier, distributor, shipper, installer, owner, repairer, re-installed, etc. As shown in Fig. 5, key pairs can be changed and re-issued at many points during the lifecycle

Figure 5. IoT device lifecycle security management

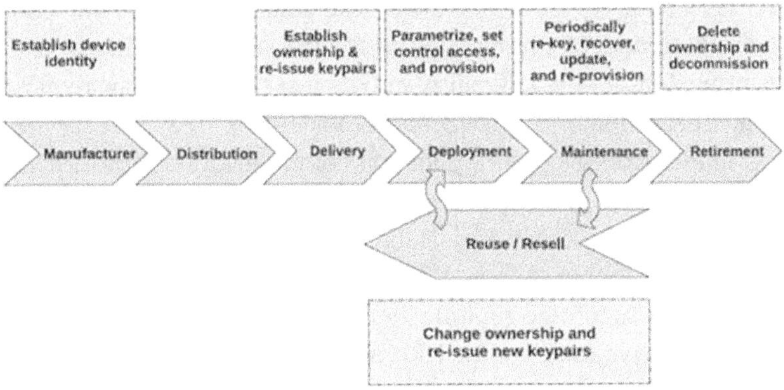

of an IoT device. Issuance of key pairs can be done firstly by the manufacturer, then by the owner, periodically after deployment.

*Data Authentication and Integrity,*By design, data transmitted by IoT devices connected to the blockchain network will always be cryptographically proofed and signed by the real sender that holds a unique public key and GUID, and thereby ensuring authentication and integrity of transmitted data. Additionally, each transaction made to or by an IoT device is recorded on the blockchain distributed ledger and can be tracked securely.

Authentication, Authorization, and Privacy, Blockchain smart contracts have the capability to provide decentralized authentication rules and logic to be able to provide single and multiparty authentication to an IoT Device.

Information Authentication and Integrity, By structure, information transmitted by IoT gadgets associated with the blockchain system will dependably be cryptographically sealed and marked by the genuine sender that holds an interesting open key and GUID, and in this manner guaranteeing confirmation and trustworthiness of transmitted information. Also, every exchange made to or by an IoT gadget are recorded on the blockchain circulated record and can be followed safely.

Validation, Authorization, and Privacy, Blockchain shrewd contracts have the capacity to give a decentralized verification tenets and rationale to have the capacity to give single and multiparty validation to an IoT Device.

Likewise, smart contracts can provide a more efficient authorization access rules to connected IoT devices with much less complexity when compared with traditional authorization protocols like Role Based Access Management (RBAC), OAuth 2.0, OpenID, OMA DM, and LWM2M. These protocols are used these days for IoT device authentication widely, authorization, and management. Moreover, data privacy can be also ensured by utilizing smart contracts which set the access rules, conditions, and time to allow certain individual or group of users or machines to own, control, or have access to data at rest or in transit. The smart contracts can spell out also who has the right to update, upgrade, patch the IoT software or hardware, reset the IoT device, provision of new key pairs, initiate a service or repair request, change ownership, and provision or re-provision of the device.

Secure Communications. IoT application communication protocols as those of HTTP, MQTT, CoAP, or XMPP, or even protocols related with routing as those of RPL and 6LoWPAN, are not secure by design. Such protocols must be wrapped inside the other security protocols such as DTLS or TLS for messaging and application protocols to provide secure communication. In the same way, for routing, IPSec is typically used to give security for RPL and 6LoWPAN protocols. DTLS, TLS, IPSec, or even the light-weight TinyTLS protocols are heavy and complex in terms of computation and memory prerequisites, and complicated with centralized management and governance of key management and distributions using the famous protocol of PKI. With blockchain, key management and distribution are totally removed, as each IoT device would have his own unique GUID and asymmetric key pair once installed and connected to the blockchain network. This will lead also to significant simplification of other security protocols as that of DTLS, with no need to handle and exchange PKI certificates at the handshake stage in case of DTLS or TLS (or IKE in case of IPSec) to negotiate the cipher suite parameters for encryption and hashing and to establish the master and session keys. Therefore, lightweight security protocols that would fit and stratify the needs for the compute and memory resources of IoT devices become more feasible.

Blockchain and IoT Related Work

In the article, research work on IoT security and blockchain is reserved, with most of the work being focused on leveraging blockchain technology to benefit IoT in general. M. Conoscenti et al. (2016) have classified 18 use cases of blockchain, out of which four cases are for IoT. The four use case categories for IoT consist of an immutable log of events and management of access control to data proposed by G. Zyskind et al. (2015), trading of collected IoT data by Y. Zhang et al. (2015) and D. Wörner et al. (2014), and symmetric and asymmetric key management for IoT devices by L. Axon et al. (2015) and C. Fromknecht et al. (2014). I. Friese et al. (2014) have laid out the issues and challenges for the identity in IoT. These challenges primarily incorporate ownership and identity relationships, authentication and authorization, governance of data and privacy. In Section 5.1, the authors discussed how blockchain can be a key enabler for resolving these challenges.

A. Bahga et al. (2016) proposed a blockchain-based framework for industrial IoT (or IIoT). The framework enables IIoT devices to communicate with the cloud and the blockchain network both. Each IIoT device is furnished with the single-board computer (SBC) having control and communication interface capabilities for both cloud and the Ethereum blockchain. IIoT devices are intended to deliver data to the cloud for storage and analysis, and send/receive transactions to other devices on the blockchain network, and also to trigger executions of smart contracts. As a proof of concept, the authors designed a simple platform using the Arduino Uno board and Ethereum smart contracts and discuss briefly how the platform can be used for machine maintenance and smart diagnostics.

The applications of blockchain smart contracts to IoT are reviewed by Christidis et al. (2016). The authors discussed how smart contracts of blockchain can facilitate and bloster the autonomous workflow and the sharing of services among IoT devices, as proposed by V. Pureswaran et al. (2014). However, the authors contend how IoT can benefit from blockchain networks in aspects regarding billing, e-trading, shipping and supply chain management. Furthermore, they discuss a scenario where blockchain can facilitate the buying and selling of energy automatically among IoT device like smart meters.

Smart contracts can be utilized to set user-defined criteria for energy trading. The authors likewise discuss another scenario for asset tracking of container shipment using smart contracts and IoT.

POSSIBLE FUTURE DIRECTIONS

Blockchain has showcased its potential in industry and academia. Authors describe possible future directions with respect to four areas: blockchain testing, stop the tendency to centralization, big data analytics, and blockchain application.

This section presents future directions in optimizing security, scalability, and capacity of Blockchain for future large-scale high-capacity IoT applications. The design of Blockchain for IoT application would also adapt to the specific attributes of IoT networks, such as immense scale, inherent partitioning incomplete network connectivity, non-trivial topology, non-zero propagation delay, heterogeneous data, and limited device memory.

- **Blockchain Testing:** Recently multiple kinds of blockchains appear and more than 700 digital currencies are listed in up to now. However, few developers might falsify their blockchain performance to attract investors driven by the huge profit. Besides that, when users want to merge blockchain into business, they have to know which blockchain meets their requirements. So blockchain testing mechanism required to be set up to test different blockchains. Blockchain testing could be separated into two phases: the standardization phase and the testing phase. In the standardization phase, all aspects have to be made and agreed. When a blockchain is introduced, it could be tested with the agreed criteria to valid if the blockchain works fine as developers claim. As for the testing phase, blockchain testing required to be performed with various criteria. For instance, a user who is in charge of online retail business cares about the throughput of the blockchain, so the examination requires to test the normal time from a user send a transaction to the transaction is packed into the blockchain, capacity for a blockchain block and etc.

- **Stop the Tendency to Centralization:** Blockchain is built as a decentralized system. However, there is a trend that miners are centralized in the mining pool. Up to now, the top 5 mining pools together own larger than 51% of the total hash power in the Bitcoin network. Aside from this, selfish mining strategy showcased that pools with over 25% of total computing power could get more revenue than a fair share. Rational miners would be mesmerized into the selfish pool and finally, the pool could easily exceed 51% of the total power. As the blockchain is not intended to serve a couple of organizations, some methods ought to be proposed to solve this problem.
- **Big Data Analytics:** Blockchain could be well integrated with big data. Here, authors roughly categorized the blend into two types: data management and data analytics. With respect to data management, blockchain could be utilized to store valuable data as it is distributed and secure. Blockchain could also guarantee that the data is original. For instance, if blockchain is used to keep the patient's health information, the information could not be altered and it is hard to steal that private information. When it comes to data analytics, transactions on the blockchain could be used for big data analytics. For instance, user trading patterns might be extracted. Users can predict their potential partners' trading behaviors with the analysis.
- **Blockchain Applications:** Currently most blockchains are utilized in the financial domain, an ever increasing number of applications for different fields are appearing. Traditional industries could take blockchain into consideration and apply blockchain into their fields to improve their systems. For instance, user reputations could be stored on the blockchain. At the same instance, the up-and-coming industry could make use of blockchain to improve performance. For example, Arcade City, a ridesharing startup gives an offer of an open commercial center where riders connect directly with drivers by leveraging blockchain technology. A smart contract is a computerized transaction protocol that runs the terms of a contract. It has been proposed for a long time and now this idea is designed with blockchain. In the blockchain, a smart contract is a code segment that could be run by

miners automatically. The smart contract has transformative potential in multiple fields like financial services and IoT.

CONCLUSION

Blockchain has showcased the capability to change the traditional industry with its key features: decentralization, firmness, privacy, and audit. In this chapter, the author presents a described outline on blockchain for IoT. Authors first review blockchain progress including the blockchain creation and the key properties of the blockchain. Some possible future titles are proposed in the same way. Nowadays, block-based apps are bouncing, and authors want to later lead exams at the top of blockchain-based applications. Blockchains and IoT were given the signal of research bearings to improve the range, security, and adaptability of the blockchains for the powerful reconciliation of the future of progress.

REFERENCES

All-In-Bits. (2017). *Introduction to tendermint.* Retrieved from https://tendermint.com/intro

Antonopoulos, A. M. (2014). Mastering Bitcoin: Unlocking Digital Crypto-Currencies. O'Reilly Media, Inc. Retrieved from https://bitcoin.org/en/

Axon, L. (2015). *Privacy-awareness in Blockchain-based PKI.* Tech. Rep. Retrieved from https://ora.ox.ac.uk/objects/uuid:f8377b69-599b-4cae-8df0-f0cded53e63b/datastreams/ATTACHMENT01

Bahga, A., & Madisetti, V. K. (2016). *Blockchain platform for industrial Internet of Things.* Tech. Rep. Retrieved from http://file.scirp.org/pdf/JSEA_2016102814012798.pdf

Biswas, K., & Muthukkumarasamy, V. (2016). Securing smart cities using blockchain technology. *Proc. 18th IEEE Int. Conf. High Performance Comput. Commun.; 14th IEEE Int. Conf. Smart City; 2nd IEEE Int. Conf. Data Sci. Syst., HPCC/SmartCity/DSS'16*, 1392–1393. 10.1109/HPCC-SmartCity-DSS.2016.0198

BitInfoCharts. (2016). *Block - BitcoinWiki.* Retrieved from https://en.bitcoin.it/wiki/Block

Buterin, V. (2014). *A next-generation smart contract and decentralized application platform.* White Paper.

Buterin, V. (2015). *On public and private blockchains*. Retrieved from https://blog.ethereum.org/2015/08/07/on-public-and-private-blockchains/

Buterin, V. (2015). On public and private blockchains. *Ethereum Blog*. Retrieved from https: //blog.ethereum.org/2015/08/07/on-public-and-private-blockchains/

Chin, W. L., Li, W., & Chen, H. H. (2017). Energy big data security threats in IoT-based smart grid communications. *IEEE Communications Magazine*, *55*(10), 70–75. doi:10.1109/MCOM.2017.1700154

Christidis, K., & Devetsikiotis, M. (2016). Blockchains and smart contracts for the Internet of Things. *IEEE Access: Practical Innovations, Open Solutions*, *4*, 2292–2303. doi:10.1109/ACCESS.2016.2566339

Conoscenti, M., Vetro, A., & Martin, J. C. D. (2016). Blockchain for the Internet of Things: A systematic literature Review. *The 3rd International Symposium onInternet of Things: Systems, Management, and Security, IOTSMS-2016*. 10.1109/AICCSA.2016.7945805

EconoTimes. (2016). *Safeshare releases first blockchain insurance solution for sharing economy*. Retrieved from https://www.econotimes.com/SafeShare-Releases-First-Blockchain-Insurance-Solution-For-Sharing-Economy-181326

EtherScan. (2016). *Ethereum Average BlockTime Chart*. Retrieved from https://etherscan.io/chart/blocktime

Friese, I., Heuer, J., & Kong, N. (2014). Challenges from the Identities of Things: Introduction of the Identities of Things discussion group within Kantara initiative. *2014 IEEE World Forum on Internet of Things (WF-IoT)*, 1–4.10.1109/WF-IoT.2014.6803106

Fromknecht, C., Velicanu, D., & Yakoubov, S. (2014). *CertCoin: A namecoin based decentralized authentication system*. Retrieved from https://courses.csail.mit.edu/6.857/2014/files/19-fromknecht-velicann-yakoubov-certcoin.pdf

Hyperledger Project. (2015). Retrieved from https://www.hyperledger.org/

IBM. (2017). *IBM blockchain based on hyperledger fabric from the linux foundation*. Retrieved from https://www.ibm.com/blockchain/hyperledger.html

International Telecommunication Union. (2015). *Measuring the Information Society Report*. International Telecommunication Union (ITU).

Johnson, D., Menezes, A., & Vanstone, S. (2001). The elliptic curve digital signature algorithm (ecdsa). *International Journal of Information Security*, *1*(1), 36–63. doi:10.1007102070100002

Korpela, K., Hallikas, J., & Dahlberg, T. (2017). Digital supply chain transformation toward Blockchain integration. *Proc. 50th Hawaii Int. Conf. Syst. Sci.* 10.24251/HICSS.2017.506

Kuhlman. (2016). *What is eris?* Retrieved from https://monax.io/2016/04/03/wtf-is-eris/

Langner, R. (2011). Stuxnet: Dissecting a cyberwarfare weapon. *IEEE Security and Privacy*, *9*(3), 49–51. doi:10.1109/MSP.2011.67

Lee KuoChuen, D. (Ed.). (2015). *Handbook of Digital Currency*. Elsevier. Retrieved from http://EconPapers.repec.org/RePEc:eee:monogr:9780128021170

Linux-Foundation. (2017). *Blockchain technologies for business*. Retrieved from https://www.hyperledger.org/

Mattila, J. (2016). *The blockchain phenomenon: The disruptive potential of distributed consensu architectures*. ETLA working papers: ElinkeinoelämänTutkimuslaitos, Research Institute of the Finnish Economy. Retrieved from https: //books.google.com.pk/books?id=StNQnQAACAAJ

Nakamoto, S. (2009). *Bitcoin: A peer-to-peer electronic cash system*. Available: https://bitcoin.org/bitcoin.pdf

Nakamoto, S. (2008). *Bitcoin: A peer-to-peer electronic cash system*. Retrieved from https: //bitcoin.org/bitcoin.pdf

Otte, M., de Vos, M., & Pouwelse, J. (2017). TrustChain: A Sybil-resistant scalable blockchain. *Future Generation Computer Systems*. doi:10.1016/j.future.2017.08.048

Perera, C., Zaslavsky, A., Christen, P., & Georgakopoulos, D. (2014). Context aware computing for the internet of things: A survey. *IEEE Communications Surveys and Tutorials*, *16*(1), 414–454. doi:10.1109/SURV.2013.042313.00197

Pticek, M., Podobnik, V., & Jezic, G. (2016). Beyond the internet of things: The social networking of machines. *International Journal of Distributed Sensor Networks*, *12*(6), 8178417. doi:10.1155/2016/8178417

Pureswaran, V., & Brody, P. (2014). *Device Democracy - Saving the future of the Internet of Things*. IBM. Retrieved from http://www-01.ibm.com/common/ssi/cgibin/ssialias?htmlfid=GBE03620USEN

Ripple. (2013). *Ripple network.* Retrieved from https://ripple.com/network

Stellar. (2014). *Stellar network overview.* Retrieved from https://www.stellar.org/developers/guides/get-started/

The-Bitcoin-Foundation. (2014). *How does Bitcoin work?* Retrieved from https://bitcoin.org/en/how-it-works

Wörner, D., & von Bomhard, T. (2014). When your sensor earns money: Exchanging data for cash with bitcoin. In *Proceedings of the 2014 ACM International Joint Conference on Pervasive and Ubiquitous Computing: Adjunct Publication, UbiComp '14 Adjunct.* ACM.10.1145/2638728.2638786

Zhang, Y., & Wen, J. (2015). An IoT electric business model based on the protocol of bitcoin. *2015 18th International Conference on Intelligence in Next Generation Networks*, 184–191. 10.1109/ICIN.2015.7073830

Zyskind, G., Nathan, O., & Pentland, A. (2015). *Enigma: decentralized computation platform with guaranteed privacy.* Retrieved from http://enigma.media.mit.edu/enigma~full.pdf

Chapter 5
A Framework on Enterprise-Grade Smart Contract Using Blockchain

Krithika L. B.
VIT University, India

Abhisek Mazumdar
VIT University, India

Rajesh Kaluri
VIT University, India

Jing Wang
Guangdong Polytechnic Institute, China

ABSTRACT

Blockchain technology is very trending and promising. It can revolutionize the traditional way of manipulation of data in many industries. There are industries which blockchain can disrupt: banking, cyber security, smart contract, insurance, cloud storage, government, healthcare, media streaming. The decentralized approach of blockchain using peer-to-peer system to verify the correct record of the ledger, which builds a trust in the system. A system can be compiled and made to get adopted with the concept of smart contract. The aim of the work is to develop a system that is flexible enough to get implemented in the industries like finance, cyber security, data storage, buying and selling of properties, healthcare, etc. This will use a one-way encryption method known as SHA-256. A block with the 256-character code bind with the other metadata of the block will be termed as a smart contract for the item.

DOI: 10.4018/978-1-7998-0186-3.ch005

INTRODUCTION

As the world is getting more connected around the globe, the data which is shared around is increasing in the rapid rate. So there a need for a proper, open and secure way to handle the whole data. The emerging of blockchain in this connected world has made the requirement of making data more secure and open to everyone. Blockchain is being adopted throughout the world as it is very advanced technology for data storage and exchange (Chen J, 2017). A blockchain offers an open ledger concept for data exchange and recording each transaction.

For buying and selling stuffs, that can be anything a property, a small item like pen can use the concept of the open ledger for keeping the data open so that everyone can see what's going into the system. As the data stays open there is need for a concept that the data can't altered by any means. So the concept of blockchain comes in with the encryption method SHA-256.

LITERATURE SURVEY

The possibilities of integrating the big data (Cachin C, 2016) concepts have been tried to explore with blockchain. The industry is adapting with the concept of big data and is required the data to be handled more and more. The big data and blockchain concept there can be many possibilities which can disrupt many interests for good. So the time with the proper systematic way of working of blockchain and big chain side by side will be really advantage for the world.

The bit coin concept (Nakamoto S, 2008) has the backend technology of blockchain where just a use case of crypto currency has its importance now. As it makes a common exchange around the globe and without the need of any middle man or industry. This technology uses the peer to peer method to transfer the block from one to another. This paper revolutionized the whole technology about the blockchain ecosystem and it provides the starting point to get the blockchain methodology.

The concept of smart contract which helps to bind stuffs into digital contract (Karafiloski & Mishev, 2017) is adopting the concept of fully open system helps to get smart contract details and the process to get things working. The smart contract system is being adopted and used in many places with is the news trending topic in terms of technology industries.

The security and enhancement (Es-Samaali & Outchakoucht, 2017) of the blockchain has been discussed where the basic requirement of proper security and quick response purpose can help the overall working of the method of the blockchain. A signature schema (Yuan C, 2017) is proposed which combined the input and the output together to perform more security and hence the overall performance of the blockchain system can be adopted to the main streamed system which can then get into a final data structure that holds the blockchain hashed data.

Many terms like the mining (Fanning K, 2016) of block and Blockchain 2.0 is considered which in return for the new version of the whole concept. This paper also highlights the principle of the upcoming fork of the system or the alteration that can be done to make the Blockchain 3.0 of the system. The concept of adding hadoop (Yeddu L K, 2016) and blockchain into one cryptographically enhanced system will be adding a next generation security into the open network of peer to peer system. As blockchain is transparent and flexible. So working with hadoop different block (Dinh, T, Wang, J, 2016) can be adopted and used to from a block full of environment.

An identity management system (Raju S, 2017) with the help of blockchain network or the open ledger structured which helps the overall structure to be open and connect all identity to one another around the whole system. As blockchain proposed the good amount of security that enables the whole system to be hacked proof. This is another example of using blockchain in different aspect of technology (Heires, K, 2016). So the implementation of the system has highlighted the proper use of the system with the help of some big data concept.

A system called Mutual distributed ledgers (MDL) helps the technology (Mainelli M, 2015) with the use of blockchain. This system will be very helpful to be adopted with IT industry (Karajovic, 2017) which in turn get affected with different attacks and will be really helpful to the industries. Blockchain is best with the technology as it was first proposed with the concept of blockchain and bit coin. The digital form (Kishigami J, 2015) of the crypto currency is using the blockchain concept that enables the scenario of adding an edge to the whole financial technology. This adds a new security layer which enables for high flexibility. The use of IOT (Kishigami J, 2015) with blockchain technology and a mechanism which can take patient's data at a hospital into the blockchain which in turn can help and record the data in such a way that the data can't be altered ever (Simic, 2016). So this type of mechanism can be adopted in our traditional hospital management system.

The importance of the concept of blockchain and smart contract in (Zheng Z, 2017) with the comparison to the traditional method is a need to be adopted with the upcoming technology which is done with the help of the blockchain. Blockchain has the potential to disrupt many industries which may add a next layer to the work of data sharing and communication.

The electronic media (Azaria, 2016) recorded in terms of blockchain and health care system have proposed a system to adopt with the old system which in turn can rapidly make some metadata requirement with the data structured they have proposed. So as blockchain is the next big thing in turn of data storage and accessing it. It became important to adapt to the changing of technology and healthcare the first big choice to be implemented.

An access control blockchain (Xia Q & Meshkov 2017) has been proposed which in turn supports the security and integrity of the whole system. There is huge demand of the integrity and the system to be very much flexible to get support to the existing system in tie to other technology to get adapted to the pure form.

SYSTEM ARCHITECTURE

The user interface is just user friendly designed to interact with the user. It can be changed according to the need. The three models in this paper uses the basic structure overall. For keeping the whole system as shown in Figure 1 needs to have a very basic structured by using javascript for the whole logical processing. As only using javascript can't be a best option so there is need more two technologies with JS - npm and browserify. Final data is formatted into a json object so that the framework gets adapted to the different database. A structured and an unstructured database can be used to keep the data at the user end and then further sending in to a private server for further verifying each block.

MODEL DESCRIPTION

In Figure 2, it is shown that there are two entities i.e. buyer and seller in both side. So in a traditional way of buying and selling things there are many middle services that make the whole process very long to follow. And some time it also become costly to make all the process get done. This process is the only reason that the

Figure 1. System architecture

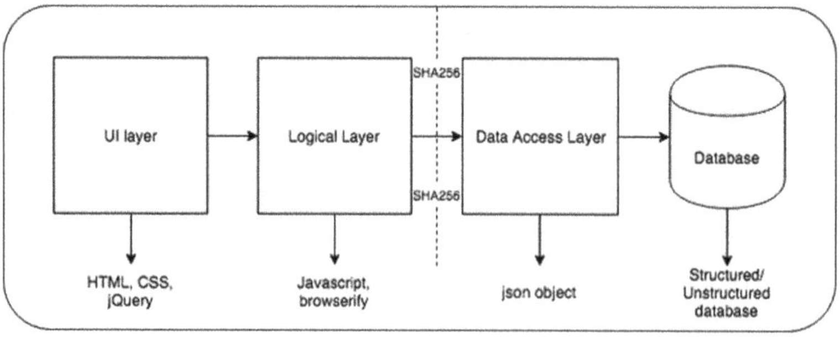

Figure 2. Buyer and seller component

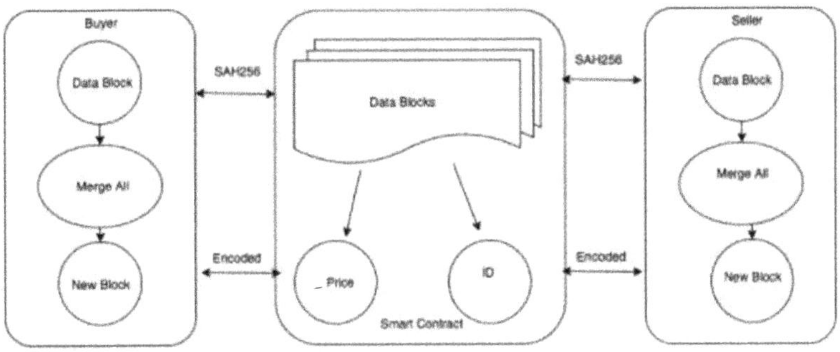

middle services exist. If enterprise starts adopting the method of smart contract, this process can be easy and less time taking.

Figure 3 shows the data from the buyer is merged in one single block using SHA256 encryption method. SHA-256 algorithm makes a unique and fixed size 256-bit (32-byte) hash string which is very much unique for the given set of data. Then the hashed code is send to the private server of Smart Contract. This whole system is backed by the concept of blockchain technology. So, once the data get into the system it can't be modified or altered any way. Any changes made in the date will create a new block and the new block will be traded as new record.

In the other side, the seller data will also be collected and same way it will be encoded and passed to the private server of Smart Contract. Its block of data will added to the set of block and the whole framework is very much flexible to get adopted in the both end so that there will be no problem to change the present system of buying and selling things.

The main use of this framework is to provide an easy way to implement the smart contract system to any existing system and adding an extra layer of security by using the concept of blockchain technology. In the perspective of transferring of data between two parties and owning it, this concept of a flexible system that

Figure 3. SHA256 encryption method

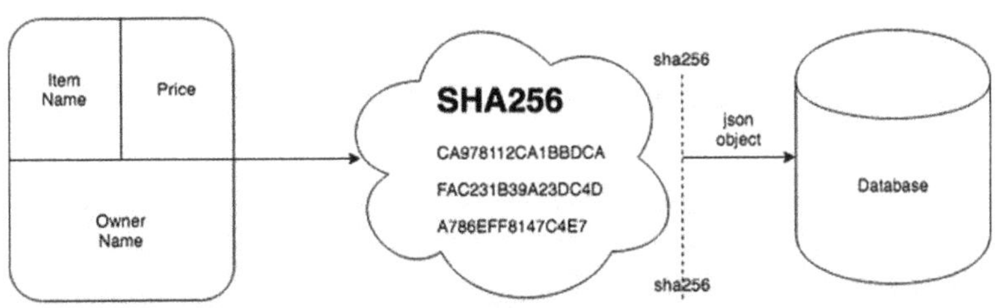

gets adopted and can handle a huge set of data. So the module which is used in the work are listed and described below

- **Add Item**: This module basically takes input from the user like name of the item, price, owner of the item. Then it sends the data to app.js file after the user presses the submit button. From those listed function there is one name saveData() that collects all the data and uses the SHA-256 object to hash all the data together and then return a hash 256 bit data which is then stored in the browser local storage.
- **List Items**: This module list all the buyer produced from the storage. So the buyer or the user can check out the product and choose which product to buy. There a display () which does all the fetching and rendering the data collects the number of values present inside the storage.
- **Buy Items**: With this module one can buy the requested or clicked item from the previous screen. This module will show all the details of the item, which is stored in JSON format. After the user modify the name and price of the item. Then app.js file then call a method name buy () which check the hash of the previous block and then new formed block and its process were shown to the user during the buying process. The hash is compared again and then its owner is changed. A new block is added into the blockchain which the new hashed and previous hashed block name. For checking the hash value it uses the way called trial and error method as SHA-256 is a one way hashing method.
- **Remove Item**: This module uses the method name removeData() from the app.js. The users put the name of the item and then it searches into the database and removes its whole block from there.

METHODOLOGY USED

Apart from using HTML, CSS for the front-end and JS for the backend there are need for many other library can be used so that it render a final result in the best way possible. So these are the few list below which is used:-

- **Node Package Manager (npm)**: is a NodeJS package manager tool which added the required library into the work and very useful tool for trying the project in different environment.
- **JS-SHA256**: A simple node JS SHA256 library to hashing the data collected from the user for the selling items. This library can be used with another framework or JS library known as Browserify.

Figure 4.

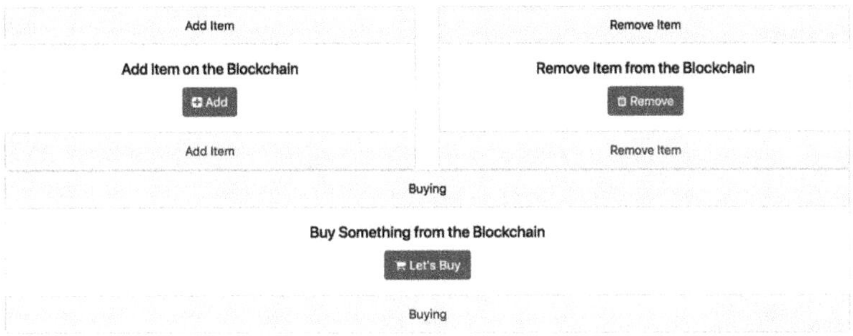

- **Browserify**: It's a type of dependence building and channelizing them for the browser to understand. The required module are added and channelized for the browser to understand it's JS
- **Beefy**: It uses the concept of Browserify to channelized rendered required library or required dependence into the local server or live environment.
- **HTML Web Storage Objects**: For the backend database this uses the local storage as this whole work focus on the framework of the blockchain.
- **Firebase:** This project prototype is hosted at Google's Firebase hosting which provided only js work to be hosted and provide secure way of modifying and accessing it.
- **Bootstrap:** This is a frontend CSS and JS library which makes the UI more importantly responsive and easy to build UI.

RESULTS AND DISCUSSIONS

The whole system has a basic prototype format to enable the overall functionality. This work aims to create and sell item over the system with the use of SHA-256. The result screenshots are given as steps

Step1: Creation of Front Page

Step2: Add an Item Page

Step3: Item Listing

Figure 5.

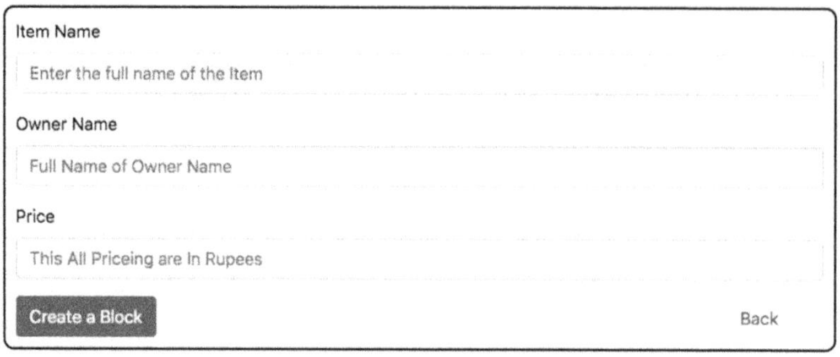

Figure 6.

Step 4: View Item Details/Buying page

Step5: Buy an Item

Figure 7.

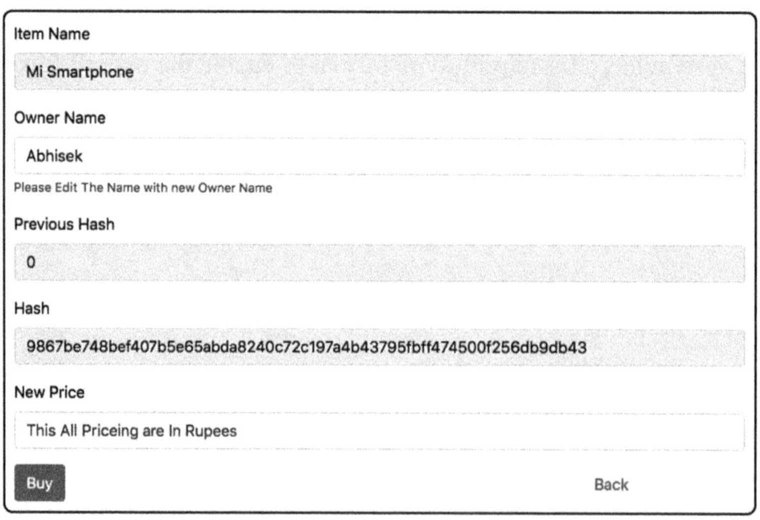

Figure 8.

CONCLUSION

As blockchain is now really a new and not understood by many, implementing it into our traditional system will be a big challenge. Lack of Government support may also happen although there banks which are trying to adopt the technology into their daily system. But all this will take a lot of time to achieve. Providing a good Framework will be changeable and accepted by any big Organization. So making a small scale system to be adopted with small market and then expanding it into a big firm will help this type of technology to grow into mainstream.

REFERENCES

Azaria, A., Ekblaw, A., Vieira, T., & Lippman, A. (2016, August). Medrec: Using blockchain for medical data access and permission management. In *2016 2nd International Conference on Open and Big Data (OBD)* (pp. 25-30). IEEE.

Cachin, C. (2016, July). Architecture of the hyperledger blockchain fabric. In *Workshop on distributed cryptocurrencies and consensus ledgers* (*Vol. 310*). Academic Press.

Chen, J., & Xue, Y. (2017, June). *Bootstrapping a blockchain based ecosystem for big data exchange. In 2017 IEEE international congress on big data (bigdata congress)* (pp. 460–463). IEEE. doi:10.1109/BigDataCongress.2017.67

Dinh, T. T. A., Wang, J., Chen, G., Liu, R., Ooi, B. C., & Tan, K. L. (2017, May). Blockbench: A framework for analyzing private blockchains. In *Proceedings of the 2017 ACM International Conference on Management of Data* (pp. 1085-1100). ACM. 10.1145/3035918.3064033

Es-Samaali, H., Outchakoucht, A., & Leroy, J. P. (2017). A blockchain-based access control for big data. *International Journal of Computer Networks and Communications Security*, *5*(7), 137.

Fanning, K., & Centers, D. P. (2016). Blockchain and its coming impact on financial services. *Journal of Corporate Accounting & Finance*, *27*(5), 53–57. doi:10.1002/jcaf.22179

Heires, K. (2016). The risks and rewards of blockchain technology. *Risk Management*, *63*(2), 4.

Karafiloski, E., & Mishev, A. (2017, July). Blockchain solutions for big data challenges: A literature review. In *IEEE EUROCON 2017-17th International Conference on Smart Technologies* (pp. 763-768). IEEE. 10.1109/EUROCON.2017.8011213

Karajovic, M., Kim, H. M., & Laskowski, M. (2017). Thinking outside the block: Projected phases of blockchain integration in the accounting industry. *Australian Accounting Review*.

Kishigami, J., Fujimura, S., Watanabe, H., Nakadaira, A., & Akutsu, A. (2015, August). The blockchain-based digital content distribution system. In *2015 IEEE Fifth International Conference on Big Data and Cloud Computing* (pp. 187-190). IEEE. 10.1109/BDCloud.2015.60

Mainelli, M., & Smith, M. (2015). Sharing ledgers for sharing economies: An exploration of mutual distributed ledgers (aka blockchain technology). *Journal of Financial Perspectives*, *3*(3).

Meshkov, D., Chepurnoy, A., & Jansen, M. (2017). Short Paper: Revisiting Difficulty Control for Blockchain Systems. In *Data Privacy Management, Cryptocurrencies and Blockchain Technology* (pp. 429–436). Cham: Springer. doi:10.1007/978-3-319-67816-0_25

Nakamoto, S. (2008). *Bitcoin: A peer-to-peer electronic cash system*. Academic Press.

Raju, S., Boddepalli, S., Gampa, S., Yan, Q., & Deogun, J. S. (2017, May). Identity management using blockchain for cognitive cellular networks. In *2017 IEEE International Conference on Communications (ICC)* (pp. 1-6). IEEE. 10.1109/ICC.2017.7996830

Xia, Q. I., Sifah, E. B., Asamoah, K. O., Gao, J., Du, X., & Guizani, M. (2017). MeDShare: Trust-less medical data sharing among cloud service providers via blockchain. *IEEE Access: Practical Innovations, Open Solutions*, *5*, 14757–14767. doi:10.1109/ACCESS.2017.2730843

Yeddu, L. K., & Yeddu, S. (2016). Hadoop: Bitcoin-BlockChain-A New Era Needed In Distributed Computing. *International Journal of Computers and Applications*, *154*(6).

Yuan, C., Xu, M. X., & Si, X. M. (2017). Research on a new signature scheme on blockchain. *Security and Communication Networks*.

Zheng, Z., Xie, S., Dai, H., Chen, X., & Wang, H. (2017, June). *An overview of blockchain technology: Architecture, consensus, and future trends. In 2017 IEEE international congress on big data (BigData congress)* (pp. 557–564). IEEE. doi:10.1109/BigDataCongress.2017.85

Section 2
Blockchain in Business

Chapter 6
An Application of Blockchain in Stock Market

Rajit Nair
Jagran Lakecity University, India

Amit Bhagat
Maulana Azad National Institute of Technology, India

ABSTRACT

Blockchain is one of the growing technologies used for financial management systems. Financial data must be kept secure otherwise it can create a huge loss. So, whenever security features or technologies are developed must keep financial security as a priority. Stock market management is another area of finance sector that works on two concepts, that is, minimize the risk and maximize the profit. In this chapter, the authors discuss how blockchain technology is used for stock market analysis. Mainly blockchain will help us to make optimal stock exchanges through automation and decentralization. Stock market across the globe is rapidly using blockchain technology for the market transaction. Some of the country is still preparing themselves to use the blockchain technology. This technology offers huge potential for tracing securities lending, margin financing, and surveillance of system risk.

INTRODUCTION

Blockchain defines as a distributed immutable ledger that contains all the transaction which has been executed (Yaga, Mell, Roby, & Sccarfone, 2018). A block is considered as a current part of blockchain which consist of some or all the recent transaction records. Once this transaction gets completed it goes into blockchain

DOI: 10.4018/978-1-7998-0186-3.ch006

as permanent database. New block is generated when previous blocks completed. Blocks are connected together in the form of chronological order. Some of the benefits of blockchain technology are as follows:

- It is a public ledger system which records and validated each and every transaction that makes it more secure and reliable.
- Miners are the one which is introduced in blockchain and they are used for auditing the transactions. This makes the transaction as immutable and prevention from unauthorized users.
- Decentralization is another approach which makes blockchain more secure. Due to decentralization approach there is no single authority which controls the entire network.
- There is no third party or central authority involved which allows us to perform peer to peer transaction.

Many of the banks and financial institutions are investing their money and time in this technology, because these sectors want to improve their services, so that they can provide safe and secure environments to the clients. Some of the famous banks and financial institutions which adopt blockchain are DBS (Sia, Soh, & Weill, 2016), Deutsche Bank (Ackermann & Trümper, 2012), NASDAQ (Irrera, 2016), EBA (Kasiewicz, 2019), SCB, Fidor Bank (Kobler, Bucherer, & Schlotmann, 2016), Standard Chartered (Batsaikhan, 2017), US Federal Reserve (Dennis, 2004) and many more. Blockchain is classified into two categories one is private and the other one is public blockchain.

Public Blockchain

In this blockchain anyone who is a participant of the platform can read or write to the platform by providing the proof of work for the same. Most of the activities are done through public blockchain and public blockchain is considered to be fully decentralized. Some of the used public blockchain technologies are as follows:

- **Ethereum**: It's a provider of decentralized platform and programming language that helps developers to build or publish smart distributed applications (Wood, 2018).
- **Factom**: It is a provider of records management and business processes for government and business (Snow, Deery, Lu, Johnston, & Kirby, 2018).
- **Blockstream**: Another provider of blockchain technology that enhances the capabilities of bitcoin. Accounting is also done with the help of this public blockchain technology (Allen, 2016).

Private Blockchain

This blockchain works on the concept of central authority, means only authority has the right to do modification. Private blockchain is very must similar to existing infrastructure where there is single owner and he has the right to make any changes in the transaction network. Most of the banking sector and financial institutions have very much interested in private blockchain. In many systems private blockchain helps in reducing the cost of system with increased efficiency. Some of industries based on blockchain are as follows:

- Blockstack is one of the organization which provides private blockchain so that financial institute or banks can perform their operations at back office which includes settlement and clearing of clients (Ali, Nelson, Shea, Freedman, 2016).
- Eric industry is another provider of shared software database using private blockchain technology (Schneider et al., 2016) .
- Multichain is an open source blockchain platform which provides distributed databases for financial transactions (MultiChain, 2018).
- Chain Inc. is the cloud blockchain infrastructure provider with APIs. It collaborated with Nasdaq Group to provide platform that allows to perform trading shares of private company with blockchain (P.R. Newswire, 2018).

There is another blockchain category which is combination of both public and private blockchain known as hybrid blockchain (Pathak, & Bhandari, 2018). Consortium blockchain is a mixed property of both that provides read and write access to certain cluster or group of peoples or nodes. It can be like when two or more different organizations come together to work on the single platform. So that they can provided restricted access to group of people based on their capability.

As already discussed there is no third party involved in Blockchain technology that enables banking and financial system to work faster specially in case of international money transfer. This technology reduced the cost or brokerage involved in transaction and at the same time it provides identification of clients in a easier way. When information of any client is created on distributed ledger then there is no need to give identification proof separately to other banks. Blockchain enables clients to identify on a single occasion and this information is stored securely so that it can be shared to all others in a network safely.

Banks and finance sectors always ensure safe transactions, deposits and loans. Still many banks are criticized for their unreliable and vulnerable behavior. A distributed ledger will help to improve the banking activities because due to decentralization approach the controlling cannot be done by single authority and this prevents the

Figure 1. View of blockchain network

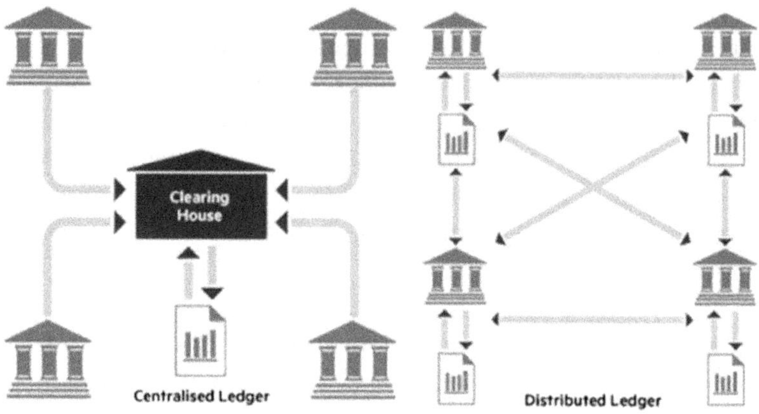

system from bankrupt. Another area of improvement in banking sector is insurance claims, this can also be improved by blockchain introducing automation payment system during insurance claims. This helps clients to receive payments immediately during insurance claims.

There are many sectors which are using the blockchain technology other than banking (Tandulwadikar, 2016) and financial sectors (Treleaven, Brown, & Yang, 2017). These are manufacturing, energy and utilities (Andoni et al., 2019), professional services, technology services (Nomura Research Institute, 2016), media, entertainment (Dutra, Tumasjan, & Welpe, 2018), gaming (Veeningen & Szirbik, 2018), health care (Angraal, Krumholz, & Schulz, 2017) goods (Abeyratne & Monfared, 2016) insurance (Getteschi, Lamberti, Demartini, Pranteda, & Santamaría, 2018) and many more.

No our main focus will be on one of the area of financial industry that is stock market. Next sections shows how blockchain works in stock market and what are the challenges that has to be faced during implementation.

How Does Blockchain Work in Stock Market Analysis?

- The first and the foremost advantage of using blockchain is to provide interoperability, trust and transparency issues in fragmented market systems.
- Time is reduced by using this technology because in stock market there are four major participants which are traders, brokers, regulators and stock exchange and all these has to go through difficult or heavy process during transaction and it need almost 3 days of time for complete process.

Figure 2. Various sectors using Blockchain Network (Hileman & Rauchs, 2017)

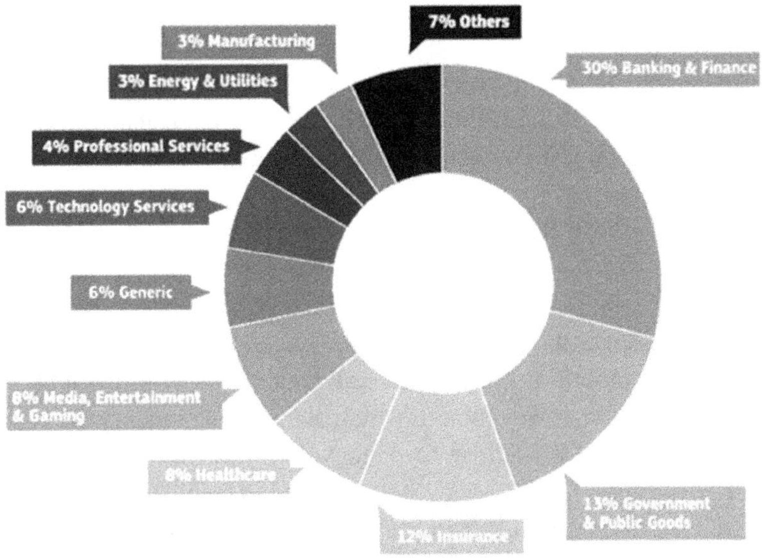

- It can make more optimal stock exchange through automation and decentralization which helps customer through reduction in costs in the form of commission which is taken to speed up the transaction process.
- It is used in clearing and settlement process also. This eases the paperwork of trade and legal ownership documents.
- The automation of the post-trade process is also done through blockchain technology.
- It can eliminate the need of third party to a large extent by keeping rules and regulations within the smart contracts through inbuilt features. This way blockchain can act as regulator for all the transactions done in stock market.

Challenges to be Faced During Blockchain Implementation

- Blockchain technology is very attractive because of its high security and reduced risk of manipulation but it also gave raze to difficult legal process and regulatory challenges (Batubara, Ubacht, & Janssen, 2018).
- Financial market is very much uncertain especially in case of capital market due to which blockchain has to face many obstructions during implementation.
- Another challenge will be the risk of maintaining security standards across a decentralized database, regulations, scalability and legal aspects. It also

combines the process like trading, clearing by separating the current legal rules and regulations.

Blockchain can be implemented by effective governance through which it can protect participants, investors and stake holders. It must also ensure that the system is resilient to systematic risk, security threats and privacy concern.

Blockchain in Stock Market

Blockchain technology is one of the hottest buzzwords among the stock market investors. It is predicted that in year 2019, this technology will reshape the stock market itself. In the month of January, a small financial operation named as tZero has introduced a significant way though which one can sell and buy the some shares of the company. tZero is owned by Overstock.com has offered a million private digital security tokens. These tokens are considered to be block chain based digital securities which are essential for investment contracts. Blockchain technology provides access to stock market like New York Stock Exchange (Officer, 1973) or Nasdaq (Heckman, 2014) without any third party involvement also helps in day to day stock market trades .

tZero has offered advanced services that can meet emerging securities and exchange communication rules on blockchain related activity. It has developed world's first SEC-kosher security token for trading. Blockchain is a potential technology that can transform or improve the security issues related to transfer, tracking and the regulation. Blockchain based securities will crack the door to change the global equity and financial markets. tZero's tokens are on a fully public blockchain, trades are effected by alternate Pro Securities trading system. Pro Securities platform are the high speed platform which are not based on blockchain but they initiates trades in blockchain based digital securities. In that case slow transaction processing speed occur in an actual blockchain stock market. Investors have to deal with broker with Pro Securities access when they need tZero tokens. Not frequently but cryptocurrency is needed for trades. In this types of trades the clearing and settlement are done using Ethereum blockchain. tZero is continuously performing research and testing the other chains. Ethereum is one of best blockchain technology that supports smart contracts which is having advantages of digital securities over traditional stock. In this token itself are programmed to perform an array of operations. Overstock's Medici Ventures announce that that took around 29% stake in Chainstone labs which is another specialist in digital securities and decentralized asset management named as Revencoin blockchain.

Figure 3. Processes in stock market

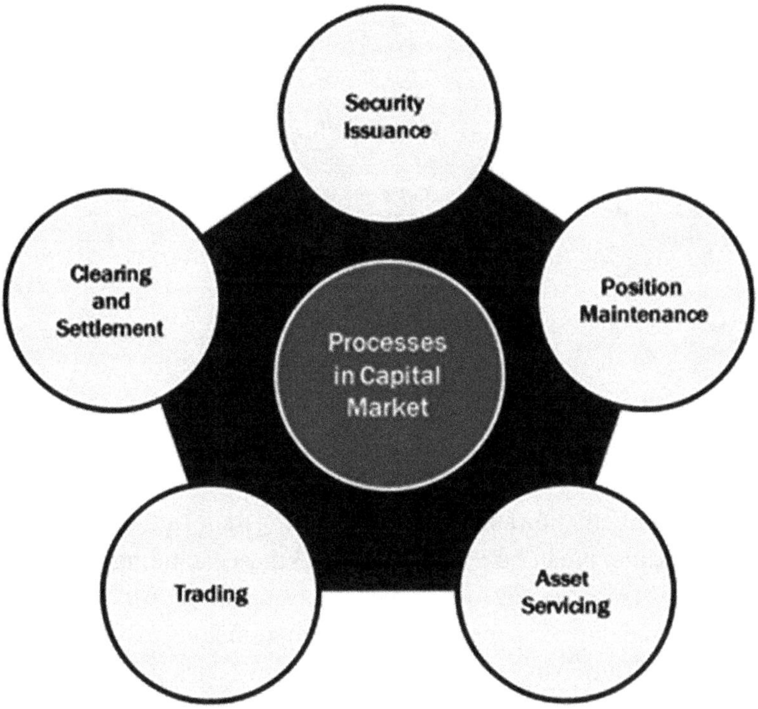

Stock Market Exchanges Using Blockchain

Nasdaq (NDAQ) and NYSE-owner Intercontinental Exchange (ICE) are two powerhouses of stock market which have implemented the blockchain technology in earlier days. ICE has already announced about federally regulated bitcoin market. It has spent more than $1.1 billion in 2018 to form scalable open platform that can control all the digital assets across global market. Overstock has generated revenue around $1.1. billion in the year 2012 with the help of bitcoin as payment system. After adding tZero, Overstock has developed their own crypto-securities. By the year 2015 they have raise $5 million in a digital bond offering. In the year 2013 stakes has been raised and received permission from SEC (U.S Securities and Exchange Commission) so that they can offer $ 13 million. The early targeting areas of blockchain in stock market are trade clearance, settlement and private equities liquidity. Nasdaq has implemented blockchain initially in the year 2015, it unveils Nasdaq Linq blockchain ledger technology that enables transaction with private blockchain property.

Figure 4. Custody and settlement value chain

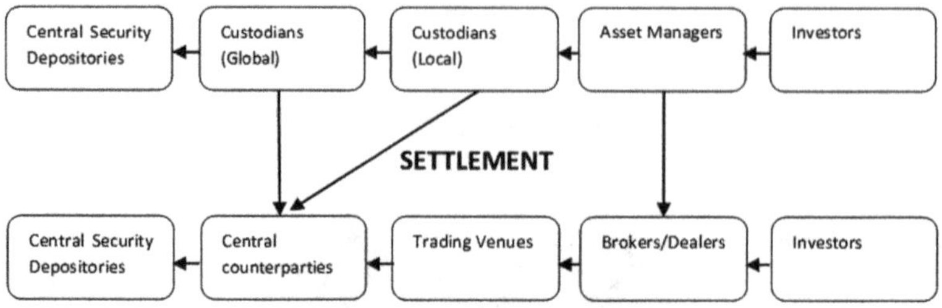

CUSTODY

Blockchain Technology and Trade Settlement

There is series of confirmation and verification during trade settlement and consumes much amount of time, it can be more than 2 or 3 days excluding trading day. This process leaves investors to wait for the receival of payment. Blockchain is the one which reduces this delay happens due to confirmation and verification process. It discards the need of third party or trusted intermediates during settlement. However this blockchain technology also causes the trouble to many clearing and settlement agencies, one of them is Depository Trust and Clearing Corporation (DTCC) (Gehde-Trapp, Gündüz & Nasev, 2015), a US based organization handling the clearing and settlement for most of the trading.

During stock exchange many intermediaries are involved, like brokers, investment managers, exchanges, custodian and central securities depositories. When there is any trading going on, all the business transaction, intermediaries update their respective ledgers which take additional amount of time and cost. Even many times it happens to complete a particular transaction they need to update some more ledger transfers in the form of realignment, securities borrowing or cash management. Due to this additional delay forms in the transaction lifecycle which are basically known as settlement in stock market.

Solutions Based on Blockchain

In the above paragraphs we have seen problem faced by investors during stock exchange market usage. But this time many of the problems are overcome by the use of blockchain technology. Some of the solutions are as follows:

Figure 5. Blockchain application in stock market

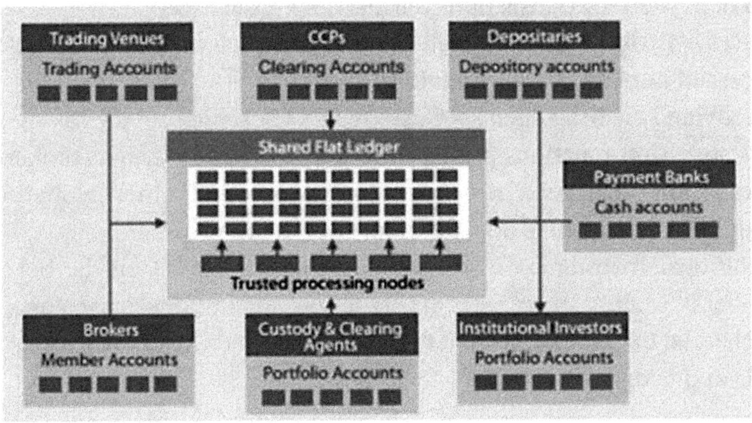

- Financial Institutions can develop a shared flat ledger using blockchain technology that can be managed by trusted processing nodes.
- Shared ledger must be encrypted so that it can protect the confidentiality of the records or data.
- Digital signatures are used by the intermediates so that they can update the ledger for completing the transaction.
- During stock exchanges there are key processes like trading, clearance, settlement and security methods that must be updated or redesigned using a blockchain.

The main components involved in stock market during blockchain transaction are as follows:

- Trading venues and accounts – This is first component involved in the activity of blockchain which is related to trading account details through which one can buy or sell the stock market shares.
- Clearing accounts – Clearing member account is the one through which securities that are bought and sold are routed for settlement is depository account.
- Depository accounts - A depository enables an investor to buy or sell securities like stocks or bonds in a paper-less manner. Depository accounts are very much similar to funds in bank accounts.
- Shared flat ledger – This ledger consist of trusted processing nodes and it is a distributed ledger that records the transactions, such as exchange of assets or data among the participants in the network.

- Payment Banks – This is related to investor bank account in which cash has been deposited for transactions during stock exchange.
- Brokers – Brokers are the medium through which many times transaction is performed in blockchain technology also.
- Custody and clearing agents - Custody and Clearing provides asset servicing and transaction functions primarily to intermediaries such as broker-dealers, banks, fund managers, insurance companies and other global investors through our proprietary network in over 60 markets.
- Institutional Investors – It's a organization that invest on the behalf of its members. Mainly there are six type on institutional investors that are commercial banks, endowment funds, mutual funds, insurance funds, pension funda and hedge funds.

Advantages of using blockchain in stock market at different aspects like pre-trade (before trading), trading, post-trade (after trading) and security services are given below:

1. Pre-Trade
    - During verification transparency is maintained
    - Credit exposures cost are minimized
    - Coordination of static data
    - KYC process has become simple due to verification
2. In between Trade
    - Blockchain offers safe, secure real time transaction with instant immutable settlements
    - Delivery versus payment (DVP) is done automatically on a cash ledger
    - Reporting is done automatically with more transparent supervision to market authorities
    - Various standards for higher Anti money laundering standards
3. Post-trade
    - Fast and efficient post-trading
    - There is no third party involved for clearing of cash transaction
    - Execution of smart contracts done automatically
    - Requirements and margin of cost is reduced
4. Security Services
    - Security protocol has been released for blockchain
    - Duplication is controlled and automation has been done
    - Central dataset is enriched with flat accounting hierarchies
    - Referencing of data is done commonly

- Subscription of funds and their redemption has done automatically through blockchain
- Processes like fund services, allocations, accounting and administration has been simplified

Challenges to be Faced During Blockchain Implementation in Blockchain

1. Upgrading of Regulation and Legislations: New rules and regulations has to be introduced so that blockchain technology get integrated with the current market infrastructure.
2. Managing operational risk of transition: Operational risk has to be reduced so that quick recovery for the participant must be done otherwise if will be flaw as that was in traditional system.
3. Governmental rules and Standards: Whenever we are ready with any project, government will play a major role in their implementation; this means industry alignment is always needed from their designing phase to implementation phase. First they look at the feasibility of the project and after that they consider different aspects of the project like security issues, cost involved, network compatibility, etc. They also look for interoperability among different networks with different protocols and create a security measures so that client must not face ant sort of problems.
4. High Standards of Technology: Various standards have to be developed so that we can provide security, robustness and increase the performance of blockchain. Integration with non existing blockchain system will also be a requirement for the near future.

Some of the blockchain companies who are providing distributed ledger technology for maintaining security are Cryptocorp, vogogo, Tradle, Sig3, Skry, Blockseer, thirdkey solutions, etc.

Blockchain Application in Other Investment Areas

Commodities - Real Asset Company enables the users across the world to buy and sell commodities securely and efficiently. This provides platform that provides an online account for buying and selling commodities or precious items. Another company that is purely based on gold investment is Goldbloc which introduced gold-backed cryptocurrency that enables additional layer of transparency and control to gold investors.

Diamonds – Diamond industry is one of the biggest natural resource industries, most of the African countries GDP depends on substantial part of diamond production.

As diamond is small so it can easily be hide and transport, due to this they are very much involved in money laundering and financial support to terrorism. To overcome from the criminal activities in this diamond smuggling area blockchain has done a decent job. One of the well known company based on blockchain named as Everledger provides an immutable ledger for diamond identification and transaction verification for various for different stake holders from insurance company to claiming clients and law enforcement agencies (Gutierrez & Khizhniak, 2017). This company generates a digital passport to individual diamond which will confirm about the each stone during transaction by unique fingerprint.

Data Management – Data management is another non financial market which also needs a blockchain for their security purpose. Factom is the company that provides distributed ledger to data management (Higgins, 2015). This use blockchain based identity ledgers in database management and data analytics to analyse different applications. During collaboration of government with businesses, Factom can be used for maintaining records and processes, managing address security and compliance issues. It maintains a fix time stamped record of data in the blockchain which reduce the company's cost and complexity involved during auditing, records management and compatibility with government rules and regulations.

Digital content – Blockchain helps artists and creators to perform digital art through Ascribe. This allows us to generate digital editions with unique id and digital certificate of authenticity. Ascribe allows to receive consignment from artist and transfer digital works to all recipient with all legal terms and conditions.

Network Infrastructure – Ethereum is one of the open source public blockchain based distributed computing platform (Sixt, 2016). This makes developer to propose, build and publish next generation based distributed application. It is very useful for developing network infrastructure that consists of trusted parties. Another platform that can be used for smart contract is ChromaWay, it also allows for digitizing and representing workflow in a private, secure and efficient way (Prisco, 2015).

Market Prediction – Blockchain also allows to built market prediction platform and it can be done by Augur.net which is an open source platform build on the concept of etherum blockchain. This helps users to perform trade and predict by providing correct information about the market.

As we come to the end of chapter, now we will list out the name of famous blockchain platforms on which various projects are implemented, they are Ethereum (Sixt, 2016), Ripple (n.d.), Eris Industries, Stellar (Sankar, Sindhu, & Sethumadhavan, 2017), MaidSafe (Yi, Xu, & Wang, 2018), Counterparty. Some more which are paving ways for projects are Hyperledger, Epiphyte, Chain.com, Peer Nova, Blockstram, Konify, etc.

CONCLUSION

In this chapter we have discussed about the blockchain, their applications in different areas. Main focus of this chapter to explain that how blockchain works in the area of stock exchange and what transformation can be done using block chain technology. Discuss about the non financial areas in which blockchain be applied to perform transaction in a secured way, also discuss about the different platforms used for implementing blockchain technology. According to Greifeld, blockchain technology collapsing clearance and settlement industry and capturing market shares from trading instruments that suffer from liquidity problems (Medici, 2018). The less frequently trades can find more ways into the blockchain based trading system. Many of the problems like trading speed challenges, brokering charges, etc, are solved by blockchain stock market revolution to some extent.

REFERENCES

Abeyratne, S. A., & Monfared, R. P. (2016). Blockchain ready manufacturing supply chain using distributed ledger. *International Journal of Research in Engineering and Technology*, *5*(9), 1–10. doi:10.15623/ijret.2016.0509001

Ackermann, J., & Trümper, F. (2012). Deutsche Bank. In *Deutsche Standards*. Retrieved from https://annualreport.deutsche-bank.com/2012/ar/managementreport/internalcontroloverfinancialreporting.html

Ali, M., Nelson, J., Shea, R., & Freedman, M. J. (2016). Blockstack : A Global Naming and Storage System Secured by Blockchains. *USENIX Annual Technical Conference*.

Allen, C. (2016). *The Path to Self-Sovereign Identity*. Retrieved from https://www.coindesk.com/path-self-sovereign-identity

Andoni, M., Robu, V., Flynn, D., Abram, S., Geach, D., Jenkins, D., ... Peacock, A. (2019). Blockchain technology in the energy sector: A systematic review of challenges and opportunities. *Renewable & Sustainable Energy Reviews*, *100*, 143–174. doi:10.1016/j.rser.2018.10.014

Angraal, S., Krumholz, H. M., & Schulz, W. L. (2017). Blockchain technology: Applications in health care. *Circulation: Cardiovascular Quality and Outcomes*, *10*(9). doi:10.1161/CIRCOUTCOMES.117.003800 PMID:28912202

Batsaikhan, U. (2017). *Cryptoeconomics - The Opportunities and Challenges of Blockchain*. Retrieved from https://bruegel.org/2017/07/cryptoeconomics-the-opportunities-and-challenges-of-

Batubara, F. R., Ubacht, J., & Janssen, M. (2018). Challenges of blockchain technology adoption for e-government. *Proceedings of the 19th Annual International Conference on Digital Government Research Governance in the Data Age - dgo '18*. 10.1145/3209281.3209317

Dennis, R. (2004). *The policy preferences of the US federal reserve*. Retrieved from https://www.frbsf.org/economic-research/files/wp01-08bk.pdf

Dutra, A., Tumasjan, A., & Welpe, I. M. (2018). Blockchain is changing how media and entertainment companies compete. *MIT Sloan Management Review*. Retrieved from https://sloanreview.mit.edu/article/blockchain-is-changing-how-media-and-entertainment-companies-compete/

Gatteschi, Lamberti, Demartini, Pranteda, & Santamaría. (2018). Blockchain and smart contracts for insurance: Is the technology mature enough? *Future Internet*, *10*(2).

Gehde-Trapp, M., Gündüz, Y., & Nasev, J. (2015). The liquidity premium in CDS transaction prices: Do frictions matter? *Journal of Banking & Finance*, *61*, 184–205. doi:10.1016/j.jbankfin.2015.08.024

Gutierrez, C., & Khizhniak, A. (2017). A Close Look at Everledger—How Blockchain Secures Luxury Goods. *Altoros*. Retrieved from https://www.altoros.com/blog/a-close-look-at-everledger-how-blockchain-secures-luxury-goods/

Heckman, L. (2014). *NASDAQ A Guide To Information Sources*. New York: Routledge.

Higgins, S. (2015). *Factom Partners With Honduras Government on Blockchain Tech Trial.* Retrieved from https://www.coindesk.com/factom-land-registry-deal-honduran-government

Hileman, G., & Rauchs, M. (2017). *Global Blockchain Benchmarking Study*. Retrieved from https://www.jbs.cam.ac.uk/fileadmin/user_upload/research/centres/alternative-finance/downloads/2017-09-27-ccaf-globalbchain.pdf

Irrera, A. (2016). Nasdaq launches blockchain-ready tech hub. *Financial News*. Retrieved from https://www.fnlondon.com/articles/nasdaq-launches-new-blockchain-ready-tech-platform-20160526

Kasiewicz. (2019). New trends in the system regulating the market of bank services. *Kwart. Nauk o Przedsiębiorstwie*.

Kobler, D., Bucherer, S., & Schlotmann, J. (2016). *Banking business models of the future*. Deloitte.

Medici. (2018). *Know more: Blockchain- Overview, Tech, Application Areas & and Use Cases*. Retrieved from https://gomedici.com/an-overview-of-blockchain-technology

MultiChain. (2018). *Open Platform for Building Blockcchains*. Retrieved from https://www.multichain.com/

Newswire, P. R. (2018). *Global Blockchain Technology Industry*. Retrieved from https://www.prnewswire.com/news-releases/global-blockchain-technology-industry-300670406.html

Nomura Research Institute. (2016). *Survey on Blockchain Technologies and Related Services*. Retrieved from https://www.meti.go.jp/english/press/2016/pdf/0531_01f.pdf

Officer, R. R. (1973). The Variability of the Market Factor of the New York Stock Exchange. *The Journal of Business, University of Chicago Press*, *46*(3), 434–453.

Pathak, N., & Bhandari, A. (2018). Understanding Blockchain. In *IoT, AI, and Blockchain for. NET*. Retrieved from https://link.springer.com/book/10.1007/978-1-4842-3709-0

Prisco, G. (2015). Nasdaq, LHV Bank, Technology Startups Develop Blockchain-Based Fintech Applications in Estonia. *Bitcoin Magazine*. Retrieved from https://bitcoinmagazine.com/articles/nasdaq-lhv-bank-technology-startups-develop-blockchain-based-fintech-applications-in-estonia-1447870921

Ripple (n.d.). *Ripple - One frictionless Experience To Send Money Globally*. Retrieved from https://www.ripple.com/

Sankar, L. S., Sindhu, M., & Sethumadhavan, M. (2017). Survey of consensus protocols on blockchain applications. *2017 4th International Conference on Advanced Computing and Communication Systems, ICACCS 2017*. 10.1109/ICACCS.2017.8014672

Schneider, J., Blostein, A., Lee, B., Kent, S., Groer, I., & Beardsley, E. (2016). *Putting Theory Into Practice*. Retrieved from https://pgcoin.tech/wp-content/uploads/2018/06/blockchain-paper.pdf.

Sia, Soh, & Weill. (2016). *How DBS bank persued a digital business strategy*. Retrieved from file:///C:/Users/jtepper/Downloads/A1%20-2%20-%20SIa%20et%20al%20-%20How%20DBS%20Bank%20Pursued%20a%20Digital%20Business%20Strategy.pdf

Sixt, E. (2016). Ethereum. In *Bitcoins und andere dezentrale Transaktionssysteme*. Springer Gabler. Retrieved from https://www.springer.com/br/book/9783658028435

Snow, P., Deery, B. L., Johnston, D., & Kirby, P. (2018). *Business Processes Secured by Immutable Audit Trails on the Blockchain*. Retrieved from https://www.factom.com/assets/docs/Factom_Whitepaper_v1.2.pdf

Tandulwadikar, A. (2016). Blockchain in Banking: A Measured Approach. *Cognizant Reports*. Retrieved from https://www.cognizant.com/whitepapers/Blockchain-in-Banking-A-Measured-Approach-codex1809.pdf

Treleaven, P., Brown, R. G., & Yang, D. (2017). Blockchain Technology in Finance. *Computer*, *50*(9), 14–17. doi:10.1109/MC.2017.3571047

Veeningen & Szirbik. (2018). Using serious gaming to discover and understand distributed ledger technology in distributed energy systems. *Proceedings of IFIP Advances in Information and Communication Technology*.

Wood. (2018). *Ethereum: A secure decentralised generalised transaction ledger*. Retrieved from https://gavwood.com/paper.pdf

Yaga, D., Mell, P., Roby, N., & Scarfone, K. (2018). *Blockchain technology overview*. Retrieved from https://nvlpubs.nist.gov/nistpubs/ir/2018/NIST.IR.8202.pdf

Yi, S., Xu, Z., & Wang, G. J. (2018). Volatility connectedness in the cryptocurrency market: Is Bitcoin a dominant cryptocurrency? *International Review of Financial Analysis*, *60*, 98–114. doi:10.1016/j.irfa.2018.08.012

Chapter 7
A Model for Extracting Most Desired Web Pages

Jayanti Mehra
Maulana Azad National Institute of Technology, India

Ramjeevan Singh Thakur
Maulana Azad National Institute of Technology, India

ABSTRACT

Weblog analysis takes raw data from access logs and performs study on this data for extracting statistical information. This info incorporates a variety of data for the website activity such as average no. of hits, total no. of user visits, failed and successful cached hits, average time of view, average path length over a website; analytical information such as page was not found errors and server errors; server information, which includes exit and entry pages, single access pages, and top visited pages; requester information like which type of search engines is used, keywords and top referring sites, and so on. In general, the website administrator uses this kind of knowledge to make the system act better, helping in the manipulation process of site, then also forgiving marketing decisions support. Most of the advanced web mining systems practice this kind of information to take out more difficult or complex interpretations using data mining procedures like association rules, clustering, and classification.

DOI: 10.4018/978-1-7998-0186-3.ch007

INTRODUCTION

Nowadays internet has become a convenient foundation and source of information in everyone's daily activity (Kumar, Ahirwar, & Singh, 2015). The World Wide Web had gone through enormous development in last two decades but its amount of swap and extent increased the trouble for different websites (Malviya & Agrawal, 2015; Agrawal & Jawdekar, 2016). To fulfill the demands of their users, the e-commerce website is quickly progressing hence their importance is obvious (Talakokkula, 2015; Xie, Yu, & Cen, 2012).

Because of several tremendous benefits of web research, it is pretty interesting thing for organizations (Anand & Hilal, 2012). It has helped to improve the profitability of the market and also for the benefit of the market intelligence (Kaur & Aggarwal, 2015), this also helps in marketing and comparative analysis for finding the customer relationships (Grace, 2011; Rana & Patel, 2013).

The web data were organized and assembled, and structured thorough the client's profiles (Yadav, Feeroz, & Yadav, 2012; Losarwar & Joshi, 2012). This advantage helps organizations to save current clients by giving more customized administrations; however, it additionally contributes in finding for potential clients (Chandra, Gupta, & Gupta, 2008; Wang & Xiuju, 2002; Parvatikar & Joshi, 2014).

WEB USAGE MINING (WUM): OVERVIEW

Data Sources

Information which is used for web study can be gathered at these three distinct locations (Jeba, Bhuvaneswari, & Muneeswaran, 2016).

Server Level: It is a sever computer that stores users' behavior so the data are collected from different sources and for different users.

Client Level: It is client computer that store user's browsing information like client browser, operating system etc.

Proxy server: It is an intermediate computer machine called proxy server. Where some browsing data are also resides therefore the weblog data should also be collected from the proxy server.

PROCEDURE OF WEB USAGE MINING

The procedure of web usage mining uses data mining techniques, to discover the interesting and fruitful patterns from web data that is understandable and which fulfills the requirements of clients searching on the web (Mobasher, Cooley, & Srivastava, 2000; Reddy, Reddy, & Sitaramulu, 2013; Singh & Badhe, 2014). Every data mining technique of web usage mining comprises these fundamental techniques i.e.

1. pre-processing,
2. pattern discovery and
3. Pattern analysis. In this work, the client performance disclosure techniques are presented with the help of log data (Koutsoukos, Alexandridis, Siolas, & Stafylopatis, 2016).

APPLICATIONS OF WEB USAGE MINING

The web usage mining has very significant applications in various domains, Some of the wildly used applications are given as follows-

Personalization

Web personalization is the procedure where web site pages are tailored for each requirements of a user (Satokar & Gawali, 2010). For the personalization, the interesting access patterns can be mined from web usage data. In many applications of web personalization, dynamic recommendations of items are made based on user's browsing behavior and his/her profile (Mobasher, Cooley, & Srivastava, 2000; Sukumar, Robert, & Yuvaraj, 2016).

System Improvement

Administration quality and performance are vital to client's satisfaction through services like databases, systems and so on. Web usage mining offer a technique to perceive different web sequential behaviors (Chand & Munishwar, 2017), it can be used for doing preparations for web page structuring and recognizes (Facca & Lanzi, 2003; Suhasini & Joshi, 2014).

Site Modification

Site improvement is a necessary task for administrator if website is effective it attracts the clients and improves the business, that is why website updating is compulsory for any e-commerce to get prosperous (Resul & Turkoglu, 2009).

Business Intelligence

The business intelligence is the prime need for every organization to grow faster in market (Zhong, 2011). Thus, it is useful for website advertisers of e-business to logical and physical structure improvement of any website (Chaofeng, 2009; Al-Asdi & Obaid, 2016).

ADVANTAGES OF WEB MINING

It helps in advertising and promoting websites on the association with the clients. The various types of web data help to sort and group to generate specific client profiles (Cooley, Mobasher, & Srivastava, 1999). The web mining isn't just causing organizations to hold clients by having the capacity to give more customized administrations, however it also contributes in the look for potential clients (Resul & Turkoglu, 2009; Muskan & Garg, 2016; Losarwar & Joshi, 2012).

NEEDS FOR WEB USAGE MINING

Some fundamental issue that is still present in web usage mining are-

1. The web data is continuously growing in volume.
2. Difficult to preprocess the data.
3. Websites contain web pages with little or absence of semantic descriptions.
4. In case of huge quantity of web usage data, the sequential pattern mining is not suitable.
5. The web usage mining contains three steps that are not correspondingly sufficient to create a comprehensible and exclusive process.

LITERATURE REVIEW

Dwivedi and Rawat (2015) have worked on different types of data preprocessing methods; it is to change raw data into appropriate format. When data is taken from server side it is not acceptable for our mining process. It is very important to preprocess the data. This paper discusses about different data preprocessing techniques. Aye (2011) described principally based on data preprocessing step of the principle scheme of web usage mining with activities like field extraction and data cleaning methods. This identifies the basic scheme of data preprocessing. In the area of field extraction and data cleaning method, the field extract method is used to secluding records for a single line. Liu, Zhou, and Hongyan (2007) have described user identification and recommended a different user identification algorithm that utilize IP address and user access time to distinguish distinct users in the logs, in particular, heuristic rule-based user identification algorithm is preferred. Kumar, Ahirwar, and Singh (2015) proposed a model to predict user behavior from the weblog data and also discussed different techniques used in data mining and described how to apply these techniques in weblog analysis. Anitha and Isakki (2016) gave a consideration on web usage mining to anticipate the web user's behavior from log files in web server. Users use website pages with a continuous way and access pages with links are stored in log file of web server and also taking about the with the respect to behavior from investigation of various algorithm and distinctive techniques. Neelima and Rodda (2016) incorporated procedure of 3 steps, specifically data_cleaning, user_identification, and session_identification. They are actualizing these three stages. Contingent on the recurrence of users visiting by each page mining is performed. By finding the session of the client and investigated the user behavior when time spent on a specific page. Koutsoukos et al. (2016) explained about the session identification algorithm for weblog data and fuzzy c means clustering has also been explained, the studied the impact of the cluster of distance framework that have on the clustering process, the proposed procedure use subtracting clustering for the partition for demonstration of the session information. The preliminary comes going to show that the proposed approach is incredible in the change of client sessions. Chaofeng (2009) has endeavored to give a propelled review of the session clustering. It has planned a system of session clustering. After that, they talked about the procedure of web session clustering. Data preprocessing is vital for performing web session clustering. This gives a few rules in each period of data preprocessing so as to plan and actualize them naturally. They reduce the log file estimate as well as increment the nature of the accessible data. Here, additionally broke down the weakness of conventional similarity measurement between web sessions. At last, attention to that various clusters, the underlying purpose of the particular clusters, and the characterizing of basis work are the three steps defined and troubles that thought in web session clustering. Investigation on Indian crime records demonstrate that the proposed strategy normally does better than the current procedures in clustering of such multivariate time series data. Chandra et al. (2008) discovered comparative crime trends among different crime series of various crime areas and therefore utilize this data for future crime patterns expectation they proposed Minkowski model. Investigation on Indian crime records demonstrate that the proposed strategy normally better than the current procedures in clustering of such multivariate time series data. Gopalan and Akilandeswari (2005) proposed a unique approach for online web mining and using it as a tool to web crawlers to recover more important significant pages. The execution of the technique with different parameters is compared and experimental result is given. Pant and Jauha (2013) proposed different types of soft computing algorithm for better and enhanced technique of supply chain management. Finally, all proposed soft computing techniques are also summarized in terms of best solution. Srivastava, Garg, and Mishra (2015) discussed about a technique of data extraction that eliminate unwanted data based on time interval and also provide sorted data based on date and time. In data cleaning all unwanted and wrong HTTP status codes are discarded and it is reduced raw log data up to 80% in the data cleaning phase. Wang and Xiuju (2002) described, rule extraction is conveyed to express data sets. A SCM is utilized to rank the significance of qualities first. As per the ranking result, diverse feature subsets are utilized as contributions to RBF classifiers. The characteristic subsets with the most minimal characterization error rates and minimal quantities of qualities are chosen. Rules are separated in view of a novel gradients-based strategy and feature subsets selection. Compare with different strategies, more compact and exact rule are removed for Iris and Breast malignancy data sets, while for Monk3 data set, the rule exactness is lower. Munk, Kapusta, and Švec (2010) described the different data preprocessing techniques like data cleaning, user identification and identification of session and described the reconstruction of activities of user's. Chitraa and Thanamani (2014) proposed a fuzzy c-means based novel approach to cluster the web user transactions. This approach is grouping the similar user navigation patterns. The algorithm enhances the FCM and Penalized FCM clustering algorithm by adding Posterior Probability to find highest membership for a member to add in a cluster. Classification is carried out by SVM and RVM for classifying a new user to a particular group. The method is evaluated based on different data and shows the better performance compared with other existing clustering techniques. Rana and Patel (2013), describes how to decide the quantity of groups. This investigation demonstrates that the auto clustering highlight of SOM is more powerful and target than the K-means method. Consequently, SOM can be used as the preliminary stage for weblog examination to decide the quantity of clusters and beginning stages. A mix of SOM with Simple K-means using Neural Network clustering technique can likewise be utilized for weblog investigation, since this grouping has been demonstrated superior over basic SOM and basic K-means strategy in different applications. In this manner, the two-label strategy, which first uses the SOM to decide the quantity of groups and afterward K-means Neural Network algorithm is used to locate the final result of clustering, can turn into a strong clustering technique for weblog investigation. Losarwar and Joshi (2012) mentioned about the data preprocessing a basic step also explained a whole methodology for preprocessing. The raw data has to be processed as it is incomplete, noisy and has lots of errors. Preprocessing is the major task to be done. This will make the mining process more effective as it converts the data in a most suitable format.

PROCESS OF FINDING MOST DESIRED WEB PAGES

Once raw data is cleaned the frequency of pages is counted. The frequency of page could be defined as the page visibility number in a particular file. The Block diagram of frequency count process for each web page is shown in Figure 1. The process for frequency count of web page for weblog analysis.

ROLES OF MOST DESIRED WEB PAGES

Statistics is critical task to any website Administrator to know useful information regarding to own Web site contents such as to find number of hits by each client on a particular page host, page and certain substance. Number of hits can be added up based on its substantial line in weblog records and further these lines can incorporate browsing, downloading and posting exercises done by various clients.

The output of this stage changed into suitable jobs like,

1. Re-structure or Re-create the website
2. Improve access (through) comparative practice.

Figure 1. Process for frequency count of web page for weblog log analysis

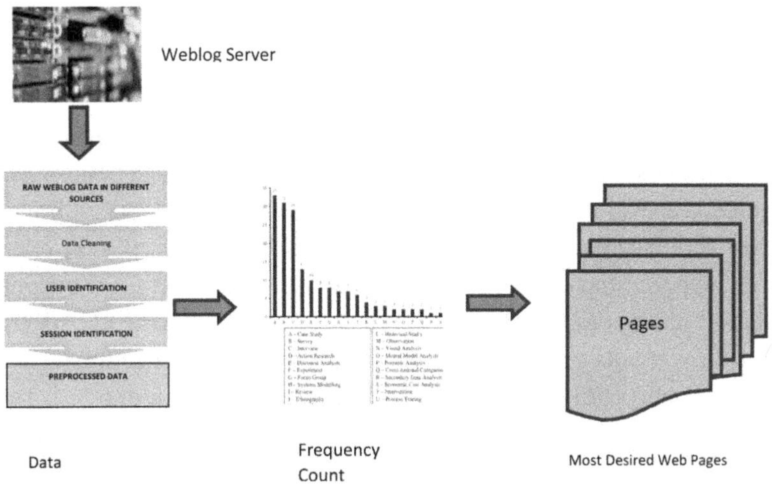

3. Different task like maximum access URL, pages, substance can be investigated and checked.
4. Monitor client's exercises towards specific page.

The statistics has been constructed here to extract useful information such as hit count of each page of site depends on content of page, no. of valid hits on the page and some other information. Figure 2 shows structure of weblog data.

As the information on WWW is growing exponentially, finding the relevant information according to the user's interest and need is a challenging issue. The user is presented with number of URLs to locate his required need. Thus, more time and efforts are required to obtain required information. Web finding most desired web page is the solution to this problem. In many commercial applications website attractiveness is a crucial feature from the business perspective. So, website structures i.e. the web pages organization needs to be improved. Web usage mining extracts the knowledge from users' behavior and helps the website designer to modify the website design, presented an approach for adaptive websites which automatically improves web structure organization by mining web usage logs from web server. Authors presented a cluster mining algorithm known as Page Gather for mining purpose.

Web usage mining for web page access frequency consists of mainly three steps; preprocessing, pattern analysis and total hits calculation. The preprocessing step mainly consists of data cleaning, user_identification and session_identification. Pattern discovery step is used to identify the interesting pattern from web usage data.

When the users browse in any website, they search for the desired information which will be placed in particular pages. If the information is significantly common to different users, those pages will be accessed with a high frequency. Thus, to identify those pages, the concept of high frequency accessed pages has been considered.

DATA FROM WEBLOGS

The standard database has taken from NASA-HTTP (textarcana, 2014) for performance evaluation of proposed models. The snapshot of raw weblog data is shown in Figure 2. Hits counted for every website can recognize the website filed, most browsed web page, most users' access, desired page requested. In case of cluster websites, we calculate the experiential cooperative probability of hits count for everyone to find the correlation of sites to which class belongs by applying page access frequency count algorithm on Hits counted for every website can recognize the website filed, most browsed web page, most users' access, desired page requested. In case of cluster websites, we calculate the experiential cooperative probability of hits count

Figure 2. Snapshot of raw data from weblog

```
199.72.81.55 - - [01/Jul/1995:00:00:01 -0400] "GET /history/apollo/
HTTP/1.0" 200 6245
unicomp6.unicomp.net - - [01/Jul/1995:00:00:06 -0400] "GET
/shuttle/countdown/ HTTP/1.0" 200 3985
199.120.110.21 - - [01/Jul/1995:00:00:09 -0400] "GET
/shuttle/missions/sts-73/mission-sts-73.html HTTP/1.0" 200 4085
burger.letters.com - - [01/Jul/1995:00:00:11 -0400] "GET
/shuttle/countdown/liftoff.html HTTP/1.0" 304 0
199.120.110.21 - - [01/Jul/1995:00:00:11 -0400] "GET
/shuttle/missions/sts-73/sts-73-patch-small.gif HTTP/1.0" 200 4179
burger.letters.com - - [01/Jul/1995:00:00:12 -0400] "GET /images/NASA-
logosmall.gif HTTP/1.0" 304 0
burger.letters.com - - [01/Jul/1995:00:00:12 -0400] "GET
/shuttle/countdown/video/livevideo.gif HTTP/1.0" 200 0
205.212.115.106 - - [01/Jul/1995:00:00:12 -0400] "GET
/shuttle/countdown/countdown.html HTTP/1.0" 200 3985
d104.aa.net - - [01/Jul/1995:00:00:13 -0400] "GET /shuttle/countdown/
HTTP/1.0" 200 3985
129.94.144.152 - - [01/Jul/1995:00:00:13 -0400] "GET / HTTP/1.0" 200 7074
unicomp6.unicomp.net - - [01/Jul/1995:00:00:14 -0400] "GET
/shuttle/countdown/count.gif HTTP/1.0" 200 40310
unicomp6.unicomp.net - - [01/Jul/1995:00:00:14 -0400] "GET /images/NASA-
logosmall.gif HTTP/1.0" 200 786
unicomp6.unicomp.net - - [01/Jul/1995:00:00:14 -0400] "GET /images/KSC-
logosmall.gif HTTP/1.0" 200 1204
```

for everyone to find the correlation of sites to which class belongs by applying page access frequency count algorithm on preprocessed input data.

EXPERIMENTAL RESULTS

The most desired web page approach is implemented in JAVA language and number of hits is counted for each page in set of web records. The experimental work is done on processor-intel(R), RAM-4GB, system type-64-bit operating system in windows 8.1 environment using MATLAB (version 8.3), JAVA language and weblog expert tool. To determine number of hits in a set of records, the weblog dataset is divided into no. of sub datasets which are shown in Table 1. Each sub dataset of weblog dataset varying in length according to no. of records. The graphical representation of daily visitors, daily hits and daily bandwidth are shown in Figure 3, Figure 4, Figure 5. Table 1 shows the daily activity of visitors.

The graphical representation of activity by hour of day shown in Figure 6. Table 2 shows the daily activity by hour of day.

The graphical representation of activity by Day of Week shown in Figure 7. Table 2 shows the daily activity by day of Week.

Figure 3. Daily visitors

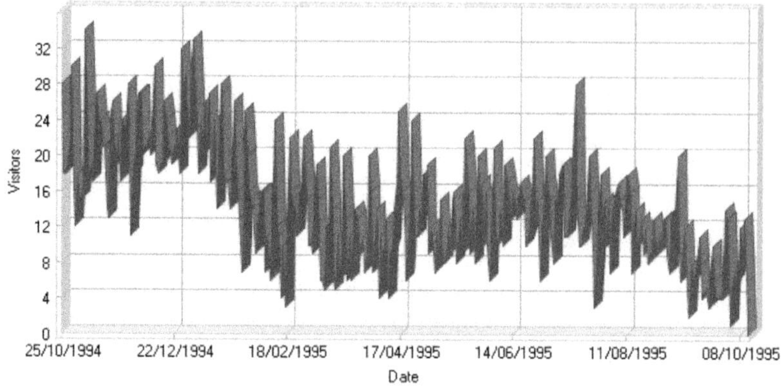

Figure 4. Daily hits

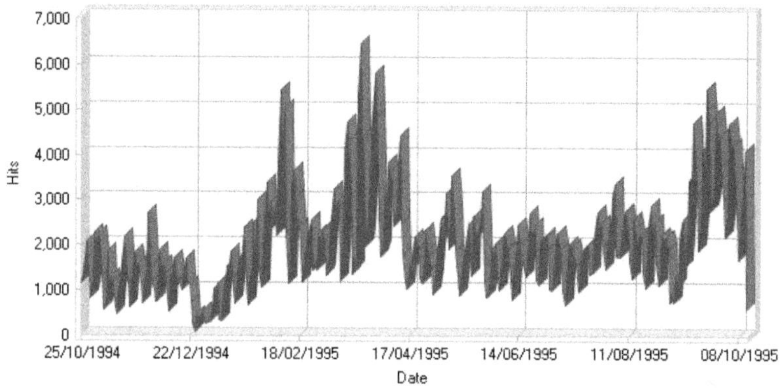

Figure 5. Daily bandwidth

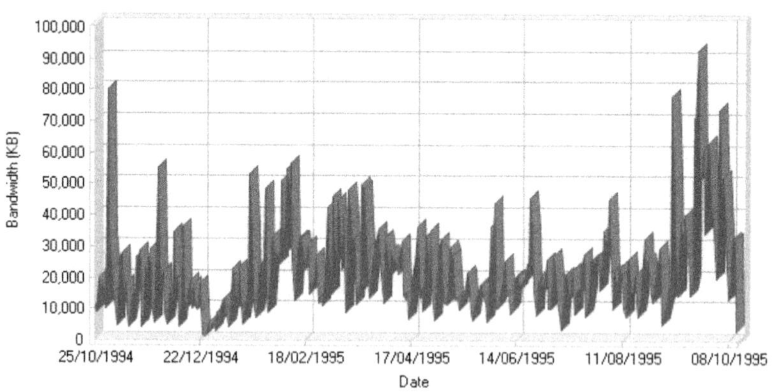

Table 1. Daily activity of visitors

Date	Hits	Page Views	Visitors	Average Visit Length	Bandwidth (KB)
Thu 24/08/1995	2,197	812	9	55:14	20,274
Fri 25/08/1995	2,529	1,026	13	29:42	25,600
Sat 26/08/1995	1,602	626	10	22:58	20,562
Sun 27/08/1995	1,109	489	9	12:19	14,160
Mon 28/08/1995	1,716	894	11	15:09	12,283
Tue 29/08/1995	2,247	930	10	41:39	20,308
Wed 30/08/1995	2,067	885	13	04:53:47	20,680
Thu 31/08/1995	2,199	904	13	24:43	29,420
Fri 01/09/1995	1,930	801	9	01:55:40	23,156
Sat 02/09/1995	742	267	7	02:28:48	5,141
Sun 03/09/1995	936	393	13	01:08:44	8,778
Mon 04/09/1995	742	348	14	02:19:21	10,783
Tue 05/09/1995	1,301	581	14	01:37:09	17,048
Wed 06/09/1995	1,109	510	20	01:28:32	12,679
Thu 07/09/1995	2,165	999	9	06:29:01	77,993
Fri 08/09/1995	2,512	1,096	6	03:24:33	50,982
Sat 09/09/1995	2,609	1,141	10	02:46:02	29,482
Sun 10/09/1995	1,542	671	12	06:38:50	14,483
Mon 11/09/1995	2,541	940	5	05:03:04	29,150
Tue 12/09/1995	3,444	1,584	2	05:26:25	37,836
Wed 13/09/1995	3,513	1,597	8	04:15:42	28,481
Thu 14/09/1995	4,711	2,060	6	07:01:21	39,882
Fri 15/09/1995	3,727	1,720	7	06:27:38	30,779
Sat 16/09/1995	3,152	1,514	8	03:28:41	26,818
Sun 17/09/1995	1,901	626	11	03:13:09	14,525
Mon 18/09/1995	2,596	1,053	8	06:07:02	18,880
Tue 19/09/1995	4,124	1,597	4	10:03:54	71,320
Wed 20/09/1995	3,614	1,657	5	07:58:36	70,317
Thu 21/09/1995	5,457	2,197	5	12:10:49	92,637
Fri 22/09/1995	4,739	1,541	3	05:37:42	53,622
Sat 23/09/1995	2,790	1,064	7	05:25:56	52,311
Sun 24/09/1995	2,893	1,006	10	08:22:56	61,079
Mon 25/09/1995	3,389	1,348	6	03:29:25	34,072
Tue 26/09/1995	4,943	2,107	4	04:26:02	61,038

continued on following page

Table 1. Continued

Date	Hits	Page Views	Visitors	Average Visit Length	Bandwidth (KB)
Wed 27/09/1995	4,278	1,761	4	16:13:55	63,493
Thu 28/09/1995	4,437	1,835	4	04:17:22	41,762
Fri 29/09/1995	3,783	1,609	4	07:21:54	40,748
Sat 30/09/1995	3,039	1,143	14	02:18:38	35,007
Sun 01/10/1995	2,194	1,019	13	03:15:10	19,874
Mon 02/10/1995	2,731	1,161	13	07:41:50	31,661
Tue 03/10/1995	4,682	2,052	1	14:12:12	73,798
Wed 04/10/1995	4,110	1,646	5	03:09:47	42,249
Thu 05/10/1995	4,222	1,588	7	02:06:14	52,448
Fri 06/10/1995	3,632	1,449	6	08:03:16	33,123
Sat 07/10/1995	2,558	1,167	8	03:50:08	22,855
Sun 08/10/1995	1,685	823	12	07:09:46	13,086
Mon 09/10/1995	2,690	1,042	8	01:45:44	19,906
Tue 10/10/1995	3,073	1,303	13	01:25:02	32,383
Wed 11/10/1995	4,106	1,691	6	02:53:54	32,137
Thu 12/10/1995	577	244	0	00:00	2,886
Subtotal	140,585	58,517	419	03:42:30	1,693,997
Total	724,837	342,632	5,139	02:04:14	7,759,572

Figure 6. Activities by hour of day

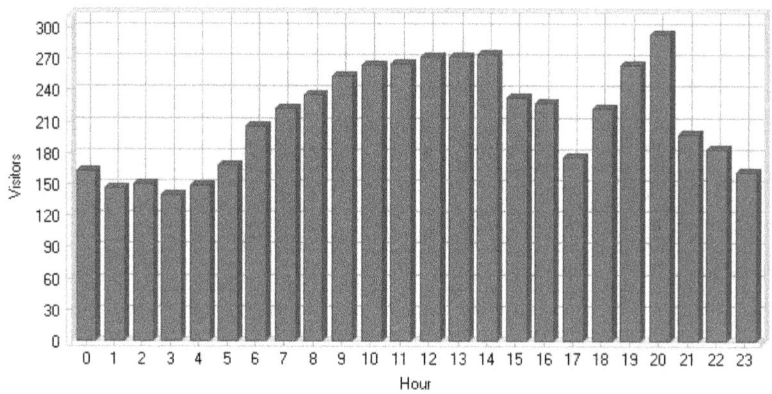

Table 2. Activity by hour of day

Hour	Hits	Page Views	Visitors	Bandwidth (KB)
00:00 - 00:59	47,211	22,381	163	539,143
01:00 - 01:59	51,083	23,883	146	537,650
02:00 - 02:59	51,850	24,645	150	574,740
03:00 - 03:59	52,935	24,704	139	484,177
04:00 - 04:59	47,406	22,219	149	462,086
05:00 - 05:59	44,194	20,695	168	418,683
06:00 - 06:59	35,590	16,598	206	355,347
07:00 - 07:59	30,722	14,700	223	318,666
08:00 - 08:59	30,266	14,445	235	299,849
09:00 - 09:59	26,798	13,392	254	231,218
10:00 - 10:59	24,401	12,253	264	235,448
11:00 - 11:59	21,364	11,183	265	193,347
12:00 - 12:59	18,752	9,709	271	171,161
13:00 - 13:59	15,392	7,586	271	181,036
14:00 - 14:59	12,627	6,151	274	156,570
15:00 - 15:59	10,597	4,955	233	130,840
16:00 - 16:59	10,105	4,684	227	130,747
17:00 - 17:59	11,411	4,947	176	150,042
18:00 - 18:59	13,879	6,106	223	168,979
19:00 - 19:59	17,386	7,800	264	200,022
20:00 - 20:59	26,973	12,367	294	367,122
21:00 - 21:59	34,267	15,490	198	446,021
22:00 - 22:59	42,912	19,601	184	473,535
23:00 - 23:59	46,716	22,138	162	533,131
Total	724,837	342,632	5,139	7,759,572

Figure 7. Activities by hour of week

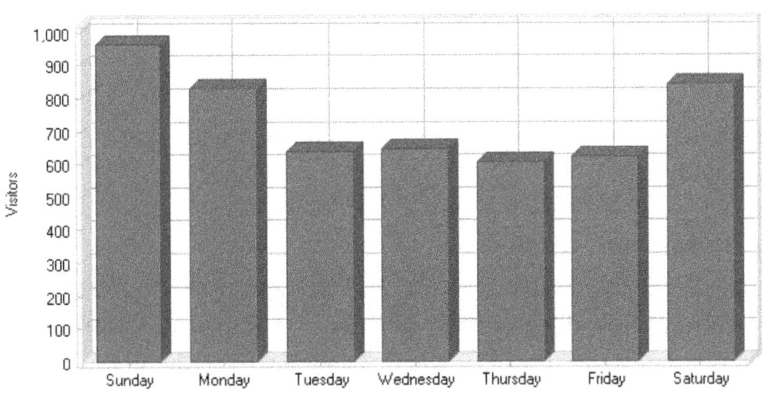

Activity by Day of Week

The graphical representation of activity by week shown in Fig.8. Table 4 shows the daily activity by week.

Table 3. Activity by day of week

Day	Hits	Page Views	Visitors	Bandwidth (KB)
Sunday	62,906	29,975	961	659,981
Monday	83,690	40,731	830	826,759
Tuesday	120,313	56,611	639	1,388,454
Wednesday	132,440	62,655	645	1,330,438
Thursday	124,919	58,126	603	1,401,380
Friday	119,584	56,012	622	1,290,239
Saturday	80,985	38,522	839	862,317
Total	724,837	342,632	5,139	7,759,572

Figure 8. Activities by week

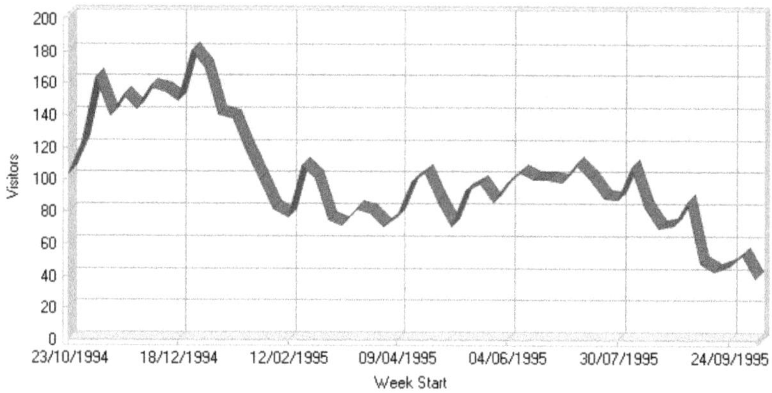

Activity by Week

The graphical representation of activity by month shown in Figure 9. Table 5 shows the activity by month.

Activity by Month

The graphical representation of daily page access shown in Figure 10 and most popular pages sown in Figure 11. Table 6 shows the most popular pages.

Table 4. Activity by week

Week Hits Page Views Visitors Bandwidth (KB)
30/10/1994 - 05/11/1994 11,689 6,434 123 188,450
06/11/1994 - 12/11/1994 7,217 3,862 164 110,114
13/11/1994 - 19/11/1994 9,327 4,797 140 124,386
20/11/1994 - 26/11/1994 9,418 4,752 153 122,547
27/11/1994 - 03/12/1994 9,632 4,950 144 153,525
04/12/1994 - 10/12/1994 8,852 4,419 158 107,858
11/12/1994 - 17/12/1994 8,458 4,532 155 110,326
18/12/1994 - 24/12/1994 7,352 3,993 149 76,685
25/12/1994 - 31/12/1994 2,449 1,387 181 26,127
01/01/1995 - 07/01/1995 4,599 2,607 170 64,453
08/01/1995 - 14/01/1995 8,634 4,795 141 110,711
15/01/1995 - 21/01/1995 10,637 5,955 138 142,684
22/01/1995 - 28/01/1995 11,746 6,313 118 137,441
29/01/1995 - 04/02/1995 16,838 8,682 100 168,050
05/02/1995 - 11/02/1995 25,672 12,356 82 297,963
12/02/1995 - 18/02/1995 18,151 9,448 77 179,845
19/02/1995 - 25/02/1995 12,881 6,982 109 140,046
26/02/1995 - 04/03/1995 13,098 7,740 101 147,181
05/03/1995 - 11/03/1995 18,134 10,558 75 237,443
12/03/1995 - 18/03/1995 21,117 12,229 72 188,206
19/03/1995 - 25/03/1995 25,728 10,028 82 208,613
26/03/1995 - 01/04/1995 28,705 17,635 79 183,159
02/04/1995 - 08/04/1995 20,665 11,624 71 172,791
09/04/1995 - 15/04/1995 18,706 9,986 77 148,009
16/04/1995 - 22/04/1995 12,319 6,744 99 147,254
23/04/1995 - 29/04/1995 11,459 6,068 105 156,463
30/04/1995 - 06/05/1995 13,527 6,552 86 129,650
07/05/1995 - 13/05/1995 17,302 7,388 71 136,239
14/05/1995 - 20/05/1995 12,036 5,202 93 102,700
21/05/1995 - 27/05/1995 16,610 5,330 98 94,042
28/05/1995 - 03/06/1995 9,873 4,967 86 143,515
04/06/1995 - 10/06/1995 11,667 5,283 98 112,760
11/06/1995 - 17/06/1995 11,757 4,608 105 108,542
18/06/1995 - 24/06/1995 13,907 5,362 100 182,015
25/06/1995 - 01/07/1995 12,656 5,372 100 128,303
02/07/1995 - 08/07/1995 11,358 4,900 99 103,335
09/07/1995 - 15/07/1995 11,145 4,606 110 104,157
16/07/1995 - 22/07/1995 11,741 5,138 101 115,849
23/07/1995 - 29/07/1995 15,624 6,519 89 153,510
30/07/1995 - 05/08/1995 16,489 6,042 88 208,415
06/08/1995 - 12/08/1995 15,187 5,735 108 123,741
13/08/1995 - 19/08/1995 14,144 4,601 83 121,350
20/08/1995 - 26/08/1995 14,499 5,847 70 139,319
27/08/1995 - 02/09/1995 12,010 5,170 72 125,149
03/09/1995 - 09/09/1995 11,374 5,068 86 207,748
10/09/1995 - 16/09/1995 22,630 10,086 48 207,431
17/09/1995 - 23/09/1995 25,221 9,735 43 373,614
24/09/1995 - 30/09/1995 26,762 10,809 46 337,203
01/10/1995 - 07/10/1995 24,129 10,082 53 276,011
08/10/1995 - 14/10/1995 12,131 5,103 39 100,400
Subtotal 717,262 338,381 5,035 7,685,351
Total 724,837 342,632 5,139 7,759,572

Daily Page Access

Most Popular Pages

The graphical representation of daily entry pages shown in Figure 12 and top entry pages sown in Figure 13. Table 7 shows Top Entry Pages.

Top Entry Pages

The graphical representation of exit pages shown in Figure 14 and top exit pages sown in Figure 15. Table 8 shows Top exit Pages.

Top Exit Pages

The graphical representation of Daily Authenticated Users Activity shown in Fig.16 and Top Authenticated Users sown in Figure 17. Table 8 shows Top Authenticated Users.

Daily Authenticated Users Activity

Top Authenticated Users

In this chapter overall process of page access frequency including required tasks has been described. Users either browse web page directly or use web site to go

Figure 9. Activities by month

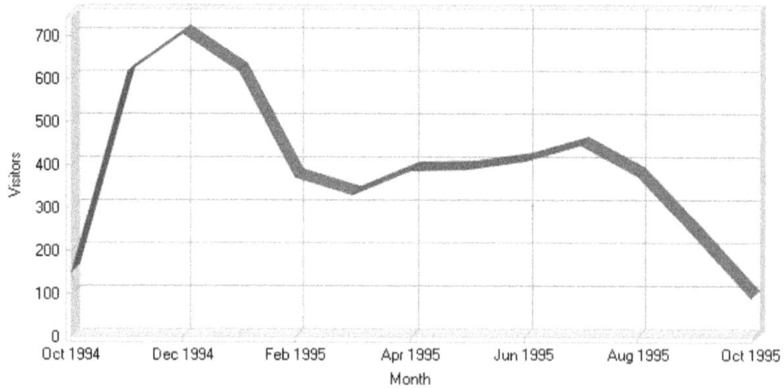

Table 5. Activity by month

Month	Hits	Page Views	Visitors	Bandwidth (KB)
Oct 1994	9,572	5,497	150	100,183
Nov 1994	41,575	21,714	615	625,368
Dec 1994	30,822	16,166	706	368,692
Jan 1995	41,139	22,585	618	518,008
Feb 1995	73,315	37,669	373	764,046
Mar 1995	98,851	53,618	333	903,158
Apr 1995	66,691	36,412	389	651,559
May 1995	63,416	26,469	390	518,935
Jun 1995	53,989	22,581	410	586,800
Jul 1995	54,227	22,760	447	544,599
Aug 1995	66,321	25,210	377	647,512
Sep 1995	88,659	36,766	239	1,154,295
Oct 1995	36,260	15,185	92	376,411
Total	724,837	342,632	5,139	7,759,572

Figure 10. Daily page access

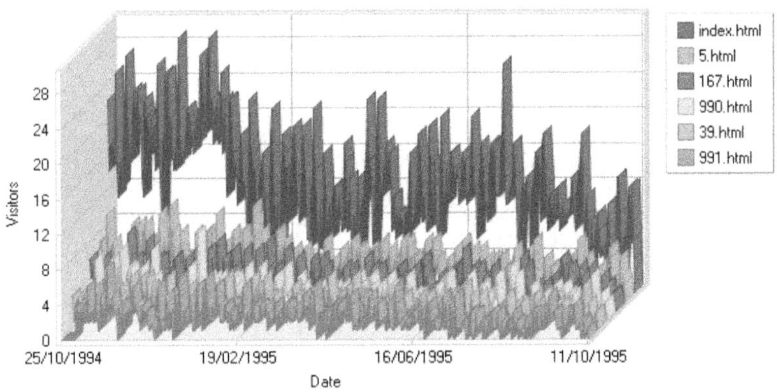

Figure 11. Most popular pages

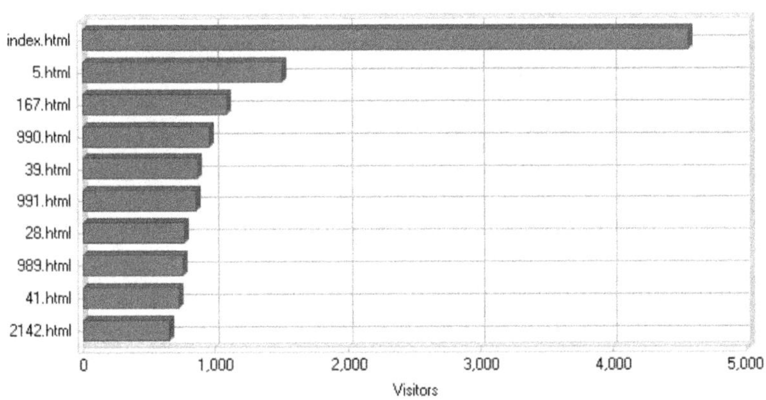

Table 6. Most popular pages

	Page	Hits	Incomplete Requests	Visitors	Bandwidth (KB)
1	http://www.weblog-expert.com/index.html	134,203	0	4,575	326,534
2	http://www.weblog-expert.com/5.html	5,010	0	1,510	3,588
3	http://www.weblog-expert.com/167.html	2,768	0	1,091	3,257
4	http://www.weblog-expert.com/990.html	2,289	0	965	9,945
5	http://www.weblog-expert.com/39.html	1,641	0	875	1,026
6	http://www.weblog-expert.com/991.html	2,008	0	856	4,142
7	http://www.weblog-expert.com/28.html	1,958	0	770	2,196
8	http://www.weblog-expert.com/989.html	1,598	0	759	1,484
9	http://www.weblog-expert.com/41.html	1,533	0	733	49,191
10	http://www.weblog-expert.com/2142.html	1,567	0	660	1,252
11	http://www.weblog-expert.com/303.html	1,491	0	634	3,766
12	http://www.weblog-expert.com/220.html	1,555	0	585	12,494
13	http://www.weblog-expert.com/34.html	1,252	0	582	3,511
14	http://www.weblog-expert.com/165.html	1,003	0	578	537
15	http://www.weblog-expert.com/627.html	1,575	0	567	1,980
16	http://www.weblog-expert.com/36.html	1,340	0	563	2,545
17	http://www.weblog-expert.com/306.html	1,337	0	561	2,511
18	http://www.weblog-expert.com/992.html	992	0	560	827
19	http://www.weblog-expert.com/153.html	914	0	535	1,715
20	http://www.weblog-expert.com/332.html	741	0	476	762
21	http://www.weblog-expert.com/216.html	809	0	468	2,313
22	http://www.weblog-expert.com/219.html	963	0	465	524
23	http://www.weblog-expert.com/974.html	1,551	0	465	8,061
24	http://www.weblog-expert.com/45.html	994	0	462	10,709
25	http://www.weblog-expert.com/706.html	1,817	0	459	13,209
26	http://www.weblog-expert.com/323.html	777	0	458	845
27	http://www.weblog-expert.com/44.html	803	0	442	500
28	http://www.weblog-expert.com/1082.html	1,064	0	441	4,212
29	http://www.weblog-expert.com/161.html	987	0	422	10,313
30	http://www.weblog-expert.com/302.html	786	0	417	339
31	http://www.weblog-expert.com/277.html	1,285	0	415	912
32	http://www.weblog-expert.com/202.html	617	0	403	1,046
33	http://www.weblog-expert.com/245.html	1,074	0	402	215
34	http://www.weblog-expert.com/170.html	547	0	389	764
35	http://www.weblog-expert.com/113.html	894	0	388	7,575
36	http://www.weblog-expert.com/267.html	1,256	0	383	2,026
37	http://www.weblog-expert.com/268.html	1,082	0	381	1,768
38	http://www.weblog-expert.com/318.html	595	0	372	375
39	http://www.weblog-expert.com/246.html	1,019	0	368	4,548
40	http://www.weblog-expert.com/276.html	1,026	0	366	1,162
41	http://www.weblog-expert.com/172.html	549	0	365	1,076
42	http://www.weblog-expert.com/275.html	572	0	338	1,123
43	http://www.weblog-expert.com/3664.html	812	0	333	3,072
44	http://www.weblog-expert.com/224.html	758	0	332	2,108
45	http://www.weblog-expert.com/1611.html	678	0	327	309
46	http://www.weblog-expert.com/1029.html	738	0	327	834
47	http://www.weblog-expert.com/29.html	559	0	323	407
48	http://www.weblog-expert.com/566.html	695	0	323	4,134
49	http://www.weblog-expert.com/188.html	461	0	317	1,120
50	http://www.weblog-expert.com/309.html	597	0	313	1,528
Subtotal		193,140	0	N/A	520,415
Total		326,836	0	N/A	1,027,013

Figure 12. Daily entry pages

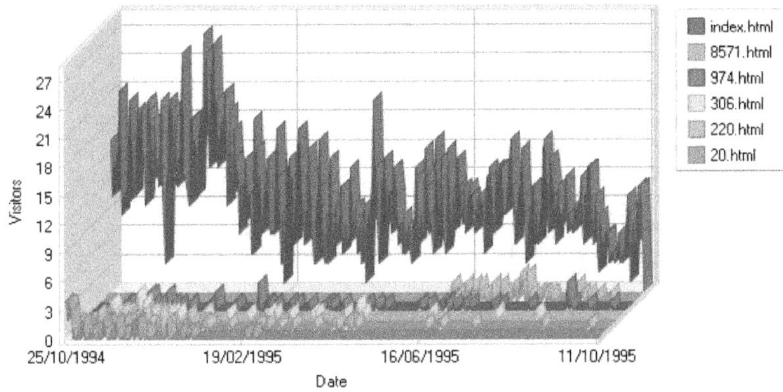

particular page. This page access frequency used for improved particular web page, re-create web sites to contain corresponding pages, upgrade user search through user clusters with similar behavior.

Website data is more useful in e-marketing, e-business and e-commerce and for this it should be updated from time to time. And if page access frequency algorithm is used, it will count no. of hits per page and will help to find which page is required to be modified. This is an effective and useful technique used in e-commerce.

Figure 13. Top entry pages

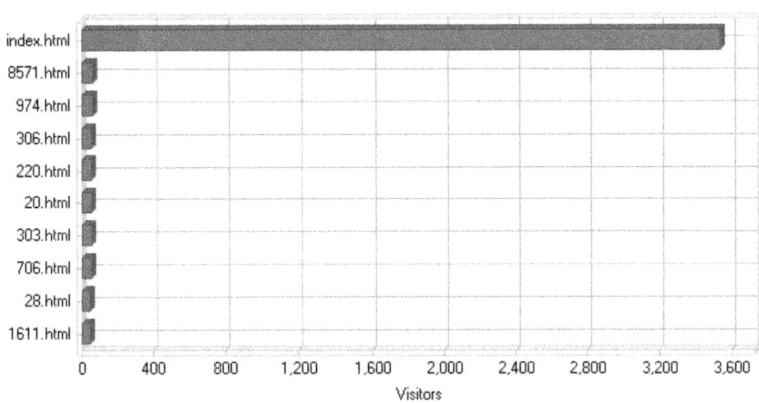

Table 7. Top entry pages

Page Visitors
1 http://www.weblog-expert.com/index.html 3,539
2 http://www.weblog-expert.com/8571.html 59
3 http://www.weblog-expert.com/974.html 58
4 http://www.weblog-expert.com/306.html 55
5 http://www.weblog-expert.com/220.html 53
6 http://www.weblog-expert.com/20.html 53
7 http://www.weblog-expert.com/303.html 51
8 http://www.weblog-expert.com/706.html 51
9 http://www.weblog-expert.com/28.html 48
10 http://www.weblog-expert.com/1611.html 44
11 http://www.weblog-expert.com/113.html 37
12 http://www.weblog-expert.com/224.html 37
13 http://www.weblog-expert.com/1082.html 37
14 http://www.weblog-expert.com/34.html 35
15 http://www.weblog-expert.com/267.html 31
16 http://www.weblog-expert.com/153.html 30
17 http://www.weblog-expert.com/161.html 29
18 http://www.weblog-expert.com/1029.html 27
19 http://www.weblog-expert.com/2130.html 25
20 http://www.weblog-expert.com/219.html 25
21 http://www.weblog-expert.com/165.html 24
22 http://www.weblog-expert.com/149.html 20
23 http://www.weblog-expert.com/3408.html 20
24 http://www.weblog-expert.com/3664.html 19
25 http://www.weblog-expert.com/151.html 19
26 http://www.weblog-expert.com/3253.html 17
27 http://www.weblog-expert.com/250.html 16
28 http://www.weblog-expert.com/6923.html 15
29 http://www.weblog-expert.com/4115.html 15
30 http://www.weblog-expert.com/627.html 12
31 http://www.weblog-expert.com/5.html 11
32 http://www.weblog-expert.com/188.html 10
33 http://www.weblog-expert.com/45.html 10
34 http://www.weblog-expert.com/8478.html 10
35 http://www.weblog-expert.com/1786.html 9
36 http://www.weblog-expert.com/14.html 9
37 http://www.weblog-expert.com/6837.html 9
38 http://www.weblog-expert.com/718.html 9
39 http://www.weblog-expert.com/1239.html 9
40 http://www.weblog-expert.com/1003.html 9
41 http://www.weblog-expert.com/1247.html 9
42 http://www.weblog-expert.com/991.html 8
43 http://www.weblog-expert.com/4468.html 8
44 http://www.weblog-expert.com/2248.html 8
45 http://www.weblog-expert.com/1051.html 7
46 http://www.weblog-expert.com/4258.html 7
47 http://www.weblog-expert.com/8462.html 7
48 http://www.weblog-expert.com/25.html 7
49 http://www.weblog-expert.com/39.html 6
50 http://www.weblog-expert.com/332.html 6
Subtotal 4,669
Total 5,048

Figure 14. Daily exit pages

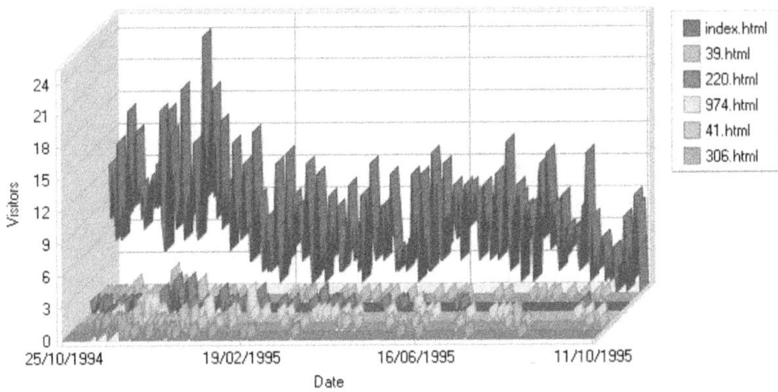

CONCLUSION

As the information on WWW is growing exponentially, finding the relevant information according to the user's interest is a challenging issue. The user behavior is presented with number of URLs to locate his required need. Thus, more time and efforts are required to obtain relevant information. Web page access frequency is the solution to this problem. In many commercial applications website attractiveness is a crucial feature from the business perspective. So, website structure i.e. the web pages organization needs to be improved. Web usage mining extracts the knowledge from users' behavior and helps the website designer to modify the website. This work has presented an approach for adaptive websites which automatically improves web structure organization by mining web usage logs from web server.

Figure 15. Top exit pages

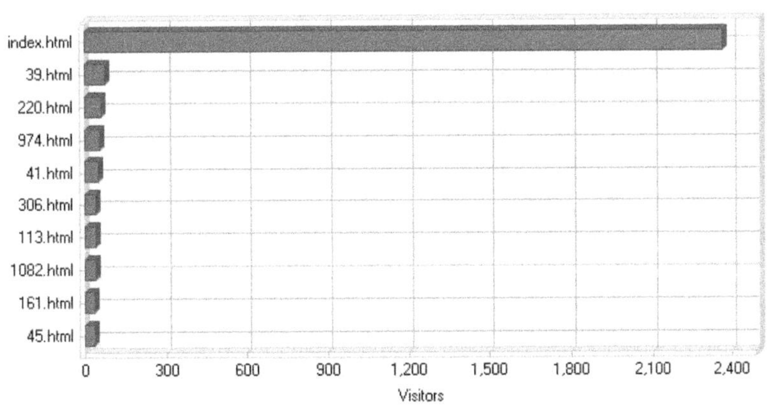

Table 9. Top exit pages

	Page	Visitors
1	http://www.weblog-expert.com/index.html	2,363
2	http://www.weblog-expert.com/39.html	75
3	http://www.weblog-expert.com/220.html	61
4	http://www.weblog-expert.com/974.html	56
5	http://www.weblog-expert.com/41.html	52
6	http://www.weblog-expert.com/306.html	42
7	http://www.weblog-expert.com/113.html	39
8	http://www.weblog-expert.com/1082.html	39
9	http://www.weblog-expert.com/161.html	36
10	http://www.weblog-expert.com/45.html	35
11	http://www.weblog-expert.com/34.html	34
12	http://www.weblog-expert.com/20.html	33
13	http://www.weblog-expert.com/10.html	31
14	http://www.weblog-expert.com/275.html	31
15	http://www.weblog-expert.com/2142.html	31
16	http://www.weblog-expert.com/216.html	31
17	http://www.weblog-expert.com/1969.html	30
18	http://www.weblog-expert.com/706.html	30
19	http://www.weblog-expert.com/219.html	29
20	http://www.weblog-expert.com/303.html	27
21	http://www.weblog-expert.com/8571.html	27
22	http://www.weblog-expert.com/224.html	27
23	http://www.weblog-expert.com/149.html	26
24	http://www.weblog-expert.com/151.html	22
25	http://www.weblog-expert.com/28.html	22
26	http://www.weblog-expert.com/715.html	20
27	http://www.weblog-expert.com/153.html	19
28	http://www.weblog-expert.com/6923.html	18
29	http://www.weblog-expert.com/267.html	18
30	http://www.weblog-expert.com/695.html	17
31	http://www.weblog-expert.com/167.html	17
32	http://www.weblog-expert.com/3427.html	16
33	http://www.weblog-expert.com/1666.html	16
34	http://www.weblog-expert.com/1611.html	15
35	http://www.weblog-expert.com/3408.html	14
36	http://www.weblog-expert.com/3664.html	14
37	http://www.weblog-expert.com/989.html	13
38	http://www.weblog-expert.com/188.html	12
39	http://www.weblog-expert.com/2248.html	12
40	http://www.weblog-expert.com/323.html	12
41	http://www.weblog-expert.com/7060.html	12
42	http://www.weblog-expert.com/941.html	12
43	http://www.weblog-expert.com/250.html	12
44	http://www.weblog-expert.com/8462.html	12
45	http://www.weblog-expert.com/5392.html	12
46	http://www.weblog-expert.com/246.html	12
47	http://www.weblog-expert.com/990.html	12
48	http://www.weblog-expert.com/10452.html	11
49	http://www.weblog-expert.com/5.html	11
50	http://www.weblog-expert.com/1051.html	11
Subtotal		3,579
Total		5,048

Figure 16. Daily authenticated users activity

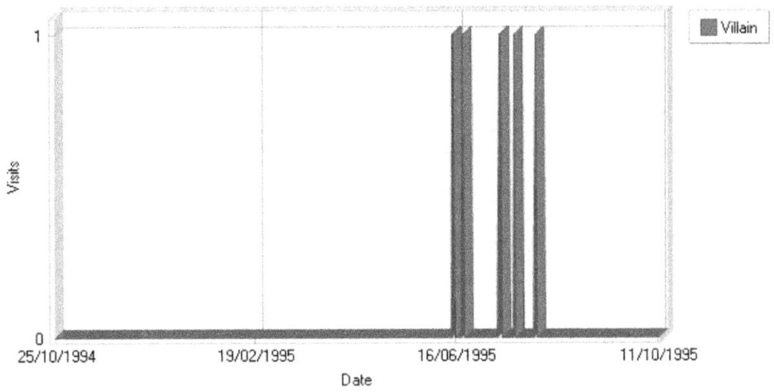

Figure 17. Top authenticated users

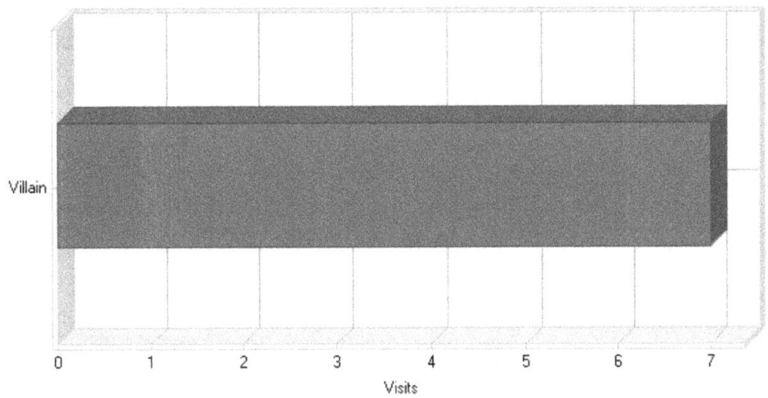

Table 9. Top authenticated users

User Name Hits Visits Bandwidth (KB)
1 Villain 16 7 301 Total 16 7 301

REFERENCES

Agrawal, N., & Jawdekar, A. (2016). User-based approach for finding various results in web usage mining. In *Proc. of Symposium on Colossal Data Analysis and Networking*. IEEE. 10.1109/CDAN.2016.7570867

Al-Asdi, T. A., & Obaid, A. J. (2016). An Efficient Web Usage Mining Algorithm Based on Log File Data. *Journal of Theoretical & Applied Information Technology*, *92*(2), 215–224.

Anand, N., & Hilal, S. (2012). Identifying the User Access Pattern in Weblog Data. *International Journal of Computer Science and Information Technologies*, *3*(2), 3536–3539.

Anitha, V., & Isakki, P. (2016). A survey on predicting user behavior based on web server log files in a web usage mining. In *Proc. of International Conference on Computing Technologies and Intelligent Data Engineering*. IEEE. 10.1109/ICCTIDE.2016.7725340

Aye, T. T. (2011). Weblog cleaning for mining of web usage patterns. *Proc. of 3rd International Conference on Computer Research and Development IEEE*, 2(1), 490-494.

Chand, S., & Munishwar, R. (2017). Customer Behaviour Analysis using Web Usage Mining. *International Journal of Scientific Research in Computer Science and Engineering*, *5*(6), 47–50. doi:10.26438/ijsrcse/v5i6.4750

Chandra, B., Gupta, M., & Gupta, M. P. (2008). A multivariate time series clustering approach for crime trends prediction. In *Proc of International Conference on Systems, Man and Cybernetics*. IEEE. 10.1109/ICSMC.2008.4811393

Chaofeng, L. (2009). Research on web session clustering. *Journal of Software*, *4*(5), 460–468.

Chitraa, V., & Thanamani, A. S. (2014). Weblog Data Analysis by Enhanced Fuzzy C Means Clustering. *International Journal on Computational Sciences & Applications*, *4*(2), 81–95. doi:10.5121/ijcsa.2014.4209

Cooley, R., Mobasher, B., & Srivastava, J. (1999). Data preparation for mining world wide web browsing patterns. *Knowledge and Information Systems*, *1*(1), 5–32. doi:10.1007/BF03325089

Dwivedi, S. K., & Rawat, B. (2015). A review paper on data preprocessing: A critical phase in web usage mining process. In *Proc. of International Conference on Green Computing and Internet of Things*. IEEE. 10.1109/ICGCIoT.2015.7380517

Facca, F. M., & Lanzi, P. L. (2003). Recent developments in web usage mining research. In *International Conference on Data Warehousing and Knowledge Discovery*. Springer. 10.1007/978-3-540-45228-7_15

Goel, R., & Jain, S. (2014). Improvisation in Web Mining Techniques by Scrubbing Log Files. *International Journal of Advanced Research in Computer Science*, *5*(5), 87–91.

Gopalan, N. P., & Akilandeswari, J. (2005). A distributed, fault-tolerant multi-agent web mining system for scalable web search. *Proc. of WSEAS 5th International conference on Applied Informatics and Communications*, 15-7.

Han, J., & Kamber, M. (2011). *Data Mining: Concepts and Techniques* (3rd ed.). Morgan Kaufmann.

Jauha, S. K., & Pant, M. (2013). Recent trends in supply chain management: A soft computing approach. *Proc. of Seventh International Conference on Bio-Inspired Computing: Theories and Applications Springer*, 465-478. 10.1007/978-81-322-1041-2_40

Jeba, J. M. P., Bhuvaneswari, M. S., & Muneeswaran, K. (2016). Extracting usage patterns from web server log. In *Proc. of 2nd International Conference on Green High Performance Computing*. IEEE. 10.1109/ICGHPC.2016.7508074

Joshila Grace, L. K., Maheswari, V., & Nagamalai, D. (2011). Analysis of Weblogs and Web User in Web Mining. *International Journal of Network Security & Its Applications*, *3*(1), 99–110. doi:10.5121/ijnsa.2011.3107

Kaur, N., & Aggarwal, H. (2015). Weblog analysis for identifying the number of visitors and their behavior to enhance the accessibility and usability of website. *International Journal of Computers and Applications*, *110*(4), 25–30. doi:10.5120/19307-0759

Koutsoukos, D., Alexandridis, G., Siolas, G., & Stafylopatis, A. (2016). A new approach to session identification by applying fuzzy c-means clustering on weblogs. In *Proc. of Symposium Series on Computational Intelligence*. IEEE.

Kumar, A., Ahirwar, V., & Singh, R. K. (2015). A Study on Prediction of User Behavior Based on Web Server Log Files in Web Usage Mining. *International Journal of Engineering and Computer Science*, *6*(2), 20233–20236.

Kumar, V., & Thakur, R. S. (2018). Web Usage Mining: Concept and Applications at a Glance. In Handbook of Research on Pattern Engineering System Development for Big Data Analytics. IGI Global.

Liu, & Zhou, & Hongyan. (2007). Data preprocessing of web usage mining. *Computer Science*, *34*, 200-204.

Losarwar, V., & Joshi, M. (2012). Data preprocessing in web usage mining. *Proc. of International Conference on Artificial Intelligence and Embedded Systems,* 15-16.

Malviya, B. K., & Agrawal, J. (2015). A Study on Web Usage Mining Theory and Applications. In *Proc. of Fifth International Conference on Communication Systems and Network Technologies (CSNT)*. IEEE.

Mobasher, B., Cooley, R., & Srivastava, J. (2000). Automatic personalization based on web usage mining. *Communications of the ACM*, *43*(8), 142–151. doi:10.1145/345124.345169

Munk, M., Kapusta, J., & Švec, P. (2010). Data preprocessing evaluation for weblog mining: Reconstruction of activities of a web visitor. *Procedia Computer Science*, *1*(1), 2273–2280. doi:10.1016/j.procs.2010.04.255

Muskan & Garg. (2016). An Efficient Algorithm for Data Cleaning of Weblogs with Spider Navigation Removal. *International Journal of Computers and Applications*, *6*(3), 6–12.

Neelima & Rodda. (2016). Predicting user behavior through sessions using the weblog mining. In *Proc. of International Conference on Advances in Human Machine Interaction*. IEEE.

Parvatikar, S., & Joshi, A. (2014). Analysis of user behavior through web usage mining. *Proc. of ICAST–International Conference on Advances in Science and Technology*, 27-31.

Pushpalatha, N., & Reddy, S. S. S. (2017). Towards an extensible web usage mining framework for actionable knowledge. *Proc. of International Conference on Inventive Communication and Computational Technologies IEEE*, 35-40. 10.1109/ICICCT.2017.7975232

Rana, H., & Patel, M. (2013). A Study of Weblog Analysis Using Clustering Techniques. *International Journal of Innovative Research in Computer and Communication Engineering*, *1*(4), 925–929.

Reddy, K. S., Reddy, M. K., & Sitaramulu, V. (2013). An effective data preprocessing method for Web Usage Mining. In *Proc. of International Conference on Information Communication and Embedded Systems*. IEEE.

Resul, D., & Turkoglu, I. (2009). Creating meaningful data from web logs for improving the impressiveness of a website by using path analysis method. *Expert Systems with Applications*, *36*(3), 6635–6644. doi:10.1016/j.eswa.2008.08.067

Satokar, K. D., & Gawali, S. Z. (2010). Web Personalization Using Web Mining. *International Journal of Engineering Science and Technology*, *2*(3), 307–311.

Singh, S., & Badhe, V. (2014). An Exclusive Survey on Web Usage Mining for User Identification. *International Journal of Innovative Research in Computer and Communication Engineering*, *2*(11), 6582–6589.

Srivastava, M., Garg, R., & Mishra, P. K. (2015). Analysis of data extraction and data cleaning in Web usage mining. In *Proc. of International Conference on Advanced Research in Computer Science Engineering & Technology. ACM*. 10.1145/2743065.2743078

Suhasini, P., & Joshi, B. (2014). Analysis of user behavior through web usage mining. *Proc. of International Conference on Advances in Science and Technology*, 65-70.

Sukumar, P., Robert, L., & Yuvaraj, S. (2016). Review on modern Data Preprocessing techniques in Web usage mining (WUM). In *Proc. of International Conference on Computation System and Information Technology for Sustainable Solutions*. IEEE. 10.1109/CSITSS.2016.7779441

Talakokkula, A. (2015). A Survey on Web Usage Mining, Applications and Tools. *Computer Engineering and Intelligent Systems*, *6*(2), 22–29.

textarcana. (2014). *A Web Log Data Set From The Web Server Workload Characterization Project*. Retrieved July 2015 from https://gist.github.com/textarcana/ef3d391178e041ee5838

Wang, L., & Xiuju, F. (2002). Rule extraction using a novel gradient-based method and data dimensionality reduction. *Proc. of International Joint Conference on Neural Networks, 2*(1), 1275-1280.

Xie, K., Yu, H., & Cen, R. (2012). Using log mining to analyze user behavior on search engine. *Frontiers of Electrical and Electronic Engineering*, *7*(2), 254–260.

Yadav, M. P., Feeroz, M., & Yadav, V. K. (2012). Mining the customer behavior using web usage mining in e-commerce. In *Proc. of Third International Conference on Computing Communication & Networking Technologies*. IEEE. 10.1109/ICCCNT.2012.6395938

Zhong, X. (2011). The research and application of weblog mining based on the platform weka. *Procedia Engineering*, *6*(12), 521–524.

Chapter 8
Global Naming and Storage System Using Blockchain

Chanti S.
Pondicherry University, Pondicherry, India

Taushif Anwar
Pondicherry University, Pondicherry, India

Chithralekha T.
Pondicherry University, Pondicherry, India

V. Uma
https://orcid.org/0000-0002-7257-7920
Pondicherry University, Pondicherry, India

ABSTRACT

The global naming systems are used to resolve the DNS (domain name system) queries by providing the IP address of a particular domain. Humans are familiar in remembering the text rather than numbers. So the DNS servers help in resolving the human-readable domain names into system understandable IP address. In the current DNS architecture, there are several threats that cost a lot of damage to the organizations. At the earlier stage, DNS protocol lacks security assurance in place. To solve this issue, they introduced DNSSEC (subsequent DNS) as an additional layer of trust on top of DNS by providing authentication. Still, the current DNS servers couldn't address issues such as DoS/DDoS attacks. To address all these issues, blockchain technology offers an innovative method to handle those challenges. The existing naming systems are centralized, which is a major problem in achieving security.. The main aim of this chapter is to provide an overview of blockchain technology and a brief introduction to blockchain-based naming and storage systems.

DOI: 10.4018/978-1-7998-0186-3.ch008

INTRODUCTION

The Domain Name System (DNS) is introduced in the early days of the internet and mainly used for an academic and military purpose (Wei-hong, Meng, Lin, Jia-gui, & Yang, 2017). DNS is used to translate the human-readable names into the numerical address of the computer. At the early stage, a host file is maintained to store the human-readable name to represent the numerical address of a computer on ARPANET (Wikipedia, n.d.). Maintaining the host files in the long turn becomes much complex and to overcome this, Paul Mockapetris created the Domain Name System in early 1980s.

The DNS lacks in security features because they didn't think that the Internet will become popular and spread globally. Denial of Service Attack (DoS) becomes a major security threat to the DNS (Bisiaux, 2014). To overcome those security issues, DNSSEC is introduced to address the security problems created on DNS (Marrison, 2015). DNSSEC provides the authenticity and integrity of the information in DNS. But, the DNSSEC fails to address the confidentiality of the data because the data is not encrypted and so anyone can see the information and there is a possibility that the manipulation of information is also carried out.

Blockchain is a decentralized peer-to-peer network, in which all the nodes in the network share the same information (Wikipedia, 2019a). It is like a public ledger that is available with all the nodes in the network and so any type of insertion or updation of records can be ubiquitous. Bitcoin is the cryptocurrency used in blockchain for transferring digital money in a peer-to-peer network more securely (Crosby, Pattanayak, Verma, Kalyanaraman, 2016). The blockchain network is fully decentralized and there is no third party in between them (Iansiti & Lakhani, 2017; Pilkington, 2016). In the initial stages, the blockchain is used for the digital transaction using cryptocurrencies. In blockchain, the miner is a peer in the network who mines the set of transaction to create a new block and miners are rewarded for successful creation of a block. Later, the technology behind the blockchain is used for many purposes. Some real-time application of blockchain technologies are: voting system using blockchain, in food industry the blockchain helps end user to see all the stages from the former to the customer, blockchain based land registration process, blockain based DNS and so on (Foroglou & Tsilidou, 2015). Blockchain can be used for global naming and storage system that is fully decentralized and it also maintains the security level as higher (Wang, Wang, Guo, Du, Cheng, & Li, 2019). The blockchain based naming system can address the security issues in the traditional DNS.

A secured naming system is required to protect the privacy of the internet users. The structure of this book chapter is given as follows: Section-1 explains the basic concepts of DNS like how it works, what are the components and parties involved in creating a domain name and so on. Section-2 is about the potential threats systems. (For example, Denial of service attack, Zero-day attack, DNS cache poisoning, DNS hijacking) that current DNS couldn't failed to address. Section-3 provides the alternative solutions that are available to provide a secure internet i.e., blockchain based naming and storage system. Namecoin, Blockstack, Nebulis, Bitforest are the existing blockchain based naming systems. Finally section-4 provides the conclusion of the book chapter.

1. DOMAIN NAME SYSTEM (DNS)

Domain Name System (DNS) is a core part of the internet that translates the human-readable domain to the system understandable IP address (Wikipedia, n.d.; Brain, Chandler, & Crawford, 2002). Humans are familiar in remembering the text rather than numbers. So DNS servers are like internet phone that maintains the IP address of all domains. When the user search for any website (for example, www.google.com), the DNS server provides the IP address (216.58.195.238) of www.google.com and by using it the user connects to that server.

1.1. Components of DNS

The DNS servers have three main components Domain Name Space, Name Server, and Resolver. Each component is explained below in detail:

1.1.1. Domain Name Space

Domain Name Space is a hierarchical representation of domain names on the internet. In this hierarchy, one root server along with number of top-level domains are present. From the top-level domains, subdomains are registered. Likewise, it can go up to 127 levels. The top-level domains will have the information of their child nodes. Figure 1 shows the hierarchy of the Domain Name Space.

1.1.2. Name Server

Name servers store the information related to domain names and their corresponding IP addresses. It is very difficult to store all the DNS entries in a single server. Therefore, a delegation of the DNS server is required. The complete namespace is divided into zones. A DNS zone is any distinct, contiguous portion of the domain name space in the Domain Name System (DNS) for which administrative responsibility has been delegated to a single manager (Wikipedia). These zones are authoritative for the

Figure 1. Hierarchy of the domain name space

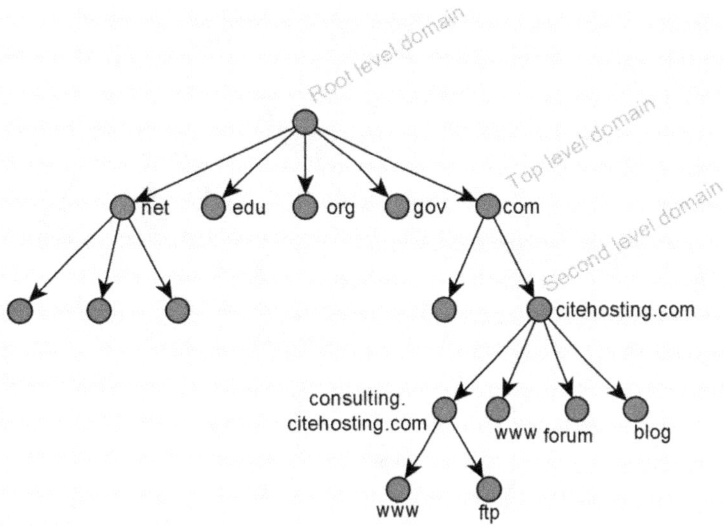

domain information they contain. Figure 2 explains the zones, where '.com' will be root, abc.com will be the primary domain and xyz.abc.com will be the secondary domain. The name servers are of two types- authoritative servers and caching server. The authoritative name server is again classified into primary name servers and secondary name servers.

1.1.3. Resolver

Resolvers are used to extract the domain name and IP address from the name server according to the user request. The resolver can directly get the information of a particular domain from the name server without any additional requirements. Resolving the DNS query can be either recursive or iterative. In recursive processes, the client asks for the IP address of google.com with Default DNS server and it provides the IP address. If it is not available, the Default DNS server contacts the root server to resolve the query. In return, the root server provides the '.com' server information. Now the Default DNS requests the IP address with '.com' server and it provides the IP address of google.com server. But in case of an iterative process, if the IP address of google.com is not available, then it queries the other DNS server to get the IP address. Figure 3 shows the recursive process and figure 4 shows the iterative process.

Figure 2. DNS Hierarchy with Zone Files

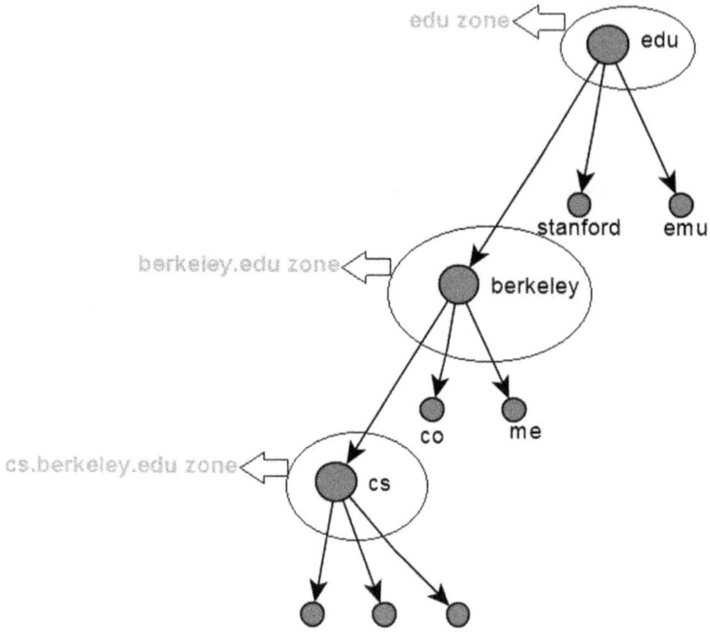

1.2. Domain Name Registration Processes

To register a domain, the registrant should register the domain with ICANN-accredited registrar (Parsons, Coffman, & Rechterman, 2011; Thoke, 2019; Network Solutions, n.d.). Later the registrar will check for the availability of the domain and the request

Figure 3. Recursive DNS Query Process

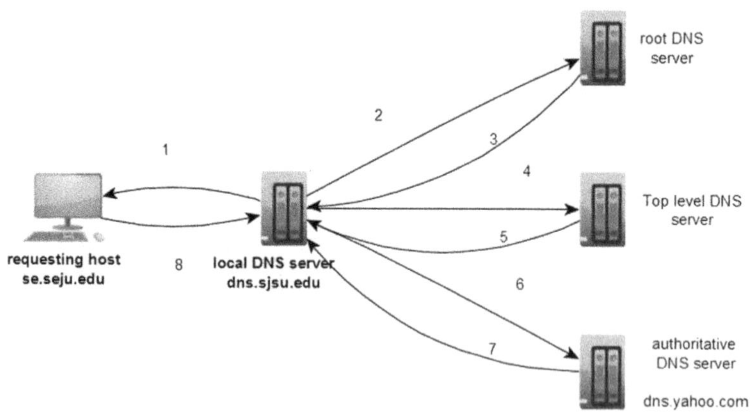

Figure 4. Iterative DNS Query Process

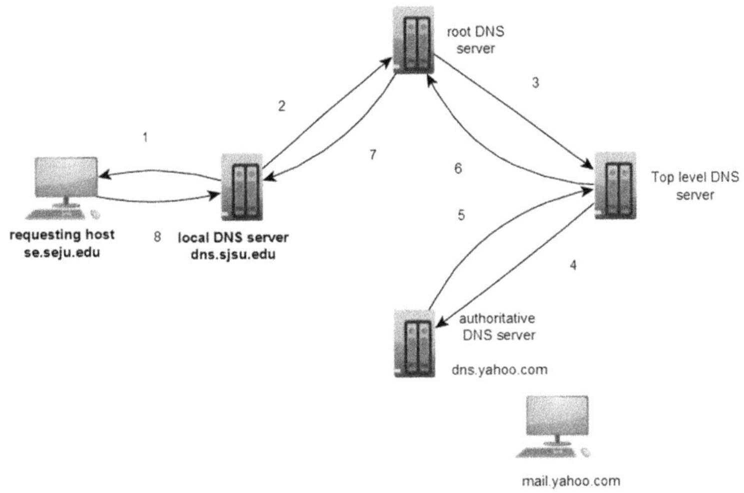

will be considered only if it is available. For every domain, there will be an expiry date and it offers the renewal of ownership. The owner of a domain can also resell their domain(s) through the registrar. There are five parties that are involved in this process of registration of the domain as shown in figure 5.

1.2.1. ICANN

The institution, Internet Corporation for Assigned Names and Numbers (ICANN) is a non-profit organization that administrates the task assigned for both IP address and domain names. ICANN is responsible for handling the root server along with the direction of Top Level Domains (TLD) name scheme process. The system makes mutual agreements between the registries and registrars that offer the foundation for the creation of the WHOIS system.

1.2.2. Registry

Registries are incharge of keeping the registry for each TLD. Normally, the registries have some obligations that comprises of accommodating registration requests from registrars. It also communicates directly from domain name registrants, preserving essential domain name registration data in a database and it broadcasts the zone file data with the help of name servers (i.e. gives details about the site information of a domain name) via Internet.

1.2.3. *Registrar*

Registrars are an organization licensed by ICANN and authorized by the registries to deal with domain names. They are tied up by the Registrar Accreditation Agreement (RAA) with ICANN and they create their contracts with the registries. The registrar responsibilities are set out by RAA which includes WHOIS database maintenance, entry of data to registries, alleviate WHOIS queries by the public, safeguarding details of domain name registrants, and obeying RAA conditions regarding termination period of the domain name registration.

1.2.4. *Reseller*

Several domain name registrants choose to register the domains via **reseller** for the organization. These organizations made an agreement with registrars and offer services like email mailboxes, web hosting, etc. Resellers sell registrar(s) services through the mutual agreement between them; because of that, they are not licensed by ICANN. However, these types of domain registration still support the registration for whom they are reselling.

1.2.5. *Registrant*

The domain name has been registered by **domain name registrant.** The registrant may be a person or organization. Generally, domain name registrant registers their domain through online or through reseller who is available at that time. In addition to the domain name registering, the domain names itemized on name servers are required in order to customize the domain name to reach the internet as quickly as possible through domain name registrant. Sometimes, if the registrar cannot compromise this service on that time, domain name registrant is accountable for obtaining or presenting his or her own name server.

2. CHALLENGES IN USING THE CURRENT DNS SERVERS

ICANN is a non-profit organization that only maintains all the registries of DNS. The DNS servers are prone to several attacks, which can increase gradually. DNSSEC is an additional layer of protection that protects users from intruders. But still, several attacks are happening by spoofing the records, poisoning the DNS entries and so on. Some major DNS attacks have been discussed here.

Figure 5. Domain registration process and the parties involved in it

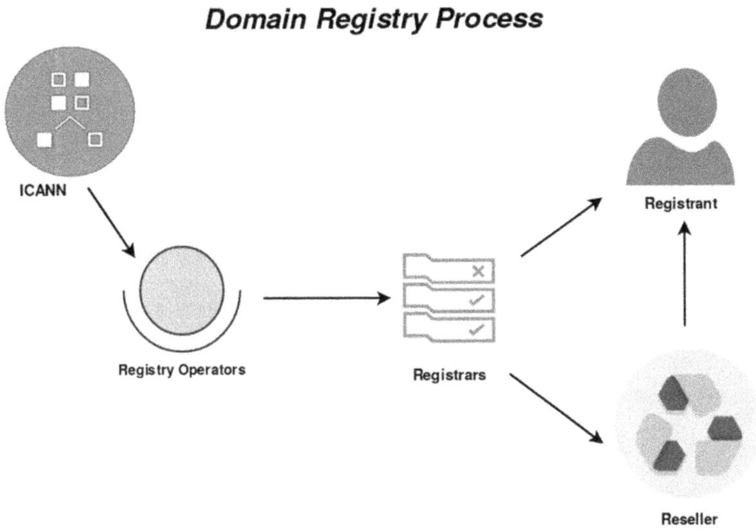

2.1. DNS Spoofing/ Cache Poisoning

In DNS Spoofing (Wikipedia, 2019b), the attackers corrupt the DNS entries of a particular domain and it is cached by the resolver. When the user tries to access the site, the resolver provides the wrong IP address that redirects the user to attackers' server. This results in redirection of users to a spoofed site. Figure 6 describes the DNS spoofing process.

2.2. Denial of Service Attack (DoS)

The Denial of Service Attacks (Fulton, 2016; Rouse, n.d.) is done to prevent the legitimate internet user to access the website by flooding or crashing the server. Rarely the attacker crashes the server and most of the time they flood the server by sending multiple spoofed packets. This slows down the system for legitimate users. For example, if a user sends a request packet to the site, in response the server has to reply the client's request as shown in figure 7. In a DoS attack, the server receives hundreds and thousands of requests which delays the intended users' service.

2.3. Distributed Denial of Service Attack (DDoS)

The Distributed Denial of Service Attack (DDoS) (Rouse, n.d.; Yusof, Udzir, & Selamat, 2019) is the advanced level of DoS attack, where the attacker targets the

Figure 6. DNS spoofing attack

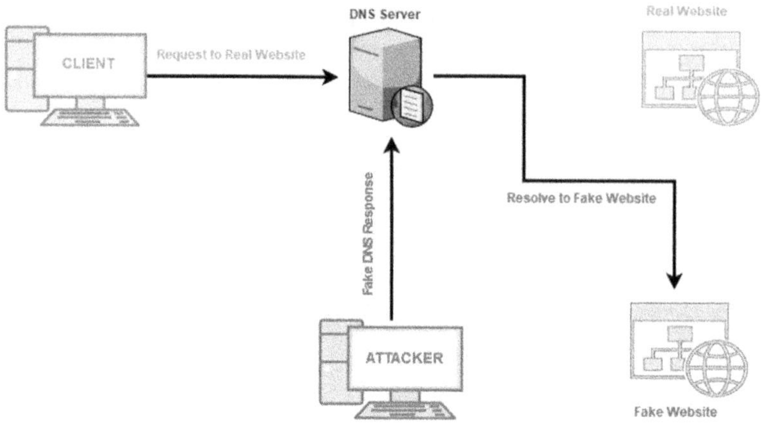

particular website or the server with multiple corrupted computers for flooding. The DoS attack uses a single computer to attack the target as shown in figure 8. But in DDoS, the attacker uses the multiple compromised computers together to shut down or crash the server.

2.4. Zero Day Attack

Zero Data vulnerability (Rijnetu, 2017) is a fault within the software, hardware which is not known to the developers. The zero-day attack occurs only when the attacker finds the loophole in the system hardware or software and attacks the system before

Figure 7. Denial of service attack (DoS)

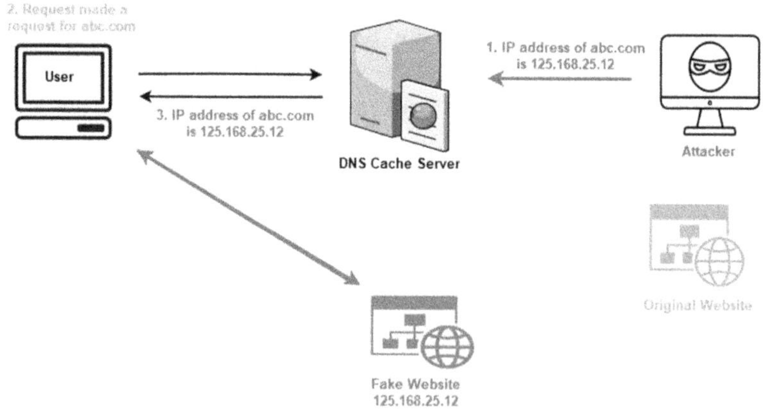

Figure 8. Distributed denial of service (DDoS)

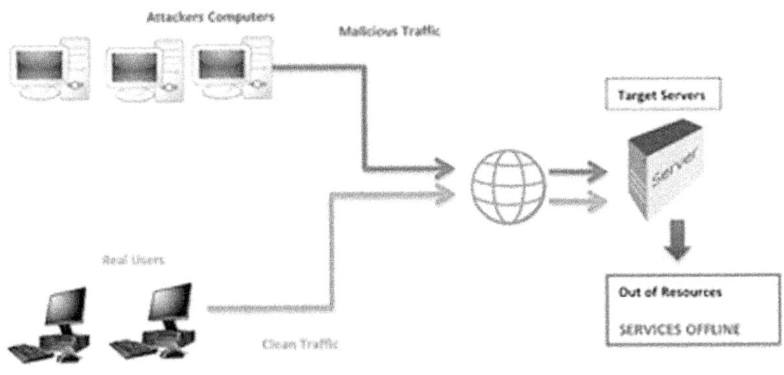

the developer comes to know about the flaw. The complete life cycle of Zero day vulnerability is shown in figure 9.

2.5. DNS Hijacking

DNS hijacking (Qadir, 2018) is one type of DNS attack, in which the user gets the wrong IP address for the requested domain. In this attack, the intruder modifies the DNS entries by installing the malicious code in the user system and modifies the host files. Otherwise, affects the DNS server by replacing IP address of a domain with the IP address of a server which is under the control of the attacker. In figure 10, it is clearly shown how the attacker changes the DNS entries.

3. BLOCKCHAIN BASED NAMING AND STORAGE SYSTEM

The blockchain-based naming system provides the internet in a decentralized manner, where there is no centralized entity to provide the service. It also addresses the current

Figure 9. Zero day attack life cycle

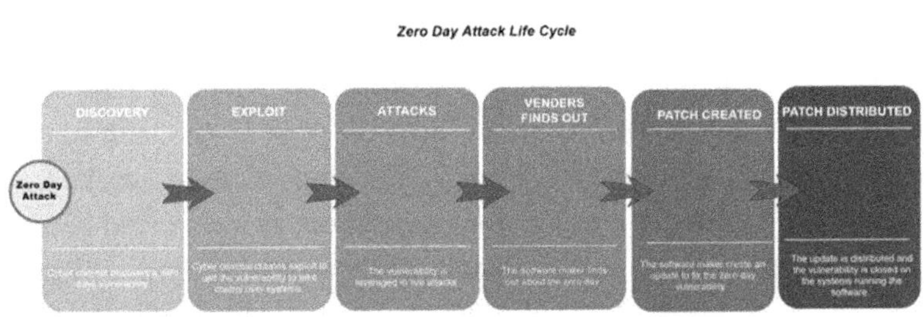

Figure 10. DNS hijacking

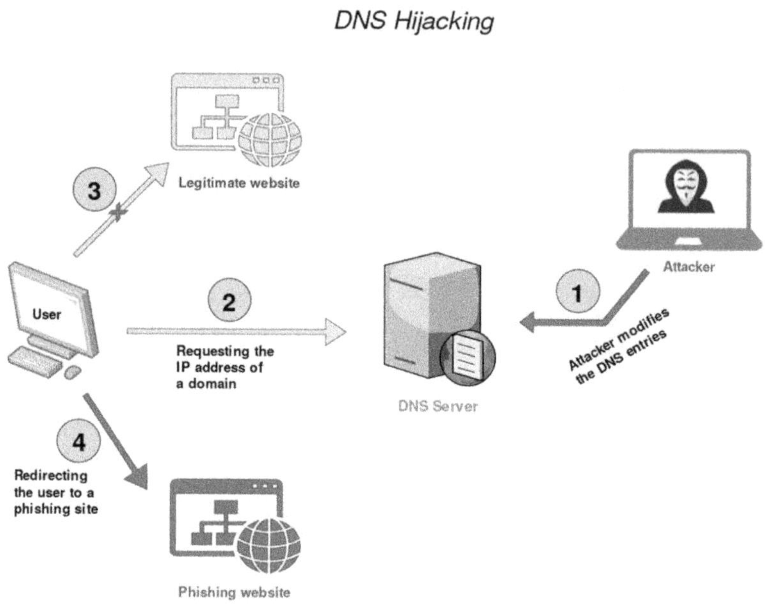

security issues facing by the traditional DNS. In recent years, many blockchain based naming system had been developed and it provides the correct information to the users in a decentralized manner. According to Zooko Wilcox-O'Hearn (2001), any naming system should satisfy the three principles of Zooko's Triangle as shown in the figure 11. Human readable, secure and decentralized are the three principles and the traditional DNS provides only two principles (i.e. human readable and secure). DNSSEC is an additional layer of traditional DNS which provides the security. But still, it fails to address many security issues like DoS, DDoS, DNS Hijacking, Poisoning the DNS entries. The blockchain is the first solution that satisfies all the principles of Zooko's triangle in developing the global naming and storage system. Namecoin, Blockstack, Nebulis, and Ethereum based naming system are the example for blockchain DNS.

3.1. Namecoin

Namecoin (Kalodner, Carlsten, Ellenbogen, Bonneau, & Narayanan, 2015) is an alternative to the current DNS system and it is the first blockchain based naming and storage system. Namecoin is originally developed based on the concept of bitcoin blockchain. Normally bitcoin stores the information related to a particular transaction that can be stored in blockchain in the form of blocks. But namecoin

Figure 11. Zooko's triangle

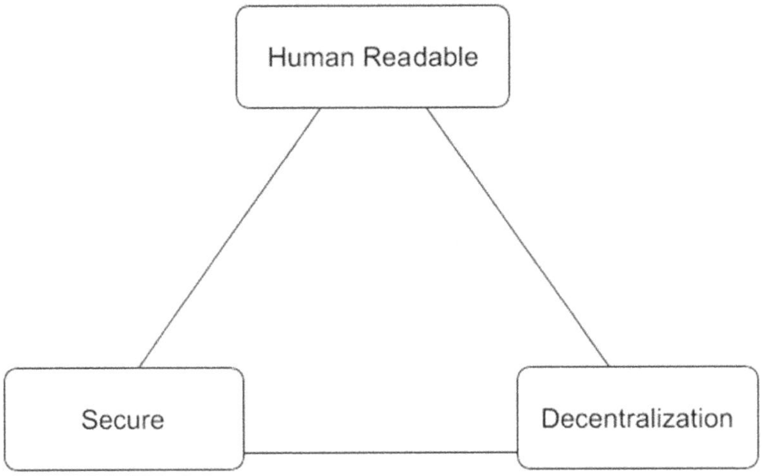

is a modified version of bitcoin that stores the content other than the transaction information like registration and storing the domain names. Namecoin follows the same mathematical logic followed by bitcoin during mining and it also introduces the concept of merged mining to reduce double spending. Merged mining helps in allowing cryptocurrencies that work on the same algorithm for mining both symmetrically. The main purpose of introducing Namecoin is:

- To provide an alternative to traditional DNS.
- It won't depend on any third-party for Censorship- resistance (Only the owner have the right to make changes on the domain that they purchased).
- It provides security, privacy and very fast.
  - **Security**: Fingerprint of the certificate owned by an owner is stored in the blockchain, which is trusted because of its proof of work.
  - **Privacy**: There is no resolver to resolve the domain name in Namecoin (all the data is stored locally). So the user can get the IP address of the required domain locally without a resolver.
  - **Fast**: It takes less time for getting the IP address of a Domain because it doesn't depend on any resolver. DNS takes 100ms to resolve a domain whereas Namecoin takes only 3ms to resolve a domain.

Namecoin is the first Blockchain based naming system that satisfies all the three conditions of Zooko's triangle (Human-meaningful, Decentralized, and secure). Using namecoin, we can register a domain, resolve the domain names registered using blockchain, renew the domains, and transfer the ownership to other users. The

Name server operator, registrars, registries are not required in Namecoin Blockchain. Unlike traditional DNS, the blockchain based naming system (namecoin) doesn't have too many top-level domains. All the domains registered using namecoin will have '.bit' as a top-level domain. Due to limited storage capacity in blocks, namecoin can only offer the domain names of 64 characters length. In Blockchain, every node in the network contains the complete information of all the transaction available locally. Namecoin provides two types of storage facilities i.e. locally stored Blockchain and remotely stored Blockchain. Namecoin can address the DNS attacks like *Packet interception, ID guessing and query prediction, Name chaining (similar to cache poisoning), Betrayal by trusted servers, authenticated denial of domain names, Denial of service attack, and wildcards*. The Namecoin addresses the following questions:

1. How does Namecoin work?

   – Using Blockchain technology.

2. What are the current shortcomings of the DNS system?

   – Centralized control and no encryption is offered.

3. Which of the shortcomings of the DNS does Namecoin address?

   – All the attacks listed above only when the data is stored locally.

4. Can Namecoin match the robustness of the DNS?

   – Yes. P2p systems that ensure all nodes with fewer resources.

5. What are the consequences for the different organizational roles like DNS operators, registrars, (root) registries, etc.?

   – Name server operators, registrars, and registries are not required in Namecoin.

6. How would a transition scenario from the DNS to Namecoin look like?

   – Using a client application and parallel resolving of queries.

3.2. Blockstack

Blockstack is a blockchain based naming system developed after the deployment of Namecoin. They found that one single miner is holding more than 51% of computational power on Namecoin blockchain (Ali, Nelson, shea, & Freedman, 2016). In Blockchain, the 51% attack is very dangerous and it impacts the security of blockchain. If the one miner or mining pool (set of miner formed as a group) contains more than 51% of computational power, they can deny the legitimate transaction and double spending is also possible. Namecoin uses merged mining, which is not practically feasible. This is the reason why they used bitcoin in their update blockchain based naming system called Blockstack and the complete architecture is shown in figure 12. The Blockstack addresses the following:

- Identified the 51% attack in Namecoin blockchain.
- The issues faced with merged mining.
- Successful migration from Namecoin to Blockstack.
- Introduced a new design for the blockchain based naming system.

In Blockstack, blockchain is at the bottom layer and on top of it, there is a logical layer for maintaining the naming system. It uses blockchain to achieve the consensus on the state of the naming system and bind these names to the data. Based on the consensus protocol of the blockchain, Blockstack can provide all operations like registering the names, updates, transferring the ownership of the domain name. This can be done by separating control pane from the data plane.

The control plane is for registering the human-readable domain names. The first layer of the control plane is blockchain and the second layer is a virtualchain (logical layer) on top of the blockchain. Once the domain name is registered, binding of domain names with the respective hash (name, hash) is done and binds with the owner's key pairs.

The data plane is to store the data and make it available for everyone. Since the blockchain has limited storage, the Blockstack uses a separate layer to store the data and access these data through zone file. It works similar to traditional DNS, but it identifies the data by hash value or URL. Storage systems like S3 and IPFS are used and the data values are signed with owners' public key before storing so that only the owner can modify the content with the help of a private key.

Blockstack contains four layers, in which two layers are in control plane and two layers are in the data plane. Each of these layers is explained below in detail.

Figure 12. Blockstack architecture (Ali et al., 2016)

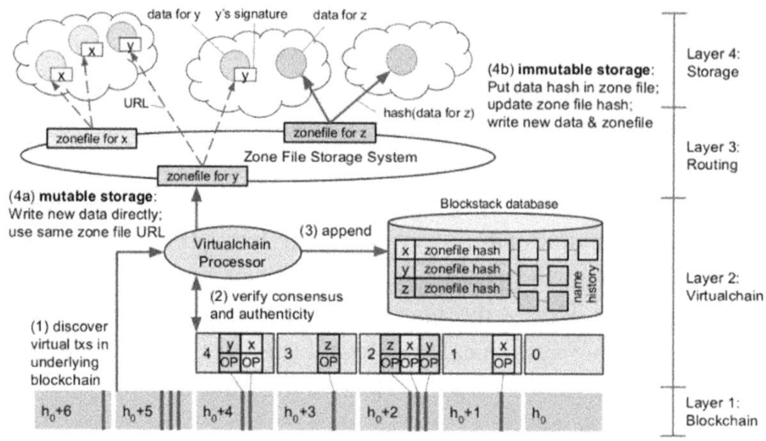

3.2.1. *Layer 1: Blockchain*

The blockchain inhabits the lowermost tier and is utilized for two purposes: it stores the series of Blockstack operations and it offers agreement on the basis of the order were the operations are written. Blockstack operations are encrypted during transactions based on the principal of blockchain.

3.2.2. Layer 2: Virtualchain

Layer 2 is the virtualchain which is present over the blockchain. Virtualchain describes novel operations that don't require any changes to the blockchain principles. Most of the Blockstack operations are carried out in virtualchain layer in addition to that the data in metadata are encrypted during a legal blockchain transaction. The execution of Blockstack operations are carried out in virtualchain layer but only the raw data transactions are shown by the Blockchain nodes. The virtualchain also outlines the rules for accepting or rejecting Blockstack operations. If the blockstack operations are accepted then the virualchain stores the data universally along with the condition that state variations at any certain state. Different kinds of state machines are developed with the help of Virtualchain. Presently, Blockstack has a distinct state machine for universal naming and storage method.

3.2.3. *Layer 3: Routing*

The blockstack maintains the routing layer apart from the storage. The routing layer helps to discover the data. Blockstacks support multiple storage providers which solve the problem of data storage. Like traditional DNS, the blockstack uses zone files to store the Routing Information. The zone files are stored in the routing layer. If the user wants to verify the integrity of the zone files, it can be done by simply verifying the hash values. The zone files contain the hash values that bind the names with their respective data.

3.2.4. *Layer 4: Storage*

The storage layer is the top layer in the blockstack that maintains the actual data. Every information stored is signed digitally with the owners key. Blockstack provides two types of storage facilities.

1. **Mutable Storage**: Mutable storage is the default way of storage provided by blockstack. The zone file contains the URI that identifies the data and the data is stored only after signing it with the owners' private key. The zone file remains the same but the data can be altered according to the owner's concern. The user can check the integrity of the data through the name owner's public key.
2. **Immutable Storage**: The immutable storage is also same as mutable storage but it maintains an additional TXT file in a zone file that stores the hash values. In immutable storage, the data once entered cannot be altered. So, when there is any modification in the data it is updated accordingly. The users can check the integrity of the zone file and the data with the hash values and the public key of the owner. In order to maintain the most updated information in the zone files, the updates are considered as a transaction.

3.3. Nebulis

Nebulis is a decentralized and uncensorable internet that uses IPFS as storage, a transport layer and ethereum based blockchain for DNS activities (Mosakheil, 2018). Nebulis contains smart contracts with some set of rules that administrates the creation of new clusters. The root contract creates the clusters and these clusters are autonomous contracts that control the top-level domains. Within the clusters, they have their own indexes that help in mapping the owners' ethereum address to a UTF-8 encoded string URL and later maps resources with IPFS Hash. Like another mining process, if a new record is created in Nebulis blockchain, the system awards a token called Dust (DST). The entire nebulis system is divided into several core contracts of the system as shown in the figure 13.

Figure 13. The nebulis system with different contracts

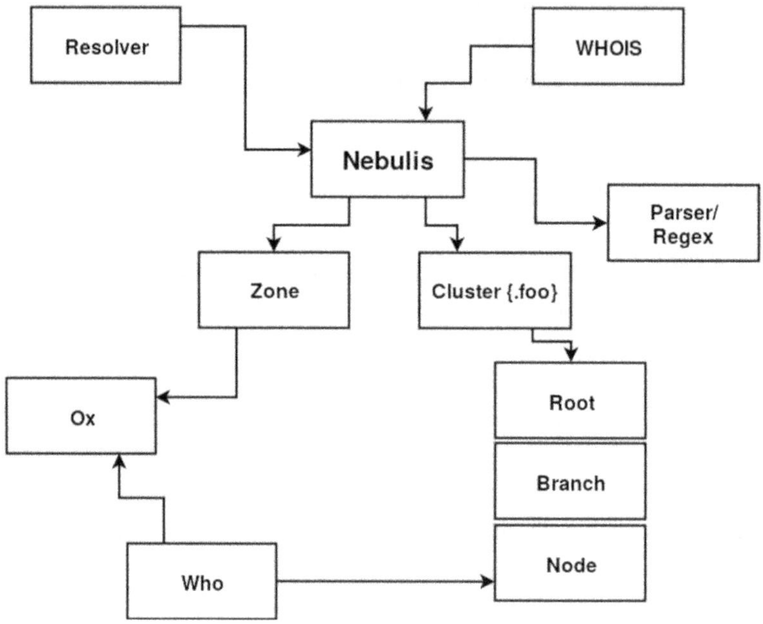

- **Nebulis:** Responsible for the creation & administration of clusters, zones, and redirection of queries.
- **Whois:** Search for the existence of domains and clusters.
- **Resolver:** Resolves the URL and returns the IPFS resource.
- **Who:** Who is a contract that holds the domains, address and the link to the database node of a new user who creates a domain.
- **Zones:** Portion of users managed as a group.
- **Clusters:** A cluster is top-level-domains that can be created by anyone by generating the Dust. Within a cluster, we can create as many domains as possible.
- **Root/Branch/Node:** All the entries in a cluster are indexed alphabetically and it can go up to three levels.
- **Parser/Regex:** Only a valid character sets is activated during the cluster creation.
- **Ox:** Ox contracts pay the miners for the domains that are ejected.

3.4. Bitforest

Bitforest is a blockchain based naming system that combines the features of Blockstack and EthIKS (Dong, Kim, & Boutaba, 2018). In Bitforest they maintain a centralized lookup service for policy enforcement and uses blockchain data structure. This is to increase the efficiency of mapping the names with their hash values. Dues to centralized storage, it is very conformable for administrators. Based on the existing blockchain, Bitforest follows the following three principles:

1. **Blockchain Portability***:* The bitforest blockchain wont't rely on any particular blockchain. The blockchains with its security based on the concept of spending the unspent transaction output at once. Bitforest adopts all blockchain based on their application and compatibility.
2. **Centralized Administration***:* Managing the namespace is done centralized to provide better security and flexible administration. A centralized provider can increase performance by indexing the blockchain and maintaining blockchain data structures as existing "hybrid" blockchain naming systems.
3. **Decentralized Identity Retention***:* The administration is centralized but no identity. There is a chance that an attacker can modify the name-value bindings without any authorization from the owner. In such cases, the identity retention is very much helpful.

CONCLUSION

In this chapter, we have explained about DNS (a naming system that resolves the human-readable domain names into the system understandable IP addresses), components of DNS, security threats and addressing mechanisms focused on current DNS. DNSSEC has been introduced to address the security issues in DNS, which is not a feasible solution. Then the blockchain is introduced as an alternative naming and storage system. Further we explained about blockchain, how it works, a complete blockchain based naming and storage system and some existing blockchain based DNS in detail. Namecoin is the first blockchain based naming system and later Blockstack, Nebulis and Bitforest are developed. Even blockchain has its own limitations like storage limit, requires more computation power, and 51% attack (a single miner holds more than 51% of computation power). Blockstack addressed the storage issue by storing the information in a separate layer. Since blockchain is an emerging technology, more research is required to address the issues.

REFERENCES

Ali, M., Nelson, J., Shea, R., & Freedman, M. J. (2016). Blockstack: A global naming and storage system secured by blockchains. In *2016 USENIX Annual Technical Conference (USENIX ATC 16)* (pp. 181-194). USENIX.

Bisiaux, J. Y. (2014). DNS threats and mitigation strategies. *Network Security*, *2014*(7), 5–9. doi:10.1016/S1353-4858(14)70068-6

Brain, M., Chandler, N., & Crawford, S. (2002). *How domain name servers work*. Retrieved from https://computer.howstuffworks.com/dns.htm

Crosby, M., Pattanayak, P., Verma, S., & Kalyanaraman, V. (2016). Blockchain technology: Beyond bitcoin. *Applied Innovation*, *2*(6-10), 71.

Dong, Y., Kim, W., & Boutaba, R. (2018, November). Bitforest: a Portable and Efficient Blockchain-Based Naming System. In *2018 14th International Conference on Network and Service Management (CNSM)* (pp. 226-232). IEEE.

Foroglou, G., & Tsilidou, A. L. (2015, May). Further applications of the blockchain. *12th Student Conference on Managerial Science and Technology*.

Fulton, S. (2015, February 20). *Top 10 DNS attacks likely to infiltrate your network*. Retrieved from https://www.networkworld.com/article/2886283/top-10-dns-attacks-likely-to-infiltrate-your-network.html#slide3

Iansiti, M., & Lakhani, K. R. (2017). The truth about blockchain. *Harvard Business Review*, *95*(1), 118–127.

Kalodner, H. A., Carlsten, M., Ellenbogen, P., Bonneau, J., & Narayanan, A. (2015, June). *An Empirical Study of Namecoin and Lessons for Decentralized Namespace Design*. WEIS.

Marrison, C. (2015). Understanding the threats to DNS and how to secure it. *Network Security*, *2015*(10), 8–10. doi:10.1016/S1353-4858(15)30090-8

Mosakheil, J. H. (2018). *Security Threats Classification in Blockchains*. Retrieved from https://repository.stcloudstate.edu/cgi/viewcontent.cgi?article=1093&context=msia_etds

Network Solutions. (n.d.). *6 Steps to Registering a Successful Domain Name*. Retrieved from http://www.networksolutions.com/education/registering-domain-names/

Parsons, R. R., Coffman, J. T., & Rechterman, B. J. (2011). *U.S. Patent No. 7,996,457*. Washington, DC: U.S. Patent and Trademark Office.

Pilkington, M. (2016). 11 Blockchain technology: principles and applications. *Research handbook on digital transformations, 225.*

Qadir, M. (2018, April 5). *What is DNS hijacking and How It Works?* Retrieved from https://www.purevpn.com/blog/dns-hijacking/

Rijnetu, I. (2017). *Security Alert: MS Office Zero Day and DNS Vulnerabilities Can Impact Users*. Retrieved from https://heimdalsecurity.com/blog/security-alert-microsoft-vulnerabilities-in-office-and-dns/

Rouse, M. (n.d.). *DNS Attack*. Retrieved from https://searchsecurity.techtarget.com/definition/DNS-attack

Thoke, O. (2019, June 24). *Understanding Domain Names and the Registration Process*. Retrieved from https://www.lifewire.com/domain-names-and-registration-process-3473709

Wang, J., Wang, S., Guo, J., Du, Y., Cheng, S., & Li, X. (2019). A Summary of Research on Blockchain in the Field of Intellectual Property. *Procedia Computer Science*, *147*, 191–197. doi:10.1016/j.procs.2019.01.220

Wei-hong, H. U., Meng, A. O., Lin, S. H. I., Jia-gui, X. I. E., & Yang, L. I. U. (2017). Review of blockchain-based DNS alternatives. *网络与信息安全学报, 3*(3), 71-77.

Wikipedia. (2019a, June 26). *Blockchain*. Retrieved from https://en.wikipedia.org/wiki/Blockchain

Wikipedia. (2019b). *DNS spoofing*. Retrieved from https://en.wikipedia.org/w/index.php?title=DNS_spoofing&oldid=891592674

Wikipedia. (n.d.). *Special*. Retrieved from https://en.wikipedia.org/w/index.php?title=Special

Wilcox-O'Hearn, Z. (2001). *Names: Distributed, secure, human-readable: Choose two*. Retrieved from https://web.archive.org/web/ 20011020191610/http://zooko.com/distnames.html

Yusof, A. R. A., Udzir, N. I., & Selamat, A. (2019). Systematic literature review and taxonomy for DDoS attack detection and prediction. *International Journal of Digital Enterprise Technology*, *1*(3), 292–315. doi:10.1504/IJDET.2019.097849

Chapter 9
Impact of Bitcoin on the World Economy:
Opportunities and Challenges

Harshita Patel
VIT University, India

Sadhana Burla
KLEF, India

Manjula Josephine B.
KLEF, India

ABSTRACT

Bitcoin has brought a revolution in digital market. Bitcoin doesn't follow any supervisory body or central authority to control it. Unlike any country's currency, it is not supervised by a government. It flows on networks and is managed by decentralized actors. Like any other innovation, bitcoin also has pros and cons associated with it. In this chapter, the authors discuss all the opportunities and challenges related to bitcoin and its impact on the world economy.

WHAT IS BITCOIN AND ITS EMERGENCE

Bitcoin is a well known cryptocurrency running over network without direct interference of any authoritative body or any financial institution that is direct transfer from one party to other. It is also known as cash running over internet. The pseudo founder of bitcoin Satoshi Nakamoto brought this concept of virtual currency which is becoming very popular in fact it could be said that over the past few years, Bitcoins

DOI: 10.4018/978-1-7998-0186-3.ch009

Figure 1. Bitcoin: A cryptocurrency (Godbole, 2019)

are gaining vital importance round the world. The system was developed with the thought of maintaining crypt proof to make possible direct transactions between two parties without the need of trusting the third one i.e. peer to peer transaction. In his paper, Satoshi Nakamoto has provided full description of Bitcoin (Nakamoto, n.d.). It is very obvious to feel the difference between functioning of the traditional currencies and Bitcoin and their impacts by the all type of financial institutions such as stock markets or any nation's finance departments. So it is becoming needed to project the direct effect of popularity of Bitcoin in world's economy. Here in this chapter we are discussing the same with possible aspects.

Effect on Different Financial Institutions

Though the effect of digital currency on the Global Economy is one of extraordinary discussion, it should be seen that how it is affecting different financial institutions in which manner; is it common for all or specific to the agency? Financial institutions may range from any country's government finance department to stock market, online transfers to Banks and GDPs or anything which may affect economy directly or indirectly.

It is a well known and generally accepted fact that world economy principally depends on the US Dollar which is being treated as reserve currency for global economy. So any ups and downs in US market directly affect the world economy, year 2008 financial slowdown is a life-size example of it. This so called US Dollar based global economy is working in traditional manner that is following the governing authorities and trusting the third parties. The ever increasing popularity of Bitcoin is somehow looking as challenging to this legendary system (Unocoin, 2017; ACQUI Technology, n.d.).

Figure 2. Governments and Bitcoin (Digdaga, 2017)

On Governments

Governments of many countries are directly rejecting the concept of cryptocurrency or Bitcoins for their nation's economy while some are getting ready to accept this global financial challenge. In both the cases of accepting or rejecting Bitcoins for their economies, countries have their own set of valid reasons. Such as at one end Bitcoins are safer currency in terms of storage because it is digital, and also secure due to high encryption while running over network and direct transaction among peers. But on the other hand as it is not bound with any centralized or authoritative system, it is not easy to control the flow of money. Beside of the advantages, Bitcoin came with some pitfalls too. Because of non existence of any superior body, transactions may be affected by threats and frauds. Money laundering and use of cryptocurrency in crime may directly be able to affect the security of any nation which will be intolerable for any government (McWhinney, 2019).

On Banks

Banking sector is one of the first financial institutions to be affected by the emergence of cryptocurrency, especially from the most popular cryptocurrency Bitcoin. Banks are playing the most important role in handling money of any country and its credibility. But because of Bitcoin, which is directly neglecting the existence of any authority in between peers, also it is highly technically strong in terms of security due to encryption, challenging the way of working of banks. Banks are also not in the

Figure 3. Bitcoin and banks (Landewednack House, n.d.)

position of just sit and watch; they need to find out the way to deal with this kind of comparatively new system of money exchange (Building Global Democracy, 2017).

On Stock Market

The effect of Bitcoin is also non deniable over stock markets, even if it is indirect in nature. It is coming into the picture of any stock exchange with the companies dealing with Blockchain or other cryptocurrency related technologies. Also it has shown its presence over the world stock exchanges with high value gains many times. Though some countries including a big economy China have ban the Bitcoin because of its high volatile nature (Pollack, 2018).

Why Control Matters

Traditionally banks are controlling the flow of currency of any country as per their financial policies under the supervision of their governments. Bitcoin is designed especially to be free from any such control. In encrypted environment Bitcoin is flowing over internet in peer to peer fashion. In traditional banking and financial system all activities related to currency will be under the control of government as all money related activities i.e. tax collection, control over criminal activities etc. While Bitcoin is emerging as less predictable and less responsible version of global currency which is not responsible to any authoritative body as bank or government. Also even after good encryptions, hackings are not getting stopped and owner of Bitcoins are being looted so far. Because of all such reasons so many countries are still in dilemma to permit the flow of Bitcoin in their country and trades (Medium, 2018).

CONCLUSION

Today's buzz word Bitcoin though sounds attractive it is also having two faces like a normal coin. At one hand, it has already left shocking impact over world economy because of its idea of direct transactions without third party intervention; on the other hand the same freedom is becoming threat to the existing centralized bank concepts. Again in the condition of hacking, the owner has to lose his money and there is no responsible board or group exist to look over it. It is needed to be known that founder himself is an elusive personality, didn't appear in front of the world, even he may one person or a group of programmers. So if one is planning to invest in Bitcoins, they should study all risk over the time. In this chapter we have discussed the benefits and loopholes Bitcoin and its impact on world economy.

REFERENCES

ACQUI Technology. (n.d.). *The Impact of Cryptocurrency on the Global Economy*. Retrieved from https://acquitechnology.com/2018/07/07/the-impact-of-cryptocurrency-on-the-global-economy/

Building Global Democracy. (2017). *The Impact of Cryptocurrency on Banks*. Retrieved from http://buildingglobaldemocracy.org/impact-cryptocurrency-banks/

Digdaga. (2017). *Debate: Are Governments Against Bitcoin & Blockchain? Or Do They Love it and Want Us to Use it?* Retrieved from https://steemit.com/bitcoin/@digdaga/is-governments-against-bitcoin-and-blockchain-or-do-they-love-it-and-want-us-to-use-it

Godbole, O. (2019). *Bitcoin Price On Track to End Six-Month Losing Streak*. Retrieved from https://www.coindesk.com/bitcoin-price-on-track-to-end-six-month-losing-streak

Landewednack House. (n.d.). *Landewednack House*. Retrieved from http://www.landewednackhouse.com/

McWhinney, J. (2019). *Why governments Are Afraid of Bitcoin*. Retrieved from https://www.investopedia.com/articles/forex/042015/why-governments-are-afraid-bitcoin.asp

Medium. (2018). *How Cryptocurrency is Disrupting the Global Economy*. Retrieved from https://medium.com/the-mission/how-cryptocurrency-is-disrupting-the-global-economy-89347581aa93

Nakamoto, S. (n.d.). *Bitcoin: A Peer-to-Peer Electronic Cash System*. Retrieved from https://bitcoin.org/bitcoin.pdf

Pollock, D. (2018). *So Is There a Correlation Between Bitcoin and Stock Market? Yes, But No*. Retrieved from https://cointelegraph.com/news/so-is-there-a-correlation-between-bitcoin-and-stock-market-yes-but-no

Unocoin. (2017). *How Has Bitcoin changed the Global Economy?* Retrieved from https://blog.unocoin.com/how-has-bitcoin-changed-the-global-economy-e33fac2e2316

Section 3
Security and Applications of Blockchain

Chapter 10
Protection to Personal Data Using Decentralizing Privacy of Blockchain.

Vilas Baburao Khedekar
https://orcid.org/0000-0003-4229-1937
VIT University, India

Shruti Sangmesh Hiremath
Jayawantrao Sawant College of Engineering, India

Prashant Madhav Sonawane
Jayawantrao Sawant College of Engineering, India

Dharmendra Singh Rajput
VIT University, India

ABSTRACT

In today's world, we deal with various online services, where each person deals with various technologies. These technologies are made for people to make our access to the new world easily. There is a tremendous use of online applications, websites which require large storage. Large data is handled by the online systems. The collection of data in the whole world is about 20% in the last few years. The data is captured from the user, controlled by the systems, and operations are performed on data. It requires more system accuracy and protection to personal data. But the person does not know about the data, where and how it is used where it is stored or whether the data is handled by some organisations for their own use or data is been hacked by another person. This chapter explores protection of data using the decentralized privacy of blockchain.

DOI: 10.4018/978-1-7998-0186-3.ch010

INTRODUCTION

In today's world we deal with various online services, where each person deals with various technologies. These technologies are made for people to make our access to new world easily. There is tremendous use of online applications, websites which require large storage. Large data is handled by the online systems. The collection of data in whole world is about 20% in last few years ("Big data, for better or worse: 90% of world's data generated over last two years," 2013). The data is captured from user, controlled by the systems and operations are performed on data. It requires more system accuracy and protection to personal data.

Ex. Email, WhatsApp, Instagram, Facebook, Bank transactions, Real-time estate etc. But the person is unknown about the data, where and how it is used where it is stored or whether the data is handled by some organisations for their own use or data is been hacked by other person (Zyskind & Pentland, 2015). Since the protection towards the personal data is been decreasing day by day. Example- Facebook one of the huge online social network collected 300 petabytes of user data during its inception (PB, n.d.). These leads to illegally accessing personal data for their own purpose without having rights on it.

WHAT IS THE PERSONAL DATA?

Every person deals with various applications nowadays, where each website or application needs authentication of user. He has must create a user id and set password to access the application. He has a unique identity .He keeps his access details up to him, where the data contains login details which he wants to keep private .Personal data is defined as the individual information which is used to identifying a person identity from others . These details may be used to trace the person .The name, identity number, account details, birth date, mothers name, biometrics and various information regarding website access, banking details and medical details is related to an individual. One of these details are enough to identify an individual. These details are not shared with others .These data is kept hidden from public. Only that person can handle or deal with his data .The data is kept private .The data is kept secured .

The Privacy Problem

In various fields, the services deploy applications for users to install. All these applications collect high resolution of personal data. The user is unknown about this process. The person is providing all the data to the applications and allow the applications to deal with his personal data on the system. The application may misuse the authentication details of the user. This results in tracing the user details whenever required . Even the hackers can easily trap the system and get access of the personal details of the system .In agriculture environment the third parties involve between farmers and customers to deal the transaction .This leads to get advantage over the other .The broker earns more profit than farmer.

What Is Blockchain?

Blockchain is a decentralised, distributed, public ledger. Blockchain is defined as collection of blocks. Block is the smallest unit of blockchain which records recent transactions. Every transactions are grouped and stored on a public ledger (*b-money*, 1998). In blockchain, the first block is called as genesis block. After genesis block the block is added accordingly by using hash of genesis block. Blockchain technology the latest word in financial service has the capacity to store, share and deal with the transactions in a different way. The Satoshi Nakamoto bought Bitcoin and Blockchain over paper in July 2009, the first blockchain was introduced and became popular. Blockchain technology is the one who builds a trust between two member or two entities. When there is a digital transaction between two persons then no a third party involved in transaction system (Nakamoto, 2007). Blockchain provides more security to the data. The aim of blockchain is to build trust among the humans. The trust should be build on both the sides in transaction as between producer and consumer. The blockchain system is build for improving the society, by reducing the frauds as illegal accessing to data and hacking the system .The blockchain is used to build the first cryptocurrency which is Bitcoin. There are various applications on where we can have blockchain technology dealing with the transaction system. The blockchain is updated by itself in each ten minutes.

The blockchain provides higher security to the storage system. The data once inserted in the block cannot be changed or deleted. Also the data cannot be updated in the system . A ledger is a list of transactions right from the start of blockchain. Block holds recent copy of ledger which is shared with each member of blockchain over the distributed network. Once the block is verified it becomes a constant part of blockchain. Using the cryptographic functions the data is validated and stored on ledger in the block .To confirm the all transactions reliability .Block time is defined as the time taken by the network to add a block into the blockchain. The block time for bitcoin is 10 minutes. In cryptography the data in encrypted and a hash code is created for every single transaction.

Blockchain technology is made for commercial transactions. The first decentralised cryptocurrency which is made using blockchain is Bitcoin. Today various institutions are changing their transactions systems into blockchain based system. This is due to the reliable and flexible nature of the blockchain .The blockchain technology

Figure 1. Blockchain architecture

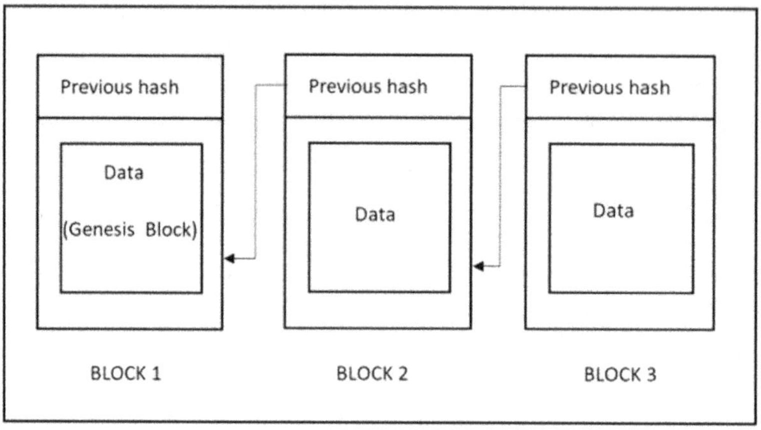

involves transaction to maintain server networks known as 'nodes'. The computer system which holds blockchain are known as nodes.

The copy of the ledger is sent to the peer-to-peer network off the blockchain. Every system has an updated replica of the ledger on the system (Tosh et al., 2017). The transactions of the blockchain are validated by nodes .If the transactions are valid then the block is added to the ledger. The blockchain makes it easy to use smart contracts such as embedded contracts in computer codes that may implement themselves automatically on the occurrence of various events ("Blockchains and the Internet of Things," n.d.).The blockchain provides high security to personal data by using hashing technique. The main advantage of blockchain are:

1. Data Ownership:

The Blockchain framework mainly ensures that the user can control and own their data. This system makes the user, the owner of their own data with permissions.

2. Data Transparency:

The user is made completely transportable to know where her/his data is being collected and accessed.

Why Blockchain Is Important?

The blockchain has capacity to modify the way data is stored, shared and managed. The most powerful aspects of the technology are the barriers to handle or deleting information which has been added to the chain . The technology is highly secure and is immutable to hacking . It is a decentralized network, so that no one owns the system. It cannot be handled by anyone due to simple structure of blockchain system. The ledger is public so copy of each transaction is stored on each node of the network. If someone wants to use and modify the data of other person it is caught easily because of blockchain. The details of transactions held between the nodes on regular basis are stored on the blockchain . The blockchain system provides encryption of data and verification of data. For a transaction the user is not charged by the system . We can transfer our money from one system to another system. The blockchain system is collection to various terms which ensures the personal data security and storage. The blockchain uses mathematics to create a distributed and secure ledger which enables the transactions without need for third parties (Moubarak & Filiol, 2018).

Aim of Blockchain

The main aim of the blockchain is to build trust among the society (Nakamoto, 2007). The society should be free of fraud systems. The public should be aware of the frauds as illegal accessing of their data by hackers or by the applications .The data should be accessed by that person only to which the data belongs . Others cannot access the details of that person. Brokers and agents are not involved in the transaction. There should be no intermediaries to the transaction .Instead of these there should be end to end transaction. The decision in the peer-to-peer network of blockchain are taken by mechanisms which are decentralised such as Proof of work (POW)(Vukoli, 2016) and proof of stake.

Smart Contracts

In 1997,the smart contracts were designed by Nick Szabo (Szabo., 1997). Smart contracts are defined as the contracts which exist between two entities using automated technique for applying conditions .Rules are defined by the smart contract around the agreement and it enforces automatically the operations .By using computer software the contracts are automatically verified and executed. They help us to have transactions, exchange money anything or shares avoiding the middleman services. This process converts the contracts into code form. Contracts means the agreement signed by two entities with pre-defined conditions. Smart is defined as the process which is automated and executes by its own using computer software. The agreement or a part of agreement are converted in its equivalent code and then send to the nodes of the blockchain. These contracts are called as self executing contracts. These contracts could be stored on blockchain network .These networks of the computer supervises the smart contracts.

The common example is the automated bill payments .In this application the computer software recognizes the details on the barcode and automatically updates the list of parameters in the bill. Then the system charges the credits of the person paying the bill.

On any network the smart contracts can be coded and executed. The computer software deals with the predefined conditions, such that the condition of agreements are agreed by both the entities .

Working of Smart Contracts

1. The code is written for the contact between the two parties. They contact using public ledger.
2. An event is created which hits the strike price and the expiration date.And according to the rules coded the contract executes itself.
3. To maintain the privacy of an individuals position, the blockchain is used by regulators to understand the market activity.

Advantages of Smart Contracts

As the smart contracts are implemented on distributed ledger, it provides advantage to both the parties, like the contracts are distributed on the blockchain network, every node ledger gets updated .The transactions between both the entities are there on the ledger of every node. Hence if one wants to delete or update the transaction, it is not possible to do. Due to the public ledger the transactions can take place easily .The customer and the sender can easily carry out transactions without involving the third parties as brokers or agents and administrators . This also reduces the transactions cost, which were associated with the third parties. Because of smart contracts the industries are benefited mostly. The smart contracts are created on blockchain peer-to -peer network allowing the buyers and sender to transact between them example:To purchase a trade art directly without involving the broker (Nakamoto, 2007). All the documents are encrypted and shared on the network. The document is replicated and stored on each system .There is a backup .The contracts save our money which are taken by the intermediaries. These contracts are cheaper and faster. The contracts also avoid errors.

Decentralised Applications

Decentralised Applications are the applications which run on peer to peer network instead on working with a single computer. DApps are stored on the blockchain system. DApps are blockchain enabled websites. Decentralised applications consist of whole parts front end and backend .Smart contract is a small part of DApp which is mostly written in solidity language. DApps are a kind of the software which cannot be controlled by any entity .In the market these applications have unlimited participants.

DApps Must Satisfy Following Criteria

1. The DApps must be on open platform where each and every one can access and use these applications
2. Using cryptographic techniques all the data should be stored.
3. The application should use cryptographic tokens.
4. Applications should generate tokens.

Advantages of dApps

1. **Autonomy**: No third parties are required for transactions. Brokers and agents are not necessary.
2 **Trust**: The documents are encrypted in ledger. A high security is provided to the data .Trust is build through blockchain.
3. **Backup**: If the documents are lost due to some reasons then there are multiple copies of ledger on nodes of network, from . where we can take details again.
4. **Accuracy**:-Smart contracts are faster and cheaper. They avoid errors that arise from manual work.

DApp Examples

1. **Blockverify**: It is a Blockchain based anti counter-feit solution. It identifies counterfeit goods, diverted products, stolen merchandise and fraudulent transactions.
2. **Ripple**: It is a network of institutional payments providers .These providers are such as banks and money services business. The providers use the solutions developed by Ripple.
3. **STORJ**: It is an open source decentralised file storage solution. It uses encryption, file shredding and a hash table of blockchain to store files on peer to peer network.
4. **Cryptokitties**: Due to large processing of transaction the cryptokitties slowed down the Ethereum network in December 2017 (Kharif, n.d.).

Difference Between DAaps and Smart Contracts

The blockchain enabled websites are DApps while connecting to blockchain is allowed by smart contracts .The DApps are similar to web applications which use frontend technologies for user interfacing. Same technologies are used by DApps for rendering the page. Instead of the API the smart contracts are used by the DApps to connect the blockchain.

Issues in Digital Transaction

Centralized Power

The every system is having a central authority which controls the whole system. The central authority has access to deal with transactions in the system .All the transacted currencies are controlled and managed by a central authority .This leads to have chances of extracting data by someone.

- **Blockchain Solution:** Blockchain is defined as public ledger. Every person is assigned the same power. The members of blockchain have equal authority to add block on blockchain.

Private Ledger

The private ledger is mostly used by banking system. The user is unknown about how transactions held in the system are done by him or by other person .The bank may invest these money somewhere else.

Blockchain Solution:

Blockchain has a public ledger. Each node of the blockchain receives updated copy of ledger after every 10 minutes .The ledger hold all transaction details right from the start of blockchain .This is a large data which is handled and stored using blockchain. The data is stored in a form that it cannot be manipulated by anyone or any system.

Prone to *Hacks*

The financial systems are been hacked by someone .The data set is released and the details are stolen (Dai, Shi, Meng, Wei, & Ye, 2017). This leads to problems of account handling by unknown person.

Blockchain Solution:

The Blockchain system is immutable to hacking. In blockchain system the data once inserted cannot be deleted or modified (Mense & Flatscher, 2018).

Double Spending

The double spending problems are faced mostly by digital platforms ("Double-spending," n.d.). The transactions using digital platform sometimes may transact money to two account simultaneously.

Blockchain Solution:

In Blockchain system the double spending are not allowed .This is due to the basic structure of blockchain.

Transaction Fees

For every transactions the financial systems charge fees near about 2-3% of the transaction amount .This leads to collecting a large amount of money in a single day.

Blockchain Solution:

The blockchain doesn't charge any kind of fees on the transaction .Hence we can transfer our money from one system to the other with no charges.

FEATURES OF BLOCKCHAIN

- Decentralised: Every organisation has a centralized authority which handles the systems task. In blockchain all the rights are equally distributed to each member in blockchain.
- Distributed: The blockchain technology is widely spread in peer to peer network, so that all the recent updates can be shared in network easily.
- Public ledger: Blockchain is a public distributed database which holds encrypted ledger. The ledger is in Encrypted format to keep the secured details of the people involved in blockchain technology.
- Trust: Blockchain reduces the need for brokers and agents and can automate the manual tasks.
- Data Security: On Blockchain, interfering the transactions is difficult because of the complex cryptography provided and also of the distributed ledger .The members can have the transaction list of the blockchain and here no one is the head of the other .
- Traceability: A distributed ledger stores the entire ownership history of an transactions.

- Immutable: The data when entered into the blockchain cannot be removed or stolen s because of its basic structure and providing security using cryptographic functions (Moubarak & Filiol, 2018).

TYPES OF BLOCKCHAIN

Public Blockchain

It can be defined as the blockchain which is by people, for people and of the people. Public Blockchain ledgers are visible to every node on internet and any member can verify block of transactions. These blockchain are open and so everyone can read and write on blockchain. Example:Bitcoin, Litecoin. In these examples any person can run, make the transaction, and can know the updates in blockchain ledger.

Private Blockchain

As the name suggest the blockchains are private means the data can be handled by a members . In private blockchain only a person in organisation is allowed to validate, verify and add transactions blocks. Here every member on the internet is only allowed to view. This makes the blockchain centralised but the blockchain is secured using cryptography e.g. Bankchain .

Consortium Blockchain

It is a combination of public and private blockchains. In this blockchain a team of organization verifies transactions and then add. There are more than one in charge in this blockchain. Here we have companies group which come together and take decisions for the network. Eg. r3,EWF.

WORKING OF BLOCKCHAIN

Public Key Cryptography

Public key cryptography has pairs of keys, a private and a public key .A private key is kept secured, and a public key is for the outside network. Encryption means converting normal data into a code. Decryption means again converting code into respective data .If we use private key for encrypting the data then it is necessary to decrypt the data using public key and vice versa.This is called a asymmetric encryption.

Peer-to-Peer Network

Peer-to-peer network is blockchain is used to have a distributed ledger .So that each person in blockchain is connected to other by means of network which is peer to peer. The peer provides disk storage and network bandwidth available to each node. Hence all the data can be shared by using the network. Distributed machines on peer to peer network helps to maintain consistency of their public ledger. This network uses digital signature to validate the transactions.

Blockchain Program

It is the technique of implementation of any solution or use cases. Blockchain can be build by any language. The most preferred default for writing programs in Ethereum blockchain is Solidity. Various other languages such as NodeJS, Kotlin, Python, Javascript, etc. are used to write program in blockchain.

Digital Signatures

The digital signatures are defined as the validation provided to the specific document user (L. Wang, Shen, Li, Shao, & Yang, 2018). They are part of the blockchain protocols. These signatures are used in transactions between the two members of the blockchain (Santra, Aleya, Maji, & Nath, 2016). Similarly using the signature we ensure the security to the sensitive information. They often use asymmetric cryptography (Merkle, 1988).This means the data is shared with other person by using public key.

Nodes

Node is defined as a blockchain device, which carry various functions and are spread over the blockchain network .A node is any electronic device which is connected to the network of internet and has an IP Address. The nodes are arranged in the binary tree format. The nodes can win rewards for validating transactions in blockchain. Node act as a point of communication in the blockchain system.

Hashing

Hashing is defined as a technique of converting a specific input into a output code form .In blockchain system the output depends on the previous transactions of blockchain. Hashing provides high security to the data .This makes blockchain immutable to hacking.

Protocols

A huge set of rules are coded in the blockchain which are known as protocols .The protocols are the program which plays an important role in networking .The blockchain builds trust among the society. The whole transactions operations are automated .The user trusts on protocol that the protocol can handle the transactions over the network and can deal with security of data .The protocol are the backbone of the blockchain network. These are a collection of rules and regulations which explains the transmission process of the blockchain .

Proof of Work

The Proof of work (POW) is a Bitcoin protocol (Salman, Member, Zolanvari, Member, & Erbad, 2018). It is mining process in which the some of the nodes act as miners. The miners validate the transactions by solving some mathematical problems .The solution on this problems are solved on the nodes. The miners which solve the mathematic puzzles, then validate the transactions .Then the miners are rewarded by some currencies

FRAMEWORKS OF BLOCKCHAIN

1. **Ethereum**: It is a decentralised open platform (Salman et al., 2018).It is a public blockchain on which we can develop various decentralised application. In the decentralised way, the contracts are run on the network .The default language for coding in Ethereum is Solidity. .Ethereum blockchains are mainly used for coding in decentralised applications like smart contracts (Salman et al., 2018).
2. **Hyperledger**: Hyperledger is a enterprise blockchain framework. It is a network with various roles .It is not a public chain .It is mostly used for business purpose .It is a global collaboration which is hosted by Linux Foundations.
3. **Corda**: Corda is an open source blockchain created for business right from start. It permits you to build blockchain which transacts in strict privacy.

Figure 2. Process to add block

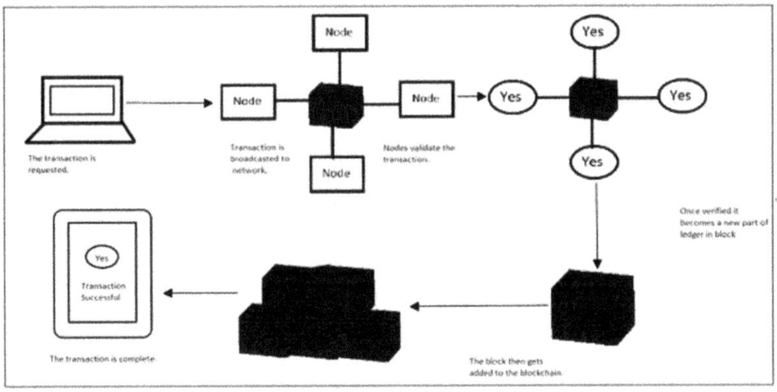

4. **Quorum**: Quorum is a distributed ledger and a smart contract platform which provides good support for privacy of transaction and privacy for network level.

PROCESS TO ADD BLOCK INTO THE BLOCKCHAIN

- When there is a request for transaction, the transaction is stored on block in ledger
- The block is send to the blockchain network.
- The nodes on the network validate the block, and then the block is approved and verified.
- After the block is verified the it is added in the blockchain.
- The transaction is successful.

SECURITY TECHNIQUES

Basic Hashing Concept

Hashing technique is specially used to identify a specific element from a group of elements.The main task of hashing is distributing the key-value pairs.

Example:

1. In universities each and every student is assigned a unique rollno which is used to identify the details of that student easily.

2. In library books are assigned a specific number through which it can be identified that either the book is in library on which shelf or it is issued by someone.

In these examples the hashing takes place, where student and the book has their own number. Using hashing technique the larger key are converted into smaller keys, the values are stored in hash table accordingly. Every element is assigned with a key-value pair through which one can search the element in O(1) time complexity.

Hashing is implemented using two ways:

1. An elements are converted into integer which acts as an index, used to store and access data from hash table.
2. The elements stored according to key values from where it can be easily accessed.
    - Hash = hashfunction (key)
    - Index = hash% arraysize

Hash Function: A function which is used to map the data into hash tables using key-value pairs.

Good hashing is achieved by following requirements:

1. It should be easy to compute.
2. The uniform distribution should be provided across the hash table.
3. Collisions should be avoided.

Hashing in Blockchain

Blockchain uses hashing from proof of work till the verification of file. Hashing is a cornerstone of cryptography .Each block consists of data, hash and hash of previous block and proof of work. Data on block chain is stored in form of amount and persons details.eg Bitcoin system stores details about the sender receiver and the transaction details. A block has a specific hash.The hash can be compared with a fingerprint . It identifies the block and its details in blockchain. Hash is always unique as a fingerprint. When the block is created accordingly the hash code is generated. Changing data or transactions of the block will cause hash to change. So the hashes are more useful when we want to protect our blocks.

The third part of block is previous block hash function, it effectively group of blocks and this technique makes the blockchain more secure. Proof of work is a mechanism which is used during validation of the block. This is a mathematical solution that we attach to block which ensure that it is a valid block. The ledger is produced using software protocol .The mathematical problems can be solved using the protocols. Ledger is distributed over the network. Everyone gets valid copy of the same. If we try to change the ledger it won't get accepted because everyone has a replica of it. Every transaction and every block is highly secured.

Hashing Technique

Hashing means to take a specific input of any length, converting it to a specific output of fixed length. Hash consists of some data structures like pointer and linked list.

Pointers are the variables which store address of another variable.

Linked lists are defined as sequence of blocks containing data which is linked to next block through pointers.

The Hash in blockchain consists of two parts:

- Data of block
- Hash of previous block

1. Data:

The block is group of recent transactions. All the transactions have an entry on ledger. In blockchain system a block gets added in blockchain after every 10 minutes.

Hence the data is stored on blockchain in block. The recent transaction ledger which is validated by miners and then gets updated on copy of every members system. A miner checks all credits and debits of the user.

2. Previous block hash:

It is a pointer which will always point to previous block of blockchain. The blockchain has a structure like linked list which consist of data and a pointer of the hash which points to hash of previous block leading to form a blockchain.

Ex. In Bitcoin system the input transactions are executed using a hashing algorithm known as SHA-256 (Secure Hashing Algorithm-256)[5][14][22], which gives fixed length output. In case of SHA-256 it matter how the input should be, and accordingly the output will be produced of length 256-bits.This becomes very difficult when we are handle with a large data. Instead of remembering the inputs we can remember hash .

Cryptographic Hash Functions

Cryptographic hash functions are special kind of hash functions which has various properties:

Figure 3. Hash key

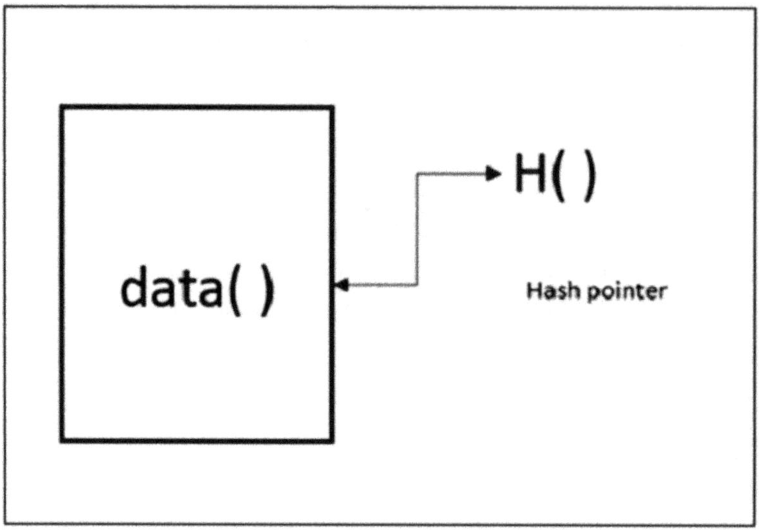

1. Deterministic:

If we parse the input for many times through hash functions the same results are obtained every time.

2. Quick Computation:

The efficiency of system should be more enough so that the system returns a hash of a particular input quickly.

3. Pre -Imaged Resistance:

If the hash code of the input is already in system then the same code is also when the input is used every time .So the hash of specific input is always the same.

4. Small changes in input changes the hash:

The hashing function treats a an individual input to get converted in hash code form.The slight changes in input results a drastic change in hash code.

5. Collision Resistant:

If collision occur in hashing algorithms, H(A) is equal to H(B) .The system breaks collision resistant as it has 50% chances to break instead of pre imaged resistance.

6. Puzzle Friendly:

This property has a huge impact on the cryptocurrencies.
Cryptographic hash functions examples:

1. MD 5 which produces 128-bit hash code .
2. SHA 1 which produces 160-bit hash code.
3. SHA 256 produces 256-bit hash which is by Bitcoin.
4. Keccak-256 which produces 256-bit hash which is used by Ethereum.

Merkle Tree

In blockchain, every single verification of data requires more number of packets which are delivered to the distributed network. Validating a single computer means to compare between an individuals transaction and the entries in ledger and make sure that information is not changed in ledger and individual transaction. This problem is solved by Merkley Tree by hashing the data in record in this ledger (Merkle, 1980). This improves efficiency of blockchain as the small packets are to be distributed across the network. Hash is an algorithm which takes input of variable length and converts it into an output of specific length. Example in Bitcoin, if A wants to send B $150, then its looks like a string of various characters .

"3cbcf3e1075b0b3357140de438336733bd6927cdle78d36cc27834fcce932ad"

This string is deterministic means that "A->B $150" is always has the same hash output. If there is a minor variation in the input as "A->B $160" the hash code of output is completely different.

In Merkley tree the transactions are hashed using hashing functions. These transactions have their own hash code .The hash codes of two transactions are combined, so that we can remember it well. Similarly the hash code of combination of two transactions are again combined with the other two transactions hash code combination (M. Wang, 2018). Hence it easy to remember the hash code for the combinations of transactions .The hash code which is formed by combinations of hash code of transactions is known as Merkle root. The hash code pointed by arrow in the figure is Merkle root. Root is the combination of two hash codes, and the two hash codes which are further combination of other two hash codes of transactions.

Every Blockchain has a Merkle root which is located in the block header .The contents of block are verified and their consistency using this. If the copy of blockchain of A has similar Merkle root for copy of blockchain of B has same transactions

Figure 4. Merkle tree

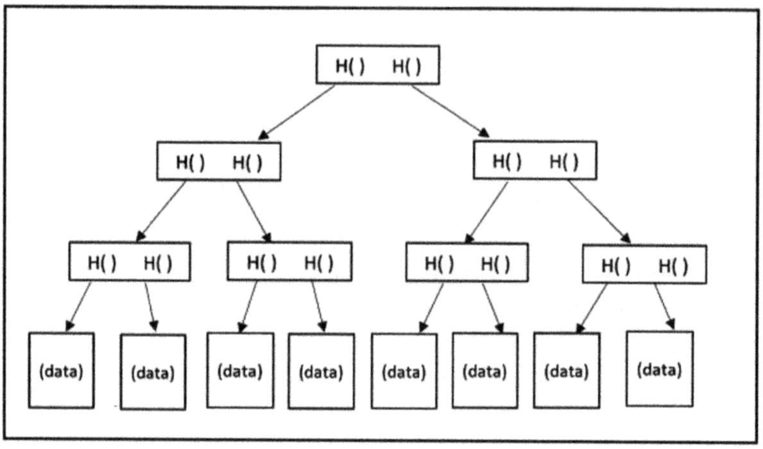

and both A and B are agreed on the ledger. If there is a change in the contents of blockchain it would lead to generating different Merkle roots due to hashing. If there is a dissimilarity in Merkle root then we may request the two sub-hashes, and we can again request the sub-hashes for their hashing code. Hence, we can find out any dissimilarity or fraud in the blockchain by using Merkle root instead of searching the code line to line.

Blockchain Transactions

The transactions are made including information on the time date of members and type of transaction. In the blockchain network each node h as a replica of the ledger .

- Miners verify the transactions after solving complex math puzzles and maintain ledger.
- Mathematical principle ensures that the nodes automatically & continuously agree to current state of ledger and each transaction .
- If changes are done in the transaction the nodes will not reach the consensus and the block is not added to the blockchain.

EXAMPLE: BITCOIN SYSTEM

Mining: Bitcoin mining is done by high powered computers which solver complex mathematical problems. Mining is a two fold.The first mining is done when the miners solve the proof of work(POW),which is solving complex mathematical issues. The second mining is done when bitcoin miners solve computational problem and makes bitcoin network secure and trustworthy by verifying the transactions.

Mining Technique: Consider A have to transfer 500 BTC(Bitcoins) & here G & H are miners .Their job is to verify whether A & D have sufficient balance or not . G & H will validate the transactions of the A & D.

G & H are going to check history old transactions of A, that A has sufficient balance(above 500)for transaction .G & H are miners who uses their resource to validate the block containing transactions.

The transactions has detailed information of the transfer of money from one member to another.Ledger gets updated with respect to every transaction .The details are stored with respect to every transaction as a part of block. Hence, no one can hack the end users money from wallet. After successful transaction the values gets updated in the ledger with respect to everyone which has copy of that ledger.

If the transactions get successful, the ledger gets updated with respect to everyone. Once the block is validated the updated block is added to the blockchain .This solves problem of double spending (Nakamoto, 2007). The total time required for validating is 10 minutes .Miners check credit and debits if the user.

FUTURE TRENDS

1. **Financial Service**: The blockchain in services changes the structure of current financial markets. The markets value will be same as on the network. Some of the financial institutions are trying to make their private blockchains. If banking system is made by blockchain hacking the banking records becomes impossible .This will solve the double spending issues. This reduces bank crisis by a large extent.
2. **Payments and Transfers**: Blockchain are mostly used in payments and transfer system. The currencies are transferred using URL code .Here public and private keys are not necessary, directly by using URL code transfer takes place. The transaction fees are not charged by the network .Easy and safe transfer of money can be done using blockchain.
3. **Healthcare**: In healthcare system blockchain(Mettler & Hsg, 2016) will be useful for storing details of patients on ledger .Getting public key of patient the doctor can access the details of patient. So that every member details are recorded on ledger .Accordingly the doctor would give the person the best treatment .All previous records of the patient will be stored on blockchain and recent data will only be added to the previous block of the patient .

4. **Law Enforcement**: In Law enforcement the blockchain can be used to store the details of the criminals and the crime details .This will reduce the crime strategy in our society. The criminals can be caught easily. The criminal details are updated on network, so we can catch them efficiently wherever they are located .
5. **Voting**: Elections need authentication of voters identity, keeping secure record and trusted tallies. Blockchains are the medium for costing tracking and counting votes without voter fraud and lost records . By using blockchain we get secured data during election and voting. The data will not be hacked due to ledger system. In coming two years blockchain will make elections get handled easily and more securely.
6. **IOT**: This field uses blockchain to transfer the data between the devices without any corruptions and without any interference (Singh, 2016).In IOT the blockchain are used to provide security to the data sensed by the sensors and it provides the best way to store the data .The structure of blockchain is such that no one can hack the data easily. The details of sensed data will be secured.
7. **Online Music**: Recently there are various remakes of the real music .By using blockchain we provide security to the music that they can only hear the music but cannot make changes in the song until we buy the validated copy of the music.

Anyone can access the online music but anyone cannot make modifications with respect to it. If the person pays for the song then all the details can be accessed.

8. **Real Estate**: In Real Estate most of the deals are conducted by an intermediary. This intermediary are the brokers and the agents which deal the process .The buyer and the seller are unknown about each other, the brokers act as bridge between them who charges commission on the transactions by both the sides .the blockchain changes all these frauds .It builds trust among the buyer and seller .The transaction using the blockchain doesn't charge any kind of transaction fees on the members. We can validate and use smart contracts for these deals.

Real Time Applications of Blockchain

1. **followmyvote.com**: This aims to modify the way we vote becoming words first open source online voting system.
2. **Arcade City**: It is a ground work to decentralized right sharing service uber killer.
3. **ShoCard**: It stores your identity onto bitcoins blockchain for easier verification.

CONCLUSION

In every centralised system the user data are accessed by organising system .These data are stored in database of system and they are not secured. Anyone can easily hack the system and access the personal details of members in the system . The blockchain system provides the solution on this problem. It collects information of user and allows the user to have control on their own data .Each user have his own private and public keys for transaction .Each user shares his public key over the decentralised, distributed, public ledger on blockchain So no one can access the details of anyone easily as it is in key form.

Since while transactions the hash code are generated and added on ledgers .Blockchain provides a high security to the personal data of user and as well as on the public network of user. Since, the details are highly secured on blockchain. The laws and regulation systems could be coded into blockchain .In some situations the ledger act as a legal evidence in case of unauthorized transactions. The Merkley tree is used by Blockchain, databases and computer networks to quickly manage the records around the multiple computer systems.

By using blockchain the transactions are validated and verified by the network nodes. The blockchain can be implemented in various fields, such as banking, health and care, voting and real estates . We discussed various future extensions of blockchain which would make the all rounded solution for building trust in society. We conclude that the blockchain provides the best way to provide the security to the data .The security is provided according to the way of storing the data in the blockchain using cryptographic techniques.

REFERENCES

b-money. (1998). Retrieved from http://www.weidai.com/bmoney.txt

Big data, for better or worse: 90% of world's data generated over last two years. (2013). *ScienceDaily*.

Blockchains and the Internet of Things. (n.d.). Retrieved from http://www.postscapes.com/blockchains-and-the-internet-of-things/

Dai, F., Shi, Y., Meng, N., Wei, L., & Ye, Z. (2017). *From Bitcoin to Cybersecurity : a Comparative Study of Blockchain Application and Security Issues*. Academic Press.

Double-spending. (n.d.). Retrieved from https://en.bitcoin.it/wiki/Double-spending

Kharif, O. (n.d.). *CryptoKitties Mania Overwhelms Ethereum Networks Processing.* Retrieved from https://www.bloombergquint.com/technology/cryptokitties-quickly-becomes-most-widely-used-ethereum-app#gs.3m37ft

Mense, A., & Flatscher, M. (2018). *Security Vulnerabilities in Ethereum Smart Contracts*. Academic Press.

Mettler, M., & Hsg, M. A. (2016). *Blockchain Technology in Healthcare The Revolution Starts Here*. Academic Press.

Moubarak, J., & Filiol, E. (2018). *On Blockchain Security and Relevant Attacks.* Academic Press.

Nakamoto, S. (2007). *Bitcoin : A Peer-to-Peer Electronic Cash System*. Academic Press.

Salman, T., Member, S., Zolanvari, M., Member, S., & Erbad, A. (2018). Security Services Using Blockchains : A State of the Art Survey 1. *IEEE Communications Surveys and Tutorials, 1*. doi:10.1109/COMST.2018.2863956

Scaling the Facebook data warehouse to 300 PB. (n.d.). Retrieved from https://code.fb.com/core-data/scaling-the-facebook-data-warehouse-to-300-pb/

Singh, S. (2016). *Blockchain : Future of Financial and Cyber Security*. Academic Press.

Szabo, N. (1997). *Formalizing and securing relationships on public networks.* Academic Press; doi:10.5210/fm.v2i9.548

Tosh, D. K., Shetty, S., Liang, X., Kamhoua, C. A., Kwiat, K. A., & Njilla, L. (2017). *Security Implications of Blockchain Cloud with Analysis of Block Withholding Attack.* Academic Press. doi:10.1109/CCGRID.2017.111

Vukoli, M. (2016). *The Quest for Scalable Blockchain Fabric : Proof-of-Work vs .BFT Replication*. Academic Press. doi:10.1007/978-3-319-39028-4

Wang, L., Shen, X., Li, J., Shao, J., & Yang, Y. (2018). Cryptographic primitives in blockchains. *Journal of Network and Computer Applications*. doi:10.1016/j.jnca.2018.11.003

Wang, M. (2018). *Research on the Security Criteria of Hash Functions in the Blockchain*. Academic Press.

Zyskind, G., & Pentland, A. S. (2015). Decentralizing Privacy : Using Blockchain to Protect Personal Data. 2015 IEEE Security and Privacy Workshops, 180–184. doi:10.1109/SPW.2015.27

Chapter 11
Preserving Data Privacy in Electronic Health Records Using Blockchain Technology

Sathiyabhama B.
Sona College of Technology, India

Rajeswari K. C.
Sona College of Technology, India

Reenadevi R.
Sona College of Technology, India

Arul Murugan R.
Sona College of Technology, India

ABSTRACT

Technology is a boon to mankind in this fast-growing era. The advancement in technology is the predominant factor for the sophisticated way of living of the people. In spite of technology, revolution happens across the world, and mankind still suffers due to various health issues. Healthcare industries take immense measures to improve the quality of life. An enormous volume of digital data is being handled every day in the healthcare industry. There arises a need for the intervention of technology in the healthcare industry to be taken to a greater extent. The prime duty of any healthcare industry is to store and maintain those data in the form of electronic health records (EHR) in a secured manner.

DOI: 10.4018/978-1-7998-0186-3.ch011

INTRODUCTION

Health care industry is one of the important industries that greatly influence the economy of a country. The present era is likely to be dominated by technology in order to fulfill the demands that arise majorly for the patient under continuous health monitoring.The healthcare industry acts as a bridge between the beneficiaries such as medical practitioners, patients, hospitals, public and private health sectors. The major issue to be addressed in this scenario is the possibility of achieving interoperability. Since the patient data is being shared between various stakeholders the data security and privacy issues are also of high concern. The affluence of block chain technology circumvents the problems related to security and privacy issues and resolves the challenges in implementing interoperability facility (Mukkamala, Vatrapu, Ray, Sengupta, & Halder, 2018). In Gordon & Catalini (2018), the block chain databases are specially designed databases created only once and never edited or deleted. Data is stored in block chain as a decentralized ledger (computer file asset) and accessibility to it is not provided as the owner holds the private keys. Additionally, the owner can hold the control to provide to access the data and transfer it from one computer to another much faster and secure manner.

Block chain technology facilitates 'smart contracts', through which patients are allowed to be compensated with tokens for their sharing of health data with providers and their research partners (Hölbl, Kompara, Kamišalić, & Zlatolas, 2018). The significance of this approach is to enable individuals to possess complete control on their own health data in order to respect and preserve the privacy of the data. Data is secured by encrypting the medical data using attribute-based encryption (ABE) and identity-based encryption (IBE) in order to implement digital signatures (Tamazirt, Alilat, & Agoulmine, 2018). This implementation ensures that EHR can be maintained with high level of security (Zhang, Schmidt, White, & Lenz, 2018). This approach also eradicates the need to use any other complex cryptographic systems. In da Conceição, Silva, Rocha, Locoro, & Barguil (2018), Data privacy and data accessibility are conflict with each other as data privacy ensures the overall control provided to access the data where as the accessibility means unconstrained information access. According to Science House (n.d.), Block chain technology possesses key properties, such as immutability, decentralization, and transparency and it also allow software apps and technology platforms to communicate securely and seamlessly in order to exchange data. Blockchain offers the opportunity to enable access to longitudinal, complete, medical records that are stored in fragmented systems in a secure and pseudo anonymous fashion (Dagher, Mohler, Milojkovic, & Marella, 2018).

NEED FOR BLOCK CHAIN TECHNOLOGY IN HEALTHCARE INDUSTRIES

Recently, Block chain technologies set it trails in the healthcare domain too. A blockchain is well-known distributed structurewhichstores healthcare transaction records securely. It is capable of sharingthese immutable recordsof peer-to-peer transactions. Blockchain is built from linked transaction blocks and stored in a digital ledger (Burniske, Vaughn, Shelton, & Cahana, 2016). Blockchain is also apublic catalog of health records that references databases, fitness and medical devices, mobile phones, and laptops. It could be used to connect every patient, healthcare provider, and payer to a secure, yet public network.

Blockchain technology has proven its worth in adecentralized digital cash system such as bit coin which was introduced as a peer-to-peer crypto currency a decade before (Calzadilla & Villa, 2017). Disruptive and innovative nature of blockchain technology, strong underpinning theoretical cryptography foundations, distributed consensus algorithms, and decentralized databases make it suitable for healthcare applications.Blockchain resembles a database which not only stores information but the data is located in a network of personal computers called nodes without any central entity to control the data. Data is shared publicly although the contents of each data are only accessible to the authenticated users. Block chain can augment intelligent miner which provides the solution to effective data management and secured access. It offers interoperable mechanism with highly immutable property and connects seamlessly all the required information on disparate networks to a common infrastructure.

Block chain is a distributed digital ledger, capable of executing smart contracts (Wang & Song, 2018). This component is responsible to record references to health transactions, such as healthappointments, clinical tests and their results, prescribed medication and treatment for cure. In a privacy layer for EHRs, a block can contain pointers to health information which is much similar to a block that has currency transactions in a crypto currency (Burniske et al., 2016). For example, when apatient has seen by a doctor in the hospital for his/her illness, a transaction is appended to theledger saying that the hospital/healthcare provider would have access to that patient information. The data is stored in the central repository or a cloud based system (Bhargava, 2019). The cloud based system enables health data access, data storage and management in a secured manner to achieve effective resource utilization.

HEALTH INFORMATION FOR IMPROVED STANDARD OF LIVING (HIISL)

It is proposed to design and develop a nationwide central repository namely Health Information for Improved Standard of Living (HIISL) to store, maintain and update the patient data when it is required. Each patient/person is owned a dedicated space in this repository and their medical history can be viewed by the healthcare practitioners/ healthcare providers with appropriate access rights.

A patient is in need of his/her medical data to be provided to a different health professional during the medical emergency, but the patient's medical history might be available with different healthcare providers. In this situation, the immediate need is to get the pre-medical history of the patient in order to take timely lifesaving decisions. HIISL eradicates the Denial-of-Access (DoA) to the patient health data during critical situations as it's intended design policy is to provide timely lifesaving measures with reduced latency. However, this information is made accessible only to certified hospitals in charge of the management with prior patient consent. The patient will be given a provision to grant/revoke permission to access their health data securely at different levels and granularities only by the certified hospitals or chain of hospitals.

A tremendous volume of electronic data available in the healthcare industry requires blockchain technology based intelligent framework in order to organize and access these data. It can be recorded and verified only with the approval of all the stakeholders who are provided with universal identifiers. Most of the healthcare data is unstructured in nature. Hence, the system adds big data analytics as constituent part to achieve eventual consistency by incorporating NoSQL databases for effective handling of voluminous data. This operational environment is backboned by block chain technology for securing the various data. This system is also supplemented by a faster information retrieval mechanism using scalable consistent hash based indexing which is much suitable for accelerating upward search performance in the distributed development environment (Xie & Chen, 2017).

INTELLIGENT BASED SERVICES IN HEALTHCARE DATA MANAGEMENT

Intelligent based Discovery Service can evolve to offerbasic services of a search for healthcare professionals or any other stakeholders. This architecture separates the transaction control from the cloud based data storage because of the well-formed push and pull methodologies. They provide the luxury of transferring any piece of data that has to pass through the secured block chain network. The system also lets various healthcare providers from various sites, access to uncorrupted secure and universal patient records, circumventing repeated tests, procedures or prescriptions (Esposito, De Santis, Tortora, Chang, & Choo, 2018). Thus, the system ensures that single version of truth (data) specific to a patient available at various points of accesses.

When the health data of any patient is maintained electronically, there must be a mechanism to ensure privacy and appropriate authorization to the people accessing the data. The patient must hold the rights to provide their own information, approving, denying and sharing changes of the data. Patients would have transparency into the entire continuum of care. The proposed decentralized system enhances the health information in healthcare exchanges/setup in a highly secured manner.

The data management is taken care through the multiple layers by tailoring the EHR for easier workflow management on a wider spectrum via Master Patient Index (MPI). MPI permitsthe stakeholders to access patient records from stern to stern linkable by unique identifier to cater population health management; coordinated care and evaluate the performance. Data management has the following all-embracing objectives to ensure greater accountability for healthcare information.They are:

1. foreseeing the issues well before it affects the quality of data
2. Reconciling the workflow issues to maintain the data quality
3. Imposing the standards by clearly defining the roles and responsibilities of data management authorities to ensure data consistency

IMPORTANT ROLES IN HEALTHCARE DATA GOVERNANCE SYSTEM

It is implicit that any data governance system must involve four important roles namely Data Owner (DO), Business Data Overseer (BDO), Technical Data Overseer (TDO) and Gatekeeper (GK). Data owner is the one who possesses overall responsibility for one or more types of data. They are also responsible to ascertain suitable solutions for the data quality related issues with the prior consent obtained from BDO and TDO.The responsibility of BDO is to ascertain optimal solutions to quality related issues. Being a subject expert, BDO shall define and devise the business rules to enhance the data quality, transformation, and aggregation.

The prime responsibility of TDO is to identify the issues related to the data quality using data profiling tools. A prior approval is obtained from the DO in order toimplement the code. GK's role is to monitor and track the status of the quality of data. In case of any issues found, that will be recorded and directed to respective BDO and tracking will be continued until they are resolved. Though the data are handled at various points by all the stakeholders, the implementation of block chain enables the interoperability across the network. The advantage of the block chain infrastructure in healthcare industries is tomake the stakeholders aware of knowhow the data manipulation was done.

EFFECTIVE DATA STORAGE AND RETRIEVAL OF EHRS

The appropriate use of indexing and hashing techniques enhance the data storage and retrieval process in EHRs. As the patient data is stored in a distributed structure there is a need for providing proper mapping between data items and storage servers, which enhances the scalability of a distributed storage system. Persistent hashing is used to access the data quickly and this feature is very much demanded in the electronic healthcare data management.It wraps around the distributed storage buffer that maintains a hash list. With the help of address to key translation mapping function the buckets are hashed. The same approach is adopted for insertion, updation and deletion of data. It promptly returns the associated bucket for both storage and retrieval of the data item with *O(1)* time. In a distributed environment, data redundancy is a frequently occurring phenomenon which is very well addressed by double persistent hashing based collision resolution technique.

ARCHITECTURE OF BLOCK CHAIN BASED HIISL SYSTEM

The proposed HIISL system is first of its kind initiative to provide patient centric platform that will eradicate the present medical scenario that lacks universal framework to cater to the needs of healthcare stakeholders. To address this, HIISL is designed to provide privacy, interoperability, security andopenness to the healthcare data. It also ensures secured transaction of medical records that is persistent throughout the course of mobility across different users. The significance of this HIISL architecture is that it adheres to Health Level7 (HL7) standard and the Health Insurance Portability and Accountability Act (HIPAA) compliance. The HL7 standard confirms EHRs remains secure at all times during mobility across the various authenticated healthcare network to create a better overall healthcare experience. Any healthcare system must confirm to this standard for exchange of patient care and clinical information. The inclusion of HIPAA in HIISL is to provide portability in terms of appropriate health coverage, administrative simplification and to avoid fraud and abuse.

The HIISL architectureillustratedin the Figure 1 has the following components: EHR, Block chain, GSM, Intelligent agent, Insurance value chain and Stakeholders.

Block chain is one of the most used buzzword in the 21st century which is the connecting core of the HIISL system for the underlying security and interoperability. The block chain renders inevitable source for health transactions by decrypting data such as clinical examinations and medications with the help of digital signature. The physicians and healthcare providers can securely connect and update medication information through block chain.

The significance of block chain technology in EHR's is it maintains a single version of the truth in a more secure manner. Patients have the privilege to decide on the choice of the viewer i.e forthose whom the data can be made visible or accessible and also the level of access. The striking benefit of this arrangement enables not only the owner of the data to hold the sole proprietorship of their own data; it also provides the patients liberty to decide the level of access that can be given even to doctors by issuing tokens every time.This is how data privacy is guaranteed for information exchange process in a more secured and authorized manner.

Moreover, the decentralized arrangement of digital ledgers in EHR's can facilitate each user to have an updated copy of the block chain and greatly challenges the intruders who may try to take control over the data. The implementation of block chain in EHR's pilots a new Digital Line Tape (DLT) based storage and this approach deems to complement the existing storage and data exchange mechanisms rather than dethrone it.

According to Figure 1 the EHR captures the patient's data in two different forms: one is obtained personally from the patient and the other one is recorded via wearable sources. The acquired data is pushed on to the cloud setup for centralized storage. A unique identifier is automatically generated for every patient data for distinct patient identification to reduce the complexity that arises due to duplication of patient data. The EHR data that are collected over a period of time fuels the intelligent based system incorporated in the HIISL.

Healthcare, and healthcare data, is more complicated than ever due to the constant changes in government mandates, insurance, EHR, and HIPAA compliance.Such difficulties are very well addressed in HIISL by providing the patients needed access to their records conveniently and securely to enable communication with the healthcare professionals. The HIISL platform provides an integrated dashboard that can handle the above mentioned complexities .The proposed dashboard is an easily readable graphical display that can visualize the Key Performance Indicators (KPIs) of a system that needs to be monitored regularly. It provides information as a single version of truth that is accessible by the authorized users across the organization in a readily accessible way. The cloud integrated EHR access enables secure anytime anywhere access capability and minimizes slowdowns in lab results sharing, prescription refill requests, and appointments.

The proposed HIISL platform provides up-to-date personal healthcare records including medications, lab results, diagnoses, care plans, immunization histories that will act as a one stop solution for all the stakeholders. The proposed real-time healthcare dashboard provides users with an instant visual representation of their healthcare KPIs. These healthcare dashboard reports will help improve operational efficiency and leads to better results and smarter decisions such as quick access to additional healthcare information (medications, lab results, diagnoses, care plans, immunization histories), educational material related to their diagnosis and receive automated reminders and alerts.

These dashboards can amalgamate numerous healthcare providers a secure access to dashboards to combine multiple data sources and find the correlations necessary to make critical healthcare decisions. These easy-to-digest healthcare dashboards are custom-built to visualize specific data the physician wants to see a specific patient's present condition or health status. In essence, the healthcare providers can quickly view the most pertinent details about the patient for preventive care.

The clinical dashboards are designed to accommodate both primary care and specialty care provided by the physicians. A primary care physician's patient-centric view might combine lab results, long-term medications, vital signs and prevention programs on one screen. Meanwhile, a specialist's more disease-specific view may capture family history, diagnostic imaging results, patient problems, vital signs and long-term medications.Based on the preference, the dashboards can create targeted visualizations that will enable better understanding of patient health status. These dashboards can educate patients and enhance their treatment compliance through snapshots, graphs and progress reports. The role-based user centric dashboards are designed for usable interaction between the patients and care providers.

The proposed HIISL system intends to address the risk of specific patient by taking appropriate decision based on the level of emergency whether to inform emergency service or to Dear one's or physicians. A thorough analysis is done with the help of machine learning platform in which analytics is performed as a batch process with multiple patients' data. The result of analytics is shared to the physician to decide on the appropriate support to be given to the patient. This is how effective life-saving decision making is achieved in concern with the specific patient data.

The GSM module is used to enable simplest reliable communication for emergency services and dear ones in case of emergency as depicted in figure.

The Intelligent agent uses the EHRs of multiple patients collected over a period of time to derive hidden meaningful patterns which could be treatment for cure, prescription and risk prediction through cutting edge machine learning techniques. The intelligent dashboards are designed to be simple yet responsive in providing all the necessary information that is required by various stakeholders. In addition, the

Figure 1. Architecture of blockchain-based HIISL system

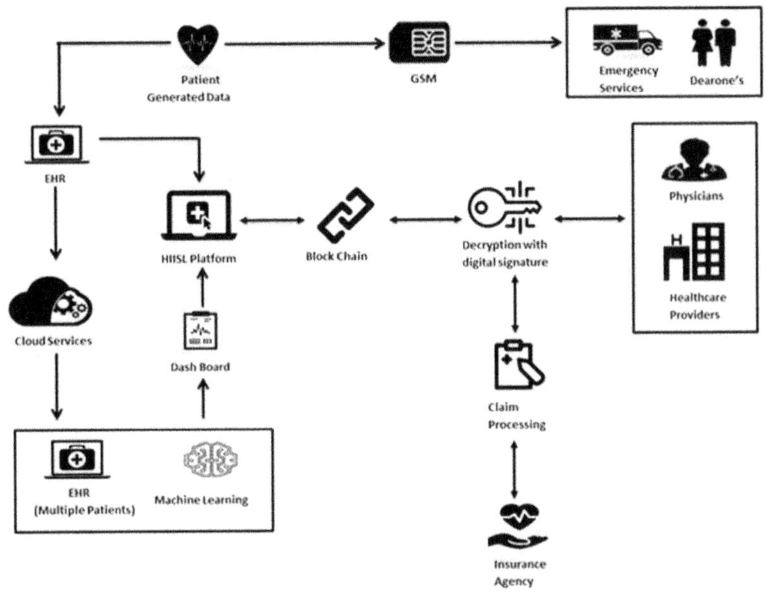

dashboards can echo the patterns derived from the intelligent agent as user-friendly reports that can influence intelligent decision making.

The cloud based HIISL platform ensures secure data storage and retrieval. Unique login are provided to various stakeholders with relevant access privileges. Audit trails are conducted for log-in, log-out, and system access to avoid potential misuse of the data. The solution also eliminates the complexities arising out of periodical system backups and in-house server maintenance thereby reduced IT expenses.

Recently, digital signatures are proven method in the healthcare data transaction systems which have provided integrity, non-repudiation, security and authentication to access the contents of electronic data set across networks.HIISL system provides authentication and immutable copies of data, securing all types of data transactions using private key signatures. Digital signatures are formed using a mathematical algorithm that creates a hash/signature using information from both the contents of the message, and information stored in the private/public key. The reason behind integrating digital signatures in HIISL is to make the transactions more secure with the help of information augmented to the key, using suitable cryptographic algorithm, and implementing advanced signature systems. The e-signatures are largely accepted as the golden standard for authentication and widely accepted due to its security enhancements.

The time stamped data records forms a chain of transactions which are encrypted using hash of the previous transaction.The digital signature is created by using the public key of the recipient, along with the private key of the signer. All these transactions require the signer to have their private key. The recipient can decrypt the transaction using public key of the signer in order to access the data.

Digital signatures and Blockchain can amalgamate the use of certificates and complex mathematical algorithms to provide authenticity and allow multiple signatures, timestamps, and distributing information across multiple systems in a network. This significant feature guarantees secure transactions that cannot be edited or removed.The use of secure, private keys in place of the public keys between the signer and the recipient enables data transactions to be maintained only by the approved parties making it a feasible choice for any type of data transaction in HIISL.

Insurance value chain connects insurance providers in ensuring the authenticity of the claim initiated by the policy holder. By issuing insurance policies and processing insurance claims on the block chain the insurance frauds can be minimized and efficiencies in claims processing can be enhanced by automating insurance audit trail.When a patient initiates services from the insurance provider, the services are recorded and assigned appropriate codes by the medical coder. The International Classification of Diseases (ICD) codes are used for diagnose that are HIPAA Compatible. Patient demographic data and insurance information are added to the claim. TheHIISL platform also automated electronic claim processing by submitting the claims via included and fully integrated clearinghouse. The platform can initiate and track automated claims submissions to both private and government insurers including Electronic Remittance Advice (ERA) retrieval.

The stakeholders play specific roles and responsibilities that are relevantly assigned to them. For instance, Patients those who receive care services from the healthcare providers can access information about their care and grant or revoke access totheir data at multiple levels. Similarly the healthcare providers can access patient's data for treatment and medications. The dearones and emergency services are intimated duringemergencies to make life saving decisions.

SUMMARY

In the proposed work, the value of personal health data is very well addressed using block chain based healthcare information management system. The main objective the system is to offer secured, interoperable patient friendly platform. The system reduces the number of repetitive clinical exams/tests and improves quality medical decision making. Since the proposed HIISL system confirms to HL7 standard and HIPAA compliance it can be very well established and profitable business model well established and profitable business model that can be successfully in a global healthcare market. As the model is patient friendly and different layers of the HIISL are imbibed with block chain based technology, it enables the users to have control of the data.

In future, a functional prototype of the proposed HIISL architecture will be implemented as a mobile (both Android and iOS) based application. Despite recent advances in Information and Communication Technology, there are lots of challenges in implementing healthcare services as a unique product for the healthcare industry. This is alleviated by the proposed HIISL as it exploits the care coordination and health information management in a secured manner. The proposed architecture is flexible in order to cater to the needs of several healthcare stakeholders. The system greatly relies on block chain technology which is an inevitable architecture for the healthcare scenario where secure data exchange is the premium importance. A well-diffused cloud setup ensures high scalability, availability, reliability, resilience and improved trust. In the near future to create reliable healthcare information network, HIISL would contribute a lot to the healthcare community as an undeniable and step ahead solution. This type of all encompassed healthcare solution undoubtedly opens new frontiers to health information management.

REFERENCES

Bhargava, R. (2019). Block chain Technology and Its Application: A Review. *IUP Journal of Information Technology*, *15*(1), 7–15.

Burniske, C., Vaughn, E., Shelton, J., & Cahana, A. (2016). *How Blockchain Technology Can Enhance HER Operability*. Retrieved from https://www.hyperledger.org/wp-content/uploads/2016/10/ARKInvest_and_GEM_Blockchain_EHR_Final.pdf

Calzadilla, J. F., & Villa, A. (2017). *Systematic Literature Review of the use of Blockchain in Supply Chain*. Retrieved from http://oa.upm.es/51171/

da Conceição, A. F., Silva, F. S. C., Rocha, V., Locoro, A., & Barguil, J. M. (2018). *Electronic health records using block chain technology.* Retrieved from https://arxiv.org/abs/1804.10078

Dagher, G. G., Mohler, J., Milojkovic, M., & Marella, P. B. (2018). Ancile: Privacy-preserving framework for access control and interoperability of electronic health records using blockchain technology. *Sustainable Cities and Society*, *39*, 283–297. doi:10.1016/j.scs.2018.02.014

Dimitrov, D. V. (2019). Blockchain Applications for Healthcare Data Management. *Healthcare Informatics Research*, *25*(1), 51–56. doi:10.4258/hir.2019.25.1.51 PMID:30788182

Esposito, C., De Santis, A., Tortora, G., Chang, H., & Choo, K. K. R. (2018). Blockchain: A panacea for healthcare cloud-based data security and privacy? *IEEE Cloud Computing*, *5*(1), 31–37. doi:10.1109/MCC.2018.011791712

Gordon, W. J., & Catalini, C. (2018). Blockchain technology for healthcare: Facilitating the transition to patient-driven interoperability. *Computational and Structural Biotechnology Journal*, *16*, 224–230. doi:10.1016/j.csbj.2018.06.003 PMID:30069284

Hölbl, M., Kompara, M., Kamišalić, A., & Zlatolas, L. N. (2018). A systematic review of the use of blockchain in healthcare. *Symmetry*, *10*(10), 470. doi:10.3390ym10100470

Mukkamala, R. R., Vatrapu, R., Ray, P. K., Sengupta, G., & Halder, S. (2018). Blockchain for Social Business: Principles and Applications. *IEEE Engineering Management Review*, *46*(4), 94–99. doi:10.1109/EMR.2018.2881149

Science House. (n.d.). *U.S. House of Representatives Committee on Science, Space, & Technology*. Retrieved from https://science.house.gov/

Tamazirt, L., Alilat, F., & Agoulmine, N. (2018). *Blockchain Technology: A new secured Electronic Health Record System*. Retrieved from https://hal.archives-ouvertes.fr/hal-01777462/document

Wang, H., & Song, Y. (2018). Secure cloud-based EHR system using attribute-based cryptosystem and blockchain. *Journal of Medical Systems*, *42*(8), 152. doi:10.100710916-018-0994-6 PMID:29974270

Xie, W., & Chen, Y. (2017). Elastic consistent hashing for distributed storage systems. In *Proceedings: IEEE International Parallel and Distributed Processing Symposium (IPDPS)*, (pp. 876-885). IEEE. 10.1109/IPDPS.2017.88

Zhang, P., Schmidt, D. C., White, J., & Lenz, G. (2018). Blockchain Technology use cases in healthcare. *Advances in Computers*, *111*, 1–41. doi:10.1016/bs.adcom.2018.03.006

Chapter 12
Decentralizing Privacy Using Blockchain to Protect Private Data and Challanges With IPFS

M. K. Manoj
VIT University, India

Somayaji Siva Rama Krishnan
VIT University, India

ABSTRACT

Blockchain technology is a distributed framework for sharing data that is validated through cryptographic functions. The nodes of the network come to a consensus regarding addition of data to the blockchain. Every blockchain operation requires a processing fee. This fee makes storing of large data on the blockchain infeasible. An indirect alternative for this challenge could be use of IPFS, which is a decentralized peer-peer network that facilitates storage of file. This is accomplished by storing the hash of the IPFS as data on the blockchain.

WHAT IS BLOCKCHAIN?

A blockchain is a time-stamped series of immutable records of data that is managed by a cluster of computers. Information held on a blockchain exists as a shared and continually reconciled database. This means that data of a blockchain is not owned by a single entity. Each of these blocks of data is secured and bound to each other using cryptographic principles (Rosic, 2016).

DOI: 10.4018/978-1-7998-0186-3.ch012

If all the data is shared then this means that there is no centralized version of this information. Thus, a blockchain has no centralized authority. The information on the chain is open for anyone and everyone in the network to see. Hence, anything that is built on blockchain is very transparent by nature and everyone involved is accountable for their actions (Hales, 2019).

WHY BLOCKCHAIN?

The blockchain is considered a disruptive technology; one that significantly alters the way businesses or entire industries operate. It often forces companies to change the way they approach their business or fear losing market share and to become irrelevant.

Blockchain brings into picture something truly unique. It gives a new no trust mechanism. Imagine a situation where a transaction made by a person A is shown to be done but due to a malicious intruder (hacker) or software error it does not show up but the amount is lost, or a case where the bank balance of A is different from the actual balance that A thinks it is. For situations like these, the third party trust is a must. A person trusts a bank and uses its features. If in case know that a bank is not trustworthy or is fraudulent then the obvious choice is to not use that particular bank's services. If an unfortunate error happens, the bank is held liable for any mistakes made.

Such situations will never arise with blockchain being similar to a public ledger with so many people acting as proof of one's transaction. There is no need to rely on a third party and hence it has become a huge concept seeking attention. The blockchain provides a trust and authentication protocol that has already disrupted banking and is on the verge of revamping healthcare, financial services, social apps and more.

Blockchain brings the proof of trust in the form of cryptographic functions i.e. mathematical equations that are solvable and can give a definitive analytical proof and not in the form of a developer who developed it (prone to human error) or any other means. So, for the first time in human existence, blockchain brings about a trust mechanism that is trustless. In other words, it is independent of where it resides and who operates it, as the trust mechanism is mathematically proven. This removes the need for human intervention in the system altogether. That is the major problem that blockchain solved for the world, which no one was able to solve before it.

Figure 1.

HOW DOES A BLOCKCHAIN WORK?

Blockchain works mainly on the basis of hashing. Hashing is a technique used to map data of arbitrary size into a fixed size. Hashing is a one-way function. It means that once converted to a hash it is not possible to get back the previous data. Now this means that sharing of a hash of a password to anyone, it would not be possible to find the original password from it.

Hashing has a lot of advantages. It is used widely in password store where a database stores the hash of a person's password in a database, so even if the database is compromised, there is no actual leakage of confidential information to a third party. When requires the site can then hash the input password and check if it matches with the one in the database to let the user have access.

Some Properties of Hashing

Deterministic: This means that no matter how many times a single input is passed through a hash function, the output will always be the same. This is critical because if there is different output over time for the same input then it will be impossible to keep track of input.

Quick Computation: The hashing function must be able to return the hash of an input quickly. If the process is not fast enough the system won't be efficient to use.

Pre-Image Resistance: What pre-image resistance states is that, given Hash A it is infeasible to determine A, where A is the input and Hash A is the output hash.

Small Changes in the Input Changes the Hash: Even if a single small change in input, the hash must have a significant change in output.

Collision Resistant: Given two different inputs A and B where Hash A and Hash B are their respective hashes, it is not possible to have Hash A equal to Hash B. This means that for each input there will be a unique output (hash).

In the above examples, it is clear that the only difference of the two string inputs is the lower case and upper case at the start but then the output is unique and differ a lot form the other. It should also be noted that the hash of a string is not impossible to crack. One may always brute force all possibility and may end up with the same hash thereby finding input. But this is very inefficient, time-consuming and cannot

Figure 2.
2^{256}= *115792089237316195423570985008687907853269984665640564039457584007913129639936*

yield many benefits. Since resource for computation is very high and time taken is also painfully high. As an example, a popular hashing algorithm SHA - 256 has a 256-bit output which may have binary values (0 or 1). Thus, making it have 2^{256} outputs.

This number is exponentially big. So brute forcing this is not a very likely option.

A Hashing function can be used to hash any data be it picture or file or text. This makes hash pretty useful in improving the integrity of a delivered file. Once a file is transferred between two parties, they can confirm the messages were not tampered with bypassing the hash of the file to check its integrity.

Similarly, a hash of a given block will be unique to that block and if changed will also be checked easily by computing its hash and checking with other computers on the node.

CONTENTS OF A BLOCK IN BLOCKCHAIN

Index: Position of the block in the blockchain. Index of genesis block (or starting block) is 0.

Timestamp: The exact time when that particular block was created.

Hash: A hash value of that block in the blockchain.

Previous Hash: Hash value of the previous block in the chain. Through this mechanism, we can link all the blocks of a blockchain. For genesis block, this value is 0.

Data: Data stored on the node. For example, transactions.

Nonce: It is a number used to determine a valid hash. To generate this number, the processing power or resources are used.

A valid hash is a term used to state a particular format of hash that is considered to be correct for a given blockchain. An example of having a hash with 5 zero's at the start is considered valid. Then, it might not be possible to have such a hash with the given/existing data input. This does not mean it is impossible to get one. Enter nonce, a random number generated and added with the data of a block to generate a hash. By changing the nonce value we can end up with a particular value for the nonce that produces a valid hash (it has 5 zero is start according to example).

Figure 3. Genesis block (Han, 2017)

Genesis Block	
Previous Hash	0
Timestamp	Thu, 27 Jul 2017 02:30:00 GMT
Data	Welcome to Blockchain CLI!
Hash	0000018035a828da0…
Nonce	56551

This process requires a lot of computation power and this adds latency in addition of a new block to the chain.

A key point here is to see that having a timestamp as an entry in the block makes it very unlikely that someone else can have even a minor possibility to produce the same hash. Since one can produce that particular hash only if all data, previous block hash and timestamp match. It is very unlikely this is possible since one cannot go back in time to get the same timestamp. An example of the same is shown in figure below.

Merkle Tree: Merkle tree takes a large amount of data and makes it more manageable for processing.

A transaction in the blockchain is represented a T_A. The hash value for the same is represented as $H_{A.}$ After each transaction has been hashed individually, the corresponding hash values are combined and hashed to produce H_{AB}. If there are odd number of hash values then the odd hash element is simply hashed with itself to obtain a new hash. Example if 5th hash value is H_E then it is hashed with itself to obtain H_{EE}.

This process is repeated to obtain the last hash value also known as a Merkle Root. Here the merkle root is $H_{ABCDEFGH}$.

Advantages of Merkle Tree Structure

- **Tamper Proof**: Organising transaction into a merkle root makes it easy to check if a transaction has been tampered with. If a transaction has been

Figure 4. Merkle Tree (Asolo, 2018)

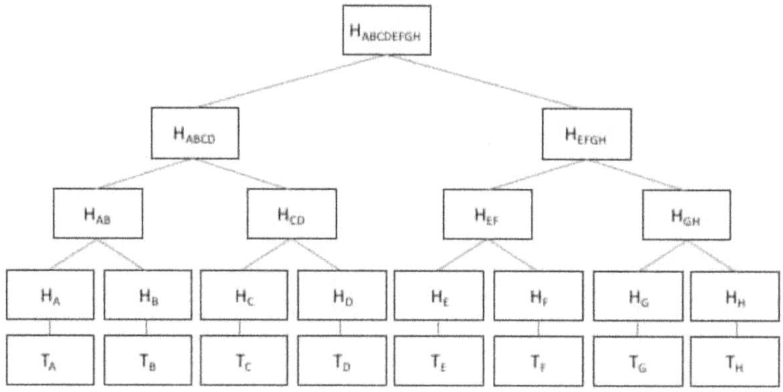

changed then its corresponding hash will also change leading to a completely different merkle root.

- **Uses Less Resources**: Organising transactions into a merkle tree uses fewer resources when compared to having to add each individual transaction hash into the block header.
- **Verification**: A merkle tree allows one to check if a transaction has been added to a block without having to download the entire blockchain (Asolo, 2018).

CONSENSUS ALGORITHM

A consensus algorithm is the root of a blockchain. It helps facilitates decision making based on the algorithm applied. It is used to arrive at a decision that helps ease the majority of the participants of the chain.

Consensus algorithms do not merely agree with the majority votes, but it also agrees to one that benefits all of them. So, it's always a win for the network.

Blockchain consensus models are methods to create equality and fairness in the online world. The consensus systems used for this agreement is called a consensus theorem.

These consensus models consist of some particular objectives, such as:

Coming to an agreement: The mechanism collects all the agreements from the group as much as it can.

- ◦ **Collaboration**: Every one of the group aims toward a better agreement that results in the group's interests as a whole.

Figure 5. Different types of consensus algorithms (Anwar, 2018)

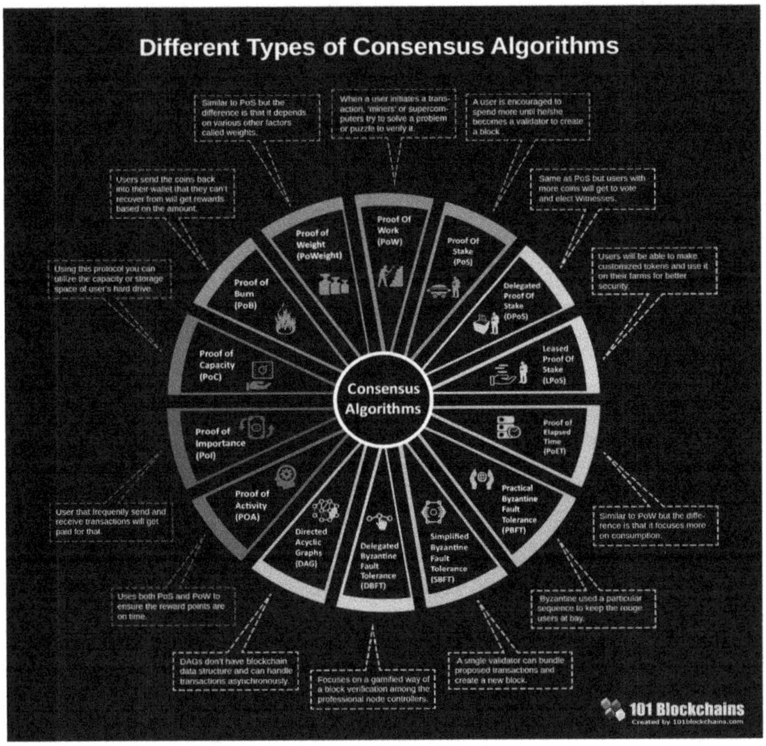

- **Co-Operation**: Every individual will work as a team and put their own interests aside.
- **Equal Rights**: Every single participant has the same value in voting. This means that every person's vote is important.
- **Participation**: Everyone inside the network needs to participate in the voting. No one will be left out or can stay out without a vote.
- **Activity**: Every member of the group is equally active. There is no one with more responsibility in the group (Hasib Anwar, 2018).

The major algorithms are:

Proof of Work

It is used in the Bitcoin network and the first algorithm to be used in a blockchain. The duty to add a block to a blockchain falls on to people called miners and the procedure they use is termed as mining. This technology works to solve complex mathematical problems.

In this method, the amount of work done by a miner decides that miner's possibility of mining a single block and the reward for mining (receiving an equivalent value of winning done in terms of the coin of the network).

What Are the Main Issues With Proof of Work Consensus Algorithm?

The majority of the Consensus algorithms have drawbacks and Proof of work is no different. The main drawbacks of the system are:

Greater Energy Consumption

Blockchain network contains huge number of microchips that hashes constantly. This process requires a lot of energy. Bitcoin currently offers 20 billion hashes per second. This procedure enables the network to add a layer of protection from a botnet attack.

The security level of the blockchain network based on proof of work requires a lot of energy, and it is intensive. The greater consumption is becoming a problem in a world where we are running out of energy. This incurs a large sum of cost due to electricity consumption.

Centralization of Miners

With the energy resource constraints, proof of work will move toward cheaper electricity solutions. However, the primary problem would be if a bitcoin miner-manufacturer rises. Within a certain time, the manufacturer can become more power hungry and try to create new rules in the mining system.

This situation will lead towards centralization within the decentralized network. That's why it's another great problem these Blockchain algorithms are facing.

The 51% Percent Attack

This attack would mean a possible control of majority of the users and taking over most of the mining power. In this scenario, the attackers will get enough power to control everything in the network.

They can stop other people from generating new blocks. Attackers can also receive rewards based on their tactics.

Less reward as chain increases in size:

This means as the chain grows it reaches a point where more resources are used mine a block than the reward obtained. Hence a loss.

Proof of Stake

Proof of stake is a blockchain algorithm that deals with the major drawbacks of the proof of work algorithm. In this, every block gets validated before the network adds another block to the blockchain. The difference is, the miners can join the mining process using their coins to stake.

The proof of stake is a new type of concept where every individual can mine or validate new blocks only based on their own coin possession. So, in this scenario the more coins one has, the better the chances are.

Although the process is entirely random, still not every miner can participate in the staking. All the miners of the network are randomly chosen. A specific amount of coins must be stored in a wallet, to be qualified to enter the staking process. New blocks will get created proportional to the number of coins based on the wallet. For example, if A owns 10% of all the coins, then A gets to mine 10% of the new blocks.

There are lot of blockchain technologies that use a variety of proof of stake consensus algorithm. However, all of the algorithms work the same for mining new blocks. Every miner will receive a block reward as well as a share of the transaction fees.

The mining capability of a miner is determined by the number of coins staked. The proof of stake community is majorly decentralized and the 51% attack is very expensive to pull off.

Proof of stake consensus algorithm blockchain is very energy efficient when compared to proof of work.

The main drawback of the system is that full decentralization is not possible ever. This is because, only a handful of nodes get to participate in the staking on the network and individuals with the most coins will eventually control most of the system.

How Much Would be the Cost Incurred for Adding a Block to the Blockchain?

One of key factors in the cost of adding a block to the blockchain is the amount of data stored in that particular block. For a block in a blockchain, the typical amount of data one can store is roughly capped at 1 MB (taking bitcoin as an example).

Why Is Storing Data on Blockchain Not Viable?

Because the amount of data one stores has to be stored by every node on the network. Everyone who is a part of the blockchain will have a copy of the data. This is why even storing KB can cost a lot.

When storing data on the blockchain, one has to pay for the base price for the transaction itself, plus an amount per byte of data stored. If smart contracts are involved, payment for the execution time of the smart contract is also added.

Every operation on a blockchain whether it is adding a block or checking an entry or finding a block, requires payment in the form of that particular coin base used in that blockchain.

Hence, storing a large amount of data would mean incurring a large sum of payment for processing it, which makes storing of data on blockchain not feasible. (CanYa, 2018).

What Is the Alternative for Storing a File on Blockchain If It Is Not Possible Directly?

Enter IPFS: [Interplanetary File System]

IPFS or Interplanetary File System, developed by the Protocol Labs is a peer-to-peer protocol where every node stores a group of hashed files. A client who wants to retrieve any of file enjoys access to an abstraction layer, where it simply needs to call the hash of the file it wants. IPFS then combs through the nodes and supplies the client with the file.

It's a decentralized way of storing and referring to files but gives more control and refers to a file by its hash (Coral Health, 2018).

If one wants to upload a file to IPFS, it is enough to put the file in the working directory and tell IPFS to add the file, which generates a hash of that file (starts with Qm for IPFS hashes). This file is then available on the IPFS network.

Now when this file has to be accessed by someone else, the hash of that file is enough for the other party to call the original file from IPFS and get a copy of the file.

There is an obvious security challenge here. As long as anyone has the hash of the file, they can retrieve it from IPFS. So sensitive files are not well suited for IPFS in their native states.

To overcome this challenge one must secure the file before uploading to IPFS. Asymmetric encryption allows us to encrypt a file with the public key of the intended recipient so that only they can decrypt it when they retrieve it with IPFS. A malicious party who retrieves the file from IPFS can't do anything with it since they can't decrypt it.

So the process changes such that before the file is uploaded to IPFS it is encrypted with the other party's public key and the encrypted file is sent to IPFS. This hash is then shared to the other party who then downloads the encrypted file and can decrypt the file using their private key to gain access to the file. A malicious party cannot decrypt the file because they lack the private key to it.

Figure 6. Asymmetric encryption (Information Commissioner's Office, n.d.)

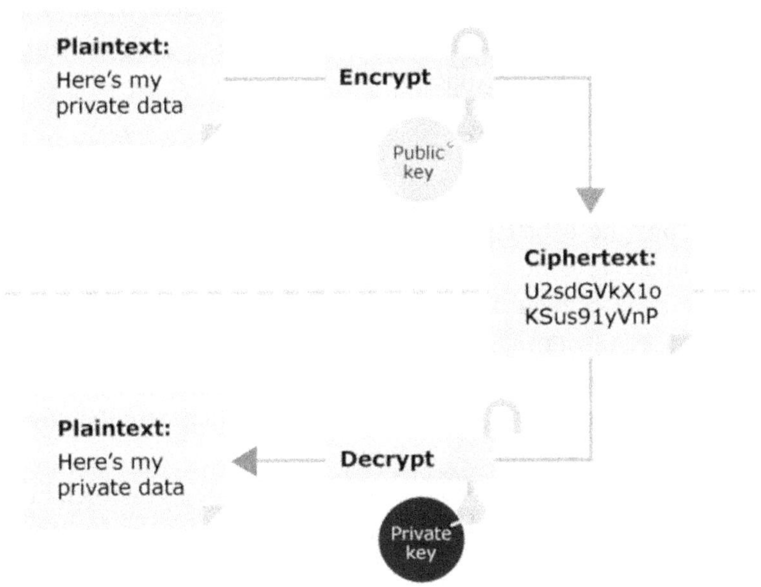

This is the reason why IPFS is powerful when coupled with blockchain. Instead of simple text, one just needs to store the hash of the IPFS file. Thus, achieving the simplicity of data that's required on the blockchain but gets to enjoy the file storage and decentralized peer-to-peer properties of IPFS.

Storing files securely on a distributed network. What does that actually mean?

It means that one can then reimagine the way one can think about how the internet itself works. For example:

- There's going to be no servers hosting websites. All the content will be served from IPFS and data pulled from the blockchain directly.
- One won't have to sign up for accounts. One's private key will grant permission and validate the identity of users to the websites/providers.
- Direct communication with another party without anyone middle man. Truly secure and private communication based applications are possible.

IPFS allows for distributed storage of data which is immune to altering and forgery. Data stored on the IPFS network cannot be altered without changing the data identifier (Hash of that file). This means non-critical data can be stored to IPFS while storing the identifier on the blockchain.

IPFS is an optimal storage platform for Decentralized applications (dApps) which are a class of applications that leverage decentralization to achieve exceptional benefits. This decentralization helps in eliminating or reducing any trading fee. Such dApps require the storage of a significant amount of data. IPFS allows this data to be stored in a distributed manner. For these reasons, IPFS is turning into a preferred storage platform for dApps.

Benefits of IPFS

- IPFS can provide a better user experience: IPFS could lead to enhanced user experience in multiple cases. For example, trying to browse through or download some content using the typical client-server model may deplete the network bandwidth and lead to network congestion. This may result in difficult user experience due to large latencies. In IPFS, contents are rendered from the closest peers that possess a copy of that content thereby removing the single-node pressure.
- IPFS allows for new online business models: In today's internet, every online content is hosted on dedicated servers. It is crucial for the content publisher to guarantee the availability of the content and adequate bandwidth to satisfy the required demand. In IPFS, instead of having a single host server serving all users, data is shared in a distributed network and can be served by any node in possession of that data.

What Are the Challenges of IPFS

IPFS is a new technology undergoing development. Yet, there are several challenges that need to be resolved in order to achieve greater usage.

- **Bandwidth Requirements**: Running an IPFS node currently takes significant bandwidth that may not be feasible for many users. Excessive bandwidth usage may harm the adoption of IPFS. One solution to this problem may be, financial incentives. Gaining rewards for hosting content on IPFS can help overcome the costs of running the nodes and encourage usage of IPFS.
- **Availability**: The current implementation of IPFS cannot guarantee data availability upon request due to lack of IPFS nodes. One way to ensure availability is through content pinning which means constantly saving copies of the published content on the node. This node is required to be online every time to ensure availability of the file.
- **Private Content**: Content published to IPFS is public by design. Anyone in possession of the content hash can access the file. Currently, IPFS does not provide a built-in solution for storage of private data. Encryption can be used

to store private data on IPFS. Another solution might be to deploy a private network (zk Capital, 2018).

CASE STUDY

E- File Sharing Using Blockchain on Ethereum DAPP and IPFS for Personal or Private Data

In this concept, the user may upload a file to IPFS and have it encrypted so that once downloaded by the recipient, only the decryption key (Asymmetric key) can help view the original contents. It is of importance to understand that this may be extended to important business files so that one server or hard disk does not contain all the required personal data and that it actually chunked and decentralized among many peers who can gain access only if authorised. Storing the hash of the file in a blockchain can help in reducing the trust issues of the file handling since IPFS makes use of hashing function thereby providing a different hash value for a different file. This helps easily track malicious changes done to file by an intruder.

The main reason as to why blockchain is of prime importance is because it makes the issue of trusting a third party unnecessary. This means all users have access to the public data ledger (blockchain) and that any changes done to a block is reflected to every block on the chain. Thus making a decentralized blockchain storage a viable option with no single point of failure and hence one will not lose any private data.

REFERENCES

Anwar. (2018). *Consensus Algorithms: The Root Of The Blockchain Technology*. Retrieved from https://101blockchains.com/consensus-algorithms-blockchain/

Asolo. (2018). *Merkle Tree & Merkle Root Explained*. Retrieved from https://www.mycryptopedia.com/merkle-tree-merkle-root-explained/

Coral Health. (2018). *Learn to securely share files on the blockchain with IPFS*. Retrieved from https://medium.com/@mycoralhealth/learn-to-securely-share-files-on-the-blockchain-with-ipfs-219ee47df54c

Hales. (2019). *What is Blockchain Technology? A Beginner's Guide*. Retrieved from https://www.uplarn.com/what-is-blockchain-technology-a-beginners-guide/

Han, S. (2017). *How does blockchain really work? I built an app to show you.* Retrieved from https://medium.freecodecamp.org/how-does-blockchain-really-work-i-built-an-app-to-show-you-6b70cd4caf7d

Information Commissioner's Office. (n.d.). *What Types of Encryption Are There?* Retrieved from https://ico.org.uk/for-organisations/guide-to-data-protection/guide-to-the-general-data-protection-regulation-gdpr/encryption/what-types-of-encryption-are-there/

Rosic. (2016). *What is Blockchain Technology? A Step-by-Step Guide For Beginners*. Retrieved from https://blockgeeks.com/guides/what-is-blockchain-technology/

Ya. (2018). *Why IPFS is the Future of Decentralised File Storage*. Retrieved from https://medium.com/canyacoin/why-ipfs-is-the-future-of-decentralised-file-storage-8958f3bd02c5

zk Capital. (2018). *IPFS: A Complete Analysis of The Distributed Web*. Retrieved from https://medium.com/zkcapital/ipfs-the-distributed-web-e21a5496d32d

Chapter 13
Conceptual Insights in Blockchain Technology:
Security and Applications

Anup Bihari Gaurav
Maulana Azad National Institute of Technology, India

Pushpendra Kumar
Maulana Azad National Institute of Technology, India

Vinod Kumar
Madanapalli Institute of Technology and Science, India

Ramjeevan Singh Thakur
Maulana Azad National Institute of Technology, India

ABSTRACT

The global popularity of digital cryptocurrencies and research in a decentralized system have led to the foundation of blockchain, which is fundamentally a public digital ledger to share information in a trustworthy and secure way. The concept and applications of blockchain have now spread from cryptocurrencies to various other domains, including business process management, smart contracts, IoT, and so on. Cryptocurrency is a mechanism designed to work for the online secure payments system using cryptography. Cryptography maintains confidentiality, integrity, and authentication. Cryptocurrency has come as a novel way of making payments that keep all the transactions secure and safe, which avoids any type of intermediaries such as a bank. This chapter will shed light on the concept of blockchain technology, security, and its applications in various domains.

DOI: 10.4018/978-1-7998-0186-3.ch013

INTRODUCTION

The system refers to organisation of different elements which collectively works for a common purpose. In the case of database and computer networking environment, this can be categorised in three basic types as Centralized System, Decentralised System, and Distributed System.

Centralized System: A centralized system has complete reliance on single point which could be turn out to be a complete failure for all associated system if the single point failures occur. Fig. 1 refers to the schematic diagram of centralized system (J. Yli-Huumo, et al., 2016).

Decentralised System: A decentralised system don't have any central authority in this system each node can take independent decisions. Decentralised system gives freedom for lower level component to compute local information to accomplish global goal (i.e. Transaction). Fig. 2 refers to the schematic diagram of decentralized system.

Distributed System: The distributed system is a network of autonomous components that cooperate, coordinate to achieve a common goal. It help in resource sharing and provide user a view of a single network. They share resources such as software (file, databases, and links), hardware (printer, processor, memory). Fig 3. Refers to the schematic diagram of distributed system (Z. Zheng et al., 2017)

The blockchain is a decentralized computation and information sharing platform that enables multiple authoritative domains, who don't trust each other, to cooperate, coordinate and collaborate in a rational decision making process.

Figure 1. Centralized System

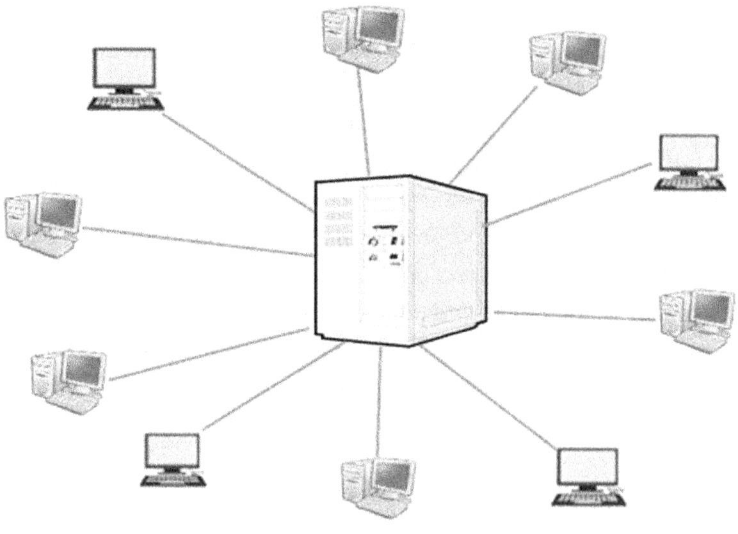

Figure 2. Decentralized System

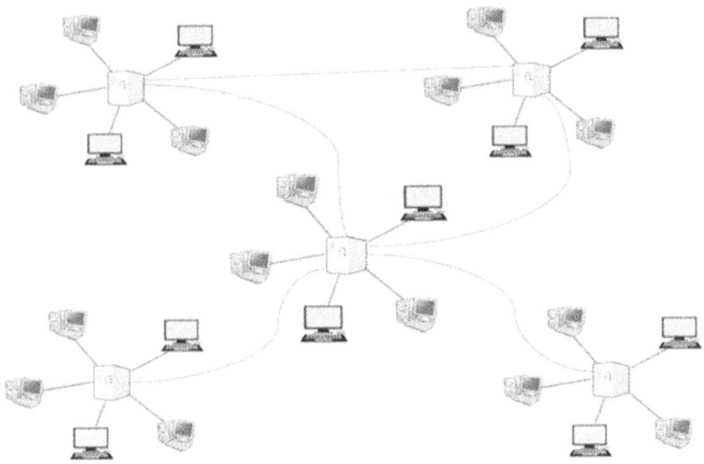

Figure 3. Distributed System

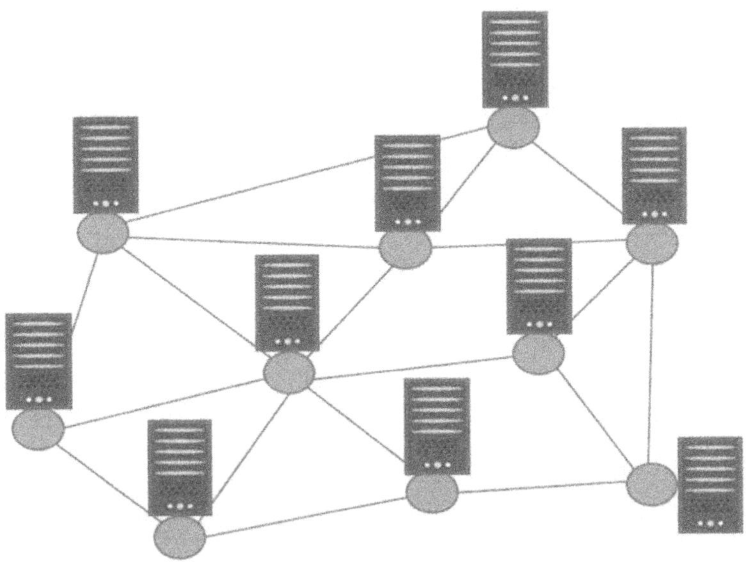

The decentralised system which exists in blockchain system provides consistent database support for every transactions that happens. It is an open, distributed ledger that can record transactions between two parties efficiently and in a verifiable and permanent way (Chen, G., *et* al. 2018).

Pros And Cons Of Distributed, Centralised, Decentralised Systems

1. **Maintenance /Points of Failure**:
   a. Decentralized have more but still finite numbers of failure.
   b. Distributed systems are the most difficult to maintain.
   c. Centralized systems are easy to maintain as there is only a single point of failure.
2. **Fault Tolerance / Stability**:
   a. **Centralized** systems can be highly unstable and intolerable due to single point failure may ruin the whole working system.
   b. **Decentralized** are stable system as compared to centralized system as if failure of the leader in decentralized doesn't harm the rest of the system and still you will have a stable network working in synchronisation.
   c. **Distributed** systems are much more stable and a single point of failure doesn't do much harm.
3. **Ease of Development / Creation**: Centralized systems can be created rapidly, and in easy way just have to build a central server for commanding/managing the connected components. For Decentralized and Distributed systems, one have to first work out the lower level details like resource sharing (Hardware/ Software), trade (Transaction) and communications (Network) and it imposes a certain level of difficulty in maintaining these system to its coherent state.
4. **Max Number of Users Added to the System/ Scalability**:
   a. **Decentralized:** Moderate
   b. **Centralized:** Low scalability
   c. **Distributed:** Infinite
5. **Diversity / Evolution:** As centralized systems shadow a single framework, they don't have diversity and grow gradually. But for distributed systems and decentralized systems, once the elementary infrastructure is in place, evolution is remarkable.

BACKGROUND

Blockchain is the central technology applied to generate the cryptocurrency, such as Bitcoin, through the maintenance of immutable distributed ledgers in thousands of nodes proposed by Satoshi Nakamoto in 2008 (Nakamoto 2008).

The cryptocurrency blockchain transaction may be shown as follows- Using a peer-to-peer blockchain network, the User 1 initiates a transaction to User 2. A pair of public key and private key is taken as a cryptographic proof of identity. These keys identifies the User 1 and the User 2 distinctively within the network. Now the transaction will be broadcasted to the memory space for the blockchain network for transaction authentication and confirmation.

If an assured number of approved nodes are gained then he fresh block is created; this is said as reaching consensus. A new "block" on the whole blockchain network is made only if the consensus is reached and every node updates its respective copy of the blockchain ledger. This block has all the transactions that happened during this period. It is now "linked" to the original block in the network with the help of digital signature. The consensus point is attained with the help of a consensus algorithm and this process is called mining.

2.1 A Simplified View Of Blockchain

The simplified view of how the blockchain technology works is mentioned below and the how blocks are chained is shown in the schematic diagram of Figure 4.

- Every single node maintain a local copy of global data sheet.
- The system guarantees the consistency among the local copies of ledger
- The local copies at every node is identical.
- The local copies are always modified based on the global information.
- The transaction is maintained over a public ledger, which is a database of historical information available at every local node within a system. This information is utilised for future computations.

2.2 Securing Data Cryptographically Within A Block

Block: A block is a container data structure which contain series of transactions. Each transaction within a block is digitally signed and encrypted and verified by the peer node of blockchain network. Cryptography security ensures that only authorised participant will be able to view information on the ledger. Fig.5 shows the transaction information that is contained in the blockchain.

A single block of bitcoin can contain more than 500 transactions on average. A block contain two component

- Block header
- List of transaction

Figure 4. A simplified view of blockchain

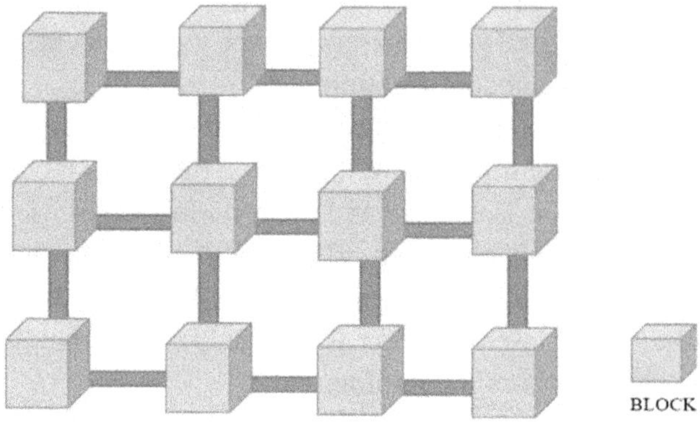

Figure 5. Transaction information in blockchain

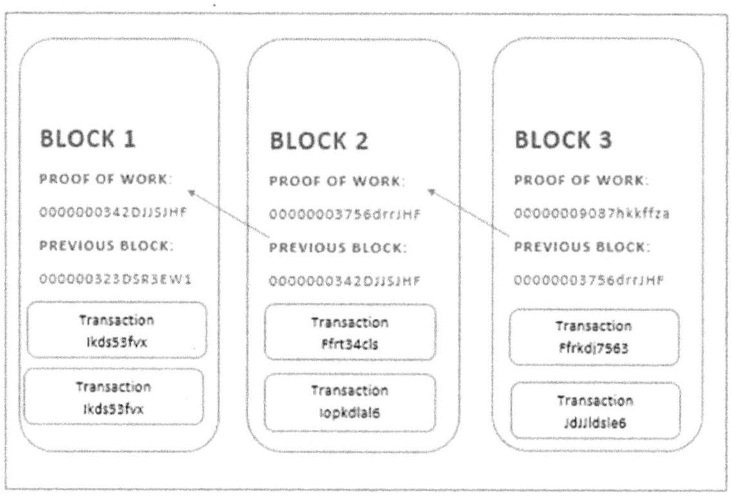

Metadata about a block

1. Previous block hash
2. Mining statistics used to construct the block
3. Merkle tree root

Every block uses previous block hash to create a new block hash thus making blockchain tamperproof. Mining mechanism generate hash which should be difficult enough to make blockchain tamperproof. The header contains mining statistics – timestamp, nonce and difficulty. Figure 6 depicts the generation of Block Hash.

Figure 6. Depiction of generation of Block Hash

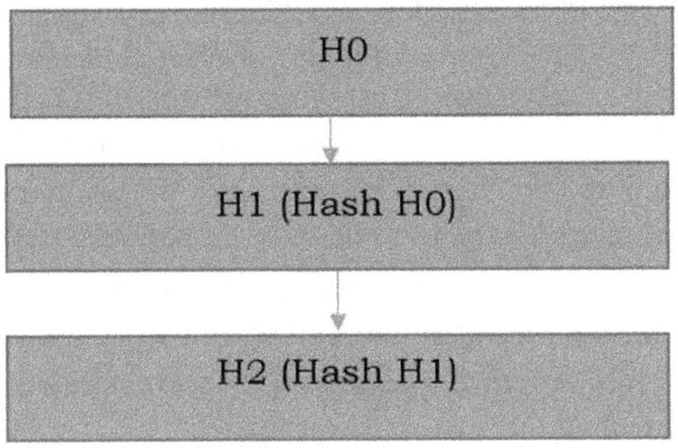

Merkle Tree Root: The transactions are organized in a Merkle Tree structure. The root of the Merkle tree is a verification of all the transactions.

There are two model where blockchain works on

1. **Permission less model (public model):** Works in an open environment and over a large network of participants. The users do not need to know the identity of the peers, and hence the users do not need to reveal their identity to others and good for financial applications like banking using cryptocurrency.
2. **Permissioned model (private model):** Blockchain can be applied just beyond cryptocurrency. The underlying notions of consensus, security and distributed replicated ledgers can be applied to even closed or permissioned network settings.

2.3 Bitcoin

Bitcoin are cryptocurrency that are generated by a complex algorithm using peer to peer network in a process referred as mining that require extensive computing resources.

Bitcoin is a decentralized digital currency without a central bank or single administrator authority Bitcoin can be sent from user-to-user on the peer-to-peer bitcoin network without the need of intermediaries. Bitcoin has many unique attributes that differentiate it from traditional currencies as it didn't require a central authority to handle transaction, and incurring cost related with it. Bitcoin also allows business to take and make payments much more easily than through usual mode of channels for payments like PayPal and credit cards. Bitcoin allows merchants to avoid the fees associated with these services, enabling frictionless transactions.

Bitcoins are not minted as traditional currency it have been generated at a predetermined rate. The program used to generate Bitcoin runs on a peer to peer network and requires very powerful computer system to operate.

Mining a Bitcoin is a result of powerful computers solving cryptographic problems in tandem with other similar computers. The computer that gets the solution will be awarded the bitcoin and the computers that are jointly solving the problems are recorded as "proof of work". Miners in the bitcoin network collect transaction for 10 minutes and start mining the proof of work. The probability of getting a proof of work is low as it is uncertain which miner will be able to generate the block. Mining bitcoin requires massive computational power of host machine and they consider to have value (F. Tschorsch & B. Scheuermann 2016).

Bitcoin uses public key cryptography to make and verify digital signatures. Spending bitcoin in a network require verification of ownership on all of the thousands of nodes in the network this prevent tampering with blockchain, double spending, attacks (Sybil, Dos services).

Proof of work: Proof of work is a process of producing data that's hard to get but easy to verify. In blockchain proof of work is about solving mathematical problems having certain level of difficulty (D. Kraft, 2016).

ISSUES AND CHALLENGES IN BLOCKCHAIN TECHNOLOGY

Blockchain technology is a revolutionary concept in the computer science and it has a variety of applications in different fields likes – banking, management, IoT's, Identity applications etc. There are still numerous challenges that are still being faced by the blockchain technology.

Lack of legal regulations: One of the major obstacle in the pursuance of blockchain technology in entrepreneurial activity. Some people are using without any obvious regulatory framework in the grey area comfortably. May countries around the world are in the way of designing the suitable laws for blockchain technology. It is expected that in a few years many country will allow to flourish business using blockchain technology with proper legal framework (A. Natchkebia, 2018)

Huge consumption of energy: In this technological functioning, a very complex and long running complex computation occurs which requires lots of computing infrastructure as a result they also need huge consumption of electrical energy (A. Natchkebia, 2018).

Cost to set up: There exists a challenge in the setting up the functional infrastructure for the blockchain technology. The system bears the complex setup which also costly tool (A. Natchkebia, 2018).

Public Perception: The prime problem in the way of the success of Blockchain is the public perception. The folks don't consider it be a portion of conventional functioning. Most of the folks consider that this technology will not last long. The characteristics like the absence of governance, easy admittance to become a member of public Blockchain spoils the image of Blockchain in public perception (A. Natchkebia, 2018).

Moreover, if a transaction has been committed in blockchain technology then the transaction roll back is not possible. Congestions generation due to cypto mining in the communication network is a big issue. All these discussed factors poses as challenges for the development of this new Technology.

APPLICATIONS OF BLOCKCHAIN TECHNOLOGIES

Blockchain technology has the wide variety of applications in the present time. The major applications of this technology has been discussed as below:

A. Cryptocurrency

1. **Bitcoin (BTC):** Bitcoin is cryptocurrency that is generated by a complex algorithm using peer to peer network in a process referred to as mining which require extensive computing resources, they have changeable value to open market, they are exchanged via a 34 character alphanumeric address that the user maintain. Managing transactions and issuing of bitcoin is carried out collectively by the network. It is exposed to all, anybody can take part in it.
2. **Litecoin (LTC):** Litecoin is another kind of open source global payment network, it is fully decentralised in nature and without any central authority Litecoin uses a peer-to-peer network to allow instant transactions. It is the internet currency incurring near-zero cost payments to anyone in the world. Mathematics secures the network and empowers individuals to control their own finances.
3. **Bytecoin (BCN):** Bytecoin is also a private, decentralized cryptocurrency where transaction is private and untraceable as well this is achieved using cryptographic algorithm. Its open source code that allows everyone to take part in development of network of Bytecoin it also incorporate privacy and security of its user. It uses CryptoNote Technology where transaction becomes untraceable and unlikable. Additionally the bytecoin API provides support for multi signature solution which will give an additional degree of security. Bytecoin encompass various features they are as follows:
    a. Bytecoin transaction

   b. Security and reliability
   c. Open source code base
   d. Multiple signature
   e. Powerful API

4. **Peercoin (PPC):** Peercoin is a cryptocurrency that launched in 2012. It holds value, offers complete anonymity, and can be sent over the internet without any central authority like a bank, just like Bitcoin, Dash, Litecoin, and the majority of other cryptocurrencies. Peercoin is different from bitcoin mining approach as it uses "Proof-of-stake" an alternative consensus protocol that was invented by Sunny King and Scott Nadal and first implemented in Peercoin in 2012. In a proof-of-stake based blockchain, coin owners are the ones who exert influence over the network, produce new blocks and secure the chain. Stakeholders of Peercoin effectively co-own the blockchain network, similar to how shareholders co-own a publicly traded corporation (Peercoin, 2019).
5. **Emercoin (EMC):** An open source cryptocurrency which originated from Bitcoin, Peercoin and Namecoin. Other than being a cryptocurrency, it is also a platform for secure distributed blockchain business services. The EMC coin is used for accessing the blockchain-based services provided by Emercoin. Emercoin inherits the reliability and security of Bitcoin, while at the same time putting more features to its own blockchain by leveraging several innovative technologies (emercoin.com, 2019).
6. **Ripple (XRP):** Ripple is a real-time gross settlement system (RTGS), currency exchange and remittance network created by Ripple Labs Inc. (US). It is built upon an open source distributed protocol it support tokens that represent cryptocurrency, commodities and other unit that represent value. Ripple network instantly enables free global financial transaction of any size incurring no additional costs.

   Ripple depends upon a common shared distributed database storing information of ripple accounts, the ripple network consists of validating servers that constantly compares their transactional records with very low latency
7. **Omni (MSC):** Omni is a digital currency and communication protocol built on bitcoin blockchain Omni is a platform for creating and trading custom digital assets and currencies. It is a software layer built on top of the most popular, most audited, most secure blockchain. Omni transactions are Bitcoin transactions that enable next-generation features on the Bitcoin Blockchain. Omni provide all feature of bicoin and also features of omni layers (omnilayer, 2019).
8. **Gridcoin (GRC):** Gridcoin is a decentralized, open-source, math-based digital asset (cryptocurrency). Gridcoin implements a "Proof of Research" which rewards user with a Gridcoin on performing useful scientific computation on

"BIONIC", while being energy-efficient, it is the first and only cryptocurrency that rewards individuals for scientific contributions and performs transactions peer-to-peer cryptographically - without the need for a central authority to distribute rewards (Gridcoin, 2019).

B. Business

- **Insurance:** Claim Processing
- **Payments:** Cross-Border Payments
- **Asset Management:** Trade Processing and settlement
- Copyright and Loyalty Protection
- Tax Regulation and Compliances
- Trading Equity

C. IOT'S Applications

- Smart Application
- Supply Chain Sensors

D. Smart Contracts

- Healthcare
- Government
- Music

E. Identity Applications

- Passports
- Personal Identification
- Birth certificate, wedding certificate and death certificates

CONCLUSION

Blockchain technology has revealed it's prospective for transmuting conventional business with its key features: anonymity decentralization, auditability, and persistency. Here, we have presented an overview over blockchain technology. We have also discussed the issues and challenges related to blockchain technology. Furthermore, the applications of blockchain technology with respect to various domains has also been discussed.

FUTURE DIRECTIONS

In this day and age blockchain technology centred applications are growing up day by day. Now our prospective effort would be to done comprehensive investigations on blockchain-centred applications in business, education. The issues and challenges will also be taken up comprehensively.

REFERENCES

Bytecoin.org. (n.d.). Retrieved from https://www.bytecoin.org/

Chen, G., Xu, B., Lu, M., & Chen, N. S. (2018). Exploring blockchain technology and its potential applications for education. Smart Learning Environments, 5(1), 1.

Emercoin.com. (n.d.). Retrieved from https://www.emercoin.com/

Gridcoin.org. (n.d.). Retrieved from https://www.gridcoin.org/

Gridcoin.us. (n.d.). Retrieved from https://www.gridcoin.us/

Kraft, D. (2016). Difficulty control for blockchain-based consensus systems. Peer-to-Peer Networking and Applications, 9(2), 397–413.

Nakamoto, S. (2019), Bitcoin: A peer-to-peer electronic cash system. Retrieved from https://bitcoin.org/bitcoin.pdf

Natchkebia, A. (2018), https://www.forexnewsnow.com/forex/analysis/cryptocurrency/ challenges-blockchain-technology/ (Retrieved on 15.03.2019)

Omnilayer.org. (n.d.). Retrieved from https://www.omnilayer.org/

https://ripple.com/(Retrieved on 20.03.2019)

Tschorsch, F., & Scheuermann, B. (2016). Bitcoin and beyond: A technical survey on decentralized digital currencies. IEEE Communications Surveys and Tutorials, 18(3), 2084–2123.

Yli-Huumo, J., Ko, D., Choi, S., Park, S., & Smolander, K. (2016). Where is current research on Blockchain technology?—A systematic review. PLoS One, 11(10).

Zheng, Z., Xie, S., Dai, H., Chen, X., & Wang, H. (2017). An overview of blockchain technology: Architecture, consensus, and future trends. In *2017 IEEE International Congress on Big Data (BigData Congress)* (pp. 557-564). IEEE. doi:10.1109/BigDataCongress.2017.8510.1109/BigDataCongress.2017.85

KEY TERMS AND DEFINITIONS

Bitcoin: Bitcoin is a cryptocurrency, a form of electronic cash. A purely peer-to-peer version of electronic cash would allow online payments to be sent directly from one party to another without going through a financial institution

Block: A block is a container data structure which contain series of transactions. Each transaction within a block is digitally signed and encrypted and verified by the peer node of blockchain network.

Blockchain: The Blockchain is a decentralized computation and information sharing platform that enables multiple authoritative domains, who don't trust each other, to cooperate, coordinate and collaborate in a rational decision making process.

Cryptocurrency: Cryptocurrency is a mechanism designed to work for the online secure payments system using cryptography.

Chapter 14
Healthcare Information Exchange Through Blockchain-Based Approaches

Rajit Nair
Jagran Lakecity University, Bhopal, India

Amit Bhagat
Maulana Azad National Institute of Technology, Bhopal, India

ABSTRACT

Blockchain is one of the fastest growing and most important technologies in the world. Most of the people think that blockchain is all about cryptocurrency or bitcoin, but it is beyond that. It is a technology that creates immutable and distributable data records that are shared between peers in network database systems and records digital events in such a way that it cannot be altered or recognized until it reaches the recipient. In recent times, many of the industries are using blockchain as a tool to innovate their functionality. Some of the well-known industries are banking sector, real estate, healthcare, internet of things, insurance, and many more. Out of these industries, healthcare is one of the industries that is adopting blockchain very rapidly. This chapter will discuss the blockchain and how it has transformed the healthcare industry.

DOI: 10.4018/978-1-7998-0186-3.ch014

INTRODUCTION

Healthcare industry is one of the fast growing industries in the world (Groves, Kayyali, Knott, & Kuiken, 2013). Day by day new innovations are taken place in this industry to provide better results. Due to these innovations average life expectancies has been increased. First of all we will discuss about the blockchain later on we will see how blockchain is performed in healthcare industry because by adopting blockchain we can develop new and efficient record system related to healthcare, wearable devices (Haghi, Thurow, & Stoll, 2017), examination systems those are based on artificial intelligence (Buchanan, 2005), cryptography (Stallings, 2011) and many more. According to survey taken by Hyper ledger's, 42.9% of healthcare organizations assumes that interoperability of digital records will use for faster blockchain implementation and out of this 28.6% have responded to use this technology in recent times. Still there is lot of improvement needed for seamless adoption of blockchain in healthcare (Mettler, 2016). Blockchain based approaches laid the foundation for Bitcoin and after that it has become more popular (Underwood, 2016). Nowadays blockchain is used almost in every area whether it is related to banking sector (Wright, 2015), agriculture sector (Tripoli & Schmidhuber, 2018), health sector (Dhillon et al., 2017), Internet of Things (IoT) (Christidis & Devetsikiotis, 2016) and so on. In today's world, health sector is one of the most important area in which block chain is used and it will become the biggest sector by year 2023. So in this chapter we will discuss how blockchain is extensively used in health sector. Blockchain technology is based on distributed approach with immutable functionality which means information will not get change till it reaches to the recipient. Due to increase number of patients, it is very much needed that we must safely keep the information like Patient health record, electronics health records, medical insurance claims, data collected from IOT devices and monitoring system. To keep these information safe blockchain plays an important role and one of the major advantages is data integrity.

Let's Discuss what is Blockchain?

Blockchain is simply a time stamped series of immutable data or records that is handles by cluster of systems and are not owned by single entity. Each of these data is in the form of blocks and these are kept secured by using cryptographic principles (Panasenko & Smagin, 2013). Immutable data means which cannot be altered or modify during transaction. Some of the important features of blockchain are as follows:

- Blockchain is not owned by single authority that's why it is decentralized.

- Each and every block which takes part are storing the cryptographically data.
- It is immutable means no one can tamper the data which is contained in the form of block chain.
- Due to its transparency nature we can trace the data vey easily whenever needed.

Relation between Blockchain and Decentralization

Before understanding the concept of decentralization, we will try to relate it with the human behavior. As we humans used to trust people by birth itself and it is accepted that to survive in this world, trust is very much required. We live in community so it is better that trusting many people is better than trusting a single one. This is what happen in decentralization also, trusting a cluster of system is better than single one. Centralization is always a problem when it comes to reliability because trusting a centralized institute like bank has generated a recession in the year 2008, which was one of the biggest financial collapses after 1930 in U.S. Later on Satoshi Nakamoto has introduced bitcoin which is based on decentralized cryptocurrency powered by blockchain technology (Satoshi Nakamoto, 2008). Decentralization is pretty simple concept in which all the records are stored within the blockchain and are not saved in a centralized storage unit. To perform this multiple systems are running within the network and that own a copy of all the data within the blockchain. That's why all the system notified once when there is any updation done.

Figure 1 shows the decentralization approach representing number of nodes and there is no single authority of control.

Figure 1. Nodes in decentralization approach

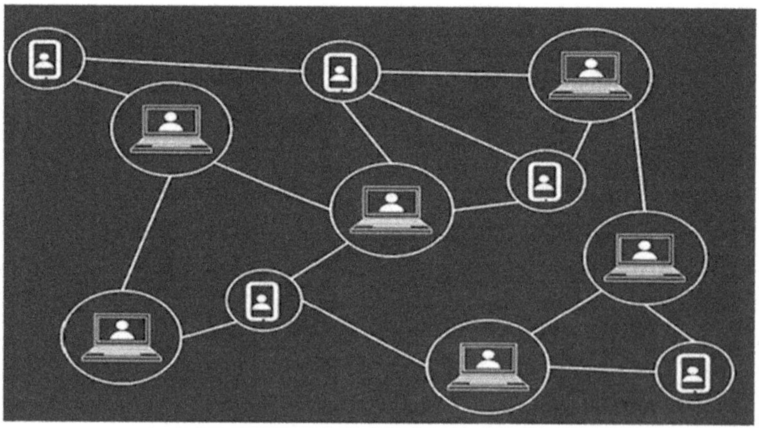

Public and Private Blockchain

Blockchain is classified into two categories one is public blockchain and the other one is private blockchain. Both are blockchain that means they provide peer to peer network which offers an immutable and decentralized framework and are synchronized using consensus protocol. Consensus protocols are the set of rules that describes about the communication and transmission of data between electronic devices (Sankar, Sindhu, & Sethumadhavan, 2017). Consensus is achieved through the agreement done by devices when decision about the data that has to be recorded in blockchain is made. Let us discuss them in details:

Public Blockchain – As the name suggest public which means accessible to all, this means public blockchain is the one which can be read and write by anyone, even anyone can join the public blockchain. In this nobody has control over the network and ensure that data cannot be changed once it is validated on the blockchain. Some well known examples based on public blockchain are Bitcoin (Antonopoulos, 2016), Etherum (Buterin, Wiederhold, Riva, & Graffigna, 2013), Litecoin (Gkillas & Katsiampa, 2018), etc. Out of these Bitcoin is the first blockchain based application that could be moved across the globe without the help of any third parties like banks or any other companies. Some of the advantages of public blockchain are as follows:

- Open read and write
- Ledger is distributed
- Immutable
- Secure due to mining

Private Blockchain - Private blockchain is accessible to limited users who are participant of any private network. This provides access though permission and work like centralized systems that provides access to limited users. This blockchain contains one or multiple entities to control the network. Sometimes for controlling there is an identity step through which we come to know about the parts of blockchain network. If we don't know who is taking part then it's become very difficult for us to define rules in the blockchain network. Hyperledger (hyperledger.org, 2016), R3 Corda (Valenta & Sandner, 2017) and Quorum (Sankar et al., 2017) are the example of private blockchain. Advantages of private blockchain are as given below:

- Enterprise permissioned
- Faster transactions
- Better scalability
- Compliance support
- Consensus more efficient

Table 1. Public and Private Blockchain

Public & Closed (Buterin, 2015)	**Public & Open**
• Voting • Voting records • Whistleblower	• Currencies • Betting • Video games
Private & Closed (Lai & LEE Kuo Chuen, 2017)	Private & Open
• Consortium • National defense • Law enforcement • Military • Tax returns	• Supply chain • Government financial records • Corporate earnings statement

Cryptographic Hash Function

Hashing is the process through which input of any string can be converted into an output of fixed length. Considering the cryptocurrencies like Bitcoin (Satoshi Nakamoto, 2008), it uses the transaction as an input and pass through hashing algorithm (Bitcoin uses Secure Hashing Algorithm-256) to generate an output of fixed length. Let us take an example that use SHA-256 (Secure Hashing Algorithm-256) as hashing algorithm for generating the output (Jung & Jang, 2017).

Some of the properties of hash function due to which it becomes very useful for blockchain are as follows:

- **Deterministic:** It's all about generating the same hash for the particular input, this is because if we generate the different hash for the same input multiple times then it become very difficult to keep the track of the input.
- **Pre-Image Resistance:** It is very difficult or even infeasible to determine input by observing hash. Suppose H(A) is the hash and for the input A, but just by watch H(A) it is very difficult to determine A.
- **Snowball Effect:** This property shows that if there is small change in input then also there will be huge change in the hash value (wierczek, 2014).

Table 2. Hash value for input

INPUT	**HASH**
Hello	67rtwththgkjgdfjghfdgkjgh7e93h439ghdgfdgh0whthgg024htroghogh04tngong
friend	38ahdbfkdbfkafbksfbsdkfjb67jdbfkjfbdbdbfkdfbdkfdfhfkbdfadfe78ee8fehf88

Figure 2 shows the different components which take participation in blockchain process which includes different steps that are as follows:

- **User Creates Transaction**: Transaction is the first step which is generated by user or nodes.
- **Transaction as a Block:** Now transaction is transformed in the form of block.
- **Block is Broadcast**: Next, this block is broadcasted though trusted network.
- **Network Nodes Approve:** Approval of the block by the participating nodes in network.
- **Block added to Chain:** The new created block is added to the chain of blocks.
- **Transaction Entered on Ledger:** Entries in the form of transaction is entered in the distributed ledger.

Blockchain in Healthcare Industry

Blockchain has proved to be one of the emerging technologies for many industries, healthcare is one of them. In this section we will discuss how blockchain works in the area of health care. Patients are increasing rapidly and the amount of data is also collected in huge volume, so the healthcare providers have to manage more and more data on a regular basis. Due to this huge volume the complexity is increase and it becomes very difficult for hospitals to manage and store information. Blockchain allows users to perform the following functions:

Figure 2. Potential Impact of blockchain on healthcare

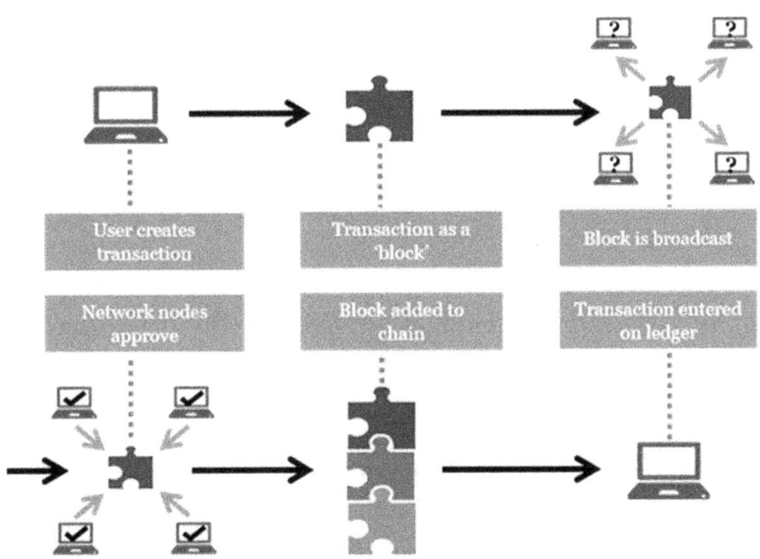

- Verifying Public Health Information Integrity
- Ensure data safety
- Maintain the integrity of clinical research reports
- Immutable auditing of medical records
- Reduction of audit expenses and regulatory compliance

Blockchain provides us more protection than ordinary encryption. This helps us in implementing the new standards in managing medical records, insurance claim, patient health information, etc. It also helps in exclusion of interruption during sharing of data. Many medical organizations hesitate to adopt blockchain due to lack of knowledge in this area. It has been seen quarter of technology experts are still at the stage of learning and exploring the blockchain. Healthcare service providers need more proofs before adopting this technology which includes:

- Technical proof of concept (PoC) (65.4%) – Through this one comes to know about the feasibility and potential of blockchain technology. It is also considered as prototype without any supporting code. This prototype is used by organizations internally who have better understanding about the project (Novo, 2018).
- Security proof (38.5%) - Security proof is very much needed in blockchain, because when any transaction is done there must be some provision through which we can prove that our system is secure (Kiayias, Russell, & David, 2017).
- Privacy proof (34.6%) - Proof techniques are used to protect our privacy
- Regulatory approval (23.1%) – Blockchain regulations are not vey emerging. So there must be some controlling authority which can regulate the blockchain (Kasiewicz, 2019).

Keeping all the above proofs in mind, it is predicted that blockchain will be widely used in healthcare industries during the coming years. Some of the following usage issues in health care that has to be processed by blockchain are as follows:

- **Drug Traceability:** One of the biggest problems in healthcare industry is drugs counterfeit. According to HRDO (Health Research Funding Organization), approx 10-30 percent of drugs manufactured in developing countries are fake. According to reports there is loss of more than $200 in the business of US due to this counterfeiting of drugs and side effect of drugs. Blockchain provides a solution for these problems by easily finding fraudulent customers. To deal with these problem blockchain is having two options one is public blockchain and the other one is private blockchain. In case of public blockchain healthcare industry has to register their products with the private company and ensure the quality and authenticity of the products. In case of private blockchain there is central authority which has access to drug blockchain. Blockchain transparency becomes useful when drug moves from retailer to manufacturer and the operational data is recorded on the blockchain. This process makes feasibility during verifying the path of the drug and determines all the chains at any time.

- **Data Security in Clinical Trials:** Clinical trials are the process through which effectiveness of the medicine is tested for specific diseases. This test sometime gets success and sometime it fails. Researchers has to maintain a record during clinical trials because statistics has been done aggressively for generating results, quality reports etc. During this trials researchers tries to make report which cannot be control by everyone. Researchers are solely responsible for specific research. These observations or data can be easily modified or hidden so that whole outcome of the research can be changed. Intruders or hackers are very much interested in recording or modifying the results even if the results do not meet the expectation. Blockchain has done a tremendous job to overcome from these problems. In this user has to prove the authenticity of the documents registered in the system. The proof is given by adding data in the form of transaction and validation is done by all the nodes. As already discussed blockchain contains immutable data that means the result generated from clinical trials can be stored in secured manner. Blockchain can discover modification by comparing a unique data code which is generated by system with the original one. SHA256 calculator is used to generate a unique hash when a modification is done.
- **Patient Data Management:** It is very much needed that PHI (Patient Health Information) must keep secure (Health and Social Care Information Centre, 2015). Information privacy is controlled by the Health Insurance Portability and Accountability Act (HIPAA) (Edemekong & Haydel, 2018). Most common problem related to PHI is that sometimes patient need to share their medical records with other parties especially when they have to buy medicine from the pharmacy store. So these are the problems which have to solve by blockchain especially partial access. Using blockchain patient can send necessary information to the third party without revealing identity. To perform this blockchain creates hash for each PHI block combined with patient ID. Through this patient can decide whom it has to provide partial access or full access. Here even patient can set specific third parties to whom they can give permission for sharing the heath information.

From the above statements it can be said that blockchain can be efficiently use for prevention of data from breaching in the healthcare sector. Through blockchain we can record, store, and share sensitive data, so that health care sector get benefitted with considering the protocol of HIPAA for trustworthy digital protection.

In the above figure 3. It is shown what problems are faced by health care industries in today's scenario and how blockchain is providing the solution to overcome from these problems.

CONCLUSION

This chapter has discussed how blockchain works and how it impacts the healthcare industry. Due to its impact, the healthcare industry can record, store and share the sensitive information related to health issues. However many industries are still in the initial stage to adopt blockchain technology. Let's see some of the facts related to blockchain technology:

Figure 3. Potential Impact of blockchain on healthcare

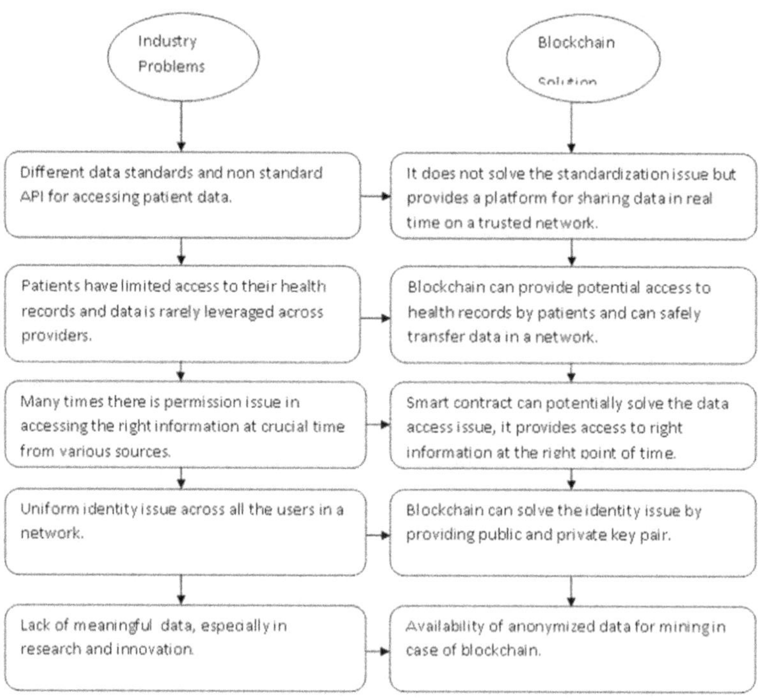

- In the first quarter of year 2018, the funding for health startups has reached to its all time high value.
- By the year 2020, it is expected that global health spending will reach to more than $8.734 trillion and this is very huge amount.

In case of healthcare industry there is no financial constraint for research and development of any new innovative technology which will always be a boost for implementation of blockchain. In the above discussions we have stated that healthcare industry will get benefitted from decentralized medical approach.

As per the research done by BIS, the reports have shown that healthcare industry can save upto $100 billion per year by using blockchain technology. The savings can be done by minimizing the cost related to data breaching, operational cost, fraud related cost, fake insurance claims, functional support and personal cost, etc. It is expected that global blockchain in the health care will grow at a CAGR of more than 64% from 2019 to 2025 which achieve a target of almost $5.7 billion by 2025. According to future predictions, we can say that blockchain in the health care industry will contribute more in the largest market share by year 2025.

Now blockchain is adopted by almost all the sectors other than healthcare like banking, agriculture, stock market, cryptocurrency, etc. So we hope that this technology will provides you horizontal innovation to boost the industries so that they can fulfill the current needs.

FUTURE WORK

In future blockchain will be applied for improving many areas in healthcare system that are as follows:

- **Consent Management:** Storing patient consent for exchanging data and privacy preferences during treatment. This will help stakeholders to access the consent of patients and can send anywhere when patient demands. Due to this approach the administrative burden will be reduced and patient care experience will be enhanced.
- **Release of Funds will Become Easier:** New methods are developed using blockchain so that remittance and micropayments can be done easy.
- Tokenization should be improved for non cash assets including the outcomes generated by blockchain.
- Consumption of electricity is very high in blockchain process. So in future there must be change in blockchain infrastructure so that electricity should be minimized.

- More and more people must be educated about the benefits and losses of blockchain which can result as implementation of high use cases.
- Genomic data should be enhanced by using blockchain technology

REFERENCES

Antonopoulos, A. M. (2016). Mastering Bitcoin. *Journal of World Trade*. doi:10.1002/ejoc.201200111

Buchanan, B. (2005). A (Very) Brief History of Artificial Intelligence. *AI Magazine*.

Buterin, V. (2015). On Public and Private Blockchains. Blog.Ethereum.Org. doi:10.5949/liverpool/9780853239963.003.0009

Buterin, V., Wiederhold, B. K., Riva, G., & Graffigna, G. (2013). *A next-generation smart contract and decentralized application platform*. Etherum. doi:10.1016/j.jchromb.2013.02.015

Christidis, K., & Devetsikiotis, M. (2016). Blockchains and Smart Contracts for the Internet of Things. *IEEE Access: Practical Innovations, Open Solutions*, *4*, 2292–2303. doi:10.1109/ACCESS.2016.2566339

Dhillon, V., Metcalf, D., Hooper, M., Dhillon, V., Metcalf, D., & Hooper, M. (2017). Blockchain in Health Care. Blockchain Enabled Applications. doi:10.1007/978-1-4842-3081-7_9

Edemekong, P. F., & Haydel, M. J. (2018). *Health Insurance Portability and Accountability Act (HIPAA)*. StatPearls.

Gkillas, K., & Katsiampa, P. (2018). An application of extreme value theory to cryptocurrencies. *Economics Letters*, *164*, 109–111. doi:10.1016/j.econlet.2018.01.020

Groves, P., Kayyali, B., Knott, D., & Van Kuiken, S. (2013). *The Big Data revolution in healthcare*. McKinsey Global Institute.

Haghi, M., Thurow, K., & Stoll, R. (2017). Wearable devices in medical internet of things: Scientific research and commercially available devices. *Healthcare Informatics Research*, *23*(1), 4. doi:10.4258/hir.2017.23.1.4 PMID:28261526

Health and Social Care Information Centre. (2015). *Hospital Episode Statistics*. Author.

hyperledger.org. (2016). *Hyperledger – Blockchain Technologies for Business*. Author.

Jung, M. Y., & Jang, J. W. (2017). Data management and searching system and method to provide increased security for IoT platform. *International Conference on Information and Communication Technology Convergence: ICT Convergence Technologies Leading the Fourth Industrial Revolution, ICTC 2017*. 10.1109/ICTC.2017.8190803

Kasiewicz, S. (2019). New trends in the system regulating the market of bank services. Kwartalnik Nauk o Przedsiębiorstwie. doi:10.5604/01.3001.0010.7450

Kiayias, A., Russell, A., & David, B. (2017). PPCoin: Peer-to-Peer Crypto-Currency with Proof-of-Stake. Proceedings of the 2016 ACM SIGSAC Conference on Computer and Communications Security - CCS'16. 10.1017/CBO9781107415324.004

Lai, R. (2017). Blockchain – From Public to Private. In Handbook of Blockchain, Digital Finance, and Inclusion. Academic Press. doi:10.1016/b978-0-12-812282-2.00007-3

Mettler, M. (2016). Blockchain technology in healthcare: The revolution starts here. In *2016 IEEE 18th International Conference on e-Health Networking, Applications and Services, Healthcom 2016*. IEEE. 10.1109/HealthCom.2016.7749510

Nakamoto. (2008). Bitcoin: A Peer-to-Peer Electronic Cash System. Academic Press. doi:10.100710838-008-9062-0

Novo, O. (2018). *Blockchain Meets IoT: An Architecture for Scalable Access Management in IoT. IEEE Internet of Things Journal*. doi:10.1109/JIOT.2018.2812239

Panasenko, S., & Smagin, S. (2013). Lightweight Cryptography: Underlying Principles and Approaches. International Journal of Computer Theory and Engineering. doi:10.7763/ijcte.2011.v3.360

Sankar, L. S., Sindhu, M., & Sethumadhavan, M. (2017). Survey of consensus protocols on blockchain applications. *2017 4th International Conference on Advanced Computing and Communication Systems, ICACCS 2017*. 10.1109/ICACCS.2017.8014672

Stallings, W. (2011). Cryptography and Network Security: Principles amd Practices. *Network*. doi:10.1007/11935070

Tripoli, M., & Schmidhuber, J. (2018). *Emerging Opportunities for the Application of Blockchain in the Agri-food Industry Agriculture*. Food and Agriculture Organization of the United Nations.

Underwood, S. (2016). Blockchain beyond bitcoin. *Communications of the ACM*, *59*(11), 15–17. doi:10.1145/2994581

Valenta, M., & Sandner, P. (2017). *Comparison of Ethereum, Hyperledger Fabric and Corda.* FSBC Working Paper.

Wierczek, A. (2014). The impact of supply chain integration on the "snowball effect" in the transmission of disruptions: An empirical evaluation of the model. *International Journal of Production Economics*. doi:10.1016/j.ijpe.2013.08.010

Wright, G. (2015). *Will Blockchain Enable Better Banking?* Global Finance.

Compilation of References

Abduvaliyev, A., Pathan, A. S. K., Zhou, J., Roman, R., & Wong, W. C. (2013). On the vital areas of intrusion detection systems in wireless sensor networks. *IEEE Communications Surveys and Tutorials*, *15*(3), 1223–1237. doi:10.1109/SURV.2012.121912.00006

Abeyratne, S. A., & Monfared, R. P. (2016). Blockchain ready manufacturing supply chain using distributed ledger. *International Journal of Research in Engineering and Technology*, *5*(9), 1–10. doi:10.15623/ijret.2016.0509001

Ackermann, J., & Trümper, F. (2012). Deutsche Bank. In *Deutsche Standards*. Retrieved from https://annualreport.deutsche-bank.com/2012/ar/managementreport/internalcontroloverfinancialreporting.html

ACQUI Technology. (n.d.). *The Impact of Cryptocurrency on the Global Economy*. Retrieved from https://acquitechnology.com/2018/07/07/the-impact-of-cryptocurrency-on-the-global-economy/

Agrawal, N., & Jawdekar, A. (2016). User-based approach for finding various results in web usage mining. In *Proc. of Symposium on Colossal Data Analysis and Networking*. IEEE. 10.1109/CDAN.2016.7570867

Ahram, T., Sargolzaei, A., Sargolzaei, S., Daniels, J., & Amaba, B. (2017). Blockchain technology innovations. In 2017 IEEE Technology & Engineering Management Conference (TEMSCON) (pp. 137-141). IEEE. doi:10.1109/TEMSCON.2017.7998367

Alaba, F. A., Othman, M., Hashem, I. A. T., & Alotaibi, F. (2017). Internet of Things security: A survey. *Journal of Network and Computer Applications*, *88*, 10–28. doi:10.1016/j.jnca.2017.04.002

Al-Asdi, T. A., & Obaid, A. J. (2016). An Efficient Web Usage Mining Algorithm Based on Log File Data. *Journal of Theoretical & Applied Information Technology*, *92*(2), 215–224.

Ali, M., Nelson, J., Shea, R., & Freedman, M. J. (2016). Blockstack: A global naming and storage system secured by blockchains. In *2016 USENIX Annual Technical Conference (USENIX ATC 16)* (pp. 181-194). USENIX.

Ali, M., Nelson, J., Shea, R., & Freedman, M. J. (2016). Blockstack : A Global Naming and Storage System Secured by Blockchains. *USENIX Annual Technical Conference*.

Allen, C. (2016). *The Path to Self-Sovereign Identity*. Retrieved from https://www.coindesk.com/path-self-sovereign-identity

All-In-Bits. (2017). *Introduction to tendermint*. Retrieved from https://tendermint.com/intro

Alvi, S. A., Afzal, B., Shah, G. A., Atzori, L., & Mahmood, W. (2015). Internet of multimedia things: Vision and challenges. *Ad Hoc Networks*, *33*, 87–111. doi:10.1016/j.adhoc.2015.04.006

Ammar, M., Russello, G., & Crispo, B. (2018). Internet of Things: A survey on the security of IoT frameworks. *Journal of Information Security and Applications*, *38*, 8–27. doi:10.1016/j.jisa.2017.11.002

Anand, N., & Hilal, S. (2012). Identifying the User Access Pattern in Weblog Data. *International Journal of Computer Science and Information Technologies*, *3*(2), 3536–3539.

Andoni, M., Robu, V., Flynn, D., Abram, S., Geach, D., Jenkins, D., ... Peacock, A. (2019). Blockchain technology in the energy sector: A systematic review of challenges and opportunities. *Renewable & Sustainable Energy Reviews*, *100*, 143–174. doi:10.1016/j.rser.2018.10.014

Androulaki, E., Barger, A., Bortnikov, V., Cachin, C., Christidis, K., De Caro, A., ... Muralidharan, S. (2018, April). Hyperledger fabric: a distributed operating system for permissioned blockchains. In *Proceedings of the Thirteenth EuroSys Conference* (p. 30). ACM. 10.1145/3190508.3190538

Angraal, S., Krumholz, H. M., & Schulz, W. L. (2017). Blockchain technology: Applications in health care. *Circulation: Cardiovascular Quality and Outcomes*, *10*(9). doi:10.1161/CIRCOUTCOMES.117.003800 PMID:28912202

Anitha, V., & Isakki, P. (2016). A survey on predicting user behavior based on web server log files in a web usage mining. In *Proc. of International Conference on Computing Technologies and Intelligent Data Engineering*. IEEE. 10.1109/ICCTIDE.2016.7725340

Antonakakis, M., April, T., Bailey, M., Bernhard, M., Bursztein, E., Cochran, J., . . . Kumar, D. (2017). Understanding the mirai botnet. In *26th USENIX Security Symposium (USENIX Security 17)* (pp. 1093-1110). USENIX.

Antonopoulos, A. M. (2014). Mastering Bitcoin: Unlocking Digital Crypto-Currencies. O'Reilly Media, Inc. Retrieved from https://bitcoin.org/en/

Antonopoulos, A. M. (2014). *Mastering Bitcoin: unlocking digital cryptocurrencies*. O'Reilly Media, Inc.

Antonopoulos, A. M. (2016). Mastering Bitcoin. *Journal of World Trade*. doi:10.1002/ejoc.201200111

Anwar. (2018). *Consensus Algorithms: The Root Of The Blockchain Technology*. Retrieved from https://101blockchains.com/consensus-algorithms-blockchain/

Armknecht, F., Karame, G. O., Mandal, A., Youssef, F., & Zenner, E. (2015, August). Ripple: Overview and outlook. In *International Conference on Trust and Trustworthy Computing*(pp. 163-180). Springer. 10.1007/978-3-319-22846-4_10

Asolo. (2018). *Merkle Tree & Merkle Root Explained.* Retrieved from https://www.mycryptopedia.com/merkle-tree-merkle-root-explained/

Axon, L. (2015). *Privacy-awareness in Blockchain-based PKI.* Tech. Rep. Retrieved from https://ora.ox.ac.uk/objects/uuid:f8377b69-599b-4cae-8df0-f0cded53e63b/datastreams/ATTACHMENT01

Aye, T. T. (2011). Weblog cleaning for mining of web usage patterns. *Proc. of 3rd International Conference on Computer Research and Development IEEE*, 2(1), 490-494.

Azaria, A., Ekblaw, A., Vieira, T., & Lippman, A. (2016, August). Medrec: Using blockchain for medical data access and permission management. In *2016 2nd International Conference on Open and Big Data (OBD)* (pp. 25-30). IEEE.

Bahga, A., & Madisetti, V. K. (2016). *Blockchain platform for industrial Internet of Things.* Tech. Rep. Retrieved from http://file.scirp.org/pdf/JSEA_2016102814012798.pdf

Banafa, A. (2016). *A secure model of IoT with Blockchain.* OpenMind.

Banerjee, M., Lee, J., & Choo, K. K. R. (2018). A blockchain future for internet of things security: A position paper. *Digital Communications and Networks*, *4*(3), 149–160. doi:10.1016/j.dcan.2017.10.006

Barenji, A. V., Guo, H., Tian, Z., Li, Z., Wang, W. M., & Huang, G. Q. (2019). Blockchain-Based Cloud Manufacturing: Decentralization. *Transdisciplinary Engineering Methods for Social Innovation of Industry 4.0.*, 1003 – 1011. doi:10.3233/978-1-61499-898-3-1003

Bashir, I. (2018). *Mastering Blockchain: Distributed ledger technology, decentralization, and smart contracts explained.* Packt Publishing Ltd.

Batsaikhan, U. (2017). *Cryptoeconomics - The Opportunities and Challenges of Blockchain.* Retrieved from https://bruegel.org/2017/07/cryptoeconomics-the-opportunities-and-challenges-of-

Batubara, F. R., Ubacht, J., & Janssen, M. (2018). Challenges of blockchain technology adoption for e-government. *Proceedings of the 19th Annual International Conference on Digital Government Research Governance in the Data Age - dgo '18.* 10.1145/3209281.3209317

BBC News. (2018). *Coincheck: World's biggest ever digital currency 'theft'.* Retrieved from https://www.bbc.com/news/world-asia-42845505

Bendiab, K., Kolokotronis, N., Shiaeles, S., & Boucherkha, S. (2018). WiP: A novel blockchain-based trust model for cloud identity management. In *2018 IEEE 16th Intl Conf on Dependable, Autonomic and Secure Computing, 16th Intl Conf on Pervasive Intelligence and Computing, 4th Intl Conf on Big Data Intelligence and Computing and Cyber Science and Technology Congress (DASC/PiCom/DataCom/CyberSciTech)*(pp. 724-729). IEEE. 10.1109/DASC/PiCom/DataCom/CyberSciTec.2018.00126

Benet, J., & Greco, N. (2018). *Filecoin: A decentralized storage network*. Protoc. Labs.

Bentov, I., Lee, C., Mizrahi, A., & Rosenfeld, M. (2014). Proof of Activity: Extending Bitcoin's Proof of Work via Proof of Stake. *IACR Cryptology ePrint Archive, 2014*, 452.

Bernstein, A. J. (1966). Analysis of programs for parallel processing. *IEEE Transactions on Electronic Computers, EC-15*(5), 757–763. doi:10.1109/PGEC.1966.264565

Bhargava, R. (2019). Block chain Technology and Its Application: A Review. *IUP Journal of Information Technology, 15*(1), 7–15.

Bhowmik, D., & Feng, T. (2017, August). The multimedia blockchain: A distributed and tamper-proof media transaction framework. In *22nd International Conference on Digital Signal Processing (DSP)* (pp. 1-5). IEEE. 10.1109/ICDSP.2017.8096051

Big data, for better or worse: 90% of world's data generated over last two years. (2013). *ScienceDaily*.

Bisiaux, J. Y. (2014). DNS threats and mitigation strategies. *Network Security, 2014*(7), 5–9. doi:10.1016/S1353-4858(14)70068-6

Biswas, K., & Muthukkumarasamy, V. (2016). Securing smart cities using blockchain technology. In *2016 IEEE 18th international conference on high performance computing and communications; IEEE 14th international conference on smart city; IEEE 2nd international conference on data science and systems (HPCC/SmartCity/DSS)* (pp. 1392-1393). IEEE. 10.1109/HPCC-SmartCity-DSS.2016.0198

Biswas, R., Das, S. K., Harvey, D., & Oliker, L. (1999). Portable parallel programming for the dynamic load balancing of unstructured grid applications. In *Proceedings 13th International Parallel Processing Symposium and 10th Symposium on Parallel and Distributed Processing. IPPS/SPDP 1999* (pp. 338-342). IEEE. 10.1109/IPPS.1999.760497

BitInfoCharts. (2016). *Block - BitcoinWiki*. Retrieved from https://en.bitcoin.it/wiki/Block

Blockchains and the Internet of Things. (n.d.). Retrieved from http://www.postscapes.com/blockchains-and-the-internet-of-things/

b-money. (1998). Retrieved from http://www.weidai.com/bmoney.txt

Botta, A., De Donato, W., Persico, V., & Pescapé, A. (2016). Integration of cloud computing and internet of things: A survey. *Future Generation Computer Systems, 56*, 684–700. doi:10.1016/j.future.2015.09.021

Boverman, A. (2011). *Timejacking & Bitcoin*. Retrieved from https://culubas.blogspot.com/2011/05/timejacking-bitcoin_802.html

Brain, M., Chandler, N., & Crawford, S. (2002). *How domain name servers work*. Retrieved from https://computer.howstuffworks.com/dns.htm

Browne, R. (2017). *An Indian state wants to use blockchain to fight land ownership fraud.* Retrieved from https://www.cnbc.com/2017/10/10/this-indian-state-wants-to-use-blockchain-to-fight-land-ownership-fraud.html

Buchanan, B. (2005). A (Very) Brief History of Artificial Intelligence. *AI Magazine.*

Building Global Democracy. (2017). *The Impact of Cryptocurrency on Banks.* Retrieved from http://buildingglobaldemocracy.org/impact-cryptocurrency-banks/

Burniske, C., Vaughn, E., Shelton, J., & Cahana, A. (2016). *How Blockchain Technology Can Enhance HER Operability.* Retrieved from https://www.hyperledger.org/wp-content/uploads/2016/10/ARKInvest_and_GEM_Blockchain_EHR_Final.pdf

Buterin, V. (2014). *A next-generation smart contract and decentralized application platform.* White Paper.

Buterin, V. (2015). On Public and Private Blockchains. Blog.Ethereum.Org. doi:10.5949/liverpool/9780853239963.003.0009

Buterin, V. (2015). On public and private blockchains. *Ethereum Blog.* Retrieved from https: //blog.ethereum.org/2015/08/07/on-public-and-private-blockchains/

Buterin, V. (2015). *On public and private blockchains.* Retrieved from https://blog.ethereum.org/2015/08/07/on-public-and-private-blockchains/

Buterin, V., Wiederhold, B. K., Riva, G., & Graffigna, G. (2013). *A next-generation smart contract and decentralized application platform.* Etherum. doi:10.1016/j.jchromb.2013.02.015

Butun, I., Morgera, S. D., & Sankar, R. (2014). A survey of intrusion detection systems in wireless sensor networks. *IEEE Communications Surveys and Tutorials, 16*(1), 266–282. doi:10.1109/SURV.2013.050113.00191

Cachin, C. (2016, July). Architecture of the hyperledger blockchain fabric. In *Workshop on distributed cryptocurrencies and consensus ledgers* (*Vol. 310*). Academic Press.

Calzadilla, J. F., & Villa, A. (2017). *Systematic Literature Review of the use of Blockchain in Supply Chain.* Retrieved from http://oa.upm.es/51171/

Cartier, L. E., Ali, S. H., & Krzemnicki, M. S. (2018). Blockchain, Chain of Custody and Trace Elements: An Overview of Tracking and Traceability Opportunities in the Gem Industry. *The Journal of Geology, 36*(3).

Castro, M., & Liskov, B. (1999, February). *Practical Byzantine fault tolerance* (Vol. 99). OSDI.

Chandra, B., Gupta, M., & Gupta, M. P. (2008). A multivariate time series clustering approach for crime trends prediction. In *Proc of International Conference on Systems, Man and Cybernetics.* IEEE. 10.1109/ICSMC.2008.4811393

Chand, S., & Munishwar, R. (2017). Customer Behaviour Analysis using Web Usage Mining. *International Journal of Scientific Research in Computer Science and Engineering*, *5*(6), 47–50. doi:10.26438/ijsrcse/v5i6.4750

Chaofeng, L. (2009). Research on web session clustering. *Journal of Software*, *4*(5), 460–468.

Chen, G., Xu, B., Lu, M., & Chen, N. S. (2018). Exploring blockchain technology and its potential applications for education. *Smart Learning Environments*, *5*(1), 1. doi:10.118640561-017-0050-x

Chen, J., & Xue, Y. (2017, June). *Bootstrapping a blockchain based ecosystem for big data exchange. In 2017 IEEE international congress on big data (bigdata congress)* (pp. 460–463). IEEE. doi:10.1109/BigDataCongress.2017.67

Chin, W. L., Li, W., & Chen, H. H. (2017). Energy big data security threats in IoT-based smart grid communications. *IEEE Communications Magazine*, *55*(10), 70–75. doi:10.1109/MCOM.2017.1700154

Chitraa, V., & Thanamani, A. S. (2014). Weblog Data Analysis by Enhanced Fuzzy C Means Clustering. *International Journal on Computational Sciences & Applications*, *4*(2), 81–95. doi:10.5121/ijcsa.2014.4209

Christidis, K., & Devetsikiotis, M. (2016). Blockchains and smart contracts for the internet of things. *IEEE Access: Practical Innovations, Open Solutions*, *4*, 2292–2303. doi:10.1109/ACCESS.2016.2566339

Conoscenti, M., Vetro, A., & Martin, J. C. D. (2016). Blockchain for the Internet of Things: A systematic literature Review. *The 3rd International Symposium onInternet of Things: Systems, Management, and Security, IOTSMS-2016*. 10.1109/AICCSA.2016.7945805

Cooley, R., Mobasher, B., & Srivastava, J. (1999). Data preparation for mining world wide web browsing patterns. *Knowledge and Information Systems*, *1*(1), 5–32. doi:10.1007/BF03325089

Coral Health. (2018). *Learn to securely share files on the blockchain with IPFS*. Retrieved from https://medium.com/@mycoralhealth/learn-to-securely-share-files-on-the-blockchain-with-ipfs-219ee47df54c

Croman, K., Decker, C., Eyal, I., Gencer, A. E., Juels, A., Kosba, A., ... Song, D. (2016, February). On scaling decentralized blockchains. In *International Conference on Financial Cryptography and Data Security* (pp. 106-125). Springer. 10.1007/978-3-662-53357-4_8

Crosby, M., Pattanayak, P., Verma, S., & Kalyanaraman, V. (2016). Blockchain technology: Beyond bitcoin. *Applied Innovation*, *2*(6-10), 71.

Czachorowski, K., Solesvik, M., & Kondratenko, Y. (2019). The Application of Blockchain Technology in the Maritime Industry. In *Green IT Engineering: Social, Business and Industrial Applications* (pp. 561–577). Cham: Springer. doi:10.1007/978-3-030-00253-4_24

da Conceição, A. F., Silva, F. S. C., Rocha, V., Locoro, A., & Barguil, J. M. (2018). *Electronic health records using block chain technology*. Retrieved from https://arxiv.org/abs/1804.10078

Dagher, G. G., Mohler, J., Milojkovic, M., & Marella, P. B. (2018). Ancile: Privacy-preserving framework for access control and interoperability of electronic health records using blockchain technology. *Sustainable Cities and Society*, *39*, 283–297. doi:10.1016/j.scs.2018.02.014

Dai, F., Shi, Y., Meng, N., Wei, L., & Ye, Z. (2017). *From Bitcoin to Cybersecurity : a Comparative Study of Blockchain Application and Security Issues*. Academic Press.

Deininger, K. (2018). *For Billions without Formal Land Rights, the Tech Revolution Offers New Grounds for Hope*. Retrieved from http://blogs.worldbank.org/developmenttalk/billions-without-formal-land-rigtechrevolution-offers-new-grounds-hope

Deng, Z., Ren, Y., Liu, Y., Yin, X., Shen, Z., & Kim, H. J. (2019). Blockchain-Based Trusted Electronic Records Preservation in Cloud Storage. *Computers. Materials & Continua*, *58*(1), 135–151. doi:10.32604/cmc.2019.02967

Dennis, R. (2004). *The policy preferences of the US federal reserve*. Retrieved from https://www.frbsf.org/economic-research/files/wp01-08bk.pdf

Desjardins, J. (2017). *Bitcoin: The Top Performing Currency For a Second Year in a Row*. Retrieved from http://money.visualcapitalist.com/bitcoin-top-performing-currency-second-year/

Dhillon, V., Metcalf, D., Hooper, M., Dhillon, V., Metcalf, D., & Hooper, M. (2017). Blockchain in Health Care. Blockchain Enabled Applications. doi:10.1007/978-1-4842-3081-7_9

Digdaga. (2017). *Debate: Are Governments Against Bitcoin & Blockchain? Or Do They Love it and Want Us to Use it?* Retrieved from https://steemit.com/bitcoin/@digdaga/is-governments-against-bitcoin-and-blockchain-or-do-they-love-it-and-want-us-to-use-it

Dimitrov, D. V. (2019). Blockchain Applications for Healthcare Data Management. *Healthcare Informatics Research*, *25*(1), 51–56. doi:10.4258/hir.2019.25.1.51 PMID:30788182

Dinh, T. T. A., Wang, J., Chen, G., Liu, R., Ooi, B. C., & Tan, K. L. (2017, May). Blockbench: A framework for analyzing private blockchains. In *Proceedings of the 2017 ACM International Conference on Management of Data* (pp. 1085-1100). ACM. 10.1145/3035918.3064033

Do, H. G., & Ng, W. K. (2017). Blockchain-based system for secure data storage with private keyword search. In *2017 IEEE World Congress on Services (SERVICES)* (pp. 90-93). IEEE. 10.1109/SERVICES.2017.23

Dong, Y., Kim, W., & Boutaba, R. (2018, November). Bitforest: a Portable and Efficient Blockchain-Based Naming System. In *2018 14th International Conference on Network and Service Management (CNSM)* (pp. 226-232). IEEE.

Dorri, A., Kanhere, S. S., & Jurdak, R. (2016). *Blockchain in internet of things: challenges and solutions*. arXiv preprint arXiv:1608.05187

Double-spending. (n.d.). Retrieved from https://en.bitcoin.it/wiki/Double-spending

Douceur, J. R. (2002, March). The sybil attack. In *International workshop on peer-to-peer systems* (pp. 251-260). Springer. 10.1007/3-540-45748-8_24

Dutra, A., Tumasjan, A., & Welpe, I. M. (2018). Blockchain is changing how media and entertainment companies compete. *MIT Sloan Management Review*. Retrieved from https://sloanreview.mit.edu/article/blockchain-is-changing-how-media-and-entertainment-companies-compete/

Dwivedi, S. K., & Rawat, B. (2015). A review paper on data preprocessing: A critical phase in web usage mining process. In *Proc. of International Conference on Green Computing and Internet of Things*. IEEE. 10.1109/ICGCIoT.2015.7380517

EconoTimes. (2016). *Safeshare releases first blockchain insurance solution for sharing economy*. Retrieved from https://www.econotimes.com/SafeShare-Releases-First-Blockchain-Insurance-Solution-For-Sharing-Economy-181326

Edemekong, P. F., & Haydel, M. J. (2018). *Health Insurance Portability and Accountability Act (HIPAA)*. StatPearls.

Ekblaw, A., Azaria, A., Halamka, J. D., & Lippman, A. (2016, August). A Case Study for Blockchain in Healthcare: "MedRec" prototype for electronic health records and medical research data. In Proceedings of IEEE open & big data conference (p. 13). IEEE.

Eldredge, M., Hughes, T. J., Ferencz, R. M., Rifai, S. M., Raefsky, A., & Herndon, B. (1997). High-performance parallel computing in industry. *Parallel Computing*, *23*(9), 1217–1233. doi:10.1016/S0167-8191(97)00049-5

Esposito, C., De Santis, A., Tortora, G., Chang, H., & Choo, K. K. R. (2018). Blockchain: A panacea for healthcare cloud-based data security and privacy? *IEEE Cloud Computing*, *5*(1), 31–37. doi:10.1109/MCC.2018.011791712

Es-Samaali, H., Outchakoucht, A., & Leroy, J. P. (2017). A blockchain-based access control for big data. *International Journal of Computer Networks and Communications Security*, *5*(7), 137.

EtherAPIs: Decentralized Anonymous Trustless APIs. (2019). Retrieved from https://etherapis.io/

EtherScan. (2016). *Ethereum Average BlockTime Chart*. Retrieved from https://etherscan.io/chart/blocktime

Eyal, I., & Sirer, E. G. (2014). Majority is not enough: Bitcoin mining is vulnerable. In N. Christin & R. Safavi-Naini (Eds.), Financial cryptography and data security (pp. 436–454). Academic Press.

Eyal, I., Gencer, A. E., Sirer, E. G., & Van Renesse, R. (2016). Bitcoin-ng: A scalable blockchain protocol. In *13th USENIX Symposium on Networked Systems Design and Implementation (NSDI 16)* (pp. 45-59). USENIX.

Eyal, I. (2017). Blockchain technology: Transforming libertarian cryptocurrency dreams to finance and banking realities. *Computer*, *50*(9), 38–49. doi:10.1109/MC.2017.3571042

Facca, F. M., & Lanzi, P. L. (2003). Recent developments in web usage mining research. In *International Conference on Data Warehousing and Knowledge Discovery*. Springer. 10.1007/978-3-540-45228-7_15

Fanning, K., & Centers, D. P. (2016). Blockchain and its coming impact on financial services. *Journal of Corporate Accounting & Finance*, *27*(5), 53–57. doi:10.1002/jcaf.22179

Faridi, O. (2018). *In Altcoins, Bitcoin Gold Hit With 51% and Double Spend Attacks, $18 Million Stolen*. Retrieved from https://www.cryptoglobe.com/latest/2018/05/bitcoin-gold-hit-with-51-and-double-spend-attacks-18-million-stolen/

Fernández-Caramés, T. M., & Fraga-Lamas, P. (2018). A Review on the Use of Blockchain for the Internet of Things. *IEEE Access: Practical Innovations, Open Solutions*, *6*, 32979–33001. doi:10.1109/ACCESS.2018.2842685

Ferrag, M. A., Derdour, M., Mukherjee, M., Derhab, A., Maglaras, L., & Janicke, H. (2018). *Blockchain technologies for the internet of things: Research issues and challenges*. IEEE Internet of Things Journal.

Foroglou, G., & Tsilidou, A. L. (2015, May). Further applications of the blockchain. *12th Student Conference on Managerial Science and Technology*.

Frankenfield, J. (2018). *SegWit (Segregated Witness)*. Retrieved from https://www.investopedia.com/terms/s/segwit-segregated-witness.asp

Friese, I., Heuer, J., & Kong, N. (2014). Challenges from the Identities of Things: Introduction of the Identities of Things discussion group within Kantara initiative. *2014 IEEE World Forum on Internet of Things (WF-IoT)*, 1–4.10.1109/WF-IoT.2014.6803106

Fromknecht, C., Velicanu, D., & Yakoubov, S. (2014). *CertCoin: A namecoin based decentralized authentication system*. Retrieved from https://courses.csail.mit.edu/ 6.857/2014/files/19-fromknecht-velicann-yakoubov-certcoin.pdf

Fulton, S. (2015, February 20). *Top 10 DNS attacks likely to infiltrate your network*. Retrieved from https://www.networkworld.com/article/2886283/top-10-dns-attacks-likely-to-infiltrate-your-network.html#slide3

Gallagher, S. (2014). *New "Shellshock" patch rushed out to resolve gaps in first fix*. Retrieved from https://arstechnica.com/information-technology/2014/09/new-shellshock-patch-rushed-out-to-resolve-gaps-in-first-fix/

Garoffolo, Stabilini, Viglione, & Stav. (2018). *Horizon Proposal to modify satoshi concensuss to enhance protection against 51% attacks*. Academic Press.

Gatteschi, Lamberti, Demartini, Pranteda, & Santamaría. (2018). Blockchain and smart contracts for insurance: Is the technology mature enough? *Future Internet*, *10*(2).

Gehde-Trapp, M., Gündüz, Y., & Nasev, J. (2015). The liquidity premium in CDS transaction prices: Do frictions matter? *Journal of Banking & Finance*, *61*, 184–205. doi:10.1016/j.jbankfin.2015.08.024

Gencer, A. E., van Renesse, R., & Sirer, E. G. (2017, April). Short paper: Service-oriented sharding for blockchains. In *International Conference on Financial Cryptography and Data Security* (pp. 393-401). Springer. 10.1007/978-3-319-70972-7_22

Gkillas, K., & Katsiampa, P. (2018). An application of extreme value theory to cryptocurrencies. *Economics Letters*, *164*, 109–111. doi:10.1016/j.econlet.2018.01.020

Godbole, O. (2019). *Bitcoin Price On Track to End Six-Month Losing Streak*. Retrieved from https://www.coindesk.com/bitcoin-price-on-track-to-end-six-month-losing-streak

Goel, R., & Jain, S. (2014). Improvisation in Web Mining Techniques by Scrubbing Log Files. *International Journal of Advanced Research in Computer Science*, *5*(5), 87–91.

Gopalan, N. P., & Akilandeswari, J. (2005). A distributed, fault-tolerant multi-agent web mining system for scalable web search. *Proc. of WSEAS 5th International conference on Applied Informatics and Communications*, 15-7.

Gordon, W. J., & Catalini, C. (2018). Blockchain technology for healthcare: Facilitating the transition to patient-driven interoperability. *Computational and Structural Biotechnology Journal*, *16*, 224–230. doi:10.1016/j.csbj.2018.06.003 PMID:30069284

Granjal, J., Monteiro, E., & Silva, J. S. (2015). Security for the internet of things: A survey of existing protocols and open research issues. *IEEE Communications Surveys and Tutorials*, *17*(3), 1294–1312. doi:10.1109/COMST.2015.2388550

Groves, P., Kayyali, B., Knott, D., & Van Kuiken, S. (2013). *The Big Data revolution in healthcare*. McKinsey Global Institute.

Guo, Y., & Liang, C. (2016). Blockchain application and outlook in the banking industry. *Financial Innovation*, *2*(1), 24. doi:10.118640854-016-0034-9

Gutierrez, C., & Khizhniak, A. (2017). A Close Look at Everledger—How Blockchain Secures Luxury Goods. *Altoros*. Retrieved from https://www.altoros.com/blog/a-close-look-at-everledger-how-blockchain-secures-luxury-goods/

Haghi, M., Thurow, K., & Stoll, R. (2017). Wearable devices in medical internet of things: Scientific research and commercially available devices. *Healthcare Informatics Research*, *23*(1), 4. doi:10.4258/hir.2017.23.1.4 PMID:28261526

Hales. (2019). *What is Blockchain Technology? A Beginner's Guide*. Retrieved from https://www.uplarn.com/what-is-blockchain-technology-a-beginners-guide/

Han, S. (2017). *How does blockchain really work? I built an app to show you*. Retrieved from https://medium.freecodecamp.org/how-does-blockchain-really-work-i-built-an-app-to-show-you-6b70cd4caf7d

Han, J., & Kamber, M. (2011). *Data Mining: Concepts and Techniques* (3rd ed.). Morgan Kaufmann.

Hari, A., Kodialam, M., & Lakshman, T. V. (2019, April). ACCEL: Accelerating the Bitcoin Blockchain for High-throughput, Low-latency Applications. In *IEEE INFOCOM 2019-IEEE Conference on Computer Communications* (pp. 2368-2376). IEEE.

Health and Social Care Information Centre. (2015). *Hospital Episode Statistics.* Author.

Heckman, L. (2014). *NASDAQ A Guide To Information Sources*. New York: Routledge.

Heires, K. (2016). The risks and rewards of blockchain technology. *Risk Management*, *63*(2), 4.

Hellman, M. E. (2002). An overview of public key cryptography. *IEEE Communications Magazine*, *40*(5), 42–49. doi:10.1109/MCOM.2002.1006971

Higgins, S. (2015). *Factom Partners With Honduras Government on Blockchain Tech Trial.* Retrieved from https://www.coindesk.com/factom-land-registry-deal-honduran-government

Hileman, G., & Rauchs, M. (2017). *Global Blockchain Benchmarking Study*. Retrieved from https://www.jbs.cam.ac.uk/fileadmin/user_upload/research/centres/alternative-finance/downloads/2017-09-27-ccaf-globalbchain.pdf

Hjalmarsson, F. P., Hreioarsson, G. K., Hamdaqa, M., & Hjalmtysson, G. (2018, July). Blockchain-Based E-Voting System. In *2018 IEEE 11th International Conference on Cloud Computing (CLOUD)* (pp. 983-986). IEEE. 10.1109/CLOUD.2018.00151

Hofman, W., & Brewster, C. (2019). The Applicability of Blockchain Technology in the Mobility and Logistics Domain. In *Towards User-Centric Transport in Europe* (pp. 185–201). Cham: Springer. doi:10.1007/978-3-319-99756-8_13

Hölbl, M., Kompara, M., Kamišalić, A., & Zlatolas, L. N. (2018). A systematic review of the use of blockchain in healthcare. *Symmetry*, *10*(10), 470. doi:10.3390ym10100470

Huckle, S., Bhattacharya, R., White, M., & Beloff, N. (2016). Internet of things, blockchain and shared economy applications. *Procedia Computer Science*, *98*, 461–466. doi:10.1016/j.procs.2016.09.074

Huh, S., Cho, S., & Kim, S. (2017, February). Managing IoT devices using blockchain platform. In *2017 19th international conference on advanced communication technology (ICACT)* (pp. 464-467). IEEE. 10.23919/ICACT.2017.7890132

Hyperledger Project. (2015). Retrieved from https://www.hyperledger.org/

hyperledger.org. (2016). *Hyperledger – Blockchain Technologies for Business*. Author.

Iansiti, M., & Lakhani, K. (2017). R. (2017). The truth about blockchain. Harvard Business Review. *Harvard University*, *27*(9).

Iansiti, M., & Lakhani, K. R. (2017). The truth about blockchain. *Harvard Business Review*, *95*(1), 118–127.

IBM. (2017). *IBM blockchain based on hyperledger fabric from the linux foundation*. Retrieved from https://www.ibm.com/blockchain/hyperledger.html

Imbrex. (2017). *Sharding, Raiden, Plasma: The Scaling Solutions that Will Unchain Ethereum*. Retrieved from https://medium.com/imbrexblog/sharding-raiden-plasma-the-scaling-solutions-that-will-unchain-ethereum-c590e994523b

Information Commissioner's Office. (n.d.). *What Types of Encryption Are There?* Retrieved from https://ico.org.uk/for-organisations/guide-to-data-protection/guide-to-the-general-data-protection-regulation-gdpr/encryption/what-types-of-encryption-are-there/

International Telecommunication Union. (2015). *Measuring the Information Society Report*. International Telecommunication Union (ITU).

Irrera, A. (2016). Nasdaq launches blockchain-ready tech hub. *Financial News*. Retrieved from https://www.fnlondon.com/articles/nasdaq-launches-new-blockchain-ready-tech-platform-20160526

Ito, K., & O'Dair, M. (2018). *A Critical Examination of the Application of Blockchain Technology to Intellectual Property Management. In Business Transformation through Blockchain* (pp. 317–335). Cham: Palgrave Macmillan.

Jarecki, S., Kiayias, A., Krawczyk, H., & Xu, J. (2016, March). Highly-efficient and composable password-protected secret sharing (or: How to protect your bitcoin wallet online). In *2016 IEEE European Symposium on Security and Privacy (EuroS&P)* (pp. 276-291). IEEE 10.1109/EuroSP.2016.30

Jauha, S. K., & Pant, M. (2013). Recent trends in supply chain management: A soft computing approach. *Proc. of Seventh International Conference on Bio-Inspired Computing: Theories and Applications Springer*, 465-478. 10.1007/978-81-322-1041-2_40

Jeba, J. M. P., Bhuvaneswari, M. S., & Muneeswaran, K. (2016). Extracting usage patterns from web server log. In *Proc. of 2nd International Conference on Green High Performance Computing*. IEEE. 10.1109/ICGHPC.2016.7508074

Jentzsch, C., Jentzsch, S., & Tual, S. (2018). *Slock.IT*. Available online: https://slock.it

Jesus, E. F., Chicarino, V. R., de Albuquerque, C. V., & Rocha, A. A. D. A. (2018). A survey of how to use blockchain to secure internet of things and the stalker attack. *Security and Communication Networks*.

Johnson, D., Menezes, A., & Vanstone, S. (2001). The elliptic curve digital signature algorithm (ecdsa). *International Journal of Information Security*, *1*(1), 36–63. doi:10.1007102070100002

Joshila Grace, L. K., Maheswari, V., & Nagamalai, D. (2011). Analysis of Weblogs and Web User in Web Mining. *International Journal of Network Security & Its Applications*, *3*(1), 99–110. doi:10.5121/ijnsa.2011.3107

Juels, A., Kosba, A., & Shi, E. (2016, October). The ring of gyges: Investigating the future of criminal smart contracts. In *Proceedings of the 2016 ACM SIGSAC Conference on Computer and Communications Security* (pp. 283-295). ACM. 10.1145/2976749.2978362

Jung, M. Y., & Jang, J. W. (2017). Data management and searching system and method to provide increased security for IoT platform. *International Conference on Information and Communication Technology Convergence: ICT Convergence Technologies Leading the Fourth Industrial Revolution, ICTC 2017*. 10.1109/ICTC.2017.8190803

Juno: Smart Contracts Running on a BFT Hardened Raft. (2019). Retrieved from https://github.com/kadena-io/juno

Kalodner, H. A., Carlsten, M., Ellenbogen, P., Bonneau, J., & Narayanan, A. (2015, June). *An Empirical Study of Namecoin and Lessons for Decentralized Namespace Design*. WEIS.

Kalra, S., & Sood, S. K. (2015). Secure authentication scheme for IoT and cloud servers. *Pervasive and Mobile Computing*, *24*, 210–223. doi:10.1016/j.pmcj.2015.08.001

Karafiloski, E., & Mishev, A. (2017, July). Blockchain solutions for big data challenges: A literature review. In *IEEE EUROCON 2017-17th International Conference on Smart Technologies* (pp. 763-768). IEEE. 10.1109/EUROCON.2017.8011213

Karajovic, M., Kim, H. M., & Laskowski, M. (2017). Thinking outside the block: Projected phases of blockchain integration in the accounting industry. *Australian Accounting Review*.

Kasiewicz, S. (2019). New trends in the system regulating the market of bank services. Kwartalnik Nauk o Przedsiębiorstwie. doi:10.5604/01.3001.0010.7450

Kasiewicz. (2019). New trends in the system regulating the market of bank services. *Kwart. Nauk o Przedsiębiorstwie*.

Kaul, A. (2016). *IBM Watson IoT and its integration with blockchain*. Academic Press.

Kaur, N., & Aggarwal, H. (2015). Weblog analysis for identifying the number of visitors and their behavior to enhance the accessibility and usability of website. *International Journal of Computers and Applications*, *110*(4), 25–30. doi:10.5120/19307-0759

Keenan, T. P. (2017). Alice in Blockchains: Surprising Security Pitfalls in PoW and PoS Blockchain Systems. In *2017 15th Annual Conference on Privacy, Security and Trust (PST)* (pp. 400-4002). IEEE.

Khadilkar, V., Kantarcioglu, M., Thuraisingham, B., & Mehrotra, S. (2011). *Secure data processing in a hybrid cloud.* arXiv preprint arXiv:1105-1982

Khan, M. A., & Salah, K. (2018). IoT security: Review, blockchain solutions, and open challenges. *Future Generation Computer Systems*, *82*, 395–411. doi:10.1016/j.future.2017.11.022

Kharif, O. (n.d.). *CryptoKitties Mania Overwhelms Ethereum Networks Processing*. Retrieved from https://www.bloombergquint.com/technology/cryptokitties-quickly-becomes-most-widely-used-ethereum-app#gs.3m37ft

Kiayias, A., Russell, A., & David, B. (2017). PPCoin: Peer-to-Peer Crypto-Currency with Proof-of-Stake. Proceedings of the 2016 ACM SIGSAC Conference on Computer and Communications Security - CCS'16. 10.1017/CBO9781107415324.004

Kirkman, S. (2018). A data movement policy framework for improving trust in the cloud using smart contracts and blockchains. In *2018 IEEE International Conference on Cloud Engineering (IC2E)* (pp. 270-273). IEEE. 10.1109/IC2E.2018.00054

Kishigami, J., Fujimura, S., Watanabe, H., Nakadaira, A., & Akutsu, A. (2015, August). The blockchain-based digital content distribution system. In *2015 IEEE Fifth International Conference on Big Data and Cloud Computing* (pp. 187-190). IEEE. 10.1109/BDCloud.2015.60

Kobler, D., Bucherer, S., & Schlotmann, J. (2016). *Banking business models of the future*. Deloitte.

Korpela, K., Hallikas, J., & Dahlberg, T. (2017). Digital supply chain transformation toward Blockchain integration. *Proc. 50th Hawaii Int. Conf. Syst. Sci.* 10.24251/HICSS.2017.506

Kouicem, D. E., Bouabdallah, A., & Lakhlef, H. (2018). Internet of things security: A top-down survey. *Computer Networks*, *141*, 199–221. doi:10.1016/j.comnet.2018.03.012

Koutsoukos, D., Alexandridis, G., Siolas, G., & Stafylopatis, A. (2016). A new approach to session identification by applying fuzzy c-means clustering on weblogs. In *Proc. of Symposium Series on Computational Intelligence*. IEEE.

Kshetri, N. (2017). Blockchain's roles in strengthening cybersecurity and protecting privacy. *Telecommunications Policy*, *41*(10), 1027–1038. doi:10.1016/j.telpol.2017.09.003

Kshetri, N. (2017). Can blockchain strengthen the internet of things? *IT Professional*, *19*(4), 68–72. doi:10.1109/MITP.2017.3051335

Kuhlman. (2016). *What is eris?* Retrieved from https://monax.io/2016/04/03/wtf-is-eris/

Kumar, K.D., & Umamaheswari, E. (2018). Efficient Cloud Resource Scaling based on Prediction Approaches. *International Journal of Engineering & Technology, 7*(4.10).

Kumar, M., Singh, A. K., & Kumar, T. S. (2018). Secure Log Storage Using Blockchain and Cloud Infrastructure. In *2018 9th International Conference on Computing, Communication and Networking Technologies (ICCCNT)* (pp. 1-4). IEEE. 10.1109/ICCCNT.2018.8494085

Kumar, V., & Thakur, R. S. (2018). Web Usage Mining: Concept and Applications at a Glance. In Handbook of Research on Pattern Engineering System Development for Big Data Analytics. IGI Global.

Kumar, A., Ahirwar, V., & Singh, R. K. (2015). A Study on Prediction of User Behavior Based on Web Server Log Files in Web Usage Mining. *International Journal of Engineering and Computer Science*, *6*(2), 20233–20236.

Kumar, K. D., & Umamaheswari, E. (2017). *An Authenticated, Secure Virtualization Management System in Cloud Computing. Asian Journal of Pharmaceutical and Clinical Research.*

Kumar, K. D., & Umamaheswari, E. (2018). Prediction methods for effective resource provisioning in cloud computing: A Survey. *Multiagent and Grid Systems*, *14*(3), 283–305. doi:10.3233/MGS-180292

Kuperberg, M., Kindler, D., & Jeschke, S. (2019). *Are Smart Contracts and Blockchains Suitable for Decentralized Railway Control?* arXiv preprint arXiv:1901.06236

Lai, R. (2017). Blockchain – From Public to Private. In Handbook of Blockchain, Digital Finance, and Inclusion. Academic Press. doi:10.1016/b978-0-12-812282-2.00007-3

Landewednack House. (n.d.). *Landewednack House*. Retrieved from http://www.landewednackhouse.com/

Langner, R. (2011). Stuxnet: Dissecting a cyberwarfare weapon. *IEEE Security and Privacy*, *9*(3), 49–51. doi:10.1109/MSP.2011.67

Lee KuoChuen, D. (Ed.). (2015). *Handbook of Digital Currency*. Elsevier. Retrieved from http://EconPapers.repec.org/RePEc:eee:monogr:9780128021170

Liang, X., Shetty, S., Tosh, D., Kamhoua, C., Kwiat, K., & Njilla, L. (2017). Provchain: A blockchain-based data provenance architecture in cloud environment with enhanced privacy and availability. In *Proceedings of the 17th IEEE/ACM international symposium on cluster, cloud and grid computing* (pp. 468-477). IEEE Press. 10.1109/CCGRID.2017.8

Li, C., & Hains, G. (2011). A simple bridging model for high-performance computing. In *2011 International Conference on High Performance Computing & Simulation* (pp. 249-256). IEEE. 10.1109/HPCSim.2011.5999831

Li, J., Liu, Z., Chen, L., Chen, P., & Wu, J. (2017). Blockchain-based security architecture for distributed cloud storage. In *2017 IEEE International Symposium on Parallel and Distributed Processing with Applications and 2017 IEEE International Conference on Ubiquitous Computing and Communications (ISPA/IUCC)* (pp. 408-411). IEEE. 10.1109/ISPA/IUCC.2017.00065

Lim, J. W., Hoong, P. K., Yeoh, E. T., & Tan, I. K. (2011). Performance analysis of parallel computing in a distributed overlay network. In TENCON 2011-2011 IEEE Region 10 Conference (pp. 1404-1408). IEEE. doi:10.1109/TENCON.2011.6129040

Linux-Foundation. (2017). *Blockchain technologies for business*. Retrieved from https://www.hyperledger.org/

Liu, & Zhou, & Hongyan. (2007). Data preprocessing of web usage mining. *Computer Science*, *34*, 200-204.

Losarwar, V., & Joshi, M. (2012). Data preprocessing in web usage mining. *Proc. of International Conference on Artificial Intelligence and Embedded Systems,* 15-16.

Luu, L., Chu, D. H., Olickel, H., Saxena, P., & Hobor, A. (2016, October). Making smart contracts smarter. In *Proceedings of the 2016 ACM SIGSAC Conference on Computer and Communications Security* (pp. 254-269). ACM. 10.1145/2976749.2978309

Luu, L., Narayanan, V., Zheng, C., Baweja, K., Gilbert, S., & Saxena, P. (2016, October). A secure sharding protocol for open blockchains. In *Proceedings of the 2016 ACM SIGSAC Conference on Computer and Communications Security* (pp. 17-30). ACM. 10.1145/2976749.2978389

Maggs, B. M., Matheson, L. R., & Tarjan, R. E. (1995). Models of parallel computation: A survey and synthesis. In *Proceedings of the Twenty-Eighth Annual Hawaii International Conference on System Sciences* (Vol. 2, pp. 61-70). IEEE. 10.1109/HICSS.1995.375476

Mainelli, M., & Smith, M. (2015). Sharing ledgers for sharing economies: An exploration of mutual distributed ledgers (aka blockchain technology). *Journal of Financial Perspectives, 3*(3).

Maksutov, A. A., Alexeev, M. S., Fedorova, N. O., & Andreev, D. A. (2019, January). Detection of Blockchain Transactions Used in Blockchain Mixer of Coin Join Type. In *2019 IEEE Conference of Russian Young Researchers in Electrical and Electronic Engineering (EIConRus)* (pp. 274-277). IEEE.

Malhotra, Y. (2013). *Bitcoin Protocol: Model of 'Cryptographic Proof'Based Global Crypto-Currency & Electronic Payments System.* Academic Press.

Malik, N. (2018). *How Criminals And Terrorists Use Cryptocurrency: And How To Stop It.* Retrieved from https://www.forbes.com/sites/nikitamalik/2018/08/31/how-criminals-and-terrorists-use-cryptocurrency-and-how-to-stop-it/#5675830c3990

Malviya, B. K., & Agrawal, J. (2015). A Study on Web Usage Mining Theory and Applications. In *Proc. of Fifth International Conference on Communication Systems and Network Technologies (CSNT).* IEEE.

Marella, P. B., Mohler, J., & Milojkovic, M. (2017). *BroncoVotes: Secure Voting System using Ethereum's Blockchain.* Academic Press.

Marrison, C. (2015). Understanding the threats to DNS and how to secure it. *Network Security, 2015*(10), 8–10. doi:10.1016/S1353-4858(15)30090-8

Martin, J. (2018). *Top Tier Colleges Offering Blockchain Education.* Retrieved from https://blockchain.wtf/2018/11/blog/top-tier-colleges-offering-blockchain-education/

Mattila, J. (2016). *The blockchain phenomenon: The disruptive potential of distributed consensu architectures.* ETLA working papers: ElinkeinoelämänTutkimuslaitos, Research Institute of the Finnish Economy. Retrieved from https: //books.google.com.pk/books?id=StNQnQAACAAJ

Maupin, J. (2017). *The G20 countries should engage with blockchain technologies to build an inclusive, transparent, and accountable digital economy for all (No. 2017-48)*. Economics Discussion Papers.

Maxeiner, L. S., Martini, J. P., & Sandner, P. (2018). Blockchain in *the Chemical Industry*. Retrieved from https://medium.com/@philippsandner/blockchain-in-the-chemical-industry-ecf703237ba6

McWhinney, J. (2019). *Why governments Are Afraid of Bitcoin*. Retrieved from https://www.investopedia.com/articles/forex/042015/why-governments-are-afraid-bitcoin.asp

Medici. (2018). *Know more: Blockchain- Overview, Tech, Application Areas & and Use Cases*. Retrieved from https://gomedici.com/an-overview-of-blockchain-technology

Medium. (2018). *How Cryptocurrency is Disrupting the Global Economy*. Retrieved from https://medium.com/the-mission/how-cryptocurrency-is-disrupting-the-global-economy-89347581aa93

Menezes, N. (2017). *UN Uses Ethereum to Distribute Funds to Jordanians*. Retrieved from https://btcmanager.com/un-uses-ethereum-todistribute-funds-to-jordanians

Mense, A., & Flatscher, M. (2018). *Security Vulnerabilities in Ethereum Smart Contracts*. Academic Press.

Meshkov, D., Chepurnoy, A., & Jansen, M. (2017). Short Paper: Revisiting Difficulty Control for Blockchain Systems. In *Data Privacy Management, Cryptocurrencies and Blockchain Technology* (pp. 429–436). Cham: Springer. doi:10.1007/978-3-319-67816-0_25

Mettler, M. (2016). Blockchain technology in healthcare: The revolution starts here. In *2016 IEEE 18th International Conference on e-Health Networking, Applications and Services, Healthcom 2016*. IEEE. 10.1109/HealthCom.2016.7749510

Mettler, M., & Hsg, M. A. (2016). *Blockchain Technology in Healthcare The Revolution Starts Here*. Academic Press.

Mills, D., Martin, J., Burbank, J., & Kasch, W. (2011). *Network time protocol version 4: Protocol and algorithms specification*. RFC 5905. Internet Engineering Task Force.

Miraz, M. H., & Ali, M. (2018). *Applications of blockchain technology beyond cryptocurrency*. arXiv preprint arXiv:1801.03528

Mitchell, R., & Chen, R. (2014). A survey of intrusion detection in wireless network applications. *Computer Communications*, *42*, 1–23. doi:10.1016/j.comcom.2014.01.012

Mobasher, B., Cooley, R., & Srivastava, J. (2000). Automatic personalization based on web usage mining. *Communications of the ACM*, *43*(8), 142–151. doi:10.1145/345124.345169

Mosakheil, J. H. (2018). *Security Threats Classification in Blockchains*. Retrieved from https://repository.stcloudstate.edu/cgi/viewcontent.cgi?article=1093&context=msia_etds

Moubarak, J., & Filiol, E. (2018). *On Blockchain Security and Relevant Attacks*. Academic Press.

Mueller, B. (2017). *Mythril—Reversing and Bug Hunting Framework for the Ethereum Blockchain*. Retrieved from https://hackernoon.com/introducing-mythril-a-framework-for-bug-hunting-on-the-ethereum-blockchain-9dc5588f82f6

Mukkamala, R. R., Vatrapu, R., Ray, P. K., Sengupta, G., & Halder, S. (2018). Blockchain for Social Business: Principles and Applications. *IEEE Engineering Management Review*, *46*(4), 94–99. doi:10.1109/EMR.2018.2881149

MultiChain. (2018). *Open Platform for Building Blockcchains*. Retrieved from https://www.multichain.com/

Munk, M., Kapusta, J., & Švec, P. (2010). Data preprocessing evaluation for weblog mining: Reconstruction of activities of a web visitor. *Procedia Computer Science*, *1*(1), 2273–2280. doi:10.1016/j.procs.2010.04.255

Muskan & Garg. (2016). An Efficient Algorithm for Data Cleaning of Weblogs with Spider Navigation Removal. *International Journal of Computers and Applications*, *6*(3), 6–12.

Nakamoto, S. (2007). *Bitcoin : A Peer-to-Peer Electronic Cash System*. Academic Press.

Nakamoto, S. (2008). *Bitcoin: A peer-to-peer electronic cash system*. Academic Press.

Nakamoto, S. (2008). *Bitcoin: A peer-to-peer electronic cash system*. Retrieved from http://bitcoin. org/bitcoin. pdf

Nakamoto, S. (2008). *Bitcoin: A peer-to-peer electronic cash system*. Retrieved from https: //bitcoin.org/bitcoin.pdf

Nakamoto, S. (2009). *Bitcoin: A peer-to-peer electronic cash system*. Available: https://bitcoin.org/bitcoin.pdf

Nakamoto, S. (n.d.). *Bitcoin: A Peer-to-Peer Electronic Cash System*. Retrieved from https://bitcoin.org/bitcoin.pdf

Nakamoto. (2008). Bitcoin: A Peer-to-Peer Electronic Cash System. Academic Press. doi:10.100710838-008-9062-0

Neelima & Rodda. (2016). Predicting user behavior through sessions using the weblog mining. In *Proc. of International Conference on Advances in Human Machine Interaction*. IEEE.

Network Solutions. (n.d.). *6 Steps to Registering a Successful Domain Name*. Retrieved from http://www.networksolutions.com/education/registering-domain-names/

Neudecker, T., Andelfinger, P., & Hartenstein, H. (2015, May). A simulation model for analysis of attacks on the bitcoin peer-to-peer network. In *2015 IFIP/IEEE International Symposium on Integrated Network Management (IM)* (pp. 1327-1332). IEEE. 10.1109/INM.2015.7140490

Newswire, P. R. (2018). *Global Blockchain Technology Industry*. Retrieved from https://www.prnewswire.com/news-releases/global-blockchain-technology-industry-300670406.html

Nomura Research Institute. (2016). *Survey on Blockchain Technologies and Related Services*. Retrieved from https://www.meti.go.jp/english/press/2016/pdf/0531_01f.pdf

Nordström, E. (2015). *Personal Clouds: Concedo*. Retrieved from http://www.diva-portal.org/smash/get/diva2:1029288/FULLTEXT02.pdf

Novo, O. (2018). Blockchain meets IoT: An architecture for scalable access management in IoT. *IEEE Internet of Things Journal*, *5*(2), 1184–1195. doi:10.1109/JIOT.2018.2812239

O'Dair, M., & Beaven, Z. (2017). The networked record industry: How blockchain technology could transform the record industry. *Strategic Change*, *26*(5), 471–480. doi:10.1002/jsc.2147

Officer, R. R. (1973). The Variability of the Market Factor of the New York Stock Exchange. *The Journal of Business, University of Chicago Press*, *46*(3), 434–453.

Oprunenco, A., & Akmeemana, C. (2018). *Using blockchain to make land registry more reliable in India*. Retrieved from https://www.undp.org/content/undp/en/home/blog/2018/Using-blockchain-to-make-land-registry-more-reliable-in-India.html

Otte, M., de Vos, M., & Pouwelse, J. (2017). TrustChain: A Sybil-resistant scalable blockchain. *Future Generation Computer Systems*. doi:10.1016/j.future.2017.08.048

Palmer, D. (2018). *Cybercrime drains $600 billion a year from the global economy*. Retrieved from https://www.zdnet.com/article/cybercrime-drains-600-billion-a-year-from-the-global-economy-says-report/

Panarello, A., Tapas, N., Merlino, G., Longo, F., & Puliafito, A. (2018). Blockchain and iot integration: A systematic survey. *Sensors (Basel)*, *18*(8), 2575. doi:10.339018082575 PMID:30082633

Panasenko, S., & Smagin, S. (2013). Lightweight Cryptography: Underlying Principles and Approaches. International Journal of Computer Theory and Engineering. doi:10.7763/ijcte.2011.v3.360

Park, S. J. (2009). An Analysis of GPU Parallel Computing. In *2009 DoD High Performance Computing Modernization Program Users Group Conference* (pp. 365-369). IEEE. doi: 10.1109/HPCMP-UGC.2009.59

Parsons, R. R., Coffman, J. T., & Rechterman, B. J. (2011). *U.S. Patent No. 7,996,457*. Washington, DC: U.S. Patent and Trademark Office.

Parvatikar, S., & Joshi, A. (2014). Analysis of user behavior through web usage mining. *Proc. of ICAST–International Conference on Advances in Science and Technology*, 27-31.

Pathak, N., & Bhandari, A. (2018). Understanding Blockchain. In *IoT, AI, and Blockchain for. NET*. Retrieved from https://link.springer.com/book/10.1007/978-1-4842-3709-0

Perera, C., Zaslavsky, A., Christen, P., & Georgakopoulos, D. (2014). Context aware computing for the internet of things: A survey. *IEEE Communications Surveys and Tutorials*, *16*(1), 414–454. doi:10.1109/SURV.2013.042313.00197

Perugini, S. (2018). The design of an emerging/multi-paradigm programming languages course. *Journal of Computing Sciences in Colleges*, *34*(1), 52–59.

Pilkington, M. (2016). 11 Blockchain technology: principles and applications. *Research handbook on digital transformations, 225.*

Pollock, D. (2018). *So Is There a Correlation Between Bitcoin and Stock Market? Yes, But No.* Retrieved from https://cointelegraph.com/news/so-is-there-a-correlation-between-bitcoin-and-stock-market-yes-but-no

Poon, J., & Buterin, V. (2017). *Plasma: Scalable autonomous smart contracts.* White Paper.

Poon, J., & Dryja, T. (2016). *The bitcoin lightning network: Scalable off-chain instant payments.* Academic Press.

Prisco, G. (2015). Nasdaq, LHV Bank, Technology Startups Develop Blockchain-Based Fintech Applications in Estonia. *Bitcoin Magazine*. Retrieved from https://bitcoinmagazine.com/articles/nasdaq-lhv-bank-technology-startups-develop-blockchain-based-fintech-applications-in-estonia-1447870921

Pticek, M., Podobnik, V., & Jezic, G. (2016). Beyond the internet of things: The social networking of machines. *International Journal of Distributed Sensor Networks*, *12*(6), 8178417. doi:10.1155/2016/8178417

Pureswaran, V., & Brody, P. (2014). *Device Democracy - Saving the future of the Internet of Things*. IBM. Retrieved from http://www-01.ibm.com/common/ssi/cgibin/ssialias?htmlfid=GBE03620USEN

Pushpalatha, N., & Reddy, S. S. S. (2017). Towards an extensible web usage mining framework for actionable knowledge. *Proc. of International Conference on Inventive Communication and Computational Technologies IEEE*, 35-40. 10.1109/ICICCT.2017.7975232

Qadir, M. (2018, April 5). *What is DNS hijacking and How It Works?* Retrieved from https://www.purevpn.com/blog/dns-hijacking/

Raju, S., Boddepalli, S., Gampa, S., Yan, Q., & Deogun, J. S. (2017, May). Identity management using blockchain for cognitive cellular networks. In *2017 IEEE International Conference on Communications (ICC)* (pp. 1-6). IEEE. 10.1109/ICC.2017.7996830

Rana, H., & Patel, M. (2013). A Study of Weblog Analysis Using Clustering Techniques. *International Journal of Innovative Research in Computer and Communication Engineering*, *1*(4), 925–929.

Raul. (2018). *The Speed of Crypto Hacks is Picking Up: This Month Alone Thieves Stole*. Retrieved from https://howmuch.net/articles/biggest-crypto-hacks-scams

Reddy, K. S., Reddy, M. K., & Sitaramulu, V. (2013). An effective data preprocessing method for Web Usage Mining. In *Proc. of International Conference on Information Communication and Embedded Systems*. IEEE.

Resul, D., & Turkoglu, I. (2009). Creating meaningful data from web logs for improving the impressiveness of a website by using path analysis method. *Expert Systems with Applications*, *36*(3), 6635–6644. doi:10.1016/j.eswa.2008.08.067

Reyna, A., Martín, C., Chen, J., Soler, E., & Díaz, M. (2018). On blockchain and its integration with IoT. Challenges and opportunities. *Future Generation Computer Systems*, *88*, 173–190. doi:10.1016/j.future.2018.05.046

Rijnetu, I. (2017). *Security Alert: MS Office Zero Day and DNS Vulnerabilities Can Impact Users*. Retrieved from https://heimdalsecurity.com/blog/security-alert-microsoft-vulnerabilities-in-office-and-dns/

Ripple (n.d.). *Ripple - One frictionless Experience To Send Money Globally*. Retrieved from https://www.ripple.com/

Ripple. (2013). *Ripple network*. Retrieved from https://ripple.com/network

Romero-Laorden, D., Villazón-Terrazas, J., Martinez-Graullera, O., Ibanez, A., Parrilla, M., & Penas, M. S. (2016). Analysis of parallel computing strategies to accelerate ultrasound imaging processes. *IEEE Transactions on Parallel and Distributed Systems*, *27*(12), 3429–3440. doi:10.1109/TPDS.2016.2544312

Rosic. (2016). *What is Blockchain Technology? A Step-by-Step Guide For Beginners*. Retrieved from https://blockgeeks.com/guides/what-is-blockchain-technology/

Rouse, M. (n.d.). *DNS Attack*. Retrieved from https://searchsecurity.techtarget.com/definition/DNS-attack

Salman, T., Member, S., Zolanvari, M., Member, S., & Erbad, A. (2018). Security Services Using Blockchains : A State of the Art Survey 1. *IEEE Communications Surveys and Tutorials*, *1*. doi:10.1109/COMST.2018.2863956

Sankar, L. S., Sindhu, M., & Sethumadhavan, M. (2017). Survey of consensus protocols on blockchain applications. *2017 4th International Conference on Advanced Computing and Communication Systems, ICACCS 2017*. 10.1109/ICACCS.2017.8014672

Satokar, K. D., & Gawali, S. Z. (2010). Web Personalization Using Web Mining. *International Journal of Engineering Science and Technology*, *2*(3), 307–311.

Sawa, T. (2018). Blockchain technology outline and its application to field of power and energy system. *Electrical Engineering in Japan*.

Scaling the Facebook data warehouse to 300 PB. (n.d.). Retrieved from https://code.fb.com/core-data/scaling-the-facebook-data-warehouse-to-300-pb/

Schneider, J., Blostein, A., Lee, B., Kent, S., Groer, I., & Beardsley, E. (2016). *Putting Theory Into Practice*. Retrieved from https://pgcoin.tech/wp-content/uploads/2018/06/blockchain-paper.pdf.

Science House. (n.d.). *U.S. House of Representatives Committee on Science, Space, & Technology*. Retrieved from https://science.house.gov/

Sfar, A. R., Natalizio, E., Challal, Y., & Chtourou, Z. (2018). A roadmap for security challenges in the Internet of Things. *Digital Communications and Networks*, *4*(2), 118–137. doi:10.1016/j.dcan.2017.04.003

Shang, Q., & Price, A. (2019). A Blockchain-Based Land Titling Project in the Republic of Georgia: Rebuilding Public Trust and Lessons for Future Pilot Projects. *Innovations: Technology, Governance, Globalization*, *12*(3-4), 72–78. doi:10.1162/inov_a_00276

Sharma, P. K., Moon, S. Y., & Park, J. H. (2017). Block-VN: A Distributed Blockchain Based Vehicular Network Architecture in Smart City. *JIPS*, *13*(1), 184–195.

Sharples, M., & Domingue, J. (2016, September). The blockchain and kudos: A distributed system for educational record, reputation and reward. In *European Conference on Technology Enhanced Learning* (pp. 490-496). Springer. 10.1007/978-3-319-45153-4_48

Shih, W. C., Tseng, S. S., & Yang, C. T. (2010). Performance study of parallel programming on cloud computing environments using mapreduce. In *2010 International Conference on Information Science and Applications* (pp. 1-8). IEEE. 10.1109/ICISA.2010.5480515

Shirani, A. (2018). Blockchain for global maritime logistics. *Issues in Information Systems*, *19*(3).

Shrier, D., Wu, W., & Pentland, A. (2016). Blockchain & infrastructure (identity, data security). *Massachusetts Institute of Technology-Connection Science*, *1*(3).

Sia, Soh, & Weill. (2016). *How DBS bank persued a digital business strategy*. Retrieved from file:///C:/Users/jtepper/Downloads/A1%20-2%20-%20SIa%20et%20al%20-%20How%20 DBS%20Bank%20Pursued%20a%20Digital%20Business%20Strategy.pdf

Sicari, S., Rizzardi, A., Grieco, L. A., & Coen-Porisini, A. (2015). Security, privacy and trust in Internet of Things: The road ahead. *Computer Networks*, *76*, 146–164. doi:10.1016/j.comnet.2014.11.008

Singh, S. (2016). *Blockchain : Future of Financial and Cyber Security*. Academic Press.

Singh, S., & Singh, N. (2016). Blockchain: Future of financial and cyber security. In *2016 2nd International Conference on Contemporary Computing and Informatics (IC3I)* (pp. 463-467). IEEE.

Singh, S., & Badhe, V. (2014). An Exclusive Survey on Web Usage Mining for User Identification. *International Journal of Innovative Research in Computer and Communication Engineering*, *2*(11), 6582–6589.

Sixt, E. (2016). Ethereum. In *Bitcoins und andere dezentrale Transaktionssysteme*. Springer Gabler. Retrieved from https://www.springer.com/br/book/9783658028435

Snow, P., Deery, B. L., Johnston, D., & Kirby, P. (2018). *Business Processes Secured by Immutable Audit Trails on the Blockchain*. Retrieved from https://www.factom.com/assets/docs/Factom_Whitepaper_v1.2.pdf

Solat, S., & Potop-Butucaru, M. (2016). *Zeroblock: Preventing selfish mining in bitcoin*. arXiv preprint arXiv:1605.02435

Sompolinsky, Y., & Zohar, A. (2013). Accelerating Bitcoin's Transaction Processing. Fast Money Grows on Trees, Not Chains. *IACR Cryptology ePrint Archive, 2013*(881).

Srivastava, M., Garg, R., & Mishra, P. K. (2015). Analysis of data extraction and data cleaning in Web usage mining. In *Proc. of International Conference on Advanced Research in Computer Science Engineering & Technology. ACM*. 10.1145/2743065.2743078

Staff, E. (2016). Blockchains: The great chain of being sure about things. *The Economist, 18*.

Stallings, W. (2011). Cryptography and Network Security: Principles amd Practices. *Network*. doi:10.1007/11935070

Statista. (2019). *Size of the Bitcoin blockchain from 2010 to 2019, by quarter*. Retrieved from https://www.statista.com/statistics/647523/worldwide-bitcoin-blockchain-size/

Stellar. (2014). *Stellar network overview*. Retrieved from https://www.stellar.org/developers/guides/get-started/

Suhasini, P., & Joshi, B. (2014). Analysis of user behavior through web usage mining. *Proc. of International Conference on Advances in Science and Technology*, 65-70.

Sukhodolskiy, I., & Zapechnikov, S. (2018). A blockchain-based access control system for cloud storage. In *2018 IEEE Conference of Russian Young Researchers in Electrical and Electronic Engineering (EIConRus)* (pp. 1575-1578). IEEE. 10.1109/EIConRus.2018.8317400

Sukumar, P., Robert, L., & Yuvaraj, S. (2016). Review on modern Data Preprocessing techniques in Web usage mining (WUM). In *Proc. of International Conference on Computation System and Information Technology for Sustainable Solutions*. IEEE. 10.1109/CSITSS.2016.7779441

Sun Yin, H. H., Langenheldt, K., Harlev, M., Mukkamala, R. R., & Vatrapu, R. (2019). Regulating cryptocurrencies: A supervised machine learning approach to de-anonymizing the bitcoin blockchain. *Journal of Management Information Systems*, *36*(1), 37–73. doi:10.1080/07421222.2018.1550550

Sun, X., & Ansari, N. (2016). EdgeIoT: Mobile edge computing for the Internet of Things. *IEEE Communications Magazine*, *54*(12), 22–29. doi:10.1109/MCOM.2016.1600492CM

Swan, M. (2015). *Blockchain: Blueprint for a new economy*. O'Reilly Media, Inc.

Szabo, N. (1997). The idea of smart contracts. *Nick Szabo's Papers and Concise Tutorials, 6*.

Szabo, N. (1997). *Formalizing and securing relationships on public networks*. Academic Press; doi:10.5210/fm.v2i9.548

Talakokkula, A. (2015). A Survey on Web Usage Mining, Applications and Tools. *Computer Engineering and Intelligent Systems*, *6*(2), 22–29.

Tamazirt, L., Alilat, F., & Agoulmine, N. (2018). *Blockchain Technology: A new secured Electronic Health Record System*. Retrieved from https://hal.archives-ouvertes.fr/hal-01777462/document

Tandulwadikar, A. (2016). Blockchain in Banking: A Measured Approach. *Cognizant Reports*. Retrieved from https://www.cognizant.com/whitepapers/Blockchain-in-Banking-A-Measured-Approach-codex1809.pdf

Tang, C., Wu, L., Wen, G., & Zheng, Z. (2019). Incentivizing Honest Mining in Blockchain Networks: A Reputation Approach. *IEEE Transactions on Circuits and Wystems. II, Express Briefs*, 1. doi:10.1109/TCSII.2019.2901746

textarcana. (2014). *A Web Log Data Set From The Web Server Workload Characterization Project*. Retrieved July 2015 from https://gist.github.com/textarcana/ef3d391178e041ee5838

The-Bitcoin-Foundation. (2014). *How does Bitcoin work?* Retrieved from https://bitcoin.org/en/how-it-works

Thoke, O. (2019, June 24). *Understanding Domain Names and the Registration Process*. Retrieved from https://www.lifewire.com/domain-names-and-registration-process-3473709

Tian, F. (2017, June). A supply chain traceability system for food safety based on HACCP, blockchain & Internet of things. In *International Conference on Service Systems and Service Management* (pp. 1-6). IEEE.

Tosh, D. K., Shetty, S., Liang, X., Kamhoua, C. A., Kwiat, K. A., & Njilla, L. (2017). *Security Implications of Blockchain Cloud with Analysis of Block Withholding Attack*. Academic Press. doi:10.1109/CCGRID.2017.111

Treleaven, P., Brown, R. G., & Yang, D. (2017). Blockchain Technology in Finance. *Computer*, *50*(9), 14–17. doi:10.1109/MC.2017.3571047

Tripoli, M., & Schmidhuber, J. (2018). *Emerging Opportunities for the Application of Blockchain in the Agri-food Industry Agriculture*. Food and Agriculture Organization of the United Nations.

Underwood, S. (2016). Blockchain beyond bitcoin. *Communications of the ACM*, *59*(11), 15–17. doi:10.1145/2994581

Unocoin. (2017). *How Has Bitcoin changed the Global Economy?* Retrieved from https://blog.unocoin.com/how-has-bitcoin-changed-the-global-economy-e33fac2e2316

Valenta, M., & Sandner, P. (2017). *Comparison of Ethereum, Hyperledger Fabric and Corda*. FSBC Working Paper.

Van Der Meulen, R. (2015). Gartner says 6.4 billion connected 'things' will be in use in 2016, up 30 percent from 2015. Gartner.

Veeningen & Szirbik. (2018). Using serious gaming to discover and understand distributed ledger technology in distributed energy systems. *Proceedings of IFIP Advances in Information and Communication Technology.*

Vukoli, M. (2016). *The Quest for Scalable Blockchain Fabric : Proof-of-Work vs .BFT Replication.* Academic Press. doi:10.1007/978-3-319-39028-4

Wang, L., & Xiuju, F. (2002). Rule extraction using a novel gradient-based method and data dimensionality reduction. *Proc. of International Joint Conference on Neural Networks, 2*(1), 1275-1280.

Wang, M. (2018). *Research on the Security Criteria of Hash Functions in the Blockchain.* Academic Press.

Wang, Y., Uehara, T., & Sasaki, R. (2015). Fog computing: Issues and challenges in security and forensics. In *2015 IEEE 39th Annual Computer Software and Applications Conference* (Vol. 3, pp. 53-59). IEEE.

Wang, H., & Song, Y. (2018). Secure cloud-based EHR system using attribute-based cryptosystem and blockchain. *Journal of Medical Systems, 42*(8), 152. doi:10.100710916-018-0994-6 PMID:29974270

Wang, J., Wang, S., Guo, J., Du, Y., Cheng, S., & Li, X. (2019). A Summary of Research on Blockchain in the Field of Intellectual Property. *Procedia Computer Science, 147*, 191–197. doi:10.1016/j.procs.2019.01.220

Wang, K., Kulkarni, A., Lang, M., Arnold, D., & Raicu, I. (2015). Exploring the design tradeoffs for extreme-scale high-performance computing system software. *IEEE Transactions on Parallel and Distributed Systems, 27*(4), 1070–1084. doi:10.1109/TPDS.2015.2430852

Wang, L., Shen, X., Li, J., Shao, J., & Yang, Y. (2018). Cryptographic primitives in blockchains. *Journal of Network and Computer Applications.* doi:10.1016/j.jnca.2018.11.003

Wang, S., Zhang, Y., & Zhang, Y. (2018). A blockchain-based framework for data sharing with fine-grained access control in decentralized storage systems. *IEEE Access: Practical Innovations, Open Solutions, 6*, 38437–38450. doi:10.1109/ACCESS.2018.2851611

Wang, X., Zha, X., Ni, W., Liu, R. P., Guo, Y. J., Niu, X., & Zheng, K. (2019). Survey on blockchain for Internet of Things. *Computer Communications, 136*, 10–29. doi:10.1016/j.comcom.2019.01.006

Weber, R. H. (2015). Internet of things: Privacy issues revisited. *Computer Law & Security Review, 31*(5), 618–627. doi:10.1016/j.clsr.2015.07.002

Wei-hong, H. U., Meng, A. O., Lin, S. H. I., Jia-gui, X. I. E., & Yang, L. I. U. (2017). Review of blockchain-based DNS alternatives. 网络与信息安全学报, *3*(3), 71-77.

Weiss, M., & Corsi, E. (2017). Bitfury: Blockchain for government. *HBS Case Study.*

Wierczek, A. (2014). The impact of supply chain integration on the "snowball effect" in the transmission of disruptions: An empirical evaluation of the model. *International Journal of Production Economics*. doi:10.1016/j.ijpe.2013.08.010

Wikipedia. (2019a, June 26). *Blockchain*. Retrieved from https://en.wikipedia.org/wiki/Blockchain

Wikipedia. (2019b). *DNS spoofing*. Retrieved from https://en.wikipedia.org/w/index.php?title=DNS_spoofing&oldid=891592674

Wikipedia. (n.d.). *Special*. Retrieved from https://en.wikipedia.org/w/index.php?title=Special

Wilcox-O'Hearn, Z. (2001). *Names: Distributed, secure, human-readable: Choose two*. Retrieved from https://web.archive.org/web/ 20011020191610/http://zooko.com/distnames.html

Wilkinson, S., Boshevski, T., Brandoff, J., & Buterin, V. (2014). *Storj a peer-to-peer cloud storage network*. Academic Press.

Wood, G. (2014). Ethereum: A secure decentralised generalised transaction ledger. *Ethereum project yellow paper, 151*, 1-32.

Wood. (2018). *Ethereum: A secure decentralised generalised transaction ledger*. Retrieved from https://gavwood.com/paper.pdf

World Bank. (2017). *Why Secure Land Rights Matter*. Retrieved from http://www.worldbank.org/en/topic/land

Wörner, D., & von Bomhard, T. (2014). When your sensor earns money: Exchanging data for cash with bitcoin. In *Proceedings of the 2014 ACM International Joint Conference on Pervasive and Ubiquitous Computing: Adjunct Publication, UbiComp '14 Adjunct*. ACM.10.1145/2638728.2638786

Wright, G. (2015). *Will Blockchain Enable Better Banking?* Global Finance.

Xia, Q. I., Sifah, E. B., Asamoah, K. O., Gao, J., Du, X., & Guizani, M. (2017). MeDShare: Trust-less medical data sharing among cloud service providers via blockchain. *IEEE Access: Practical Innovations, Open Solutions*, *5*, 14757–14767. doi:10.1109/ACCESS.2017.2730843

Xie, K., Yu, H., & Cen, R. (2012). Using log mining to analyze user behavior on search engine. *Frontiers of Electrical and Electronic Engineering*, *7*(2), 254–260.

Xie, W., & Chen, Y. (2017). Elastic consistent hashing for distributed storage systems. In *Proceedings: IEEE International Parallel and Distributed Processing Symposium (IPDPS)*, (pp. 876-885). IEEE. 10.1109/IPDPS.2017.88

Xu, X., Pautasso, C., Zhu, L., Gramoli, V., Ponomarev, A., Tran, A. B., & Chen, S. (2016, April). The blockchain as a software connector. In *2016 13th Working IEEE/IFIP Conference on Software Architecture (WICSA)* (pp. 182-191). IEEE. 10.1109/WICSA.2016.21

Xu, Y., Zhao, S., Kong, L., Zheng, Y., Zhang, S., & Li, Q. (2017, October). ECBC: A high performance educational certificate blockchain with efficient query. In *International Colloquium on Theoretical Aspects of Computing* (pp. 288-304). Springer. 10.1007/978-3-319-67729-3_17

Xu, R., Chen, Y., Blasch, E., & Chen, G. (2018). Blendcac: A blockchain-enabled decentralized capability-based access control for iots. In *2018 IEEE International Conference on Internet of Things (iThings) and IEEE Green Computing and Communications (GreenCom) and IEEE Cyber, Physical and Social Computing (CPSCom) and IEEE Smart Data (SmartData)* (pp. 1027-1034). IEEE. 10.1109/Cybermatics_2018.2018.00191

Ya. (2018). *Why IPFS is the Future of Decentralised File Storage*. Retrieved from https://medium.com/canyacoin/why-ipfs-is-the-future-of-decentralised-file-storage-8958f3bd02c5

Yadav, M. P., Feeroz, M., & Yadav, V. K. (2012). Mining the customer behavior using web usage mining in e-commerce. In *Proc. of Third International Conference on Computing Communication & Networking Technologies*. IEEE. 10.1109/ICCCNT.2012.6395938

Yaga, D., Mell, P., Roby, N., & Scarfone, K. (2018). *Blockchain technology overview*. Retrieved from https://nvlpubs.nist.gov/nistpubs/ir/2018/NIST.IR.8202.pdf

Yeddu, L. K., & Yeddu, S. (2016). Hadoop: Bitcoin-BlockChain-A New Era Needed In Distributed Computing. *International Journal of Computers and Applications, 154*(6).

Yiannas, F. (2018). A New Era of Food Transparency Powered by Blockchain. *Innovations: Technology, Governance, Globalization, 12*(1-2), 46–56. doi:10.1162/inov_a_00266

Yi, S., Qin, Z., & Li, Q. (2015). Security and privacy issues of fog computing: A survey. *International Conference on Wireless Algorithms, Systems, and Applications*, 685–695. 10.1007/978-3-319-21837-3_67

Yi, S., Xu, Z., & Wang, G. J. (2018). Volatility connectedness in the cryptocurrency market: Is Bitcoin a dominant cryptocurrency? *International Review of Financial Analysis, 60*, 98–114. doi:10.1016/j.irfa.2018.08.012

Yuan, C., Xu, M. X., & Si, X. M. (2017). Research on a new signature scheme on blockchain. *Security and Communication Networks*.

Yue, X., Wang, H., Jin, D., Li, M., & Jiang, W. (2016). Healthcare data gateways: Found healthcare intelligence on blockchain with novel privacy risk control. *Journal of Medical Systems, 40*(10), 218. doi:10.100710916-016-0574-6 PMID:27565509

Yusof, A. R. A., Udzir, N. I., & Selamat, A. (2019). Systematic literature review and taxonomy for DDoS attack detection and prediction. *International Journal of Digital Enterprise Technology, 1*(3), 292–315. doi:10.1504/IJDET.2019.097849

Zarpelao, B. B., Miani, R. S., Kawakani, C. T., & de Alvarenga, S. C. (2017). A survey of intrusion detection in Internet of Things. *Journal of Network and Computer Applications, 84*, 25–37. doi:10.1016/j.jnca.2017.02.009

Zhang, Y., & Wen, J. (2015). An IoT electric business model based on the protocol of bitcoin. *2015 18th International Conference on Intelligence in Next Generation Networks*, 184–191. 10.1109/ICIN.2015.7073830

Zhang, Y., Wu, S., Jin, B., & Du, J. (2017). A blockchain-based process provenance for cloud forensics. In *2017 3rd IEEE International Conference on Computer and Communications (ICCC)* (pp. 2470-2473). IEEE. 10.1109/CompComm.2017.8322979

Zhang, P., Schmidt, D. C., White, J., & Lenz, G. (2018). Blockchain Technology use cases in healthcare. *Advances in Computers*, *111*, 1–41. doi:10.1016/bs.adcom.2018.03.006

Zheng, Z., Xie, S., Dai, H., Chen, X., & Wang, H. (2017, June). *An overview of blockchain technology: Architecture, consensus, and future trends. In 2017 IEEE international congress on big data (BigData congress)* (pp. 557–564). IEEE. doi:10.1109/BigDataCongress.2017.85

Zhong, X. (2011). The research and application of weblog mining based on the platform weka. *Procedia Engineering*, *6*(12), 521–524.

zk Capital. (2018). *IPFS: A Complete Analysis of The Distributed Web*. Retrieved from https://medium.com/zkcapital/ipfs-the-distributed-web-e21a5496d32d

Zraick, K. (2019). *Crypto-Exchange CEO dies in India, platform can't pay investors as he had the passwords*. Retrieved from https://economictimes.indiatimes.com/small-biz/startups/newsbuzz/crypto-exchange-ceo-dies-in-india-platform-cant-pay-investors-as-he-had-the-passwords/articleshow/67861832.cms

Zyskind, G., & Pentland, A. S. (2015). Decentralizing Privacy : Using Blockchain to Protect Personal Data. 2015 IEEE Security and Privacy Workshops, 180–184. doi:10.1109/SPW.2015.27

Zyskind, G., Nathan, O., & Pentland, A. (2015). *Enigma: decentralized computation platform with guaranteed privacy*. Retrieved from http://enigma.media.mit.edu/ enigma~full.pdf

About the Contributors

Dharmendra Singh Rajput completed their Ph.D. (January 2015) in the area of Document Clustering from National Institute of Technology Bhopal, India. They have 9+ Years' Experience in Teaching, Research, and Industry field. Currently, they are working as an Associate Professor in School of Information Technology & Engineering, VIT University, Vellore (India). They have published 10+ Reputed Journals paper and 12 paper presented in International Conferences. They have visited four countries i.e. Malaysia, UK, France, and UAE to attend the various International Conferences. They received various awards from Indian Government like DST, CSIR Travel Grant, MPCST Young Scientist Fellowship.

Ramjeevan Singh Thakur received his BSc from Sagar University in 1995, MCA from SATI Vidisha in 1999 and a PhD degree from RGPV, Bhopal in 2008 in Computer Science and Applications. He worked as an Assistant Professor in RGPV Technical University, Bhopal from July 2000 to July 2007. After then, he joined NIT, Trichy from July 2007 to June 2010. Currently, he is an Associate Professor in Maulana Azad National Institute of Technology, Bhopal, India. His research interests include data/document warehousing, and data/text mining. He is a member of the IAENG, IACSIT and CSI.

Syed Muzamil Basha is working as an assistant professor in the Department of Information Technology at Sri Krishna College Of Engineering and Technology (Autonomous). In 2019, he Completed this Ph.D. from School of Computer Science and Engineering at VIT University, Vellore, India. He completed his M.Tech at VIT university in 2011. He has five years of teaching experience and three years of Fulltime research experience. He published 40+ research articles in reputed SCI and Scopus Indexed journals. He is the editor of four other Textbooks. His exciting area of research is Text Analytics, Machine Learning algorithms, Blockchain Technology.

* * *

Taushif Anwar is a Ph.D. scholar in the Department computer science at Pondicherry University, Pondicherry, India. He received MCA degree from, Punjab Technical University and B.C.A degree from JAMIA HAMDARD University, New Delhi, India. His research interests include the area of Machine Learning, Data Mining and Recommender System.

Sathiyabhama B. is presently working as a Professor and Head in the department of Computer Science and Engineering at Sona College of Technology, Salem India. She has 25 years of teaching and 15 years of research experience. She has completed PhD degree from National Institute of Technology, Tiruchirappalli. She has obtained grant from DST and AICTE for various healthcare projects. She has published over 70 research papers in both international journals and conferences. She has membership in IEEE, CSI, ISTE professional societies. She Co-authored a book titled "Professional Ethics". She has delivered several invited lectures in various national level seminars.

Anup Bihari Gaurav, born in Bihar grew up in Ranchi Jharkhand and graduated from Birla Institute of Technology at Ranchi in Computer Application course, during my years of study in this institute become project Engineer during my 2nd year and core member of R&D wing of BIT ranchi. Currently pursuing MCA from Maulan Azad National Institute of Technology, Bhopal and constantly engaged in learning process.

Jay Jain has completed his Ph. D. degree in Mobile Ad hoc Networks from Department of Computer Applications, MANIT, Bhopal in 2015 and he has completed his M.C. A. degree from UIT-RGPV Bhopal Madhya Pradesh, India in 2007. He has published many research papers in International Journal and Conferences. He is having research as well as teaching experience of about 10 years and currently working as an Assistant Professor, in MANIT, Bhopal His research interests include Wireless Sensor Networks, IoT and MANETs.

Varsha Jain has completed her M. Tech. in Next Generation Networks from Bansal Institute of Science and Technology, Bhopal, India. Her area of research includes Next Generation Networks and IPv6, IoT.

Rajeswari K. C. is at present working as Assistant Professor (SG) at Sona College of Technology, Salem, India. She received her Ph.D. degree from Anna University, Chennai, Tamil Nadu, India in 2016. The focus of her research dissertation is on the enrichment of spontaneous speech synthesis. Her research interests include natural language processing, artificial intelligence, speech processing and Internet of Things. She is associated with the Computer Society of India and Indian Society for Technical Education as a member. She has co-authored a book on artificial intelligence in 2009 under Umayam publications. She also holds the credit of 21 publications across various international, national conferences and journals. She has executed several consultancy projects

Rajesh Kaluri obtained B. Tech in CSE from JNTU, Hyderabad, India and did M.Tech in CSE from ANU, Guntur, India. He has completed Ph.D in Computer Vision at VIT University, India. Currently, he is working as an Assistant Professor (Senior) in School of Information Technology and Engineering, VIT University, India. He is having 8.5 years of teach experience. He was a visiting professor in Guangdong University of Technology, China in 2015 and 2016. His current research are in the areas of Computer Vision, Human Computer Interaction. He has published research papers in various reputed international journals.

Vartika Koolwal is a research scholar of Computer Science in Central University of Rajasthan, India. She was awarded the Bachelor's degree in Computer Application from St. Xavier's College (2014), Master's degree in Computer Application from Banasthali University (2017). Her research interest are data mining, big data and location-based prediction.

K. Dinesh Kumar is currently pursuing the Ph.D., in the School of Computing Science and Engineering, VIT University, Chennai. He received his B.Tech and M.Tech degrees under JNTU-Hyderabad. He has published national and International publications to his credit and participated in various national and international conferences. His research area is cloud computing and also interests in machine learning, computer networks, and grid computing.

Sunil Kumar is a research scholar of Computer Science in Central University of Rajasthan, Ajmer, India. He was awarded the Bachelor's degree in Computer Application from NIMITS Patna (SMUDE, 2014), Master's degree in Computer Application from Patna University (2017). His research interest are data mining, data science and utility mining.

Krithika L. B. is a Professor at School of Information Technology and Engineering, VIT University. Her area of research interest is Image Processing.

Praveensankar Manimaran is currently pursuing M.Tech. in Computer Science and Engineering from National Institute of Technology Puducherry, India. He has completed his B.E. in Computer Science and Engineering from PSG College of

Technology, India. He has worked as Software Engineer for 8 months at Accolite Software India Pvt. Ltd.

Jayanti Mehra received Graduation degree From Barkatullah University Bhopal MP in 2003 and Post Graduation Degree in Computer Science from Makhanlal Chaturvedi National University of Journalism and Communication University Bhopal in year 2008. She is currently pursuing the PhD. Degree in the Department of Computer Applications, Maulana Azad National Institute of Technology Bhopal. M. P. His Research interests include Web Mining, Fuzzy c means and Clustering.

Krishna Kumar Mohbey is an Assistant Professor of Computer Science at Central University of Rajasthan, India. He received his Bachelor's degree in Computer Application from MCRPV Bhopal (2006), Master's in Computer Application from Rajiv Gandhi Technological University Bhopal (2009) and PhD from Department of Mathematics and Computer Applications from National Institute of Technology Bhopal, India (2015). His areas of interest are data mining, mobile web services, big data analysis and user behaviour analysis.

Harshita Patel has done her Ph.D. from Maulana Azad National Institute of Technology, Bhopal, India in 2017. She has earned various years of teaching and research experience. Presently she is working as an Assistant Professor Senior in VIT University, Vellore, India. Her area of interests in research are Data Mining, Machine Learning and IoT.

Ravi Kumar Poluru received M.Tech. from JNTU Anantapur, Anantapuram in 2014. Currently, he is a Research Scholar in the School of Computer Science & Engineering, Vellore Institute of Technology, Vellore and pursuing his Ph.D. work in the field of Internet of Things. His main areas of research include the Internet of Things, Wireless Sensor Networks and Nature Inspired Optimization Techniques.

Arul Murugan R. is currently working as an Assistant Professor in Computer Science and Engineering Department at Sona College of Technology, Salem, Tamil Nadu, India. He received his Bachelor degree in Information Technology from K.S.R College of Engineering, Namakkal with First Class. He obtained his Master degree in Information Technology from K.S.R College of Engineering, Namakkal with distinction. He has worked in web application development, Big Data and Machine Learning projects in the industry. His areas of specialization include Internet of Things, Cloud Computing and Machine Learning. He has published three papers in International Journals. He has also participated in various National-level Workshops and Seminars conducted by various reputed organizations.

Reenadevi R. is at presently working as Assistant Professor at Sona College of Technology, Salem, India. She received her B.E degree in Computer Science and Engineering from Bharathiar University, Tamil Nadu, India in 2003 and M.E degree in Computer Science and Engineering from Anna University, Tamil Nadu, India in 2009. Her general research interests include Data Mining, Data Analytics, Cyber Security and Computational Intelligence. She has published research papers in both national and international journals and conferences.

Venkata Ramana R. is currently working as Assistant Professor at the department of Computer Science and Engineering in SVCE- Tirupati, JNTUA. He received his master's degree from JNTUA in 2012 and Bachelor's degree in 2008. He has 5 years of experience and has taught various subjects in computer science stream and organized various national conferences and workshops in the organization. His research interests are Knowledge Engineering, Image mining, Image Analytics, Recommender Systems. He also published various National and International Journals.

Venkata Rathnam is currently working as Assistant Professor in the Department of Computer Science & Engineering in AITS, Tirupati - JNTUA. Received Master's Degree from JNTUA in 2012 and Bachelor's Degree in 2008 & has Six Years of Experience and taught various subjects in Computer Science stream, organized various national conferences & workshops, guided many students in developing their projects in both UG & PG level and Published papers in conferences and journals. My Research interests are Big Data analytics and Image Processing.

Chandrasekar Ravi is currently working as an assitant professor at National Institute of Technology Puducherry, India. He has completed his Ph.D. from Vellore Institute of Technology. He has completed his M.Tech. and B.Tech. from Pondicherry Engineering College, Pondicherry University.

M. Sudhakar currently works as Research Associate at Vellore Institute of technology, Chennai Campus. He finished master's degree in the stream of Computer Science and Engineering in the year of 2012 from JNTU University, Anantapur. He finished graduation from the same university in the year of 2010. He has 4 years of teaching experience as Assistant Professor in reputed engineering colleges in Andrapradesh, India. He started his research career in 2015 in the school of Computing Science and Engineering at VIT Chennai Campus. He published several UGC and Scopus Indexed journals. His research interests include Image Analytics, Image Processing and Deep Learning in computer vision.

Jing Wang is a Doctor of Computer Software and Theory, Associate Professor of Computer Software, Member of Chian CCF, Oracle Java Certification Trainer, Big Data Analyst, Baidu Yun ABC Advanced Certification. Now she works in Guangdong Polytechnic Institute. She has presided over and participated in more than 10 educational research projects at all levels, including 3 provincial projects, 3 provincial projects and 2 municipal projects. More than 20 high-level papers have been published, including 2 papers indexed by SCI, 6 papers indexed by EI, 7 papers indexed by CPCI and 3 core journals. It has one software copyright, one invention patent and two utility model patents. Research areas include personalized recommendation.Jing Wang, Doctor of Computer Software and Theory, Associate Professor of Computer Software, Member of Chian CCF, Oracle Java Certification Trainer, Big Data Analyst, Baidu Yun ABC Advanced Certification. Now she works in Guangdong Polytechnic Institute. She has presided over and participated in more than 10 educational research projects at all levels, including 3 provincial projects, 3 provincial projects and 2 municipal projects. More than 20 high-level papers have been published, including 2 papers indexed by SCI, 6 papers indexed by EI, 7 papers indexed by CPCI and 3 core journals. It has one software copyright, one invention patent and two utility model patents. Research areas include personalized recommendation.

Index

H

I

N

P

R

S

T

W

Premier Reference Source
Emerging GIS Applications for Emergency and Disaster Management

Premier Reference Source
Managerial Strategies and Green Solutions for Project Sustainability

Premier Reference Source
Comparative Approaches to Using R and Python for Statistical Data Analysis

Premier Reference Source
Solutions for High-Touch Communications in a High-Tech World

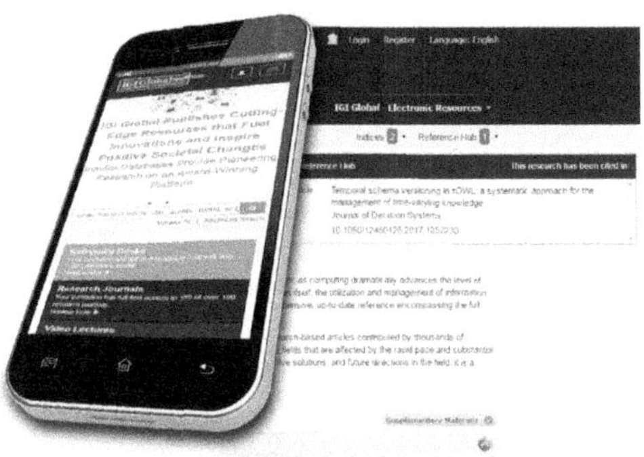

www.ingramcontent.com/pod-product-compliance
Lightning Source LLC
LaVergne TN
LVHW081332300926
849161LV00008B/1955
* 9 7 8 1 7 9 9 8 0 1 8 6 3 *